ORGANIZATION OF AMERICAN HISTORIANS

MAGAZINE OF HISTORY

FOR TEACHERS OF HISTORY

American Stories: Collected Scholarship on Minority History from the *OAH Magazine of History*

AMERICAN STORIES: COLLECTED SCHOLARSHIP ON MINORITY HISTORY
FROM THE *OAH MAGAZINE OF HISTORY*

Copyright © 1998 by the Organization of American Historians

Printed in the United States of America

ISBN 1-884141-02-1

Printed by Indiana University Printing Services
First Printing, April 1998

Organization of American Historians
112 North Bryan Street
Bloomington Indiana 47408
(812) 855-7311
oah@oah.org

Contents

LATINOS IN THE UNITED STATES

Lesson Plan

ASIAN AMERICAN HISTORY

Lesson Plans

Chronological Contents

(Lesson plans have been underlined.)

FROM THE EDITORS

THEMATIC/SURVEY

COLONIAL AND REVOLUTIONARY PERIOD

EARLY NATIONAL PERIOD

CIVIL WAR AND RECONSTRUCTION

GILDED AGE AND PROGRESSIVE ERA

EARLY TWENTIETH CENTURY

POST-WORLD WAR II

Introduction

Early in this century, the American reformer Jane Addams warned that "the accumulations of knowledge possessed by one age are [not] adequate to the needs of another." The last two decades have seen an explosion of new research and writing in U.S. history. This new research has challenged the tradition of attending mostly to Western European sources of American politics and culture. If citizens are to share a common memory of where our society has been, we need to enrich our knowledge of the past by absorbing additional information—new to many of us—about those aspects of U.S. history that have been shaped by Native Americans and by those who came from Africa, Asia and Latin America. Our continuing education as historians and as teachers demands that we widen our horizons.

Enlarging our own accumulations of knowledge and simultaneously teaching students who are struggling to understand basic concepts and themes is not easy, however. Responding to this challenge, the Organization of American Historians published four special issues of the *OAH Magazine of History*. We asked master teachers to prepare surveys of new work and lesson plans that would enable colleagues to situate themselves in the new research and take advantage of teaching strategies already being employed in classrooms all over the country. Together, these essays and lesson plans are a resource with many uses. We take great pleasure in reprinting them together and in this way putting them in the hands of more teachers and on the shelves of more libraries.

This volume is testimony to the commitment of the Organization of American Historians to sustaining and strengthening the teaching of history in our schools and colleges. We have included membership information throughout this book. Virtually all our members are teachers, whether they perform in K-12 classrooms, community and four-year colleges, universities, museums, archives and libraries, or as writers who teach their readers. The *OAH Magazine of History* appears four times a year and is attentive to new developments in the teaching of minority history; this collection is a beginning, not an end.

We live at a time in which we hear many demands for a renewed national commitment to high achievement standards for all students. The OAH is determined to play a significant part in reaching that goal.

—Linda K. Kerber
President, Organization of American Historians, 1996-97
May Brodbeck Professor in the Liberal Arts and
Professor of History, University of Iowa

—George Fredrickson
President, Organization of American Historians, 1997-98
Edgar E. Robinson Professor in United States History
Stanford University

Acknowledgements

We would like to thank the many contributors to this special compilation of articles from the *OAH Magazine of History:* guest editors Charles Chatfield, R. David Edmunds, Paul Finkelman, Dan Flores, James B. LaGrand, Earl Lewis, Stuart McConnell, Gary Y. Okihiro, and Vicki L. Ruiz, and the fine group of scholars they enlisted to write for us; the many suppliers of images and photographic material; the OAH *Magazine* Advisory Board; OAH Presidents Linda K. Kerber and George M. Fredrickson; the OAH staff in Bloomington who assisted with this publication: Arnita Jones, Executive Director; Roark Atkinson; Bradley Birzer; Jeanette Chafin; John Dichtl; Damon Freeman; Ginger Foutz; Kara Hamm; Monica Hendren; Tamzen Meyer; Michael Regoli; and Deneen Snyder; OAH editorial interns: Scott Dafforn, Adriana Don, April D. Lindsay, Katherine O. Givens, Kris Harned, Erin Katzman, Michelle Lewis, Cheryl E. Morell, and Sarah Rudy; Claire Mitchell for the cover design; and finally, the superb team of printing professionals at Indiana University Printing Services.

M.R.

Reconsidering and Teaching the Familiar in African-American History

To understand 1950s African-American history, we must understand the three generations who lived, struggled and died between the 1860s and the 1950s.

Earl Lewis

Earl Lewis, Associate Professor of history and Afroamerican and African Studies, is also the former director of the Center for Afroamerican and African Studies at the University of Michigan. He is the author of In Their Own Interests: Race, Class, and Power in Twentieth Century Norfolk, Virginia, as well as several essays and reviews. Recently, he served on the planning committee for the NAEP project in American history.

Some of the most important works of social history written over the last two decades have explored the intricacies of African-American life. Among the many topics covered in these works are the work regimes, family life, and cultural patterns of enslaved Africans in the colonial and antebellum periods; the felicitous strategies adopted by the first generation of free men and women as they negotiated their new freedoms and campaigned to realize all that America promised; and the acts of empowerment and acts of subordination that occurred during the formative years of the Jim Crow South. More recently, some scholars shifted the lens of analysis to explore the inner workings and differences that united and divided members of various black communities. Examples of this explosion in research and methodology are explored in this issue.

No single volume can truly capture the complexity of African-American life, of course. Therefore, the authors have been selective in highlighting several key aspects. Of particular concern is slavery, emancipation, and African-American life in the early twentieth century. The essays in this issue also have an overwhelmingly urban focus; three of the seven examine black life in the state of Virginia.

Joe Trotter frames the issue's primary concerns in his important and informative historiographical essay. Tracing African-American history from the work of ministers in the nineteenth century through the efforts of George Washington Williams, W. E. B. Du Bois, Carter G. Woodson, and contemporary scholars, he situates the changes in emphasis, methodology, and social conscience. Although noting the rise of "scientific" scholarship, he also makes it clear that African-American history long has been at the center of pressing social concerns as well.

In light of this point, only Rossiter's selection actually explores black life during or under slavery, and then with greater attention to events in Africa than to events in the United States. Most of the articles force us to take a new look at African-American history between 1865 and 1945. As a consequence, a detailed accounting of the modern Civil Rights movement goes untreated. In all fairness a special issue on that topic is warranted. But, as these essays suggest, to understand the 1950s, we must understand the three generations who lived, struggled and died between the 1860s and the 1950s.

More important, as Nancy Mirabal reminds us, critical questions about race and African-American history have not been effectively examined. Her essay forces us to look at African Americans who speak Spanish, in particular, Afro Cubans. As she notes, turn-of-the-century Afro-Cuban immigrants in Ybor City, Florida consciously distanced themselves from African Americans because of their reading of the social script. Being black in Jim Crow-era Florida brought few rewards, and as a result, many worked at being Cuban. Ethnicity was not a perfect shield, however. So-called "white Cubans" practiced racial discrimination as well, although the larger Florida community ignored such distinctions. This essay forces us to puzzle over what black and African American meant at the turn-of-the-century and what it means today.

Essays by Victoria Wolcott, Elsa Barkley Brown, Michael Hucles and Rita Koman raise intriguing questions about the many versions of "community." Wolcott describes the story of Ossian Sweet's struggle to live in a predominantly white neighborhood in 1920s Detroit. In this instance, the boundaries of community were designed to keep some out. With support from state and federal courts, Sweet and others routinely lost the right to live where they wished. But as Wolcott explains, the enabling actions of African Americans altered the traditional script: blacks would fight with guns and in the courts to protect their interests. Hucles provides a related portrait of black life in postbellum Norfolk. The community, once formed, fought to secure improved education. Paradoxically, he notes, the victories—while noteworthy—were often inconsequential.

Brown forces us to reconsider the whole meaning of community. Her brief biography of noted businesswoman Maggie Lena Walker underscores the various ways community worked in and against the interests of segments of the African-American "community." Both Brown and Koman illustrate the role that gender played in the lives of active women. Although quite different in many respects, both essays pose important questions for anyone interested in the many histories of African Americans. More important, the essays require us to re-examine the role that identity played in the lives of blacks. The net result is a collection of essays that propose key themes that should go into any new synthesis of African-American life. ❏

"The object of the Organization shall be to promote historical study and research in the field of American history and to do all things necessary and proper to accomplish this purpose."

Constitution of the Organization
of American Historians, Article II

Membership in the OAH is your way of actively supporting this simple, straightforward goal . . . to promote historical study and research in American history. As a member of the OAH you'll receive either the *Journal of American History*, the leading publication in the field, or the *Magazine of History*, our publication especially for members in the History Educator program.

You'll also receive the *OAH Newsletter*, with articles, commentary, professional opportunity ads, fellowship announcements, and other valuable information about the organization and the profession, plus a copy of our Annual Meeting *Program* containing a complete list of the sessions planned for the OAH convention.

Join us.

— —

Please start my membership in the Organization of American Historians.

Name_____

Address_____

City_____ State_____ Zip_____

___ Check or money order enclosed (must be drawn in U.S. funds, on U.S. bank)
___ Charge my ___ Visa ___ Mastercard Exp. Date_____
    Card No._____
    Signature_____

Check appropriate income/dues category:

Individual Membership Options

Individual members in the following categories receive four issues each of the *Journal of American History* and the *OAH Newsletter* as well as a copy of the Annual Meeting *Program*. Member rates are based on annual income.

- ❏ $40, income under $20,000
- ❏ $55, income $20,000-29,999
- ❏ $75, income $30,000-39,999
- ❏ $85, income $40,000-49,999
- ❏ $95, income $50,000-59,999
- ❏ $105, income $60,000-69,999
- ❏ $115, income $70,000-79,999
- ❏ $130, income over $80,000
- ❏ $150, Contributing Member
- ❏ $55, Associate
- ❏ $45, Emeritus

- ❏ $40+, Dual, receive one copy of JAH (select income category for one member, add $40 for second member)
- ❏ $25, 50 Year OAH Member (must be OAH member for 50 or more years)
- ❏ $25, Student (five-year limit; proof of student status required)
- ❏ $1,200, Life Membership (may be paid paid in two installments)
- ❏ $1,500, Patron (may be paid in four installments)
- ❏ $20, Postage **outside** U.S.

History Educator Membership

Individual members in this category receive four issues of the *OAH Magazine of History* and the *OAH Newsletter* and one copy of the Annual Meeting *Program*.

- ❏ $40, Primary/Secondary Teacher

OAH Magazine of History Subscription Only

❏ $20 per year (members)   ❏ $25 per year (nonmembers) ❏ $30 per year for institutions/libraries

Remit to: OAH, 112 N. Bryan Street, Bloomington IN 47408
(812) 855-7311 • member@oah.indiana.edu • http://www.indiana.edu/~oah

African-American History: Origins, Development, and Current State of the Field

Joe W. Trotter

Over the past three decades, African-American history has matured as a scholarly field within United States history. Under the impact of the modern Civil Rights and Black Power Movements, studies of black life and history proliferated. Black history stimulated as well as drew sustenance from larger trends in American historiography, which emphasized the study of American society "from the bottom up" (1). Despite the vital impact of what was sometimes referred to as the "new social history," scholars soon found this approach wanting, particularly its gender bias and insufficient attention to the ways that class and race unfolded within particular historical contexts. This scholarship nonetheless deepened our knowledge of life at the bottom, while slowly revamping our understanding of life in the middle, at the top, and between and within the sexes. A brief assessment of the origins, development, and current state of the field suggests the gradual ascent of a new African American synthesis.

In a 1986 historiographical essay, John Hope Franklin argued that every generation of historians has the opportunity to write its own history and that it was obliged to do so. According to his calculations, four generations of unequal length characterized the development of Afro-American history.

With some modifications, particularly during the nineteenth century, this essay builds upon Franklin's general periodization (2).

The first generation emerged before the Civil War and persisted through the 1890s. The nineteenth century pioneers included Robert Benjamin Lewis, William Wells Brown, Martin R. Delaney, William Cooper

The early writers of African-American history included many ministers who used the Bible as both source material and inspiration.

Nell, James C. Pennington, George Washington Williams, and W. E. B. Du Bois. These black historians produced seminal studies of black life, which linked the experiences of Africa, the United States, and other parts of the diaspora. Only Du Bois—educated at Fisk University, Harvard, and the University of Berlin—brought university training to the task. The early writers included many ministers with a deep commitment to theological interpretations of the world. They used the Bible as both source material and inspiration. Much like their white counterparts during the period, their work was narrative rather than analytical in style: it eschewed strict adherence to the emergent canons of historical scholarship and enlisted history as a tool in advancing the "progress of the race" (3). The nineteenth century pioneers also believed, as historian Clarence Walker has noted, that "self-conscious elevation of mind and manners would put prejudice to flight" (4).

Scholarship on black history changed during the late nineteenth and early twentieth centuries. Historian George Washington Williams helped usher in a new type of African-American history in 1882, when he published his two-volume *History of the Negro Race in America* (5). Although Williams adopted the fundamental conceptual framework of his forebears, he moved beyond the use of biblical texts and employed a wide-range of primary sources—newspapers, organizational records, statistics, archival manuscripts, and personal interviews. In effect, Williams reflected to a great extent the growing emphasis in America and Europe on a systematic or "scientific" approach to historical scholarship. Still, Williams remained committed to the notion that "in the interpretation of *History* the plans of God must be discerned. 'For a thousand years in Thy sight are but as yesterday when it is passed, and as a watch in the night'" (6). Thus, rather than making a fundamental break with the "idealist tradition," Williams served as a bridge leading to the second generation of scholarship on black history (7).

During World War I and the 1920s, the professional and scholarly activities of W. E. B. Du Bois and Carter G. Woodson symbolized the rise of a second generation of black historians. Supplementing his 1896 study *The Suppression of the African Slave Trade to the United States, 1638-1870*, Du Bois in 1915 published *The Negro*, signalling the slow emergence of university-trained professionals in the field. It was Carter G. Woodson, however, who would become most influential. Educated at Berea College in Kentucky, the Sorbonne in Paris, the University of Chicago (M.A., 1908), and Harvard, where he received the Ph.D. in 1912, Woodson pursued an energetic schedule of professional, promotional, and publishing activities. In rapid succession, he helped to found the Association for the Study of Negro Life and History (1915), the *Journal of Negro History* (1916), Negro History Week (1926), and the *Negro History Bulletin* (1933). Building upon the research methodology of the expanding historical profession, Woodson and Du Bois developed a more rigorous, systematic, and analytical approach to black history. They also emphasized the contributions of African Americans to the development of American society, particularly its literary, artistic, and musical traditions (8). Woodson expressed this new sentiment in a famous statement about the obligation of black historians. They must, Woodson argued, "save and publish the records of the Negro, that the race may not become a negligible factor in the thought of the world" (9). In short, such studies highlighted the positive side of black participation in American culture as a means of combating white racist portrayals of African Americans and as a way of instilling racial pride.

Under the onslaught of the Great De-pression and the continuing profes-sionalization of the field, however, students of black history questioned aspects of the analytical but nonetheless contributionist paradigm. At a time when black workers suffered rising unemployment, poverty, and homelessness, it seemed less meaningful to highlight the extraordinary doings of edu-cated black elites. Du Bois would once again play a leading role in rethinking Afri-can-American history just as he had partici-pated in other phases of black historiography. Although his writings had taken an increas-ingly separatist turn by the early 1930s, Du Bois's *Black Reconstruction* (1935) exhib-ited faith in the efficacy of interracial class unity (10). Emphasizing the role that slaves played in their own emancipation, Du Bois advanced an original interpretation of the Civil War and Reconstruction.

Other black historians also expressed growing dissatisfaction with the liberal per-spective which the depression had brought into sharp relief. In 1937, for example, in an essay entitled "A New Interpretation of Negro History," historian Lawrence Reddick de-cried the liberal approach to black history. Trained at Fisk University and later at the University of Chicago, where he completed his doctoral studies in history in 1939, Reddick criticized established studies for failing to systematically analyze the factors that shaped black life, and for ignoring which forces were "influential" and "under what circumstances" (11). Along with Du Bois, Reddick advocated a new interpreta-tion of black history—one that emphasized "the record of the clashes and rationaliza-tions of individual and group impulse against an American social order of an unfolding capitalism, within which operates semiarticulate arrangements and etiquettes of class and caste" (12).

The radical sensibilities of scholars like Reddick and Du Bois were subordinated in subsequent years to an integrationist agenda. With the onset of World War II, the economy recovered and stimulated the resurgence of black migration into the urban industrial centers of the nation. Re-employment dur-ing the war years rekindled hope that per-haps blacks would enter the mainstream of American life after all. The number of university-trained black historians increased markedly, although their numbers remained relatively small; they were joined by an increasing number of white historians who largely adopted the prevailing black per-spective, which emphasized the impact of Afro Americans on the history of the nation (13).

Stimulated by the expanding Civil Rights movements, post-World War II scholars also sought ways to reinforce the black struggle for full citizenship rights. As histo-rian John Hope Franklin noted, "Historians of the third generation were compelled by circumstances to fight for the integration of Afro-American history into the mainstream of the nation's history. Their fight to inte-grate Afro-American history into the main-stream was a part of the fight . . . to gain admission to the mainstream of American life—for the vote, for equal treatment, for equal opportunity, for their rights as Ameri-cans" (14). As might be expected, then, this third generation of historians turned to the experiences of the free black population in the late antebellum years and to the events of Reconstruction for subject matter. In so doing, they countered prevailing notions that ex-slaves were illiterate, corrupt, and politically unprepared to participate in a democracy.

By overturning demeaning stereotypes, scholars of black history believed that they could help to complete America's unfin-ished revolution which began with emanci-pation and create a truly multiracial and pluralist society. Kenneth Stampp, a highly sympathetic white historian of the period, captured the essence of the liberal integra-tionist perspective when he wrote in 1956 that "innately Negroes *are,* after all, only white men with black skins, nothing more, nothing less" (15). This perspective sug-gests how far the third generation had trav-elled toward reversing the racist portrait of African Americans in U.S. history, but also reflected how far succeeding genera-tions would have to travel in order to correct remaining cultural and gender biases.

A fourth generation of scholars chal-lenged the liberal, integrationist paradigm and pushed black history in new and often radical directions. During the 1970s, black

Carter G. Woodson, shown here in the early years of his directorship of the ASNLH, later helped to found the *Journal of Negro History,* Negro History Week, and the *Negro History Bulletin.*

historians and their white allies broke ranks with the older revisionist perspectives. Spurred on by the Black Consciousness Movement, new writers used slavery rather than Reconstruction or free blacks as a springboard to alter the shape of black history. They adopted interpretive strategies and techniques that illuminated the interior lives of slaves and outlined the development of "a distinct Afro-American culture" (16). Like their white counterparts, many of the black scholars of this era received their training in the major graduate schools of the nation. By the late 1980s, however, some of these scholars had started to question the prevailing "community and culture" focus. Such studies invariably overlooked the gendered nature of black history, and, for the industrial era, only slowly apprehended the dynamics, meaning, and significance of a working class forming within the African-American community (17). A closer look at the historiography of slavery, emancipation, and black life in the industrial era brings the development of African-American history into sharper focus.

In 1918, the white historian U. B. Phillips published *American Negro Slavery: A Survey of the Supply, Employment and Control of Negro Labor as Determined by the Plantation Regime.* Using plantation records, which offered unusual insight into the words and deeds of the planter class, Phillips portrayed slavery as a paternalistic institution. He recognized the coercive nature of the slave regime, but justified the institution as a mechanism for introducing "backward Africans" to the fruits of western culture. Although W. E. B. Du Bois, Carter Woodson, and a few other black historians rejected this portrait, Phillips nonetheless became the principal authority on black life under bondage.

During the 1950s, scholars gradually revamped our understanding of slavery and overturned the paternalistic thesis. Stampp in 1956 published *The Peculiar Institution: Slavery in the Ante-Bellum South* and Stanley Elkins released his *Slavery: A Problem in American Institutional and Intellectual Life* in 1959. Both Stampp and Elkins emphasized the coercive nature of slavery, an institution designed to reap profits rather than incorporate slaves into the mainstream of western culture. Stampp showed in substantial detail how slaves resisted bondage through a variety of tactics, including running away, work slowdowns, feigning sickness, and, at times, by violent rebellions and plots to rebel. Unlike Stampp, however, Elkins conceptualized slavery as a concentration camp, using the Nazi analogy, and treated slaves as uniformly subdued by the system. As Elkins understood it, slavery divorced Africans from their heroic traditions and transformed "men" into "boys" (18). Only during the 1970s did scholars challenge these perspectives on slaves and slavery.

As the non-violent Civil Rights movement gave way to the separatist Black Power movement during the late 1960s and early 1970s, historians challenged the image of slaves as culturally impoverished, devoid of family life, isolated from community, and largely passive in the face of a dehumanizing experience. John Blassingame, Eugene

Genovese, Lawrence Levine, and the late Herbert Gutman all helped to establish a new portrait of African-American cultural and community life under slavery (19). These scholars moved beyond plantation records to examine sources left by slaves themselves which revealed unique family and religious practices, songs, dances, folklore, and oral traditions. These studies demonstrate how slaves responded to their lowly position by promoting group solidarity, building self-esteem, and supporting both covert and sometimes overt forms of resistance to bondage. John Blassingame argued, for example, that "however oppressive or dehumanizing the plantation was, the struggle for survival was not severe enough to crush all of the slave's creative instincts" (20). During the 1980s and early 1990s, while scholars continued to elaborate upon the community and culture perspective, they deepened our understanding of slavery by adding new chronological, regional, and topical dimensions, including studies of slave religion, women, and the process of emancipation and community formation in the antebellum North (21).

Research on emancipation and Reconstruction has also highlighted the role of blacks in shaping their own history. Studies by Barbara Fields, Eric Foner, Thomas Holt, Leon Litwack, Nell Painter, Armstead Robinson, and others, all have shown how ex-slaves defined their own freedom and took steps to establish a new life after the Civil War (22). This scholarship reveals, for example, that the sharecropping system was not merely an unequal and exploitative relationship between landowners and workers, but an intense bargaining arrangement: landowners reluctantly gave black laborers access to land and a measure of independence in its cultivation. Building upon their cultural experiences in the slave community, ex-slaves also founded a plethora of new institutions, especially churches, fraternal orders, and social clubs, which in turn stimulated the growth of small business, professional, political, and civil rights organizations. Although black workers and the poor would often articulate goals and aspirations at odds with emerging black economic and political elites, they nonetheless supported elite efforts to advance the interests of the race.

Paralleling the growth of scholarship on the early emancipation era were studies of the origins, causes, and consequences of Jim Crow. C. Vann Woodward helped to launch this field of inquiry in 1955 when he published *The Strange Career of Jim Crow*. He emphasized the proliferation of state statutes prescribing a separate place for blacks and whites in the institutional, social, and political life of the South. In the "rigid and universal" form that it had taken by the mid-twentieth century, Woodward argued that the segregationist system was a product of the 1890s and early 1900s. Before disfranchisement, lynchings, and *de jure* racial separation fully triumphed, he said that there had transpired a period of experimentation, alternatives, and roads not taken, including some evidence of a liberal philosophy of integrationism. In this way, similar to the post-World War II scholars of slavery, Wood-

George Washington Williams developed a new type of African-American history when he published his two-volume *History of the Negro Race in America* in 1882.

ward held out hope that contemporary de-segregation efforts would find fruitful southern soil and grow.

The modern segregationist system produced no scholarly defense comparable to U. B. Phillips's defense of the antebellum slave South. This was undoubtedly a consequence of the prevailing social climate. For at the time that historians turned their attention to this important subject, African Americans and their tiny core of white supporters were hard at work dismantling the system. Nevertheless, students of Reconstruction like Joel Williamson soon challenged the Woodward thesis. Williamson downplayed the importance of the law, located the origins of segregation in the racist mentality of whites, and pushed its beginnings back toward the early emancipation years. With the exception of August Meier's groundbreaking study *Negro Thought in America, 1880-1915* (1963), the debate between Woodward and his critics unfolded with little sense of blacks as agents in the making of the segregationist era. In 1978, however, Howard Rabinowitz published his *Race Relations in the Urban South, 1865-1890*, and changed the terms of the debate.

Focusing on the responses of blacks, as well as the nature of black-white interactions, Rabinowitz moved the discussion onto new terrain. He stressed the importance of black exclusion, alongside issues of integration and segregation. In the region's institutional life, he argued that segregation sometimes replaced exclusion, making the integration-segregation dichotomy untenable. Moreover, Rabinowitz demonstrated that segregated institutions, such as schools, were not gifts of an increasingly racist society, but the product of demands from a highly politicized black community. In subsequent years, using different approaches, a variety of scholars advanced the study of black life in the Jim Crow South, by giving increasing attention to workers in rural and urban contexts (23).

Scholars of American and African American urban history are also transforming our understanding of black life. Studies of the Great Migration of World War I and

its aftermath reflect these changes. Until recently, scholars of black population movement emphasized how blacks were *pushed* out of the rural South by intolerable socio-economic and political conditions on the one hand, and *pulled* into the urban North by the labor demands of wartime production, restrictions on European immigration, better race relations, and access to citizenship rights on the other. Recent studies by Earl Lewis, James Grossman, and Peter Gottlieb have challenged this static image of black migration. These scholars demonstrate how African Americans used their kin and friendship networks, pooled their resources, shared information, and in general played a pivotal

---

During the late 1960s and ear-ly 1970s, historians challenged the image of slaves as culturally impoverished and largely passive.

---

role in organizing their own movement into the expanding cities of the North and South (24).

Even before scholars turned to the Great Migration, however, they had focused—and continued to focus—on the transformation of black urban life itself. By the mid-1970s, Gilbert Osofsky, Allan Spear, and Kenneth Kusmer had documented the rise of black urban ghettos. They illustrated the impact of white racism on various aspects of black urban life, highlighted sharp differences between blacks and European immigrants, and established a uniquely racial and spatial interpretation of black urban history. By the mid-1980s, an increasing number of new studies addressed significant blind spots in this scholarship. Books by Dennis Dickerson, Robin D. G. Kelley, Peter Rachleff, and Joe W. Trotter, to name a few, emphasized the emergence of new classes and social relations within the black urban community

(25). In varying degrees, they document the development of the black community and the transformation of black institutions and politics. Either explicitly or implicitly, they also conclude that the process of class formation or proletarianization is as critical to understanding the black urban experience as is the process of residential and institutional segregation.

Despite important strides in the development of African American history as the 1990s got underway, important conceptual and substantive gaps remained. The role of black women and gender analysis only slowly entered the field. Helping to pave the way, however, were books and essays by Elsa Barkley Brown, Sharon Harley, Evelyn Brooks Higginbotham, Darlene Clark Hine, Dolores Janiewski, Jacqueline Jones, Earl Lewis, Rosalyn Terborg-Penn, and Deborah Gray White, among others (26). These studies illuminate the interactive impact of gender, class, and race dynamics on the black experience. They also suggest essential components of a new synthesis—the specific outlines of which will be complex. But its central theme is quite clear: In the face of external hostility and substantial internal fragmentation, African Americans created a unified (if not unitary) cultural, political, and community life. ❑

Bibliography

Cox, LaWanda, "From Emancipation to Segregation: National Policy and Southern Blacks" in John B. Boles and Evelyn Thomas Nolan, ed., *Interpreting Southern History: Historiographical Essays in Honor of Sanford W. Higginbotham.* Baton Rouge: Louisiana State University Press, 1987.

Franklin, John Hope, "On the Evolution of Scholarship in Afro-American History" in Darlene Clark Hine, ed., *Afro-American History: Past, Present, and Future.* Baton Rouge: Louisiana State University Press, 1986.

———, "Afro-American History: State of the Art," *Journal of American History* (June 1988): 163-173.

———, *George Washington Williams: A Biography*. Chicago: University of Chicago, 1985.

Harris, Robert L., "Coming of Age: The Transformation of Afro-American Historiography," *Journal of Negro History* 57 (1982): 107-121.

Higginbotham, Elizabeth and Sarah Watts, "The New Scholarship on Afro-American Women," *Women's Studies Quarterly* 1 and 2 (1988): 12-21.

Higginbotham, Evelyn Brooks, "African-American Women's History and the Metalanguage of Race," *Signs: Journal of Women in Culture and Society* 17 (1992): 251-274.

Hine, Darlene Clark. *Afro-American History: Past, Present, and Future*. Baton Rouge: Louisiana State University Press, 1986.

Hoover, Dwight W., ed. *Understanding Negro History*. Chicago: Quadrangle Books, 1968.

Kusmer, Kenneth L., "The Black Urban Experience in American History," in Darlene Clark Hine, ed., *The State of Afro-American History: Past, Present and Future*. Baton Rouge: Louisiana State University Press, 1986.

Meier, August and Elliott Rudwick. *Black History and the Historical Profession*. Urbana: University of Illinois Press, 1986.

Rabinowitz, Howard, "From Exclusion to Segregation: Southern Race Relations, 1865-1890," *Journal of American History* 63 (Sept. 1976).

Redding, J. Saunders, "The Negro in American History: As Scholar, as Subject," in Michael Kammen, ed., *The Past Before Us: Contemporary Historical Writing in the United States*. Ithaca: Cornell University Press, 1980.

Reddick, Lawrence, "A New Interpretation of Negro History," *Journal of Negro History* 22 (Jan. 1937): 17-28.

Thorpe, Earl E. *Black Historians: A Critique*. New York: William Morrow Company, 1971.

Trotter, Joe William, Jr., "Afro-American Urban History: A Critique of the Literature," in Joe William Trotter, Jr., *Black Milwaukee: The Making of an Indus-trial Proletariat, 1915-45*. Urbana: University of Illinois Press, 1985.

———, ed. *The Great Migration in Historical Perspective: New Dimensions of Race, Class, and Gender*. Bloomington: Indiana University Press, 1991.

———, "African American Society," in Peter N. Stearns, ed., *Encyclopedia of Social History*. New York: Garland Publishing, 1993.

Walker, Clarence E, "The American Negro as Outsider, 1836-1935," *Canadian Review of American Studies* (Summer 1986): 137-154.

Williamson, Joel. *The Crucible of Race: Black-White Relations in the American South since Emancipation*. New York: Oxford University Press, 1984.

Woodman, Harold D., "Economic Reconstruction and the Rise of the New South, 1865-1900" in John B. Boles and Evelyn Thomas Nolan, ed., *Interpreting Southern History: Historiographical Essays in Honor of Sanford W. Higginbotham*. Baton Rouge: Louisiana State University Press, 1987.

Woodward, C. Vann. *American Counterpoint: Slavery and Racism in the North/South Dialogue*. New York: Oxford University Press, 1971.

Endnotes

1. Darlene Clark Hine, *Afro-American History: Past, Present, and Future* (Baton Rouge: Louisiana State University Press, 1986); August Meier and Elliott Rudwick, *Black History and the Historical Profession* (Urbana: University of Illinois Press, 1986); Peter N. Stearns, ed., *Expanding the Past: A Reader in Social History, Essays from the Journal of Social History* (New York: New York University Press, 1988).

2. John Hope Franklin, "On the Evolution of Scholarship in Afro-American History," in Hine, ed., *Afro-American History,* 14-22; J.H Franklin, "Afro-American History: State of the Art," *Journal of American History* (June 1988): 163-173.

3. Robert L. Harris, "Coming of Age: The Transformation of Afro-American Historiography," *Journal of Negro History* 57 (1982): 107-121; Clarence E. Walker, "The American Negro as Outsider, 1836-1935," *Canadian Review of American Studies* (Summer 1986): 137-154; Earl Thorpe, *Black Historians: A Critique* (New York: William Morrow Company, 1971), 27-61.

4. Walker, "The American Negro as Outsider," 137.

5. John Hope Franklin, *George Washington Williams: A Biography* (Chicago: University of Chicago Press, 1985).

6. Quoted in Franklin, *George Washington Williams,* 113; Harris, "Coming of Age," 111.

7. For an insightful discussion of the "idealist tradition" in early black historiography, see Walker, "The American Negro as Outsider."

8. Meier and Rudwick, *Black History and the Historical Profession,* 1-71; Thorpe, *Black Historians,* 65-124; Franklin, "Afro-American History," 162-163; Franklin, "On the Evolution of Scholarship," 50-51; Harris, "Coming of Age," 111.

9. Quoted in Meier and Rudwick, *Black History and the Historical Profession,* 9; Franklin, "On the Evolution of Scholarship," 51.

10. Harris, "Coming of Age," 112-113; Walker, "The American Negro as Outsider," 144; Franklin, "On the Evolution of Scholarship," 51-52; Meier and Rudwick, *Black History and the Historical Profession,* 101-102.

11. Lawrence Reddick, "A New Interpretation of Negro History," *Journal of Negro History* 22 (Jan. 1937): 17-28; Meier and Rudwick, *Black History and the Historical Profession,* 103-104.

12. Reddick, "A New Interpretation," 26.

13. Meier and Rudwick, *Black History and the Historical Profession,* especially chapters 2 and 3. Also see C. Vann Woodward, "Clio with Soul," *Journal of American History* (June 1969): 5-20.

14. Franklin, "On the Evolution of Scholarship," 56-57.

15. Kenneth M. Stampp, *The Peculiar Institution: Slavery in the Ante-Bellum South* (New York: Vintage Books/Random House, 1956), vii-viii.

16. Leslie H. Owens, "The African in the Garden: Reflections about New World Slavery and its Lifelines," in Hine, ed., *The State of Afro-American History,* 25-36; Harris, "Coming of Age," 114-115; Meier and Rudwick, *Black History and the Historical Profession,* 239-276.

17. Darlene Clark Hine, "Lifting the Veil, Shattering the Silence: Black Women's History in Slavery and Freedom," in Hine, ed., *The State of Afro-American History,* 223-249; Elizabeth Higginbotham and Sarah Watts, "The New Scholarship on Afro-American Women," *Women's Studies Quarterly,* 1 and 2 (1988): 12-21; Evelyn Brooks Higginbotham, "African-American Women's History and the Meta-language of Race," *Signs: Journal of Women in Culture and Society* 17 (1992): 251-274; Kenneth Kusmer, "The Black Urban Experience in American History," in Hine, ed., *The State of Afro-American History,* 91-122; Joe W. Trotter, "Afro-American Urban History: A Critique of the Literature," in *Black Milwaukee: The Making of an Industrial Proletariat, 1915-45* (Urbana: University of Illinois Press, 1985), 264-282.

18. See David Brion Davis, "Slavery and Post-World War II Historians," *Daedalus* 103 (1974): 2-16.

19. Meier and Rudwick, *Black History and the Historical Profession,* 239-276.

20. John W. Blassingame, *The Slave Community: Plantation Life in the Antebellum South* (New York: Oxford University Press, 1979), 105.

21. Margaret Washington Creel, *"A Peculiar People": Slave Religion and Community-Culture Among the Gullahs* (New York: New York University Press, 1988); Mechal Sobel, *Trabelin' On: The Slave Journey to an Afro-Baptist Faith* (Princeton: Princeton University Press, 1988); Deborah Gray White, *Ar'n't I a Woman?: Female Slaves in the Plantation South* (New York: W.W. Norton and Company, 1985). For a review of recent studies of black life in the antebellum North, see James Oliver Horton, *Free People of Color: Inside the African American Community* (Washington: Smithsonian Institution Press, 1993), 1-19.

22. Useful reviews of this extensive scholarship include Armstead Robinson, "The Difference Freedom Made: The Emancipation of Afro-Americans," in Hine, ed., *The State of Afro-American History,* 51-74; LaWanda Cox, "From Emancipation to Segregation: National Policy and Southern Blacks," in John B. Boles and Evelyn Thomas Nolen, ed., *Interpreting Southern History: Historiographical Essays in Honor of Sanford W. Higginbotham* (Baton Rouge: Louisiana State University Press, 1987), 199-253; Harold D. Woodman, "Economic Reconstruction and the Rise of the New South, 1865-1900," in Boles and Nolen, ed., *Interpreting Southern History,* 254-307; and Eric Foner, *Reconstruction: America's Unfinished Revolution, 1863-1877* (New York: Harper and Row, 1988).

23. C. Vann Woodward, "The Strange Career of a Historical Controversy," in Woodward, *American Counterpoint: Slavery and Racism in the North-South Dialogue* (New York: Oxford University Press, 1983), 234-260; Howard Rabinowitz, "From Exclusion to Segregation: Southern Race Relations, 1865-1890," *Journal of American History* (Sept. 1976): 325-350; Joel Williamson, *The Crucible of Race: Black-White Relations in the American South Since Emancipation* (New York: Oxford University Press, 1984). Cf. C. Vann Woodward, *"Strange Career* Critics: Long May They Persevere," *Journal of American History* 75 (Dec. 1988): 857-868; Howard N. Rabino-witz, "More Than the Woodward Thesis: Assessing *Strange Career of Jim Crow,"* *Journal of American History* 75 (1988): 842-856.

24. A review of this literature is in Joe W. Trotter, ed., *The Great Migration in Historical Perspective: New Dimensions of Race, Class, and Gender* (Bloomington: Indiana University Press, 1991).

25. Dennis Dickerson, *Out of the Crucible: Black Steelworkers in Western Pennsylvania, 1875-1980* (Albany: State University of New York Press, 1986); Robin D. G. Kelley, *Hammer and Hoe: Alabama Communists During the Great Depression* (Chapel Hill: University of North Carolina Press, 1990); Peter Rachleff, *Black Labor in the South: Richmond, Virginia, 1865-1890* (Philadelphia: Temple University Press, 1984); Trotter, *Black Milwaukee.* Cf. Eric Arnesen, "Following the Color Line of Labor: Black Workers and the Labor Movement before 1930," *Radical History Review* 55 (1993): 53-87.

26. Hine, "Lifting the Veil," in Hine, ed., *The State of Afro-American History,* 223-249; Higginbotham and Watts, "The New Scholarship on Afro-American Women," 12-21; Higginbotham, "African-American Women's History," 251-274; Elsa Barkley Brown, "Womanist Consciousness: Maggie Lena Walker and the Independent Order of Saint Luke," *Signs: Journal of Women in Culture and Society* 14 (1989): 610-633; Dolores Janiewski, *Sisterhood Denied: Race, Gender, and Class in a New South Community* (Philadelphia: Temple University Press, 1985); Jacqueline Jones, *Labor of Love, Labor of Sorrow: Black Women, Work, and the Family, from Slavery to the Present* (New York: Vintage Books/Random House, 1985); Earl Lewis, *In Their Own Interests: Race, Class, and Power in Twentieth-Century Norfolk, Virginia* (Berkeley: University of California Press, 1991), esp. 101-109; Deborah Gray White, *Ar'n't I a Woman?.*

Joe W. Trotter is Professor of history at Carnegie Mellon University. His books, Black Milwaukee and Coal, Class, and Color, are seminal studies in the history of African-American working class formation.

The Afro-Cuban Community in Ybor City and Tampa, 1886-1910

Nancy Raquel Mirabal

In 1886, the same year that Cuba eliminated slavery, Vicente Martinez Ybor built the first cigar factory in the Tampa area of Florida and established a company town known as Ybor City. Once the cigar factory was constructed, Martinez Ybor had little trouble finding workers. As a result of severe depressions in Cuba during the mid-1880s, the arrival of a million Spanish workers between 1882 and 1894, and the introduction of two hundred former slaves into the Cuban labor force, thousands of Cuban immigrants, both black and white, travelled to the United States in search of employment (1).

When Afro Cubans arrived in Ybor City to work in the cigar factories, local laws and customs defined them as black and assigned them to the same legal category as African Americans, despite the differences in language and heritage (2). At the same time, they maintained an identity with and cultural ties to the larger Cuban community, which was viewed as white (3). Since being both black and Cuban (meaning white) was incompatible with the racial mores of Florida during the Jim Crow era, Afro Cubans created a separate community and a fluid identity which reflected both their cultural heritage and race. The manner in which they negotiated their identity and positioned themselves in Ybor City, especially during the late nineteenth and early twentieth centuries, complicates the history of race and ethnicity in the United States—especially African American history.

Many Afro Cubans attempted to transcend racial segregation laws in Ybor City by privileging their ethnicity over their race.

Moreover, the difficulty in defining Cubans solely on the basis of race becomes increasingly clear when one considers that during this period, the Anglo population in Tampa often referred to the Cuban community, regardless of race or background, as "Cuban niggers" (4). By using negative racial references to characterize Cubans, some in the Anglo community in Tampa easily dismissed and devalued the Cuban immigrant community in Ybor City. While those outside the Cuban community failed to differentiate Cubans on the basis of race, within the Cuban community race factored in the participation of Afro Cubans in the Cuban nationalist movement and in the creation of cultural clubs.

To better understand the complex relationship between race and ethnicity it is necessary to briefly explore certain "sites" where contestation and negotiation of identities occurred. In Tampa, these included the cigar factories, nationalist movements and the Afro-Cuban club and mutual aid society *La Union Marti Maceo*. Afro Cubans who immigrated to Ybor City encountered a community where residents could be heard speaking Spanish, where Spanish newspapers were readily available, and where Cuban immigrants owned grocery stores known as *bodegas* that sold Cuban and Spanish products. Cubans could be found discussing politics over their *café con leche* in "hole in the wall cafes," while old Cuban men played dominoes surrounded by the odors of hot Cuban bread and the tang of "bright leaf tobacco mellowing in the dungeons of the cigar factories." The cit

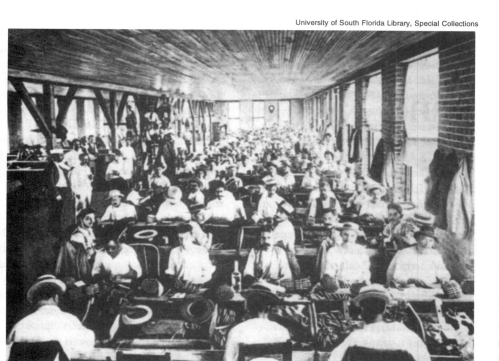

Cigar factories gave immigrants valuable economic and social security within their community. Ninety percent of the men who immigrated to Tampa worked in cigar factories.

that Vicente Martinez Ybor founded in 1886 would later be called the "Havana" of America by the Florida Branch of the Federal Writers Project Archives in 1941 (5).

Because immigrants were not expected to "fit in" or to radically alter their lifestyles to accommodate a standing community, Ybor City differed greatly from other cities located in the South. Not only did the city provide Afro Cubans with the space and independence to form a Black immigrant community, but the cigar factories that employed Afro Cubans offered them the needed economic security and social connections to sustain themselves and their community. Although the number of them who immigrated to Tampa was relatively low, ninety percent of the men and fifteen percent of the women worked in the cigar factories (6). More important, the cigar factories were not racially segregated and Afro Cubans sat next to white Cubans rolling cigars and listening to a *lector* read a variety of books and newspapers, including radical presses. This practice, also evident and popular in cigar factories in Cuba, kept cigarworkers informed of political developments in both

Cuba and the United States. The *lectura* was taken very seriously by cigarmakers who depended on *el lector* to disseminate news, translate local English language newspapers and entertain them with novels (7).

The cigarworkers transferred a series of Cuban customs and traditions which gave them a degree of control over the workplace. Individual workers arrived and departed freely, drank *el cafecito* throughout the day and smoked an unlimited amount of cigars while in the factory. Although the cigar factories were not racially segregated and Afro Cubans received the same wages as white Cubans for comparable work, labor was divided into several departments and stratified on the basis of sex. The majority of women worked as stemmers while the men rolled the cigars. Initially a boy's occupation, stemming was viewed as a stepping stone to a cigarmaking job. By 1870, however, it was fast becoming a separate occupation and manufacturers usually hired women for this "dirty, dead-end low wage labor" (8).

While Afro Cubans moved freely within Ybor City and worked next to white Cubans

in the cigar factories, Florida's segregation laws sharpened racial realities for Cuban immigrants elsewhere in the area and state. Schools, hospitals, certain businesses and private clubs all subscribed to Florida's Jim Crow laws (9). Afro Cubans often travelled to the African American section of Tampa to attend school, receive medical attention or go to the only movie theater that was open to blacks. As a result, many Afro Cubans attempted to transcend the seemingly selective applications of racial segregation laws in Ybor City by privileging their ethnicity over their race. Resisting any formal interactions or alliances with African Americans during this period, Afro Cubans viewed themselves as primarily Cuban and participated in clubs and movements that addressed the concerns of Cubans on the island and in the United States (10). While some Afro Cubans responded in this manner because they believed that their stay in the United States was temporary, others, cognizant of the social, economic and political ramifications of being considered black in the United States, chose to alter their status rather than question racial segregation.

Ironically, racial divisions within the Cuban community marred certain pretenses of ethnic solidarity. During the late nineteenth century the emigre community in Ybor City worked to liberate Cuba from Spanish control. Those involved in the nationalist movement were dedicated to a "Cuba Libre" (11). Yet for many of the Afro Cubans who joined white Cubans in providing critical economic, political, and military support, race remained a factor and at times a barrier in organizing efforts for the Cuban War for Independence. Prominent Afro-Cuban leaders, including Bruno Roig, Cornelio Brito, and Paulina and Ruperto Pedroso, endured racial animosities within and outside of revolutionary organizations.

When the Cuban patriot and national hero Jose Marti was invited by the Club Ignacio Agramonte in November 1891 to visit Ybor City, he was determined to directly confront the racism within the Cuban community. Marti recognized the importance of incorporating Afro Cubans into the nationalist movement. In his famous "Liceo" speech, Marti demanded that white Cubans alter their racist attitudes in the name of a "Cuba Libre" by reminding Cubans that this would be a "revolution [in which] all Cubans, regardless of color have participated" (12). To maximize his base of support, Marti's words had to be inclusive and yet critical of those who employed racist tactics and practices. He achieved this tenuous balance by requesting that Cubans put aside the racial divisions that stood in the way of a unified nationalist movement. His tactic for diffusing racial divisions was to construct an ethnic identity, a *Cubanidad*, strong enough to overcome racial differences. Moreover, the need to do so underscored the fact that racism was not exclusively a problem of the United States.

Marti recognized the importance of incorporating Afro Cubans into the nationalist movements and made a point of interacting and working closely with prominent Afro Cubans to show his dedication to racial solidarity. His speech in Ybor City indicated the value of Afro Cuban participation and even the very necessity of it if Cuban independence was to be successful. Attempts at unifying a nationalist movement had previously failed, which made Marti fully aware of the destructive consequences of racism to the cause of independence. During the 1890s, Afro Cubans helped found the Cuban Revolutionary Party known as the Partido Revolucionario Cubano (PRC), served as delegates to the PRC, wrote for and assisted in the publication of revolutionary newspapers, collected dues and donations, and raised funds. Nonetheless, despite their dedication to the nationalist cause, few recognized their efforts. Afro Cubans rarely held any positions of power within the nationalist movement and were expected to form separate revolutionary and cultural clubs.

Despite Marti's efforts, however, the Cuban community remained essentially divided and stratified. Revolutionary and cultural clubs formed on the basis of race, ethnicity, gender, and class testify to the degree to which Cubans of all backgrounds sought to separate themselves. Ironically, many of these clubs were founded on Marti's nationalist and patriotic principles. Clubs like La Union Marti-Maceo, the Obreras de

La Independencia and El Circulo Cubano were active in raising funds, printing revolutionary pamphlets and working with the PRC. Not one of the clubs, however, was racially integrated. By the late nineteenth and early twentieth centuries, La Union Marti Maceo was a male Afro-Cuban club, La Obrera de la Independencia included only white Cuban women, and white Cuban males comprised the membership of El Circulo Cubano.

The experience of Afro-Cuban immigrants in Ybor City during the turn of the century raises important questions concerning race, politics, ethnicity and power. For example, why did Cuban immigrants form separate revolutionary and social clubs if they were all working toward the same goal? Did Florida's Jim Crow laws force Cuban immigrants to adhere to racial segregation or did it simply magnify the racial divisiveness already present in the Cuban community? Why were women expected to organize separate clubs if their participation in the nationalist movement was extensive and invaluable? Why were Afro Cubans able to distance themselves from African Americans while at the same time depending on the resources located in the African-American section of Tampa? These questions help to demonstrate the complex and intricate relationship among race, ethnicity, gender and class.

While these questions provide a skeletal framework for studying the history of Afro Cubans in Ybor City and Tampa during the turn of the century, more research is needed to understand the experiences of Afro-Latino immigrants, a broader and even more diverse group (13). Rarely included in the history of African Americans and/or Latinos in the United States, the histories of Black Cubans, Puerto Ricans, and Dominicans in the United States often fall through the cracks of historical study. The failure to incorporate the experiences, stories and lives of Afro-Latino immigrants in the United States may render incomplete examinations of racial and ethnic constructions. Perhaps by taking a closer look at the early history of Afro Cubans in Ybor City and Tampa, we can begin to unravel and study the relationship between race and ethnicity in the United States. ❑

Segregation based on gender was common in many cigar factories. These women are stemming, which was a male precursor to cigar-making before becoming a separate occupation for women.

Endnotes

1. Please refer to Durward Long's "The Historical Beginning of Ybor City and Modern Tampa," *Florida Historical Quarterly* 45 (1966), Susan Greenbaum's "Afro-Cubans in Exile: Tampa, Florida, 1886-1984," *Cuban Studies/ Estudios Cubanos* 15 (Winter 1985), and Louis A. Perez's "Cubans in Tampa: From Exiles to Immigrants, 1892-1901," *Florida Historical Quarterly* 576 (October 1978) for more details on the establishment of Ybor City and the development of an immigrant community. For more information concerning Cuban history and how it affected Cuban migration to Tampa please see Louis A. Perez Jr.'s *Cuba Between Empires, 1878-1902* (Pittsburgh: University of Pittsburgh Press, 1983), 22-23 as well as Perez's *Cuba Under the Platt Amendment, 1902-1934* (Pittsburgh: University of Pittsburgh Press, 1986).

2. To better understand how racial segregation laws affected legal definitions of race for African Americans in Florida, please refer to Jerrell H. Shofner, *Nor Is It Over Yet: Florida in the Era of Reconstruction, 1863-1877* (Gainesville: University Presses of Florida, 1974), and Wali Kharif's "Black Reaction to Segregation and Discrimination in Post Reconstruction Florida," *Florida Historical Quarterly* (Fall 1987).

3. Susan Greenbaum characterizes the history of Afro Cubans in Tampa during the turn of the century as a "conceptual relationship between race and ethnicity in American society." Greenbaum, "Tampa's Afro-Cubans," *Cuban Heritage* 1 (Fall 1987), 5.

4. Gary R. Mormino and George E. Pozzetta, *The Immigrant World of Ybor City: Italians and their Latin Neighbors in Tampa, 1885-1985* (Urbana: University of Illinois Press, 1987), 241. This quote was taken from an oral interview of Frank Urso conducted in 1982 by Mormino and Pozzetta. In the interview, Urso stated that "If the crackers (Tampa's Anglo community) really wanted to make us Latins mad they'd call us Cuban niggers."

5. "Ybor City: Tampa's Latin Colony," produced by the Florida Branch of the Federal Writer's Project of the WPA, Special Collections Department, University of South Florida, Tampa, 31 March 1941. While the descriptions were documented by writers visiting the city in 1941, it is clear that from works such as Gary R. Mormino and George E. Pozzetta's *The Immigrant World of Ybor City* and Jose Rivero Muniz's, "Los Cubanos en Tampa," *Revista Bimestre Cubana* 74 (1958), from its inception, Ybor City was an immigrant community where Cubans easily transferred Cuban customs and traditions.

6. Susan Greenbaum, "Afro-Cubans in Ybor City: A Centennial History," Tampa: A publication of the University of South Florida, 1986, 9.

7. Louis A. Perez Jr., explains the importance of *lectores* to Cuban cigarworkers and the threat *lectores* posed to cigar manufacturers. *Lectores* assisted in the nationalist cause by informing Cuban cigarworkers of political developments in Cuba and requesting funds to aid the nationalist cause. At the same time, *lectores* read newspapers and books that discussed the plight of workers in the United States. In November 1931, as Perez notes, "cigar manufacturers, supported by city and county authorities and vigilante groups, announced the decision to abolish the *lectura*." Perez, "Reminiscences of A Lector: Cuban Cigar Workers in Tampa," *Florida Historical Quarterly* 53 (April 1975).

8. Patricia A. Cooper, *Once A Cigar Maker: Men, Women and Work Culture in American Cigar Factories, 1900-1919* (Urbana: University of Illinois Press, 1987), 15.

9. During the turn of the century, African Americans in Florida challenged a series of racial segregation laws and were active in changing oppressive and unjust conditions. Both Wali R. Kharif's "Black Reaction to Segregation and Discrimination in Post-Reconstruction Florida," *Florida Historical Quarterly* (Fall 1987) and August Meier and Elliot Rudwick's "Negro Boycotts of Segregated Streetcars in Florida, 1901-1905," *South Atlantic Quarterly* (Autumn 1970) show the strategies African Americans developed and used to affect change in a period of intense racial discrimination and disenfranchisement.

10. While it is difficult to document informal alliances between African Americans and Afro Cubans, the records of La Union Marti-Maceo, an Afro-Cuban club and mutual aid society, dated 17 October 1915, indicate that Afro Cubans finally voted to permit all Black individuals regardless of nationality, as members of La Union Marti-Maceo. However, as the vote count reveals, the Afro-Cuban members were not fully content with the decision. Out of sixty-two members present, only twenty-six members voted in favor, four voted against it and thirty-two abstained.

11. Translated this means a free Cuba. I have used the term "Cuba Libre" throughout the text to show how the notion of a free Cuba, that is a Cuba independent from Spain, fueled nationalist rhetoric and reflected the goals of the exiled Cuban community.

12. Quoted in Joan Marie Steffy, "Cuban Immigration to Tampa, 1886-1898," (Unpublished M.A. Thesis, University of South Florida, 1975), 48.

13. For the purposes of this article I have used the term Afro-Latino to describe Latinos of African ancestry and descent. However, it is an inadequate term, one that in no way considers cultural, political and social ties and experiences. The fact that imprecise terms have to be used to describe these communities shows to what extent a language which speaks to their experiences still needs to be established and developed.

Nancy Raquel Mirabel is a doctoral candidate in American history at the University of Michigan. She is working on a dissertation that explores the relationship among race, ethnicity, and identity.

Defending the Home: Ossian Sweet and the Struggle Against Segregation in 1920s Detroit

Victoria W. Wolcott

"When I opened the door I saw the mob and I realized I was facing the same mob that had hounded my people throughout our entire history. I was filled with a fear that only one could experience who knows the history and strivings of my race" (1). To understand these words and to know the history of the Sweet case, in which Ossian Sweet and ten other African Americans were acquitted of murder for defending Sweet's home against a white mob, is to know the history of segregation in America. Although much American history has been written as if segregation was not effectively challenged before the 1954 Supreme Court decision of *Brown* v. *Board of Education*, a more careful examination of African-American racial struggle in the twentieth century reveals a legacy of resistance to segregation in the courts and in the streets. The Sweet case gripped the nation's attention in 1925 and 1926 as race riots became commonplace, the Ku Klux Klan's influence grew, and rapid urbanization and industrialization created an array of new urban problems. Indeed, a close examination of the events surrounding the Sweet case reveals a neglected side of the seemingly upbeat Jazz age—a side of violence, racial intolerance, and segregation. How-

ever, it also demonstrates the ongoing growth of African-American self-determination and struggle in a rapidly changing urban America.

In June of 1925, Sweet purchased a house in the northeast section of Detroit, a largely white immigrant neighborhood. Because the previous owners had been an interracial couple, Sweet harbored few fears

---

The Sweet case reveals a neglected side of the seemingly upbeat Jazz age — a side of violence, racial intolerance, and segregation.

---

of a violent reaction from his neighbors. The residents believed, however, that their light-skinned African American neighbor, Edward Smith, had been white. When they heard the house was sold to an African American family the residents organized the "Waterworks Improvement Association," named for the nearby Waterworks park. Like other neighborhood associations orga-

nized in Detroit during this period, this group was formed exclusively for the purpose of maintaining a "whites only" neighborhood. Cognizant of the growing resistance in the area, and hopeful that the tumult over a number of racial incidents in the city that summer would die down, the Sweets decided to delay their move until September.

On 8 September 1925, Sweet and his family moved into their newly purchased house after requesting police protection from the local precinct. Along with Gladys Sweet, his wife, Ossian was joined by his brothers Otis Sweet, a dentist, Henry Sweet, a college student, three friends, a large supply of food, nine guns, and ammunition. Although crowds formed near the house sporadically that first day, the night passed relatively peacefully. The crowd, however, became increasingly belligerent the next day so the Sweets invited four more friends to help protect their property. That evening, as Otis Sweet and a friend arrived from work in a taxi, a white crowd caught sight of them and began to hurl rocks and racial epithets. After Otis and his friend had narrowly escaped injury by racing into their home, the mob began to hurl stones at the house itself, shattering an upstairs window. The Sweets and their friends took position inside and

Housing conditions similar to those in this eastside neighborhood of Detroit in the 1930s were not uncommon due to overcrowding which often resulted from segregation.

the rapid development of the automobile industry dramatically increased the demand for unskilled labor. The Emergency Immigration Act of 1921, however, had closed off the primary source of unskilled labor in the North—European immigrant workers. Thus, two major waves of African-American migration hit Detroit, the first in 1916-17 when the war-induced labor shortage was at its most acute, and the second during 1924-25 when the decrease in foreign immigration led Detroit's automakers to open up more jobs to African Americans. As a result, between 1910 and 1930 there was a *twenty-fold* increase of Detroit's African-American population, outpacing the growth of any other industrial city.

The city's African-American migrants were usually forced to the eastside where absentee landlords took advantage of the overcrowded conditions by demanding high rents. In 1923, the State Supreme Court of Michigan upheld the constitutionality of restrictive covenants (agreements restricting the use or occupancy of a residence by a person of a particular race) in *Parmallee* v. *Morris*, a legal precedent that stood until 1948. Thus, neighborhood improvement associations and realtors had the legal right to draft contracts that excluded persons on the basis of race. As a result, African Americans who tried to move into white neighborhoods often faced not only mob violence but legal barriers.

When relatively affluent migrants, like Sweet who was a physician, sought housing outside of the eastside neighborhood, small-scale riots often ensued. In 1925, a series of these disturbances led up to the Sweet riot. In June 1925, Dr. Alex L. Turner bought a house in an all-white northwest Detroit neighborhood. When the Turner family attempted to move into their new home, a mob of five thousand jeering and stone-throwing whites greeted them. They escaped only under police protection. The leader of the Tireman Avenue Improvement Association, who had orchestrated the forced removal of the Turners, helped form the Waterworks Improvement Association, whose members formed the bulk of the September 9 mob. A few weeks after the Turner affair, an African-American undertaker, Vollington A. Bristol,

shots rang out both from the house and from the guns of police stationed nearby. A member of the mob, Leo Breiner, was shot in the back and killed, and another man, Erik Halberg, was injured by a bullet to the leg. Police immediately entered the house and arrested all eleven residents for murder.

The Detroit that Ossian Sweet knew in 1925 was a dynamic urban center. The city had been transformed by the Great Migration and the growth of the industrial sector. The defense industries of World War I and built a home in a white neighborhood and withstood several nights of violent demonstrations before being forced from his house. When it appeared that Bristol might hold out against the mob, a white woman was reported to have stood on a box and shouted, "If you call yourselves men and are afraid to move these niggers out, we women will move them out, you cowards!" (2). In addition to these and other attempts to challenge segregation, in the two years before the Sweet case, fifty-five African Americans were killed by Detroit police with impunity.

On top of unrelenting police brutality and mob violence, there was a series of election campaigns during 1924 and 1925 in which the Ku Klux Klan openly ran a mayoral candidate, Charles S. Bowles. In 1924, Bowles nearly won the mayoral election as a write-in candidate. His opponent, John W. Smith, who was supported by the African American and immigrant communities, was declared the winner only when fifteen thousand ballots were disqualified by the city. On the Saturday prior to this election, the largest meeting of Klansmen and Klanswomen in Detroit's history congregated in a field in nearby Dearborn (3). Thus, the mid-1920s in Detroit was a time of tremendous racism, nativism and violence.

However, there was another side to the racial struggles of the 1920s. African Americans in Detroit and other urban centers were forming strong community institutions that provided an organizational base from which to fight battles such as the Sweet case. Detroit in this period was also a major center for Marcus Garvey's United Negro Improve-

Archives of Labor and Urban Affairs, Wayne State University

Henry Sweet, at left, stands with his legal counsel team. The jury in the case found Sweet not guilty and the charges for the remaining ten defendants were later dropped.

ment Association (UNIA) which preached African-American self-help and self-defense. The National Association for the Advancement of Colored People (NAACP), an extremely important national organization, lent its resources to fight racism at the local level. Its agreement to back the Sweet case with financial and legal support was key to a three-pronged national attack on segregation. In 1917, the NAACP had successfully argued, in *Buchanan* v. *Warley*, that the state could not pass legislation limiting individuals' right to own or use property because of their race. In 1925, just as the Sweet case began, the NAACP argued *Corrigan* v. *Buckley* in the U.S. Supreme Court in an attempt to overturn a residential covenant in Washington, D.C. Having addressed housing segregation sanctioned by the state and by private agreement, they hoped to win a third battle against segregation through mob violence by defending the eleven accused in Detroit. Thus, thirty years before *Brown* v. *Board of Education*, the NAACP was directly challenging both legal and extra-legal attempts to draw a color line in American towns and cities.

In addition to the NAACP leadership, African Americans in many communities outside of Detroit rallied to support the Sweet defendants. Fundraisers were held in major cities to raise the money necessary to try the case which had captured national attention. After a mass fund-raising meeting in New York City, Walter White, assistant secretary of the NAACP, telegrammed Rev. Robert L. Bradby, president of the local chapter, and explained, "It is felt here in New York that in making the fight you are making for Dr. Sweet you are fighting the battle of every one of the eleven million Negroes in the U.S." (4).

The NAACP felt that in order to win the case, the best legal representation should be sought, and although African-American lawyers from Detroit would be allowed to assist in the defense, they recommended a white lawyer be found in order to appeal to an all-white jury. Therefore, James Weldon Johnson, secretary of the NAACP, in early October contacted celebrated lawyer Clarence

Darrow who agreed to take the case for a nominal fee of five thousand dollars. Darrow's acceptance of the Sweet case made front-page news in African-American newspapers across the country. By 4 November a jury had been picked in the initial trial of all eleven defendants, and opening arguments were ready to be heard.

Judge Frank Murphy, who later became Mayor of Detroit, Governor of Michigan and a Supreme Court Justice, presided over the trial. Hundreds packed the courtroom each day, and after Darrow complained that African Americans were not being allowed seating, Murphy set aside half of the spectators' section for them. The prosecutor,

---

Clarence Darrow transformed the courtroom into a classroom and the jury into students of African-American history.

Robert M. Toms, relied on a conspiracy theory to present his case because he could not prove who had shot the bullet that had killed Breiner, or even if the shot had come from the house. Much of the prosecution's presentation consisted of seventy-five witnesses who testified that they saw no crowds near the Sweet's house on the night of September 9. Apparently the irony of having seventy-five witnesses testify to the absence of a crowd was lost on the prosecution. Darrow's skillful cross-examinations of these witnesses delighted court spectators and reporters. At one point he caught a young boy in a direct lie as his assistant Arthur Garfield Hays remembered: "'There was a great crowd—no, I won't say a great crowd, a large crowd—well, there were a few people there and the officers were keeping them moving.' Darrow was on his feet. 'Have you talked to any one about the case?' 'Lieutenant Johnson' (the police detective). 'And

when you started to answer the question you forgot to say a few people, didn't you?' 'Yes, sir'" (5).

After discrediting the prosecution's witnesses, Darrow based his defense on sociological evidence describing race relations in America. John C. Dancy, the influential director of the Detroit Urban League, testified about housing conditions in Detroit, and Walter White testified about the history of lynching and racial violence that had pervaded American society since emancipation. However, the most effective witness was Ossian Sweet himself. During his testimony Sweet discussed his childhood in a small town in Florida where the fear of lynching was ever-present. He went on to explain how he witnessed race riots in Washington, D.C. while studying medicine at Howard University and how he had reacted to the series of racial incidents in Detroit that preceded the events that had landed him in jail. Using this strategy, Darrow showed both the defendant's state of mind during the night of the shooting and transformed the courtroom into a classroom and the jury into students of African American history.

"There are persons in the North and South who say a black man is inferior to the white and should be controlled by the whites." Darrow said in his eloquent closing argument which moved many spectators to tears, "There are also those who recognize his rights and say he should enjoy them. To me this case is a cross-section of human history; it involves the future, and the hope of some of us that the future shall be better than the past" (6). The jury deliberated for forty-six hours, arguing so loudly that at times those waiting in the halls could hear them. Finally they announced they were unable to reach a verdict. Expectations had been raised in the African-American community that an acquittal was imminent because of Darrow's skillful defense; therefore, a hung jury was a severe disappointment. However, White concluded that "the case has largely changed public sentiment in Detroit," as evidenced by white newspapers' sympathetic portrayal of the defendants by the close of the trial (7).

The defendants were released on bail after the verdict, but on 20 April 1926, a second trial began. The state had decided to try the defendants separately and began with the prosecution of Henry Sweet, Ossian's younger brother, and the only defendant who admitted firing his gun. This trial proceeded in a similar fashion as the first, with Darrow skillfully uncovering the lies of the prosecution witnesses and providing the sociological background to support his argument of self-defense. Darrow was again passionate in his closing argument:

"Eleven people, knowing what it meant, with the history of the race behind them, with the picture of Detroit in front of them, with the memory of Turner and Bristol . . . with the knowledge of shootings and killings and insult and injury without end, and eleven of them go into a house, gentlemen, and no police protection, in the face of a mob, and in the hatred of a community, and take in guns and ammunition and fight for their rights and for your rights and for mine, and for the rights of every being that lived" (8).

After deliberating four hours on 19 May 1926, the jury found Henry Sweet not guilty, and the charges were eventually dropped for the remaining ten defendants. African Americans across the country had finally gotten the victory they had been seeking.

Race relations in Detroit did improve somewhat after the Sweet trial, but it proved to be a short-lived peace. In 1942, Detroit's Seven-Mile Fenelon Improvement Association attempted to ban African Americans from the desperately needed Sojourner Truth housing project, and one year later, the worst race riot the nation had yet witnessed took place on Detroit's streets. Legal efforts to fight segregation also had a mixed legacy. Although the NAACP's attempt to eradicate residential covenants in 1925 was defeated with the dismissal of the *Corrigan* v. *Buckley* case by the Supreme Court, in 1948 the Court's ruling in *Shelley* v. *Kraemer* finally declared implementation of restrictive covenants in private housing unconstitutional. Ironically, Justice Frank Murphy, who twenty-two years earlier had presided over the Sweet case, cast a key vote in this decision.

The Sweet case marked an early victory against housing segregation both by the lawyers and leaders of the Civil Rights movement and by individual African Americans willing to face a white mob with strength and pride. Paradoxically then, the Sweet case foreshadowed both the non-violent Civil Rights movement and the ideology of self-defense of Malcolm X and the Black Panthers. ❏

Bibliography

Asher, Cash. Papers. Bentley Historical Library. Ann Arbor, Michigan.

Capeci, Dominic J., Jr. *Race Relations in Wartime Detroit: The Sojourner Truth Housing Controversy of 1942*. Philadelphia: Temple University Press, 1984.

Dancy, John C. *Sand Against the Wind: The Memoirs of John C. Dancy*. Detroit: Wayne State University Press, 1966.

Darrow, Clarence. *The Story of My Life*. New York: Charles Scribner's Sons, 1932.

Fine, Sidney. *Frank Murphy: The Detroit Years*. Ann Arbor: University of Michigan Press, 1975.

Gellein, Hilmer. Papers. Bentley Historical Library. Ann Arbor, Michigan.

Haldeman-Julius, Marcet. *Clarence Darrow's Two Great Trials: Reports of the Scopes Anti-Evolution Case and the Dr. Sweet Negro Trial*. Girard, Kansas: Haldeman-Julius, 1927.

Hays, Arthur Garfield. *Let Freedom Ring*. New York: Horace Liveright, 1928.

Jackson, Kenneth T. *The Ku Klux Klan in the City, 1915-1930*. New York: Oxford University Press, 1967.

Lilienthal, David E. "Has the Negro the Right of Self-Defense?" *Nation* 121 (23 December 1925): 1-3.

Meier, August and John Bracey, eds. *Papers of the N.A.A.C.P.* Microfilm. Frederick, MD: University Publications of America, 1986.

Thomas, Richard W. *Life for Us Is What We Make It: Building Black Community in Detroit, 1915-1945*. Bloomington: Indiana University Press, 1992.

Vose, Clement E. *The Supreme Court, the NAACP, and the Restrictive Covenant Cases*. Berkeley: University of California Press, 1959.

Weinberg, Kenneth G. *A Man's Home, a Man's Castle*. New York: McCall Publishing, 1971.

Widick, B.J. *Detroit: City of Race and Class Violence*. Detroit: Wayne State University Press, 1989.

Endnotes

1. Quoted in August Meier and John Bracey, eds., *Papers of the N.A.A.C.P., microfilm* (Frederick, MD: University Publications of America, 1986). Speech by Arthur Garfield Hays at the annual meeting of the N.A.A.C.P., 3 January 1926, pp. 5-6, reel 3.

2. Marcet Haldeman-Julius, *Clarence Darrow's Two Great Trials: Reports of the Scopes Anti-Evolution Case and the Dr. Sweet Negro Trial* (Girard, KS: Haldeman-Julius, 1927), 39.

3. Kenneth T. Jackson, *The Ku Klux Klan in the City, 1915-1930* (New York: Oxford University Press, 1967), 136.

4. *Papers of the N.A.A.C.P.*, telegram from Walter White to Rev. Bradby, 21 September 1925, reel 2.

5. Arthur Garfield Hays, *Let Freedom Ring* (New York: Horace Liveright, 1928), 209.

6. Quoted in Kenneth G. Weinberg, *A Man's Home, A Man's Castle* (New York: McCall Publishing, 1971), 119.

7. Quoted in *Papers of the N.A.A.C.P.*, Press Release, 28 November 1923: "Sweet Jury Disagrees, New Trial in January," reel 3.

8. *Papers of the N.A.A.C.P.*, Transcript of Darrow's closing argument, p. 31, 11 May 1926, reel 3.

Victoria W. Wolcott is writing a dissertation on labor, race, and gender in Detroit during the interwar period. A doctoral student at the University of Michigan, she has presented her work at several professional conferences.

Constructing a Life and a Community: A Partial Story of Maggie Lena Walker

Elsa Barkley Brown

'I was not born with a silver spoon in my mouth: but instead with a clothes basket almost upon my head" (1). In this way, Maggie Lena Walker—early twentieth century bank president, political activist, and club woman—described her entry into the world and her understanding of her place in a hierarchical southern society.

Maggie Lena Draper Mitchell Walker was born in Richmond, Virginia, ca. 1867 (2). Her mother, Elizabeth Dra-per, was a young domestic servant in the mansion of Civil War spy Elizabeth Van Lew. Her father, Eccles Cuthbert, was a northern white journalist who frequented the Van Lew house (3). Shortly after Maggie Lena's birth, her mother married William Mitchell, a butler in the same household and soon-to-be waiter in the St. Charles Hotel. The family moved to College Alley, a location that put them within view of Broad Street, one of Richmond's main thoroughfares, and just around the corner from First African Baptist Church, Richmond's oldest and largest black congregation. By engaging in the social life of the neighborhood, Maggie Mitchell could witness firsthand many of the social and political activities of black Richmonders; she also became a fervent (and lifelong) member of First African (4).

As will be seen, Maggie Walker was in many ways a remarkable individual who influenced her Richmond community in profound ways, and as such she is certainly deserving of biographical treatment. Unfortunately, in the case of Maggie Walker, there are some gaps in the sources which historians have traditionally used to write biography. Many social historians, in fact, have encountered this problem in their wish to study individuals other than politicians, industrialists, and other elites. Fortunately, such problems can be surmounted by looking to different types of sources. In Walker's

---

Walker pointed out that black women had only three occupations available to them: domestic worker, teacher, and church builder.

---

case, community records viewed in conjunction with her diary and various personal papers provide important context for her life's work. Although we still do not know all we would like to know about individuals like Maggie Walker, her story is important and should be told.

On the streets and especially in the church, Maggie Mitchell from an early age had a view of women engaging in public life, developing community institutions, and con-

testing race and gender prescriptions. African-American women during Walker's time often faced dire economic straits. When she wanted to emphasize the paucity of jobs available to black women, especially as work in the city's tobacco factories closed to them, she would point out that black women had only three occupations: domestic worker, teacher, and church builder. The last reference signaled how seriously she took the notions expressed years earlier; she continued to argue that women's contributions were indeed a vital form of labor, even though unwaged.

In constructing her political arsenal, Maggie Mitchell Walker frequently turned to the church (6). Biblical language undergirded most of Walker's speeches and scripture served as her most effective means of arguing for women's rights (7). Certainly she had learned her Bible in First African but she may also have been influenced by the women who were known throughout the community as the authors of prominent male ministers' sermons or those few women who themselves established reputations as "soul-stirring" preachers. One of these was the Rev. Mrs. Carter, of whom it was said, "Many fell out at her preaching" (8).

Maggie Walker's prominence provided a sharp challenge to the complex gender relations that existed in the African-American community during the last years of the nineteenth century. A local black newspaper, the *Richmond Planet*, reported intra-racial gender disagreements as if they were commonplace occurrences. First African debated women's attendance at church meetings. The *Virginia Baptist* saw a threat to "womanliness" when women exceeded their proper place in the church by attempting to preach and their proper place in the community by the "deplorable" effort to "exercise the right of suffrage" (9). Thus, by the early twentieth century when Walker had established her own leadership, things had not changed much within First African, and she was nearly unique in her ability to speak in church meetings and participate in church business. (She was chief financial advisor, developing the church budget.) Yet it would be hard not to imagine the women within her church and her community who petitioned, wrote sermons and preached establishing a precedent for Walker's own sermonizing and her understanding of women's rights.

Other communities of women also influenced her development. After William Mitchell's mysterious death in 1876, Maggie helped her mother in her work as a laundress and with the care of her younger brother, Johnnie. Laundry work was a traditional occupation of African American women, especially married women who desired time at home to care for children and time to partake in community activities (10). Rather than confine themselves to their individual homes for a day of solitary drudgery, however, women often organized to collectively scrub, rinse, starch, iron, and fold the pounds of laundry. Some laundry women actually became entrepreneurs, contracting all of the work themselves and hiring the other women who worked with them (11). Many of these days spent scrubbing were also spent organizing; a number of churches, schools and recreational centers grew out of the discussions among washerwomen about the need for these community institutions (12).

Maggie Mitchell's early start in the world of work was fairly typical for African-American children in the nineteenth century. In fact, Mitchell was quite fortunate for, despite the need for her to assist her mother, she was able to still attend school regularly. Many others had to forego school-

ing in order to contribute to the family income. Mitchell, however, graduated in 1883 from Colored High and Normal, becoming a teacher at Valley School that fall. It was perhaps the requirement that she relinquish her teaching assignment upon her 1886 marriage to Armstead Walker, a Colored High graduate and brick contractor, that pushed Walker into her business career.

Having studied accounting and sales while teaching, Walker joined several other women in founding the Woman's Union insurance business. At the same time, she worked her way up through the Independent Order of St. Luke (IOSL), a mutual benefit society which she had joined at age fourteen, becoming an elected delegate at age sixteen and an elected officer by age seventeen. After her marriage, Walker devoted more time to the St. Lukes, traveling throughout Virginia and West Virginia to develop new Councils, and working to establish a juvenile branch of the Order in 1895. In 1899, Walker, by then the mother of two sons, became Grand Worthy Secretary, the highest executive officer of the IOSL. In 1903, she spearheaded the founding of St. Luke Penny Savings Bank and became its president. Three decades later, she would oversee its reorganization as the present-day Consolidated Bank and Trust Company, the oldest continuously existing black-owned and black-run bank in the country.

Maggie Lena Walker's occupational and economic advancement was in one sense a singular success. On another level, however, her rise to schoolteacher represented the chief form of occupational advancement for black women in the late nineteenth and early twentieth centuries; a number of other women from both poor and more well-to-do backgrounds had traveled this route (13). Walker was not alone among members of Richmond's African-American community in pursuing other careers after marrying effectively prevented her from teaching. Sarah G. Jones, for example, left Richmond temporarily to attend Howard University Medical School and returned to develop a successful practice, becoming the first black woman physician in the state of Virginia (14).

Walker's climb in mutual benefit soci-

ety work, while more spectacular than mos also suggests a particular avenue for blad women's occupational and economic m bility. When Maggie Walker assumed th position of Grand Worthy Secretary in 189 her "first work was to draw around n *women*." In fact, after the executive boa elections in 1901, six of the nine membe were women (15). Walker's plan to have th bank be run solely by women was thwarte when her inability to find an experience black woman cashier allowed the men in th Order to insist that this not be totally women's venture (16). However, wome were still instrumental; eight of the fir nineteen directors of the St. Luke Penn Savings Bank were women.

A department store, set up by the IOS in 1905, provided further opportunities fc Richmond's African-American community The St. Luke Emporium, collectively forme by twenty-two women, aimed at providin quality goods at affordable prices, as well a a place where black women could earn living and get a business education. The S Luke Emporium employed fifteen wome as salesclerks, an insignificant number i comparison to the thousands of black wome working outside the home, but in the contex of the occupational structure of Richmonc it represented a significant percentage of th white-collar and skilled working-clas women in the community. In 1910, only 22 of the more than thirteen thousand em ployed black women listed their occupa tions as typists, stenographers, bookkeepers and salesclerks. Black secretaries and clerk were entirely dependent on the financia stability of black businesses and, in thi regard, the IOSL was especially important With its fifty-five clerks in the home office over one-third of the black female clerica workers in Richmond in the 1920s worke for this Order. The salaries of these clerica workers, moreover, often surpassed eve those of teachers (17).

Additionally, black women worked fo the St. Lukes, as for other mutual benefi societies, organizing adult and juvenile coun cils and recruiting members. Organizer were paid for each council organized an member recruited, and for travel expenses Apart from the financial benefits it brought he position allowed many African-American women in Richmond a significant amount of independence, visibility, and occasionally a foothold in politics. Lillian Payne, for example, one of the chief organizers for the St. Lukes, became a popular political speaker throughout the Northeast as a result of her organizing work (18). Whether working as clerks in the home office or organizers in the field, these women engaged in political and community work along with their St. Luke work. The work routine of the St. Luke Home Office regularly included detailing a segment of the clerks to community projects such as fundraising for the Community House for Colored People, the Afro-American Old Folks Home, the Friends Orphan Asylum, the Council of Colored Women, and the NAACP (19).

Many of these women faced with Walker the challenge of balancing a home life with a professional life outside the home. Even among those African-American women who were married and had children, a significant portion engaged in wage labor. Additionally, it was more common for middle-class black clubwomen to be married and to have children than for middle-class white women undertaking club and community work (20). Walker's balancing efforts were not together successful, as surely many women's were not. And her life was not without its tragedy and scandal. In 1915, her eldest son, Russell, shot and killed his father. After a sensational trial Russell was acquitted, the death ruled accidental. Yet the trial itself, combined with Walker's few scattered and cryptic diaries, is the best evidence we have of life inside the Walker home, where Maggie Walker lived at various times with her mother, relative/housekeeper, husband, two sons,

and later their wives and children. The evidence points to a household that pivoted around a prominent and successful businesswoman: her husband spent much of his time away from home, rumors of a liaison between Maggie Walker and another man

Maggie L. Walker National Historic Site

Maggie Mitchell Walker, daughter of a laundress, became a teacher in the Richmond public school system and an active member of the Independent Order of Saint Luke.

persisted, and her sons were disgruntled at the amount of attention and funds their mother expended on other people's children. Becoming prominent and successful (or even just engaging in community and/or wage work) had its personal costs. Maggie Walker seems to have paid them—usually

quietly, privately, and for a few months, quite publicly (21).

This is but a small part of Maggie Lena Walker's story. But examining the life of one black woman prominent in her time and little-known in historical scholarship suggests ways to take other women and use the reconstruction of their lives to explore African American women's history and the internal dynamics of African American community life.
❑

Endnotes
1. Maggie Lena Walker, "Stumbling Blocks," Second Baptist Church, February 17, 1907, bound in Maggie Lena Walker, *Addresses 1909*, Maggie Lena Walker Papers, Maggie L. Walker National Historic Site, Richmond, Virginia (hereafter MLW Papers).
2. The traditional date given for Walker's birth is 15 July 1867; however, Gertrude Marlowe, Director of the Maggie Lena Walker Biography Project, Department of Anthropology, Howard University, suggests that her actual year of birth was probably two years earlier. Marlowe, "Maggie Lena Walker," in Darlene Clark Hine, Elsa Barkley Brown, and Rosalyn Terborg-Penn, eds., *Black Women in America: An Historical Encyclopedia* (Brooklyn: Carlson Publishing, 1993), 1214.
3. For basic biographical information on Walker, see Wendell P. Dabney, *Maggie L. Walker and the Independent Order of Saint Luke: The Woman and Her Work* (Cincinnati: Dabney, 1927); Marlowe, "Maggie Lena Walker," 1214-1219; Sadie Iola Daniel, *Women Builders* (Washington, D.C.: Associated Publishers, 1931), 28-52. On her political thought, see Elsa Barkley Brown, "Womanist Consciousness:

Maggie Lena Walker and the Independent Order of Saint Luke," *Signs* 14 (Spring 1989): 610-633.

4. For an excellent discussion of the network of institutions—church, mutual benefit societies, and families—in post-Civil War black Richmond, see Peter J. Rachleff, *Black Labor in the South: Richmond, Virginia, 1865-1890* (Philadelphia: Temple University Press, 1984), especially chapter 2.

5. For an eyewitness account of the women's drills, see Wendell P. Dabney, "Rough autobiographical sketch of boyhood years," n.d. (microfilm), Wendell Phillips Dabney Papers, Folder 3, Cincinnati Historical Society, Cincinnati, Ohio. Dabney was a boyhood friend of Walker.

6. Debates over gender roles within black churches occured on congregational and denominational levels. Church minutes are an excellent source for examining gender relations within the black community; in addition to the division of labor within the church and church policy, one can also examine the disciplinary measures taken against men and women for various offenses. First African's minutes, 1841-1930, are available on microfilm at the Archives Division, Virginia State Library, Richmond, Virginia. For studies which examine these debates at the state and/or national level, see, for example, Evelyn Brooks Higginbotham, *Righteous Discontent: The Women's Movement in the Black Baptist Church* (Cambridge: Harvard University Press, 1993); Glenda Gilmore, "Gender and Jim Crow: Women and the Politics of White Supremacy in North Carolina, 1896-1920," Ph.D. diss., University of North Carolina, Chapel Hill, 1992 (on the A.M.E. Zion); Cheryl Townsend Gilkes, "'Together and in Harness': Women's Traditions in the Sanctified Church," *Signs* 10 (Summer 1985): 678-699.

7. Maggie Lena Walker, "Speech to the Negro Young People's Christian and Educational Congress," Convention Hall, Washington, D.C., August 5, 1906; "Women at the Sepulchre," both in

MLW Papers, Maggie L. Walker National Historic Site, Richmond, Virginia.

8. *Richmond Planet*, 26 July 1890, 17 and 24 September 1898, 19 November 1898, and 9 September 1899.

9. *Virginia Baptist* cited in *Woman's Era*, 1 and 6 September 1894.

10. An excellent study of black domestic and personal service workers, including laundresses, is Tera W. Hunter, "Household Workers in the Making: Afro-American Women in Atlanta and the New South, 1861 to 1920" (Ph.D. Diss., Yale University, 1990). See also, Jacqueline Jones, *Labor of Love, Labor of Sorrow: Black Women, Work, and Family From Slavery to Freedom* (New York: Basic Books, 1985).

11. For examples of laundry women who became entreprenuers, see Elsa Barkley Brown, "Mothers of Mind," *Sage: A Scholarly Journal on Black Women* 6 (Summer 1989): 7; Sara Lawrence Lightfoot, *Balm in Gilead: Journey of a Healer* (Reading, Mass.: Addison-Wesley, 1988), 23-24.

12. See, for example, the 1896 founding of St. James Baptist Church which grew out of the discussions of three women's discussions as they did their laundry about the need in their area for a "building to be used as a Sunday School and a place for community entertainment." The resulting building also served as a school. Rev. D. J. Bradford, "An Historical Sketch of St. James Baptist Church, Goochland County, Va.," (typescript, n.d.), St. James Baptist Church.

13. An examination of any black college's records—catalogues, alumni correspondence, school newspapers, etc.—will demonstrate the number of black women in the late nineteenth and early twentieth centuries who came from, often were sent by, impoverished families and communities to train for teaching. They will also, obviously, suggest the curriculum the women took and report on their activities in their careers, communities, and families after leaving the school.

14. Interestingly, Jones' husband, Miles,

followed her example, left his teaching assignment to attend Howard and returned to practice medicine alongside his wife. For a biographical sketch of Jones, see *Richmond Planet*, 26 January 1895.

15. Maggie Lena Walker, Diary, 6 March 1928, MLW Papers; *50th Anniversary—Golden Jubilee Historical Report of the R.W.G. Council of the I. O. St. Luke, 1867-1917* (Richmond, Va.: Everet Waddey, 1917), 41.

16. William Sydnor, "Early Leadership with the Independent Order of Saint Luke," presentation at "Maggie Lena Walker: Perspectives in Her Innovative Leadership," Symposium, Richmond Virginia, July 18, 1992.

17. This paragraph is taken from Brown, "Womanist Consciousness," 610-633. Nevertheless, black women in Richmond, as elsewhere, overwhelmingly remained in employed in domestic service.

18. See Lillian Payne Papers, Valentine Museum, Richmond, Virginia.

19. See, for example, Maggie Lena Walker, Diary, 30 and 31 January 1920, January 1920 memoranda. See also Lillian Payne Papers.

20. Linda Gordon, "Black and White Visions of Welfare: Women's Welfare Activism, 1890-1945," *Journal of Amercian History* 78 (September 1991): 559-590.

21. See Walker, Diaries, esp. 1925; *Richmond Planet*, June-November 1915.

Elsa Barkley Brown is an Instructor in history and Afroamerican and African Studies at the University of Michigan. Her essays have appeared in Signs, Feminist Studies, Sage, *and the* History Workshop Journal *The current essay is selected from her larger study of blacks in Richmond, Virginia during the late nineteenth and early twentieth centuries.*

Emancipation's Impact on African-American Education in Norfolk, Virginia, 1862-1880

Michael Hucles

The importance of the changes brought by emancipation can scarcely be exaggerated. While enslaved, African Americans were denied the opportunity to participate in the political arena, own property, receive an education, and enter into a free contractual arrangement with employers. With emancipation, African Americans embarked on a vigorous affirmation of their newly-won status by insisting on directing their lives in these and other areas. These changes, however, varied depending upon the political economy and location of the African-American community. The African-American community in Norfolk, for example, asserted itself in ways essential to its perceived interests. One of the areas uppermost in the minds of many black Norfolk residents was education. The educational opportunities that the Civil War and Reconstruction presented to the African-American community were significant, but education in the urban context also brought special problems. With changes in the urban political climate over time, the very real gains made by Norfolk African Americans often appeared illusory (1).

Norfolk in 1865 differed in many respects from the pre-Civil War city. Federal occupation of Norfolk on 10 May 1862 provided enslaved African Americans from the surrounding countryside a safe haven from rebel masters. Large numbers of African Americans came to the city in the hopes of finding freedom, and by 1870, the city's black population had nearly doubled since the outbreak of war almost ten years previous.

This dramatic increase in the city's black population (2) fueled the political aspirations of many African Americans who sought to affirm and debate the equality of "mankind." Others in the African American community simply rejoiced in their newly acquired status, supported their leaders, and sought to improve their lives materially in light of postwar economic adjustments. Still others, including many recent arrivals from the countryside, struggled to make the transition from rural to urban life.

African American definitions of freedom gained full eloquence in a document issued by Norfolk's black male elite in June 1865. In the *Equal Suffrage* statement, Norfolk blacks outlined a three-part program that called for male suffrage, property acquisition, and fair labor practices. As an expression of their class and gender, the authors focused their attention on obtaining the vote. And yet, they were aware that rights denied in one area affected the quality of life in other areas. Thus, they called for the formation of land and labor associations. They hoped that this multiple approach would provide a suitable organizational framework (3).

The vast majority of African Americans in the city, although not part of the political elite, supported the efforts of these leaders and participated in the numerous political gatherings. Most African Americans, however, focused on acquiring jobs and education. They perceived the ability to provide for their families and to have the opportunity to advance as far more critical than casting the ballot. Former slave and Norfolk resident Cornelius Garner recalled that "de fust school was Nicholson Street School." Staffed by primarily white school teachers, "dey had dat school an' two er three other schools heah den" (4).

Norfolk's African-American commu-

> *Most African Americans perceived the ability to provide for their families and to have the opportunity to advance as more critical than casting the*

nity briefly enjoyed public school education as early as 1863, when missionaries sent to liberated Norfolk obtained two buildings formerly used to teach white students. These schools were returned to white use, however, with the close of the war. Black children, therefore, were without schools for two years until a new political climate and the efforts of missionaries led to the opening of several schools for African-American students in 1867. The success of these schools was immediately apparent. The conservative white paper, the *Norfolk Journal*, for example, expressed praise and surprise "at the display of the intelligence by the pupils" who attended the Fenchurch Street school (5).

The school located on Fenchurch Street was one of three sponsored by the American Missionary Association. It was known as Southgate's Institute and had three teachers. The other schools were Wilson Institute, located at the corner of Bute and Union Streets, and the Calvert Street school. Wilson Institute had two teachers while the Calvert Street school had three. In addition, missionaries sponsored a night school for adults at Southgate's Institute four nights during the week. Prior to the Civil War, legal prohibitions forbade teaching blacks; hence, the night classes enabled a larger group of African Americans to receive what had been denied previously. These schools continued to provide valuable service to the black community until 1871, when the city councils passed an ordinance establishing a black public school in each of the four wards of the city. The schools within the black community would then be under the supervision of the superintendent of all schools (6).

Unfortunately, black educational progress in Norfolk was tied to the political climate of the city. In 1870, the newly elected city council redrew the boundaries of the four wards. A disproportionate number of blacks came to live in a new fourth ward. At the same time, the ward's representatives declined from eleven to five, which diluted the potential political power of blacks. Ironically, however, it also assured black representation on the council, which to some was tremendous progress since none had

Norfolk's Population, 1850-1870						
	Total Pop.	Black Pop.			White Pop.	% Black
		Total	Free	Slave		
1850	14,326	5,251	956	4,295	9,075	37
1860	14,610	4,319	1,035	3,284	10,290	30
1870	19,229	8,765	—	—	10,462	46

Source: Superintendent of the Census, *The Seventh Census of the United States: 1850* (Washington, D.C.: Robert Armstrong, Public Printer, 1853), p. 258; Superintendent of the Census, *Population of the United States in 1860; Compiled from the Original Returns of the Eighth Census* (Washington, D.C.: Government Printing Office, 1864), p. 519; U.S. Census Bureau, Eighth Census, 1860, Manuscript Population Schedules, Norfolk County (microfilm), RG 29, National Archives, Washington, D.C.; and U.S. Census Bureau, *The Statistics of the Population of the United States* (Washington, D.C., 1872), 1:281.

previously existed (7). Although this appeared promising, it proved less than satisfactory for black educational efforts. No clearer illustration of this can be seen than in the efforts of one black councilman, Jacob Riddick.

Riddick was elected to council in 1872 along with two other African Americans from the fourth ward, A. A. Portlock and J. D. Epps. Reflecting their minority status on council, conservative opposition appeared slight when minor issues were brought to its attention, such as when Riddick offered a resolution "to put into proper condition the pump on the southeast corner of Hawk and Liberty streets." When Riddick, who was a member of the Committee on Schools, requested a "special committee" be appointed to study "the location and condition of the colored public schools," his efforts were less than fruitful. Riddick remained a tireless proponent of black education and was appointed as a member of the Board of School Trustees in 1883 (8).

Throughout the 1870s, however, the efforts of Riddick and others proved ephemeral. The council ultimately limited opportunities for African-American students despite passing legislation in 1871 to create a black public school in each of the four wards. In reality, only two schools were created, although under missionary effort there had been at least three schools. According to the 1872 city directory, these schools were located on Church and Bute

Streets. The directory listed a private school for blacks on James Street run by a J. D. S. Hall, but the number of children attending and the type of instruction received were not reported and thus, it is difficult to determine the success of its operation. By contrast, white students attended four public schools in the city, thus receiving greater opportunities to advance (9).

In his 1877 annual report to the councils concerning educational progress, Mayor John S. Tucker stated that the Bute Street school was dilapidated and in need of extensive repair. Further, the school staff consisted of two persons: the rector, R. A. Tucker; and a grammar instructor, Miss M. E. Melvin, who would therefore be able to instruct only a limited number of students. Mayor Tucker informed the councils that the city rented this property and did not own it, which he saw as a waste of city expenditures, given the condition of the structure. He proposed, therefore, that the councils appropriate sufficient funds to "build another school-house for colored children and dispense with the one now rented for that purpose." This, he felt, could be accomplished because certain revenues were already available and others were anticipated (10).

The councils, however, appeared reluctant to respond to the mayor's request. The mayor was not alone in his urgings. School Trustee W. Talbot Walke and School Superintendent R. L. Page supported the mayor's

Many African Americans fled to cities in search of economic and educational freedom after emancipation. Oyster shuckers in Norfolk, for instance, soon discovered the difficulties that came with urban life.

request. Indeed, the Norfolk African-American community had impressed upon Walke their own sense of urgency as well. Walke noted that "there is a great demand on the part of the colored population, for additional School room . . . ." This was certainly necessary as Walke further indicated that "several hundred children in the Primary Departments are ready and anxious to enter the Public Schools." Certainly, Walke and others felt the pressures coming from black demands to provide more adequate facilities. Poor conditions were not new, however, as Cornelius Garner had noted that even the earliest "School was held in an ole buildin'" (11).

Council was not immune to pressures from blacks either, although they proceeded at a snail's pace. In response to the pressures, in 1877, the councils appropriated funds to purchase two lots "to erect a School House on each, one for the White and the other for Colored Pupils. . . ." Property was acquired and Walke suggested the following year that the purchased Cumberland Street lot was "conveniently located, and well-suited for the purpose" of constructing a new school for black students. Instead of following Walke's suggestion, council in 1879 obtained a "superior well-ventilated building on Queen Street at a less rent than we have paid for the other" to house African-Ameri-

can students. Norfolk's African-American student population appeared to be pleased with the new facility as attendance rates soared that year to a rate that exceeded white attendance by six percentage points (12).

Despite the addition of a new facility, the number of schools for African Americans remained at two. In an effort to accommodate more black students, the superintendent instituted a two-session structure, one in the morning and the other in the afternoon. In particular, the superintendent hoped to provide additional primary education to African Americans. Although the number of students accommodated increased, the needs of the African-American community were not met. As the superintendent noted, "We cannot accommodate all who are anxious to enter the Public Schools."

If we use the history of educational attainment as a barometer of African American advancement after the Civil War, the results are mixed. The Civil War ended slavery but did not guarantee black advancement. African Americans realized this. But as they jockeyed for political, social, and economic power, they constantly reassessed the meaning of freedom. In the process, they championed the cause of education. ❑

Endnotes

1. There have been many works produced recently describing Reconstruction's impact on African Americans. Perhaps the most comprehensive work on the period is *Eric Foner, Reconstruction: America's Unfinished Revolution, 1863-1877* (New York: Harper and Row, 1988). Foner has also published a very useful small volume that describes the meaning of freedom. See his *Nothing But Freedom: Emancipation and Its Legacy* (Baton Rouge: Louisiana State University Press, 1983). Another useful resource describing various aspects of Reconstruction is Eric Anderson and Alfred A. Moss, Jr., eds., *The Facts of Reconstruction: Essays in Honor of John Hope Franklin* (Baton Rouge: Louisiana State University Press, 1991). For an examination of political Reconstruction in Norfolk see Michael Hucles, "Many Voices, Similar Concerns: Traditional Methods of African-American Political Activity in Norfolk, Virginia, 1865-1875," *The Virginia Magazine of History and Biography* 100 (1992): 544-66; and Earl Lewis, *In Their Own Interests: Race, Class, and Power in Twentieth-Century Norfolk, Virginia* (Berkeley: University of California Press, 1991), chapter 1.

2. The published population schedules of the Eighth Census (Table III) incorrectly states a total African American population in Norfolk of 4,330. This consisted of 1,046 "free colored" and 3,284 slaves. It is the free colored category that was inaccurately computed as the published gender breakdown indicated 358 males and 678 females, or 1,036. One of the free colored indicated in the individual schedules is listed as an Indian. If removed from the African American count, the number would then be 1,035. See U.S. Census Bureau, *Population of the United States in 1860; Compiled from the Original Returns of the Eighth Census* (Washington, D.C., 1864), p. 519; and U.S. Census Bureau, Eighth Census, 1860, Manuscript Population Schedules, Norfolk County (microfilm), RG 29, National Archives, Washington, D.C.

3. See *Equal Suffrage: Address from the Colored Citizens of Norfolk, Va., to the People of the United States. Also an Account of the Afitation among the Colored People of Virginia for Equal Rights. With an Appendix Concerning the Rights of Colored Witnesses before the State Courts* (Norfolk, 1865), 1 (microfilm). See also Lewis, *In Their Own Interests*, 11-17, 20.

4. Charles L. Perdue, Jr., Thomas E. Barden, and Robert K. Phillips, eds., *Weevils in the Wheat: Interviews with Virginia Ex-Slaves* (Charlottesville: University Press of Virginia, 1976), 103.

5. Quoted in Luther P. Jackson, "The Origin of Hampton Institute," *Journal of Negro History* 10 (April 1925): 138-139. Also, in a letter written to American Missionary Association headquarters, missionary W. L. Coan reported, "I have now got possession of two of the *City School Houses. . . ."* See, Coan to Whiting, October 21, 1863, Roll 2, in *American Missionary Association Manuscripts*, hereinafter cited *AMA* (microfilm, Collis P. Huntington Library, Hampton University). See also, Woodbury to S. S. Jocelyn, October 20, 1863, Roll 2, in *AMA*; and Woodbury to S. S. Jocelyn, October 29, 1863, Roll 2, in *AMA*.

6. J. F. Milligan and Company, *Norfolk City Directory for 1869* (Norfolk, 1869), xxiv. See also, George Holbert Tucker, *Norfolk Highlights, 1584-1881* (Portsmouth, Va., 1972), 121.

7. See *The Revised Ordinances of the City of Norfolk to Which are Prefixed the Original Charter of the Borough, and City, and a Collection of Acts and Parts of Acts of the General Assembly, Relating to the City* (Norfolk, 1866), 159-160; and *The Ordinances of the City of Norfolk to Which is Appended the Charter of the City* (Norfolk, 1875), 156.

8. Hucles, "Many Voices, Similar Concerns," 562-563.

9. J. H. Chataigne and W. Andrew Boyd, compilers, *Norfolk and Portsmouth Directory, 1872-1873*. Throughout the first half of the 1870s, the number of students attending Norfolk's schools was slightly more than 6,000. Of that number, African American school attendees numbered slightly more than 1,000.

10. See *Message of John S. Tucker, Mayor of the City of Norfolk, Virginia, to the Select and Common Councils Together With Municipal Reports for the Year Ending December 31st, 1876* (Norfolk, 1877), 13.

11. See *Message of John S. Tucker, Mayor of the City of Norfolk, Virginia, to the Select and Common Councils, Together With Municipal Reports for the Twelve Months Ending June 30th, 1878* (Norfolk, 1878), 73. See also, Perdue, *Weevils in the Wheat*, 103.

12. See *Message Ending June 30th, 1878*, 73. See also, *Message of John S. Tucker, Mayor of the City of Norfolk, Virginia, to the Select and Common Councils, Together With Municipal Reports for the Twelve Months Ending June 30th, 1879* (Norfolk, 1880), 82.

Michael Hucles, Assistant Professor of history at Old Dominion University, is the author of essays on blacks in postbellum Norfolk, Virginia and is currently working on a coauthored history of the city's postbellum black community.

The Struggle for Black Freedom before Emancipation

Wayne K. Durrill

The Civil War has recently become a hot ticket. The movie *Glory*, the PBS series "The Civil War" by Ken Burns, and James McPherson's recent Pulitzer Prize-winning account of the conflict have all dramatized the continuing relevance of the war as a defining experience for a people and a nation. These stories, however, have often neglected an important part of that defining experience: the role of black people in securing their own emancipation. Most accounts of war date emancipation from Lincoln's famous proclamation and the military campaigns that followed. Even *Glory*, which traces the heroic deeds of black soldiers from Massachusetts, portrays slaves in the lowcountry of South Carolina as incompetent and ineffectual, persons who simply waited for Northern free black liberators to march South and rescue them from bondage.

However, even this relatively enlightened view of the role of black people in their own emancipation is historically inaccurate. As Ira Berlin and his colleagues have shown in their monumental multi-volume series, *Freedom: A Documentary History of Emancipation*, slaves throughout the South squeezed freedom in dribs and drabs from their own local situation as opportunities arose in wartime. In Kentucky, where blacks remained in bondage until after the Civil War, slaves fled to Tennessee where they could join the

Union army as laborers and later as soldiers, and thereby free themselves and sometimes their families. Others stayed home, testing the limits of servitude in a volatile and dangerous situation, always with an eye toward establishing claims to property and place, as well as to their own humanity. These black struggles for freedom within slavery are sometimes difficult to visualize. Indeed, they seem to be a contradiction in terms. Yet they did occur, and with an

---

Slaves throughout the South squeezed freedom in dribs and drabs from their own local situation as opportunities arose in wartime.

---

intensity and regularity that historians have only just begun to uncover. As an example of such struggle, let us examine the story of how one group of North Carolina slaves redefined the rules of slavery in the crisis of war so as to create for themselves a larger space in which to carry on a life separate from their white masters.

In September of 1861, after the fall of

federal forces of Hatteras Island on North Carolina's Outer Banks, Major General John Wool, Union commander of the island, reported that "negro slaves" were "almost daily arriving at this post from the interior." They came in small groups, many traveling over one hundred miles from the counties bordering the Albemarle Sound. At Columbia, on the eastern edge of the Sound and about five miles from William Pettigrew's plantation, a certain planter had brought his slaves to town for "safekeeping." The militia had already mustered there and the town had a jail if he needed it. But shortly after their arrival, thirteen of the man's slaves quietly stole a boat and sailed for Hatteras, setting in motion a chain of events that quickly spread through counties all around the Sound. One planter complained that news of the escape had spread among slaves in the area, and he reasoned, "We may look for others to leave soon." In response, slave owners throughout the Sound region began to move to the upcountry, taking with them as many of their slaves as they could support on the land available to them.

William Pettigrew, one of the richest planters in Washington County, North Carolina, grasped the crisis early on and resolved to remove his slaves before planting began the following spring. On 4 March 1862, the planter arranged for twenty-five Confederate cavalrymen to descend upon Magnolia plantation. The move took the slaves by surprise, and all were captured. That day, men, women, and children were loaded onto wagons guarded by armed troopers, and began a long journey upcountry. After a nine-day forced march, Pettigrew and the slaves came to Haywood, a small crossroads community about fifty miles west of Raleigh where the planter had located a small farm for sale. He purchased the farm as his base camp in the upcountry, but it was too small to support any but a handful of his slaves. The others he drove on foot fifty miles further west where he leased out eighty-seven of them in nineteen groups to fifteen different planters.

The exchange of slaves for promissory notes, however, signified more than simply a purchase of labor. It included a broader transfer of power from one planter to another. For this reason, William Pettigrew insisted that persons who hired his slaves provide them with certain goods in the coming year, mostly food, clothing, and shoes. The planter might have provided the goods himself and factored the cost into his asking price. But he did not. Instead, he included in the contract detailed directions specifying what each slave should receive. In doing so, Pettigrew ensured that his slaves' new master would become the sole source of some crucial goods for them, thus giving the new master enormous leverage over the hired-out slaves. By his actions, Pettigrew produced not merely new employers for his slaves, but new masters.

Such contracts, however, did not settle all questions of a planter's dominance and a slave's submission in the upcountry. Planters and slaves, in fact, had always created their own mutual expectations, in part by contesting the rules by which they lived. Before the war, this had not been a conflict among equals, to be sure. Instead, the struggle between planter and slave presumed an unequal resolution; the master would rule and the slave submit. But in 1862, the relations between planters and slaves had changed dramatically, even in the upcountry. Many of the Pettigrew slaves worked for new masters who might or might not be skilled in managing human property. Would these men have the wherewithal to nail the

meat-house door shut, call in the slave patrol, or face down a personal challenge? No one knew. But William Pettigrew's slaves were determined to find out.

Mary Jane, for example, decided early on to see just what kind of master she had been assigned. William Pettigrew had hired her out as a cook to a planter named George Foushee, along with a slave named Dick Lake, his wife Jenny, and their five children. Mary Jane complained "mostly of colick" during her first three weeks at Foushee's place. In that period, she rendered "very little service" in the planter's view. According to Foushee, "She don't seem to be very bad off, just sick enough to keep her from work." The planter further wondered if "a good deal of it is deception." To find out, Foushee asked Dick Lake about her, and the slave's answer confirmed the planter's suspicions. According to Lake, Mary Jane had "never done much the year she was in a family way." Mary Jane had a history of probing the limits of her master's power.

Similarly, Jenny took advantage of the change of masters to renew work rules she had known at Magnolia plantation. She had just borne a child and informed Foushee that she had "never been required to do any work until her child was eight weeks old." She also objected to Foushee's plan to put her to work in the fields. At Magnolia she always had labored as a cook and now complained that she "could not work out."

Mary Jane, Jenny, and their fellow slaves did not wish simply to avoid work by refusing to labor for their masters. Most, in fact, worked steadily and with a will. In late March, a friend of William Pettigrew's who saw some of the planter's slaves "most every Sunday" in church, reported them at work and "well satisfied" with their new circumstances. Therefore, the action taken by Mary Jane and Jenny must be interpreted as having some more specific purpose. Mary Jane had succeeded in making pregnancy a privileged status at their old plantation. Here, she renewed the rule by making a public event of her refusal to work while pregnant. Similarly, she served notice upon George Foushee that Pettigrew slaves could not be required to work when ill, no matter how slight the planter thought evidence of any malady

appeared. Jenny, for her part, sought to reinforce two rules. The first would give women a special status when pregnant. The second would renew a long-standing division between housework and fieldwork that served as the basis for some very important and very sharp distinctions among the Pettigrew slaves themselves.

George Foushee understood all of this on a practical level. Doubtless, he could never admit publicly, or perhaps even to himself, that Mary Jane and Jenny's actions constituted a challenge to the local rules that governed relations between masters and slaves. But Foushee did have the presence of mind to remain calm. He reported by letter to William Pettigrew the two slaves' failure to work diligently. But Foushee did not propose that either he or Pettigrew take any action. The planter concluded his account of Mary Jane's behavior by saying simply, " hope she will be better hereafter."

Mary Jane did become better. After she had made her point, she returned to work as usual. Other planters, however, did not fully appreciate the give-and-take that an exercise of a master's power required, particularly when the power of masters had been so undermined by Union military activity on the North Carolina coast. Or perhaps some planters sensed in small challenges larger issues that George Foushee had overlooked

A. E. Caveness is a case in point Caveness had hired one slave family from William Pettigrew—Jack, his pregnant wife Venus, and their six young children. The children must have been young because the entire family hired out for twenty-five dollars, less than the cost of hiring a single prime male field hand. Caveness got a good deal more than he bargained for, however, when he paid his pittance to William Pettigrew. When members of the slave family initiated the same contest that took place on the Foushee plantation, Caveness could not comprehend their actions for what they were. In his view, the slaves attempted to "overrun" him. Finally, in a fit of ill-temper, the planter whipped the oldest child, a girl named Sarah, for what he considered her "laziness and disobedience."

The girl's parents objected violently to this. They "made a great ado about it,

Leslie's Illustrated

Union officials sign up escaped slaves for military service.

according to one account, so much so that Caveness felt compelled to "take Venus in hand." At that point, Venus "started off" down the plantation road and, as she walked, turned to the planter and told him off. What exactly she uttered that day remained a matter of dispute. Caveness claimed that she shouted, I am "going to the Yankees." Doubtless, she had no such intention—if she even spoke these words. Venus and her family had just made the nine-day trek from the coast on foot. She well knew that she needed food and extra clothing for such a journey, that Confederate troops blanketed eastern North Carolina and would demand a pass from her, and that William Pettigrew would hire a slave catcher to find her long before she reached federal lines. Later, Venus's husband claimed that she had said no such thing. By the slave's account, Venus told Caveness that she intended to walk to the plantation of William Campbell, Pettigrew's friend, presumably to lodge a complaint against her new master for his actions. Whatever the exact words, Venus had made her point in producing this small drama—publicly and loudly. She feared no man, planter or otherwise, and if she chose to oppose that man, she would make her claim a matter of public debate.

Caveness "ordered her to come back," but Venus refused and continued walking down the road. The planter then got his whip and followed her. Some distance from the house, he finally caught up with her. Again, Caveness commanded Venus to return to the plantation. Once more, the slave refused and voiced her intention to leave. At that point, the planter lost all patience and good sense. Caveness began to whip Venus, at which time Jack, who evidently had followed the two, "got in between them." The planter then "fell to work on Jack, and drove both slaves back to the house."

But Venus had succeeded in her purpose, even as she and her husband bore the lashes of the planter's whip. Caveness complained that "the fuss might have been heard all over the neighborhood." If he hoped to exercise any power over Pettigrew's slaves, Caveness now would have to submit to the scrutiny of his neighbors, both black and white. Each side in this conflict would mobilize its supporters. The battle between master and slave over who would rule the family, and particularly the children of Venus and Jack, became a public controversy.

The next day, Caveness traveled to Wil-

liam Campbell's plantation, where he hoped to make his case to the county's planters. To Campbell, he gave an account of the basic facts in the matter. But Caveness made no attempt to justify his actions. Instead he simply announced a solution. He demanded that Campbell, who had been charged with managing William Pettigrew's interest in Chatham and Moore counties, write to the slaves' owner seeking "permission to conquer them." If Pettigrew refused to grant him such authority, Caveness demanded that their master "take them away." By this ultimatum, Caveness cast the conflict in terms of fundamental issues—in this case, the interest of planters in dominating their slaves. Essentially, Caveness argued that all planters must stand with him, no matter what the specifics of this case, in order to preserve their power over slaves as a whole.

Meanwhile, Venus and Jack also made their opinions known throughout the neighborhood. The couple communicated their interpretation of the conflict to slaves belonging to William Campbell who, in turn, approached their master after Caveness returned home. They told Campbell that Caveness had "not been good" to Pettigrew's slaves. They argued that Caveness was "a man of bad temper," and he acted "very ill" to Jack and his family. In particular, Campbell's slaves charged that Caveness had refused to give Jack and his family "enough to eat," even though he had "plenty of meat and bread" to sell to other persons in the neighborhood.

During the next two weeks, Jack and Venus appealed directly to William Campbell. When Campbell visited the family, Jack accused Caveness of abusing them "without any just cause." To support the charge, the slave pointed out that recently Caveness had "knocked Edith [his youngest child] down with a handspike." The blow cut the little girl "severely on the head." And "since the first difficulty with Venus," Caveness had "knocked [her also] down with a chair." That piece of viciousness caused Venus to miscarry. On 10 June, she was reported "very bad off." Moreover, after he struck Venus, Caveness "threatened to kill her if she did not get up and go to work," according to Jack's account.

Jack therefore requested that Campbell write to William Pettigrew in order to give the planter the slaves' version of events. In the letter, Jack argued that he and his family had "worked harder" that spring than they had "ever worked in their lives," but Caveness could not be satisfied. Therefore, he implored William Pettigrew to remove them from Caveness's plantation. Jack declared his family "willing to live anywhere," even "on half feed," as long as they would "not be abused." We "did not want to put you to any trouble," Jack told his master, but we can "not stand it."

In the end, Jack and his wife prevailed. Their story had a ring of truth that even Caveness himself made no attempt to deny. Moreover, Caveness's poor reputation in the area precluded his attempt to mobilize planter opinion in his cause. Campbell considered Caveness "very hard to please" and "a very passionate man." Finally, Caveness did not help his own case when he admitted to Campbell that if he had carried his gun along, he would have "killed some of them."

But all of this might have come to nothing if Venus had not made the dispute a public event. By mobilizing local opinion, both black and white, Jack and Venus forged a means by which the Pettigrew slaves could shape their own destiny, at least in some small part. William Campbell considered his slave's version of events "only negro news" and therefore, "only to be used as such." Yet, he recommended to William Pettigrew that Jack and his family be removed from Caveness's plantation to a place where they would be "well cared for." "If Caveness is not willing to keep them and treat them humanely as other negroes are treated in this part of the country," wrote Campbell, "I should take them away."

In one sense, the customary rights of slaves acting within the rules of paternalism had been renewed. Yet, there was more to the story than a restoration of peaceable relations between masters and slaves. The abuse by Caveness of Venus and her children provided an unprecedented opportunity to challenge a slaveholder. Caveness had made certain guarantees to Pettigrew—physical safety and an adequate subsistence for the slaves—that he failed to fulfill. And ironically, by insisting on Pettigrew's rights in his property, Venus advanced her own claim as a human being. Indeed, she used those double-edged claims to turn Caveness's own class against him; she forced Pettigrew and others to recognize not only her right to safety and a subsistence but also her right to be heard and recognized as a person. In doing so, Venus and Jack and all the other Pettigrew slaves participated in a much larger defining moment, the self-emancipation of America's slaves in the crucible of the Civil War. ❑

Wayne K. Durrill teaches American history at the University of Cincinnati. This article is adapted from his book War of Another Kind: A Southern Community in the Great Rebellion *published by Oxford University Press in 1990.*

Escaped slaves make their way from Hampton, Virginia, to Fortress Monroe, a Union army post.

Henry David Thoreau, Martin Luther King Jr., and the American Tradition of Protest

Brent Powell

Henry David Thoreau and Martin Luther King, Jr. fundamentally altered the American tradition of protest and reform. Thoreau was the first American to define and use civil disobedience as a means of protest. Ever since his essay "Civil Disobedience" was published in 1846, Thoreau's ideas have influenced the world. In the most famous case of all, Martin Luther King reified the ideas in Birmingham, Alabama. "During my early college days, I read Thoreau's essay on 'Civil Disobedience' for the first time," King remembered, "I became convinced then that non-cooperation with evil is as much a moral obligation as is cooperation with good" (1). King best articulated his convictions in his "Letter from Birmingham Jail." The 1963 letter supported and expanded the concepts first presented in Thoreau's essay, injecting nonviolent direct action into the American tradition of protest.

Although the ideas expressed in "Civil Disobedience" and "Letter from Birmingham Jail" are quite similar, the authors were radically different. Henry David Thoreau was a white, northern, nature-loving individualist; Martin Luther King was a black, southern leader of masses. Thoreau was an uninspiring public speaker;

King was an exhilarating Baptist minister. Thoreau was thought to be eccentric and aloof; King, a hero to millions, was compared to Mohandas Gandhi and Jesus Christ (2).

Despite the significant differences, both fought for the freedom of blacks—Thoreau by aiding fugitive slaves and writing essays attacking slavery; King by

> *Although the ideas expressed in "Civil Disobedience" and "Letter from Birmingham Jail" are quite similar, the authors were radically different.*

leading a nonviolent army against segregation. Both believed that individuals had a right and an obligation to oppose injustice and to disobey unjust laws.

The American tradition of protest, strongly influenced by Thoreau's writing on civil disobedience, includes the notion of nonviolent, direct action. Martin Luther King, "fascinated" and "deeply moved"

by Thoreau's essay, built upon the work of both Thoreau and Gandhi (3). Likewise, Gandhi also admitted that, "Thoreau's ideas greatly influenced [his] movement in India" (4). In the 1950s and 1960s, King proved that civil disobedience and nonviolence could be effective tools of mass protest. Today, although they sometimes deviate from the message of nonviolence and civil disobedience, pro-choice and pro-life advocates, gay rights supporters, and radical environmentalists frequently invoke the language and techniques of Thoreau and King to defend their causes.

Background

Henry David Thoreau (1817-1862) repeatedly expressed disappointment in the people of his hometown, Concord, Massachusetts. He believed they were simply too concerned with making money and not concerned enough with opposing slavery. Thoreau lived what he preached. In opposition to slavery, he stopped paying taxes in 1842. He defended his actions, claiming he would not support an institution that tolerated injustice. "I did not pay a tax to, or recognize the authority of, the state which buys and sells men, women, and children," he wrote in *Walden* (5). Concord authorities arrested Thoreau and placed him in jail for one night (after six years of noncompliance). By breaking a law and willingly accepting the punishment, he was the first American to practice nonviolent civil disobedience.

In a January 1848 lecture, Thoreau described the night he spent in jail. The lecture entitled "The Relation of the Individual to the State" became "Civil Disobedience" when it was published eighteen years later. In it, Thoreau opposed slavery and the Mexican-American War and he urged people to pursue their lives based on conscience and morality. Martin Luther King further developed many of the ideas in the essay in his effort to desegregate the South.

King embodied much of what Thoreau advocated. As with Thoreau, King's conscience guided him. As the leader of the Montgomery Bus Boycott and the first president of the Southern Christian Leadership Council, King led civil rights protests based on Thoreau's theories of nonviolence. In 1963, King took his campaign of civil disobedience and direct action to "the most thoroughly segregated city in this country"—Birmingham, Alabama (6). There, he organized a massive nonviolent protest, hoping to force the city leaders to

desegregate the lunch counters, fitting rooms, rest rooms, and drinking fountains. He ultimately hoped to attain city-wide desegregation (7).

On April 12, nine days after the campaign began, King took a giant leap of faith. In spite of the movement's lack of bail money, King violated a court injunction prohibiting him from leading demonstrations. He found his decision agonizing,

Francis H. Allen, *A Bibliography of Henry David Thoreau*, 1908

Henry David Thoreau (1817-1862) believed an individual must live according to his/her conscience.

later writing, "[I] was standing at the center of all that life had brought me to be (8). Although King had been to jail before, the lack of money created an uncertain situation. On the one hand, he had pledged to join his fellow demonstrators in jail, but, on the other he was the movement's most effective fund raiser. Either choice—to go to jail or to stay out—risked the momentum of the campaign. In the end, King decided to break the law and accept punishment.

Unlike Thoreau who "did not for moment feel confined" in jail (Thoreau in fact experienced a sense of freedom there), King abhorred his thirteenth time behind bars, describing his imprisonment as "nightmare of despair" (9). Birmingham authorities locked King in solitary confinement where he faced the possibility of violence and even death. While in jail, the minister read smuggled newspapers highly critical of his movement. One article entitled, "White Clergymen Urge Negroes to Withdraw from Demonstrations" particularly enraged him. In response, King wrote his famous "Letter from Birmingham Jail."

Different Views on Government, Different Risks

Though King risked a great deal in the

irmingham jail and relied on the Constitu-
on and the national government to protect
m, Thoreau risked little in the Concord
il. In fact he openly attacked the Constitu-
on and national government. Thoreau
pposed both of these institutions because
e believed they protected slavery and hin-
ered individual freedom. He urged each
an to "make known what kind of govern-
ent would command his respect"; doing so
ould protect the natural rights of all people,
crease respect for individual decisions,
d provide economic freedom. In compari-
n, King had faith in the Constitution,
nended since Thoreau's time, and in the
stice of the national government. Rather
an fighting the government or Constitu-
n in broad terms, he fought the specific
stem of segregation. King believed that
acks, like all Americans, deserved protec-
n under the Constitution, and appealed to
e national government to grant them equal
ghts. In fighting for equality, King risked,
d eventually gave, his life.

Compared to King, Henry Thoreau
sked little by his protest. As a member of
established Concord family, he had a
rsonal security that King did not have.
'ith no wife, children, or substantial prop-
ty, Thoreau had few to hurt and little to
se by going to jail. While there, he suf-
red and feared nothing from the jailor. In
ntrast, King faced the possibility of a
ngthy jail sentence, the depletion of bail
oney, and the possibility of violence and
ath. "Some of the people sitting here
day will not come back alive from this
mpaign," King feared at the beginning of
s protest (10).

Connecting the Documents

Despite these differences, the documents
oreau and King wrote share five impor-
nt themes: 1) the problem in a democracy
the majority oppressing the minority (a
ncept first articulated by James Madison
d later developed by Alexis de
cqueville); 2) the presence of injustice; 3)
e need for immediate action; 4) the appro-
iate method of protest; and 5) the obstacles
reform.

Both men observed inherent problems
th majority rule in a democratic society.

Thoreau said that sheer physical strength
alone allowed the majority to rule. He noted
that majorities, in wanting to maintain their
position, failed to look within and to correct
themselves; they were, therefore, inherently
unjust. King went a step further saying that
"privileged groups seldom give up their
privileges voluntarily. We know through
painful experience that freedom is never
voluntarily given by the oppressor; it must
be demanded by the oppressed." Both King
and Thoreau called for the individual to
combat the injustice being maintained by
the majority.

Thoreau never precisely defined his concept of injustice, though much of "Civil
Disobedience" attacks the injustice of slavery. Most likely, he assumed that his
audience recognized the immorality of the
institution, and he saw no need to warrant it.

King, however, specifically addressed
the notion of injustice. He wrote that a law
is unjust 1) if it does not agree with God's
law; 2) if it does not apply to the majority
who made it; 3) if the people it affects had no
say in its creation; or 4) if it interferes with
a constitutional right. King said, "Any law
that uplifts human personality is just. Any
law that degrades human personality is unjust." He, therefore, concluded segregation
was unjust. In addition, he criticized the
court injunction prohibiting his right to protest, saying that it interfered with his "First
Amendment privilege."

Both men expressed the need for immediate action. Thoreau asked, "shall we be
content to obey [unjust laws], or shall we
transgress them at once?" His answer was
obviously the latter. He argued that people
must act on their consciences and bring
change through action. Thoreau set an
example by not paying his taxes and by
breaking the fugitive slave law. He said that
one is an accomplice to injustice when, in
finding fault with the government, a person
does not withdraw his or her support. He
urged the abolitionists to sever their ties with
the government immediately, and for people
to "break the law" and "cast your whole
vote, not a strip of paper merely, but your
whole influence."

King echoed Thoreau's call for immediate action. "Human progress never [comes]

inevitability," he stated, "it comes through
the tireless efforts of men." He preached that
American blacks had suffered for three centuries; thus, the time for action was upon
them.

The documents also contain a guide for
protest. King defined a practitioner of civil
disobedience as one "who breaks a law that
conscience tells him is unjust, and who
willingly accepts community." Just over a
century earlier, Thoreau had written that if
governments imprison a just man, jail is the
just man's only "true place." He predicted
that if a government was given the choice
between imprisoning all men or changing an
unjust law, "the State will not hesitate" to
change the law. "This" he declared, "is the
definition of a peaceful revolution."

King's "peaceful revolution" in Birmingham implemented Thoreau's ideas of
filling the jails to combat injustice. His
nonviolent army, by fighting on the highest
moral ground, earned the respect of the
President, the northern press, the nation, and
the world. Thoreau had called for a "whole
vote." King promised to "present our very
bodies as a means of laying our case before
the conscience" of the community. King
used nonviolence because "injustice must
be exposed, with all the tension its exposure
creates. . . before it can be cured."

Both men agreed on the obstacles to
reform. While they advocated nonviolence
and civil disobedience, they recognized that
majorities often failed to step aside peaceably. Violence might result from civil disobedience, they wrote, but this should not
keep one from protesting. Thoreau believed
that even if "blood should flow," one should
not back down from the violence. With-
drawing from the protest because of violence, he wrote, would cause greater
psychological harm to the protestor than the
physical harm brought on by accepting it.
Thoreau asserted that by turning away, "the
conscience is wounded. . . a man's real
manhood and immortality flow out, and he
bleeds to an everlasting death." King con-
curred, saying that one should work to "gain
his basic constitutional rights" even if that
pursuit precipitates violence.

Much of King's success lay in his ability
to convince his followers that pain and pun-

ishment were small prices to pay for equality under the law. Indeed, King's demonstrators risked the threat of death. Yet without violent retaliation, they endured the police beatings, the dog bites, and the high-pressure fire hoses.

Thoreau and King also shared a disappointment in people who recognized injustice but refused to combat it. Thoreau castigated people in Massachusetts for their inaction, saying that it was not southern politicians who stood in the way of justice, but Northerners who where "more interested in commerce and agriculture than. . . in humanity," thereby blaming these people for blocking reform. King aimed his criticism at white moderates, people who agreed in principle with the movement, yet urged blacks to wait for gradual change. He argued that people often favor stability over the necessary tension of change.

Even so, both men remained optimistic about the future. Thoreau explained that he was combating not a "brute force" but a "human" one and wrote, "I see that appeal [for justice] is possible." He concluded his essay not only by applauding the western progress from absolute monarchy to democracy, but also by questioning whether or not individuals could go further. He sought a state which "recognize[d] the individual as a higher and independent power." King, too, expressed confidence: "We will reach our goal of freedom in Birmingham and all over this nation, because the goal of America is freedom."

Conclusion

Thoreau lacked the broad influence of King. He also failed to command the respect of his peers. Unable to convert others to his ideas or arouse them from the lectern, Thoreau had to remain content with his own actions guided by his own principles. Admittedly, he faced the difficulty of convincing others to act on ideas of justice and humanity when there was little threat to their immediate freedom. Despite his lack of followers in Concord, his writings had a lasting and profound influence on both Mohandas Gandhi and on Martin Luther King, Jr.

King, unlike Thoreau, had an audience thirsting for freedom. King led workshops, taught nonviolence, and used the media to his advantage. He galvanized the blacks in Birmingham and much of the nation behind his cause for equality under the law. After the jailing of nearly 2,500 civil rights protestors, Birmingham Alabama finally desegregated itself. King's plan had been a grand success.

In calling for individuals to follow their consciences, for unjust laws to be challenged, and for all people to be treated equally, Henry David Thoreau and Martin Luther King articulated principles of protest which remain vital today. Thoreau would have found in King a man who lived his life on principle and who persuaded others to follow his powerful example. After the Birmingham campaign, a *Saturday Evening Post* journalist wrote, "What [blacks] see is a powerful crusader for equality who does something instead of just talking, who sticks lighted matches to the status quo [and who] endows this American struggle with qualities of messianic mission" (11). Indeed, Martin Luther King had produced Henry Thoreau's "peaceful revolution." ❏

Endnotes

1. King quoted in John H. Hicks, ed., *Thoreau in Our Season* (Amherst, Mass.: University of Massachusetts Press, 1967), 13.
2. Stephen B. Oates, *Let the Trumpet Sound: The Life of Martin Luther King, Jr.* (New York: Mentor, 1985), 213.
3. King quoted in Hicks, 13.
4. Gandhi quoted in William Stuart Nelson, *Thoreau and American Non-Violent Resistance*, found in Hicks, 14.
5. Henry David Thoreau, *Walden and Civil Disobedience* (New York: Penguin Books, 1983), 217.
6. King quoted in Oates, 202.
7. Flip Schulke and Penelope McPhee, *King Remembered* (New York: Pocket Books, 1986), 122.
8. Martin Luther King, Jr., *Why We Can't Wait* (New York: Mentor, 1964), 72.
9. King quoted in Oates, 213.
10. King quoted in Oates, 205.
11. *Saturday Evening Post* quoted in Oates, 236.

Bibliography

Adams, Raymond. "*Thoreau's Sources fo 'Resistance to Civil Government.'* *Studies in Philology* 42 (1945).

Branch, Taylor. *Parting the Waters*. Nev York: Simon and Schuster, 1988.

Broderick, John C. "Thoreau, Alcott, an the Poll Tax." *Studies in Philology* 5 (1956).

Buranelli, Vincent. "The Case Again Thoreau." *Ethics* 67 (1957).

Chatfield, Charles, ed. "Peacemaking i America." *Magazine of History* (1994).

Eulau, Heinz. "Wayside Challenger." *Th Antioch Review* 9 (1949).

Glick, Wendell. "Thoreau's Attack Again: Relativism." *Western Humanities Re view* 7 (1953).

Harding, Walter. *A Thoreau Handboo* New York: New York Universit Press, 1959.

———. *The Days of Henry Thoreau*. Nev York: Dover Publications, 1982.

Herr, William A. "A More Perfect Stat Thoreau's Concept of Civil Goverr ment." *Massachusetts Review* 1 (1975).

Hicks, John H., ed. *Thoreau in Our Sec son*. Amherst: University of Massa chusetts Press, 1967.

King, Martin Luther, Jr. *Why We Can Wait*. New York: Mentor, 1964.

McPhee, Penelope, and Flip Schulke. *Kir Remembered*. New York: Pock Books, 1986.

Oates, Stephen B. *Let the Trumpet Soun* New York: Mentor, 1982.

Richardson, Robert D. *Henry Thoreau: Life of the Mind*. Berkeley: Unive sity of California Press, 1986.

Thoreau, Henry David. *Civil Disobed ence and Other Essays*. New Yor Dover Publications, 1993.

———. *Walden and Civil Disobedienc* New York: Penguin Books, 1986.

Brent Powell graduated from Willian College in 1991. He taught history for tw years at Trinity-Pawling School Pawling, New York, and is currently teac ing at the Winter Term in Lenk, Switze land.

The Right to Marry:
Loving v. Virginia

Peter Wallenstein

In June 1958, Mildred Jeter and Richard Loving left their native Caroline County, Virginia, for a visit to Washington, D.C., where they got married. They then returned to Virginia and took up residence in the home of the bride's parents. Early in the morning a few weeks later, everyone in the house was asleep—Mr. and Mrs. Loving downstairs, Mr. and Mrs. Jeter upstairs—when the Lovings awoke to find three policemen in their bedroom with flashlights. The intruders arrested and jailed the Lovings. The charge? Their marriage violated state law. He was white, and she was black. By marrying in D.C. to avoid a Virginia law prohibiting interracial marriage, they had committed a serious crime.

In January 1959, Judge Leon M. Bazile sentenced the couple to a year in jail. He suspended the sentences on the condition that "both accused leave Caroline County and the state of Virginia at once and do not return together or at the same time to said county and state for a period of twenty-five years." They moved to Washington, D.C., where they lived with Mrs. Loving's cousin Alex Byrd and his wife Laura. They continued to live in their home away from home, and this is where they raised their three children, Sidney, Donald, and Peggy.

In 1963 they determined to take a stand against the injustice that had forced

> *The law that the Lovings broke originated in 1691 when the House of Burgesses sought to reduce the number of mixed-race children born in the Virginia colony, particularly mixed-race children whose mothers were white.*

them into exile. They wrote United States Attorney General Robert F. Kennedy asking for help. He directed their letter to the National Capitol Area Civil Liberties Union, and the ACLU assigned the case to Bernard S. Cohen, a young lawyer practicing in Alexandria, Virginia. Some months later another young lawyer, Philip A. Hirschkop, who had been working in Mississippi assisting civil rights workers, joined Cohen on the case.

The law that the Lovings broke originated in 1691, when the House of Burgesses sought to reduce the number of mixed-race children born in the Virginia colony, particularly mixed-race children whose mothers were white. The Burgesses enacted a measure designed "for prevention of that abominable mixture and spurious issue which hereafter may encrease in this dominion, as well by negroes, mulattoes, and Indians intermarrying with English, or other white woman, as by their unlawfull accompanying with one another." It outlawed interracial marriage for white men and white women alike. While it did not ban the marriage *per se*, it did mandate the banishment of the white partner in any interracial marriage that occurred, at least if that person was not an indentured servant and, thus, did not owe labor to any planter: "Whatsoever English or other white man or women being free shall intermarry with a negroe, mulatto, or Indian man or woman bond or free, shall within three months after such marriage be banished and removed from this dominion forever."

Thus, the white wife of a nonwhite man was forced to have mixed-race children outside of Virginia. If she tried to evade banishment from the colony by skipping the marriage ceremony but then had a mixed-race child in Virginia out of wedlock, she would have to pay a heavy fine. If unable to pay the fine, she would be sold as a servant for five years. Either way, the child would be sold into servitude until he or she reached the age of thirty.

Only the specifics of the law changed in the years that followed. Through the American Revolution and the Civil War, Virginia law placed a severe penalty on any white person who married a nonwhite. The law was amended in 1705 to eliminate banishment; the new penalty was a fine and six months in prison. In 1848, the legislature changed the term of imprisonment for the white partner in an interracial marriage to a maximum of twelve months. The Code of 1849 declared interracial marriages "absolutely void."

In 1865, slavery came to an end in Virginia. Interracial marriages remained "absolutely void," but the laws began to take on the more specific shape of those that the Lovings encountered nearly a hundred years later. Both partners in an interracial relationship—the black Virginian and the white—became subject to prosecution. Andrew Kinney, a black man, and Mahala Miller, a white woman, wished to live as husband and wife but could not marry under Virginia law. In 1874, after living together nearly eight years and having three children, they went to Washington, D.C., to get married. When they returned home to Augusta County, authorities brought charges against them for "lewdly associating and cohabiting" together without being married. At his trial, Mr. Kinney urged the judge to instruct the jury that the marriage was "valid and a bar to this prosecution." Instead, the judge instructed the jury that the marriage was

"but a vain and futile attempt to evade the laws of Virginia." The question, simply put, was: Did the defendant have a valid marriage that gave him an effective defense against the charge he faced? Or, was his living as though he were married precisely the basis for that charge? Was he married? Or was he guilty?

After being convicted and sentenced to pay the heaviest fine the law allowed, $500, Mr. Kinney appealed to the Virginia Supreme Court. That court upheld the conviction. As to whether the law of Washington, D.C., or that of Virginia governed the case, Judge Joseph Christian, speaking for a unanimous court, declared, "There can be no doubt as to the power of every country to make laws regulating the marriage of its own sub-

---

"Mr. Cohen, tell the Court I love my wife, and it is just unfair that I can't live with her in Virginia."

---

jects; to declare who may marry, how they may marry, and what shall be the legal consequences of their marrying." The judge went on to say that "purity of public morals, the moral and physical development of both races, and the highest advancement of our cherished southern civilization, under which two distinct races are to work out and accomplish the destiny to which the Almighty has assigned them on this continent—all require that they should be kept distinct and separate, and that connections and alliances so unnatural that God and nature seem to forbid them, should be prohibited by positive law, and be subject to no evasion." What "God and nature" had sundered, let no man seek to bring together. The law would not allow the marriage of Andrew Kinney and Mahala Miller to persist, at least in Virginia. "If the parties desire to maintain

the relations of man and wife, they must change their domicile and go to some state or country where the laws recognize the validity of such marriages." Despite their loss in the courts, the couple made their own stand. Five years later, they were still living together and had had five sons. They remained subject to additional prosecution, but local authorities seem to have been content with winning the one case against them.

In 1878, the Virginia General Assembly made two changes—the most significant since the 1691 law. Not only would both partners in an interracial marriage be subject to prosecution but if convicted, they would also both be sentenced to the state penitentiary for a term of two to five years. And if, like the Kinneys, they sought to evade the law by marrying outside of Virginia, "they shall be as guilty, and be punished as if the marriage had been in this state. The fact of their cohabitation here as man and wife shall be evidence of their marriage." By the time of the Lovings the legislature had changed the minimum sentence from two years to one year.

But what about the Fourteenth Amendment? Approved in 1868, its first section declared, in part, that no state could "deny to any person within its jurisdiction the equal protection of the laws." Indeed, in 1872 the Alabama Supreme Court ruled Alabama's law against interracial marriages unconstitutional. The court said that the Civil Rights Act of 1866 had conferred "the right to make and enforce contracts amongst which is that of marriage with any citizen capable of entering into that relation," and that the Fourteenth Amendment had placed the Civil Rights Act's "cardinal principle" in the United States Constitution. Yet, the Alabama Supreme Court itself soon overruled that decision, and no other court adopted its position for many years.

Thus, the Fourteenth Amendment failed to help couples like the Lovings. As a black man in Alabama, Tony Pace and a white woman, Mary Jane Cox ound out. Convicted of carrying on an interracial relationship, each was sentenced to two years in the Alabama penitentiary, the minimum term the law permitted. They appealed their convictions, but the Alabama Supreme Court ruled against them. Each defendant's punishment, "white and black," was "precisely the same." They appealed again to the nation's highest court, but the United States Supreme Court ruled in 1883 as had the Alabama court. Tony Pace served his sentence in the Alabama penitentiary.

Gradually, laws like Virginia's and Alabama's came under successful attack. In 1948, in *Perez v. Sharp*, the California Supreme Court ruled that a California law against interracial marriage was unconstitutional—the first

such ruling since Alabama's short-lived effort in 1872. In the years that followed, states outside the South repealed their laws and left the question of marriage up to individuals regardless of their race. When the Lovings returned to court in the 1960s, however, all southern states retained such laws. As late as 1966, Oklahoma plus every state that had had slavery as late as the Civil War—Texas, Arkansas, Louisiana, Mississippi, Alabama, Tennessee, Georgia, Florida, the Carolinas, Virginia and West Virginia, Maryland, Delaware, Kentucky, and Missouri—still had such laws on the books.

At about the same time, the United States Supreme Court breathed new life into the Fourteenth Amendment's equal protection clause. For example, in 1948

the court ruled in *Shelley v. Kraemer* that state courts could not enforce restrictive covenants in housing documents that prevented nonwhite families from moving into white communities. Several rulings declared against states' banning black students from enrolling in state law schools. And in 1954, the nation's highest court ruled in *Brown v. Board of Education*, on Fourteenth Amendment grounds, that "in the field of public education the doctrine of 'separate but equal' has no place."

The Supreme Court ruled on various cases in the area of privacy at about the same time. How much control should people have over their lives, and how much power should state governments have to restrict people's freedom? What fundamental rights did people have—

Mildred and Richard Loving at their news conference on 12 June 1967, the day the U.S. Supreme Court ruled unanimously in their favor.

even if those rights are not explicit in the United States Constitution? The Court declared that people had the right to teach their children a foreign language (*Meyer v. Nebraska*, 1923) and the right to send their children to private schools (*Pierce v. Society of Sisters*, 1925). Married people had the right to have children; the Court voided a law that mandated that people convicted of certain types of crime be sterilized (*Skinner v. Oklahoma*, 1942). In the leading privacy case up to the time of the Loving case, the Court ruled that married people also had the right to decide whether to use birth control information and devices to prevent pregnancy (*Griswold v. Connecticut*, 1965). In 1973, in *Roe v. Wade*, the Court extended its rulings on matters of privacy when it struck down statutes that prohibited women from obtaining abortions, especially in the first three months of pregnancy. Thus, across a fifty-year period between 1923 and 1973, the Court determined that people had a zone of privacy—the right, at least under certain circumstances, to go about their lives without having authorities intervene and tell them what they must and must not do.

These various developments in twentieth-century American constitutional history came together in the case of the Lovings. There was no reason to assume that the Lovings would be successful. They had not even tried to contest their exile in 1959 but had waited more than four years before contacting the Attorney General's office. Only a few years before their marriage, convictions, and exile, other couples had tried unsuccessfully to get the United States Supreme Court to rule laws like Virginia's unconstitutional. In 1955, a black woman named Linnie Jackson, who had been sentenced to the Alabama penitentiary for an interracial relationship, appealed her conviction to the United States Supreme Court. The Court refused to hear her case. At about the same time, a Chinese man in Virginia, Ham Say Naim, tried to take a case to the United States Supreme Court to have his

marriage to a white woman recognized, but the Court turned a deaf ear to him too. That left intact a ruling by the Virginia Supreme Court which had insisted that "regulation of the marriage relation" is "distinctly one of the rights guaranteed to the States and safeguarded by that bastion of States' rights, somewhat battered perhaps but still a sturdy fortress in our fundamental law, the tenth section of the Bill of Rights."

In 1963, despite the obstacles, the Lovings renewed their quest to live together as husband and wife and to raise their three children in Caroline County, Virginia. Their lawyers, Bernard Cohen and Philip Hirschkop, consulted with

> *"Under our Constitution, the freedom to marry, or not marry, a person of another race resides with the individual and cannot be infringed by the State."*

various ACLU lawyers in preparing the case. They began where the Lovings had finished previously, in Judge Bazile's courtroom. The judge saw no reason to change his mind about anything. The Lovings' marriage, he said, was "absolutely void in Virginia," and they could not "cohabit" there "without incurring repeated prosecutions" for doing so. He declared his convictions on the law in dispute: "Almighty God created the races white, black, yellow, malay and red, and he placed them on separate continents. And but for the interference with his arrangement there would be no cause for such marriages. The fact that he separated the races shows that he did not intend for the races to mix."

The Lovings appealed their case to the Virginia Supreme Court, but that

court saw nothing that required change since its ruling in the Naim case ten years earlier. Richard and Mildred Loving then went to the United States Supreme Court to challenge their convictions for having violated Virginia's laws against racial intermarriage. In the months ahead, the nation's high court faced squarely, for the first time, the question of whether such laws as Virginia's violated the Fourteenth Amendment. Cohen and Hirschkop quoted one judge in the 1948 California decision on interracial marriage: "If the right to marry is a fundamental right, then it must be conceded that an infringement of that right by means of a racial restriction is an unlawful infringement of one's liberty." They also asserted that "caprice of the politicians cannot be substituted for the minds of the individual in what is man's most personal and intimate decision. The error of such legislation must immediately be apparent to those in favor of miscegenation statutes, if they stopped to consider their abhorrence to a statute which commanded that 'all marriages must be between persons of different racial backgrounds.'" Such a statute, they contended, would be no more "repugnant to the constitution"—and no less so—than the law under consideration. Something "so personal as the choice of a mate must be left to the individuals involved," they argued; "race limitations are too unreasonable and arbitrary a basis for the State to interfere." They reviewed the history of Virginia's antimiscegenation statutes—going all the way back to the seventeenth century—to characterize them as "relics of slavery" and, at the same time, "expressions of modern day racism." And, finally, in oral argument, Bernard Cohen conveyed Richard Loving's own words. "Mr Cohen, tell the Court I love my wife, and it is just unfair that I can't live with her in Virginia."

Speaking for a unanimous Court on 12 June 1967, Chief Justice Earl Warren declared that states' rights had to defe to the Fourteenth Amendment when it came to the claim of "exclusive state control" over the "regulation of marriage." The argument that Virginia's "miscegenation statutes punish equally both the white and the Negro participants in an interracial marriage" could not pass constitutional muster in the 1960s. The burden of proof rested on the state, for "the fact of equal application does not immunize the statute from the heavy burden of justification" required by the Fourteenth Amendment, particularly when racial classifications appeared in criminal statutes. "The fact that Virginia prohibits only interracial marriages involving white persons demonstrates" that those laws were "designed to maintain White Supremacy." Indeed, the statute's original purpose held no interest for the Court; the Chief Justice declared the racial classifications "repugnant to the Fourteenth Amendment, even assuming an even-handed state purpose to protect the 'integrity' of all races." According to Warren the Fourteenth Amendment's clear and central purpose was to "eliminate all official state sources of invidious racial discrimination."

The Chief Justice was sure of the Court's recent history in civil rights cases. He wrote: "We have consistently denied the constitutionality of measures which restrict the rights of citizens on account of race. There can be no doubt that restricting the freedom to marry solely because of racial classifications violates the central meaning of the Equal Protection Clause." As for the Due Process Clause, the Chief Justice noted that "the freedom to marry has long been recognized as one of the vital personal rights essential to the orderly pursuit of happiness by free men. . . . To deny this fundamental freedom on so unsupportable a basis as the racial classifications embodied in these statutes, classifications so directly subversive of the principle of equality at the heart of the Fourteenth Amendment, is surely to deprive all the State's citizens of liberty without due process of law. The Four-

teenth Amendment requires that the freedom of choice to marry not be restricted by invidious racial discriminations. Under our Constitution, the freedom to marry, or not marry, a person of another race resides with the individual and cannot be infringed by the State." Chief Justice Warren's final sentence put an end to the Lovings' odyssey through the courts: "These convictions must be reversed."

Richard and Mildred Loving finally won the case ten days after their ninth wedding anniversary. From their temporary farm home in Bowling Green, near Fredericksburg, Mr. and Mrs. Loving drove north to Alexandria for a news conference at their lawyers' office. There Mr. Loving said, "We're just really overjoyed," and Mrs. Loving said, "I feel free now." A photographer snapped a picture, law books in the background, of two happy people sitting close together, his arm around her neck. "My wife and I plan to go ahead and build a new house now," said Richard Loving the construction worker about the permanent new home in Virginia that Richard Loving the husband and father wanted his family to live in. And they did so.

Reporting on the decision, the *New York Times* noted its larger significance. "In writing the opinion that struck down the last group of segregation laws to remain standing—those requiring separation of the races in marriage—Chief Justice Warren completed the process that he set in motion with his opinion in 1954 that declared segregation in public schools to be unconstitutional." Bernard S. Cohen, the Lovings' lawyer, offered a similar benediction on the proceedings. At his clients' press conference, he said: "We hope we have put to rest the last vestiges of racial discrimination that were supported by the law in Virginia and all over the country."

The black-owned newspaper in Virginia's largest city, the *Norfolk Journal and Guide*, led off its front page with the headline "Top Court Junks Marriage Bars" and printed an editorial on "Freedom of Choice at the Altar." It predicted "no notice-

able increase in the number of mixed marriages in Virginia." As it explained, "prospective grooms" would continue to enjoy "the privileges of withholding their requests for the bride's hand," and brides would retain "the privilege and authority to prevent mixed marriages simply by saying 'no.'" Nonetheless, the *Journal and Guide* insisted on the importance of the Court's ruling: "What makes this Supreme Court decision so desirable is that it lifts an onerous and brutalizing stigma from Negro Virginians by knocking down that psychological barrier which, in effect, told them and the world that no Negro is good enough to be the husband or wife of a white Virginian." Furthermore, it saluted the Lovings for having taken a stand. "They have done an incalculably great service for their community, their state, and their nation. Had they been less persevering, the legal battle to end Virginia's oppression on the marital front might have been forfeited long ago." ❑

Bibliography

Garrow, David J. *Liberty and Sexuality: The Right to Privacy and the Making of Roe v. Wade.* New York: Macmillan, 1994.

Grossberg, Michael. *Governing the Hearth: Law and the Family in Nineteenth-Century America.* Chapel Hill: University of North Carolina Press, 1985.

Ross, William G. *Forging New Freedoms: Nativism, Education, and the Constitution, 1917-1927.* Lincoln: University of Nebraska Press, 1994.

Schwartz, Bernard. *Super Chief: Earl Warren and His Supreme Court—A Judicial Biography.* New York: New York University Press, 1983.

Sickels, Robert J. *Race, Marriage, and the Law.* Albuquerque: University of New Mexico Press, 1972.

Wallenstein, Peter. "Race, Marriage, and the Law of Freedom: Alabama and Virginia, 1860s-1960s." *Chicago-Kent Law Review* 70 (1995).

Peter Wallenstein is Associate Professor of History at Virginia Polytechnic Institute and State University.

Legacy for Learning: Jennie Dean and the Manassas Industrial School

Introduction

Though less famous than contemporaries such as Frederick Douglass, Harriet Tubman, and Booker T. Washington, Jane Serepta Dean, known to her friends as "Miss Jennie," also strove to improve the quality of life for African Americans and their communities. Born into slavery in 1852, Dean was entering her teens when emancipation came. She spent her lifetime serving others. In the process, she became a symbol of what one person can achieve if determined. Her example can serve as a model for young people and can help motivate them to search out and identify other unknown local individuals who also made a difference in their communities.

Background

Four years of war ravaged Virginia, the major battleground of the nation's Civil War. Manassas Junction in Prince William County, the focal point of two major battles, was frequently traversed by the opposing armies throughout the war, each taking turns at building up supply stations to be looted and burned by their opponents as control of the land and the railway changed hands. The life once known there changed regularly, forcing county residents to adjust. Some left for other parts of the state; others simply went out to replant their crops. Most of the 118 families in the vicinity were farmers raising wheat and corn. Of these inhabitants, the 1860 census listed 548 whites, 260 slaves and 45 free blacks (1).

The Civil War and the resultant emancipation changed the status of many African Americans. Among the slave population freed by emancipation was the Dean family. It consisted of parents, Charles and Annie Dean, four children, Jane (called Jennie by her family), Ella, Mary, and Charles, Jr., and grandparents, Mildred and Ruben. They lived on land owned by Christopher Cushing near the Sudley Springs Methodist Church, attended by white people. Caught in the crossfire of many battles, the church served as a hospital for the wounded of both armies.

In mid-1865, about the same time an enterprising property owner William Fewell systematically plotted nine blocks for the village of Manassas, Charles Dean, Sr. initiated his ownership of a farm some six miles away near the former battlefield known as Catharpin (2). Charles apparently had been a house servant, for he was taught to read and write early in life in violation of state law

forbidding slaves any education. We can assume that these skills were urged upon his children, of whom at least two received advanced educations. The oldest child, Jennie, received just a few months of formal learning in a very primitive public elementary school after the war. Unfortunately for the family, Charles Dean died long before he completed the purchase of his land. Not wishing her mother and siblings to be dispossessed by overzealous mortgage lenders, Jennie decided to venture into the working world of Washington, D.C., some forty miles away. She planned to save her wages and to use them to pay off the balance owed on the farm.

As a young woman of fourteen, Jennie Dean was probably the first member of her family to leave Prince William County to seek employment. The restoration of rail service from Manassas Junction made such a venture possible. Domestic work was plentiful in the city, and Dean had no problem finding jobs. Membership in the 19th Street Baptist Church connected her to a larger Washington. In addition, Dean knew well the expectations of southern whites—she was respectful, obedient, and hardworking—which endeared her to everyone and created a demand for her services. Consequently, she never wanted for work and won important friends among her employers. Within a few years, she bought the family farm and was able to contribute toward seminary educations for her sisters—all by hoarding her wages.

An astute individual, Dean observed the difficulties that befell her fellow African Americans, especially after the end of the Freedmen's Bureau and formal Reconstruction. As her perspective matured and her finances stabilized, she played an active role in church affairs. Ultimately, she helped found a Sunday School (3).

During her many visits home, Dean noticed the absence of black churches and used her limited free time to establish Baptist missions there. These missions evolved into churches, several of which continue to operate today. Her sincerity of purpose, unfailing good nature, and consistent reputation for accomplishment convinced many black friends to join the churches and many white friends to provide financial assistance. By the mid-1880s, Miss Jennie, as she became known, began to formulate another plan (4).

Even before incorporation as a town in 1873, the hamlet of Manassas received state literary funds to build the first public elementary school in Virginia which was reserved for white children

This action was not lost on Dean. She used her missions as places to teach black children to read and write, for many of the freedmen schools established by humanitarian northerners after the war disappeared with time. Well-meaning whites recognized the educational needs of blacks by the 1880s, but were not anxious to mix the races in public schools. Nor were state monies readily available for separate black schools. But, inspired by the success of Tuskegee Institute, founded in 1881 by Booker T. Washington, and encouraged by her growing friendships with influential white matrons and church contacts in the nation's capitol and Prince William County, Dean took a bold step: she decided to establish an industrial school for the black youth of the county (5).

In the spring of 1888, Dean convinced black Baptist ministers from all sections of the county to discuss the worthiness of an industrial school with their congregations. A superior, strong-willed organizer herself, Dean was highly motivated to succeed in this newest endeavor. She also appealed to every white person she knew in the county for financial support and then campaigned aggressively with her white employers in Washington, as well as their friends. She spoke informally but with devoted sincerity of her people's needs at women's club meetings and church fellowship gatherings. Her carefully worded pleas eventually led her listeners to introduce her to others, like industrialist Andrew Carnegie and professor-orator Edward Everett Hale. She also continued to save her own wages, diverting her resources when contributions slipped or using them to solicit matching funds from those less financially well off. Slowly, as the year advanced, momentum to establish a school grew and she began to give serious thought to a potential location (6). In trying to decide where the school should be built, Dean learned that the Hampton Brenton farm at the junction of the Southern Railroad (formerly the Orange and Alexandria line) and the main line to Strasburg (one mile from the center of Manassas) was for sale. After two years of behind-the-scenes work, a public meeting was held in Manassas in 1890 to solicit financial backing to buy the Brenton farm for $2,650. Dean's savings of sixty dollars was added to forty dollars from a Washingtonian to show an intent to buy. Thereafter, a committee of prominent white men studied the needs of the 24,000 blacks in five adjoining counties, half of whom were of school age, and concluded that a vocational school could be put to good use in an overwhelmingly agricultural county.

Jennie Dean soon discovered that fund-raising would become a full-time endeavor. In 1892, to maintain both interest and cash flow, she organized a huge picnic dinner on the fourth of July that involved all of the county neighborhoods from as far west as Gainesville, Sudley Springs, and Bull Run to nearby Conklin and Wellington. Advertised widely throughout the county as an old fashioned picnic with singing and speeches, the response from the entire community was outstanding. Seventy-five dollars was earned selling foods ranging from ten cents to fifty cents (7).

In 1893, a school charter was written. The school was expected to serve boys and girls over fourteen years by improving their "moral and intellectual condition" through "such instructions in the Common English Branches, the Mechanical Arts and Trades, in farming,

housework, needlework and other occupations as . . . shall be practicable and also useful in enabling the said youth to earn a livelihood." Dean wished to empower young people through education to take care of themselves by learning skilled trades. The academic subjects of English, spelling, and arithmetic were taught to all students. Young men studied blacksmithing, carpentry, shoemaking, wheelwrighting and agriculture. Young women learned laundering, cooking, canning, and sewing (8). Given the geographical spread of the students, a boarding school proved a necessity. And, like the Hampton and Tuskegee models on which the school was based, boarding enabled poor students to work in exchange for tuition and linked pedagogy and practical skills. Gradually fourteen hundred dollars was raised to meet the first land payment.

Once the land was purchased, Dean obtained assistance in constructing the first school building. Emily Howland, a wealthy New Yorker active in women's suffrage, befriended Dean at a Washington suffrage convention and agreed to underwrite the construction of the school's first building. In return, Dean called the building Howland Hall. Meanwhile, Dean enlisted local men (both black and white) to donate skills, time, and supplies to renovate a farmhouse that came to be called Charter Cottage (9).

It was a proud occasion when the school was formally dedicated on Labor Day, 3 September 1894. Prominent local attorney, realtor, and politician, George C. Round, headed the dedication committee. He had drafted the charter approved by the Commonwealth of Virginia and would oversee the day's formalities. Local and state politicians, judges, and black and white supporters, gathered under a newly donated American flag to hear Frederick Douglass deliver the major address of the afternoon. On 1 October 1894, six pupils came to learn. The faculty consisted of a principal and three teachers, all of whom worked only for their board the first year. Within months of its opening, the school population reached seventy-five students (10).

Until her death on 3 May 1913 at age sixty-one, Dean served on the board of trustees, as a matron in the women's dorm, and as the major, indefatigable fundraiser. Sadly for her, Dean's influence waned as individuals perceived to be more knowledgeable in the education profession took over the school's direction. At the height of its existence, the campus of more than one hundred acres had a dozen buildings, all constructed from private finances and donated labor and materials, and helped train an average of 152 students per year. A prosperous farm provided food and dairy products, and made the school somewhat self-sufficient. The Manassas Industrial School for Colored Youth was a private institution publicly acknowledged for its importance to the education of black youth in Virginia. As a result of Jennie Dean's efforts and foresight, over 6,500 young black people from Virginia, the District of Columbia, and at least ten other states received an education.

In 1938, after several years of effort to gain public funding due to dire financial straits, the school was approved for public takeover by the Virginia State Department of Education. It became a regional high school serving black students of Prince William, Fairfax, Fauquier, and Rappahannock Counties. As the population of

The Manassas Museum

Students at the Manassas Industrial School learned practical skills in addition to traditional subjects like English and arithmetic.

northern Virginia expanded, similar schools were built and the Manassas school became the Prince William County High School. In 1959, the county school board demolished the old industrial school buildings, replacing them with a new, large building for black day students. In 1966, the school board renamed the newly integrated school Jennie Dean Middle School. Today, this modernized building serves as the Jennie Dean Elementary School of Manassas (11).

Objectives and Goals

Participation in this lesson will enable students to:

1. Learn how a former enslaved, unknown woman initiated vocational education for African Americans in Northern Virginia, creating a model for young people.
2. Enhance their skills of interpretation of primary source materials.
3. Write creatively to express how Jennie Dean influenced her community.
4. Compare and contrast vocational education during the first and last decades of the twentieth century.
5. Research and identify local African American leaders in their communities.

This lesson can be used as an enrichment of a unit on Reconstruction and late nineteenth-century southern life, or it can become the focus of lessons highlighting the accomplishments of African Americans.

Procedures

1. Introduce Jennie Dean as a local black leader, unknown nationally, who developed vocational education in the county of her birth. (The map of Virginia indicates this information which you can then relate to the map of the United States).
2. Show the pictures of Dean and the campus of the Manassas Industrial School, followed with these questions for general discussion.
   a. How could a young woman with a very limited education manage to establish such an institution?
   b. What characteristics might such an individual possess to propel her actions?
3. Divide the class into small groups of three to five students and supply each group with the information in handout one.
   a. Direct students to:
      (1). Read the quotes underlining key phrases of information.
      (2). Work together to draw up a list detailing background and characteristics of Dean obtained from the quotes.
      (3). Report their findings to the entire class.
   b. Ask students what other information they might want to know about Jennie Dean. As they raise questions, answer what is possible based upon the information in the background material.

4. Distribute copies of handouts two and three to the groups previously selected. Show the pictures depicting student activities to the class. Then:
   a. Direct students to read handout two looking for the following information:
      (1). School "selling" points
      (2). Objectives of school
      (3). Who can go to the school
      (4). What the requirements are for admission
      (5). How attendance will be secured
   b. Direct students to read handout three looking for the following information:
      (1). Unusual elements of class schedule
      (2). Changes in course work, requirements from handout two
   c. Ask representatives of each group to give parts of the information requested. Get them to explain the necessity of boarding at the school and why tuition had to be paid.
   d. Prior to class, obtain current copies of your school's general regulations and curriculum for academics and vocational programs.
      (1). Distribute copies of your school's regulations and requirements to students.
      (2). Direct each group to find similarities and differences between their present school and the 1903 and 1915 school regulations and curriculum.
      (3). Ask representatives of each group to present three differences or similarities to the entire class.

   (4). Discuss whether a similar curriculum would have been taught in the white schools of Northern Virginia in 1903 and 1915. Why or why not?
5. Follow-up activities: Direct students to:
   a. Write a speech Jennie Dean might have used to gain monetary support for her school from a men's or women's group.
   b. Write a letter Jennie Dean might have sent to a prominent white or black person enlisting their financial support.
   c. Design a broadside advertising Manassas Industrial School to potential students and their parents.
   d. Design a public program of dedication for the opening of Manassas Industrial School.
   e. Write a one-act play depicting Jennie Dean appealing for funds or students arriving at the Manassas Industrial School expressing their hopes and educational expectations.
   f. Prepare a list of questions you might use to interview Jennie Dean if she were to come to class. Role play this interview with another student acting as Jennie Dean for the class.
   g. Research how Tuskegee Institute was operated and compare it to the Manassas Industrial School in an oral report to the class.
   h. Research local African-American history to find people who have provided leadership for your community. Write a report to be given to the class. ❑

The Manassas Museum

At Manassas, young men were taught such things as carpentry and shoemaking while women learned cooking and sewing.

Bibliography

Altschuler, Glenn C. *Race, Ethnicity, and Class in American Social Thought, 1865-1919.* Arlington Heights, Ill.: Harlan Davidson, Inc., 1982.

Ayers, Edward. *The Promise of the New South.* New York: Oxford University Press, 1992.

Barden, Thomas E. *Virginia Folk Legends.* Charlottesville: University Press of Virginia, 1991.

Dabney, Virginius. *Virginia: The New Dominion.* Charlottesville: University Press of Virginia, 1971.

Foner, Eric. *Reconstruction: America's Unfinished Revolution.* New York: Harper and Row, 1988.

———. *Nothing But Freedom: Emancipation and Its Legacy.* Baton Rouge: Louisiana State University Press, 1983.

Franklin, John Hope. *From Slavery to Freedom: A History of Negro Americans.* New York: Alfred A. Knopf, 1980.

Goodheart, Lawrence B., Richard D. Brown and Stephen G. Rabe, eds. *Slavery in American Society.* Lexington, Mass.: D.C. Heath and Co., 1992.

Gutman, Herbert. *The Black Family in Slavery and Freedom.* New York: Vintage Books, 1976.

Jaynes, Gerald D. *Branches Without Roots: The Genesis of the Black Working Class in the American South, 1862-1882.* New York: Oxford University Press, 1986.

Novak, Daniel A. *The Wheel of Servitude: Black Forced Labor After Slavery.* Lexington: University of Kentucky Press, 1978.

Perdue, Charles L., Jr., Thomas Barden and Robert K. Phillips. *Weevils in the Wheat: Interviews With Virginia Ex-slaves.* Charlottesville: University Press of Virginia, 1976.

Endnotes

1. VanLoan Naisawald, *Manassas Junction and The Docto* (Manassas: Lake Lithograph, 1981).
2. Stephen J. Lewis, *Undaunted Faith* (Catlett, Va.: The Circui Press, 1942).
3. These points are gleaned from oral histories with members of th 121 year-old First Baptist Church in Manassas.
4. Lewis, *Undaunted Faith.*
5. Glenn C. Altschuler, *Race, Ethnicity, and Class in America. Social Thought, 1865-1919* (Arlington Heights, Ill.: Harla. Davidson, Inc., 1982).
6. Lewis, *Undaunted Faith.*
7. Ibid.
8. *The Word From the Junction,* the newsletter of the Manasa Museum of May-June, 1992.
9. Lewis, *Undaunted Faith.*
10. *The Word From the Junction.*
11. Ibid.

Rita G. Koman was an American history and government teacher fo seventeen years. She is currently an educational consultant i Manassas, Virginia.

During its early years, the Manassas Industrial School occupied more than one hundred acres and housed one hundred and fifty students per year.

Handout I
Descriptive Quotes about Jennie Dean

Stephen Johnson Lewis, one of the early graduates of Manassas Industrial School and a Trustee in the 1920s, who became a dentist in town:

"Miss Dean possessed a wonderful vision, a capacity for planning and a technic (sic) for winning friends to her causes and then making them succeed."

"Dean was strong-willed, highly determined, devoted and willing to make many sacrifices for a school. She was a good organizer too."

Oswald Garrison Villard, grandson of William Lloyd Garrison and Board of Trustees member of the Manassas Industrial School for twenty years:

"I think it was her (Dean) own straightforward honesty and refusal to pretend to be anything else than what she was, a plain woman, unashamed of being a cook who made money to help the school and her people. I was much interested by the deep impression she made upon my Southern wife. There was nothing serville (sic) about her; she did not play up to or toady to the whites. She was just a plain, simple, dignified black woman with no gift of oratory and no charm beyond what I have said—her straightforwardness and sincerity . . . to win the Southern home friends to her cause first as a basis upon which to start the movement for the School, she overcame much greater handicaps of prejudice, disregard for Negroid capacity for schooling and training, intolerance and indifference as to the negro's possibilities as a citizen of the local regions, State, and Nation, than she had to overcome in winning more liberal minded friends of the North and East."

The Manassas Museum

Jennie Dean, founder of the Manassas Industrial School.

Richard C. Haydon, Superintendent of Prince William County Public Schools when the county School Board bought the Manassas Industrial School in 1938:

" . . . she (Dean) had done for Negro education in this limited Northern Virginia area what Booker T. Washington had done for the nation in the field of industrial education . . . That the State (Virginia) Department of Education, upon due investigation, was willing to finance the original setup (entire campus and farm) into the State's educational system through a loan of $20,000 from the Literary Fund to a three member County Board, constitutes another tribute to the wisdom, vision, and constructive service Jennie Dean rendered both to her community and her State. The School is considered by the State Department of Education as a pioneer in the regional high school movement."

An unnamed church member upon Dean's death in 1913:

"All of her (Dean) life's efforts had been directed towards a main objective: that of building for better, more productive and progressing (sic) living among her people. The establishment of missions, chapels and churches, community missionary and social service work were all preliminary steps preparatory to the main objective: . . . an educational institution for the influencing of human minds and lives . . . she taught that life is a privilege as well as a responsibility and that birth or origin have but little bearing on success or failure if the will to help one's self is cultivated and encouraged . . . Dean's influence went far in teaching many Southern whites in both private and public life, that an ignorant, uneducated, untrained and idle Negro youth was a direct liability to both the community and the State."

Source of all quotes: Stephen J. Lewis. *Undaunted Faith.* Catlett, Va.: The Circuit Press, 1942.

Handout 2
The Manassas Industrial School, 1902-1903

Location

This school for colored youths of both sexes is situated upon the historic battle grounds of Manassas, and is located about one mile from the centre of the town. Manassas is conveniently located on the Southern Railroad, 33 miles from Washington, D.C. There are ten trains daily. The place is elevated and healthful, and surrounded by picturesque scenery. Free from the seductive influences of a city, this school offers a rare opportunity to those desirous of placing their children under elevating and purifying influences. The farm contains over one hundred acres.

The Objects of the School

1. To train in habits of usefulness those committed to its care, by developing them mentally, morally, and physically.
2. To teach the dignity and importance of labor, and by means of trades to perform it skillfully and with pride.
3. To give a sound, English, common school education.
4. To teach the value and use of money.
5. To train young men and women for useful, intelligent citizenship.
6. To make its students self-reliant, careful thinkers, thorough in their work, manly and womanly in their bearing and to cultivate habits of industry.

Trades Taught

For Girls—Dressmaking, mending, and plain sewing, cooking, housekeeping, laundry work, poultry raising, and wood-work.

For Boys—Carpentry, farming, gardening, and blacksmithing. Wheelwrighting and other trades will be added from time to time as the school progresses.

Religious Worship

Each day's work is begun with devotional exercises, and each student is required to be present.
Students must attend Sabbath school, and are required to attend preaching whenever the weather permits.
A Christian Endeavor Society exists at the school.

The School Year of Three Terms will begin the first Tuesday in October, and end the last week in May.
First Term . . . . . October, November and December.
Second Term . . . . January and February.
Third Term . . . . March, April and May.

Students intending to board at the school will be received the Saturday before the opening day.
Persons applying for admission to this school must be able to furnish satisfactory evidence of good character.
The school is in charge of competent and experienced teachers.

Admission of Students

Persons seeking admission into the school should write to the Principal.
Examinations will take place the first Monday in October of each year.
Students are urged to be present upon the first day of the fall term. Admission at any other time than the beginning will be allowed only in special cases.
Candidates for admission to the school must be at least sixteen years of age.
Those entering either Academic or Trade Departments, must be able to read well in the fourth reader, write in a fair hand a paragraph or letter in simple English, with proper regard to capitalization, punctuation, and spelling; and to pass a satisfactory examination in both mental and written work, in the first four rules in arithmetic, in United States money and common fractions.
The estimated cost of books is from $2.50 to $5.00 according to classes. Books and stationery must be paid for in cash.
Each Student will be charged $10.00 a month for tuition, this will include room, board, washing, fuel and light; $4.50 of this amount may be paid by their labor. The entrance fee is $10.00.
The cost of board is paid partly in cash and partly in work.

Trade Students

Trade students receive instructions in their trades four and a half days each week.

When trade students become efficient they will receive pay for a part of their work in the shops or on the premises.

Trade students will be given an opportunity to earn a part of their expenses at common labor one and a half days each week when necessary.

Trade students attend night classes.

Students in the manual training and literary departments attend School four or five days in each week and work for a part of their board one or two days.

Wages

Good workers may earn as much as $5.00 by working one or two days each week, but the school does not guarantee any fixed amount regardless of the value of the services rendered. Wages are paid according to value of work done. Students' labor is accepted as pay only when it is satisfactory. When otherwise they may be suspended from school.

The earnings of students are expected to be used only to pay school expenses. If the school is indebted to any student at the end of the year or at time of withdrawal, the amount due stands to his credit and may be used by him as part payment of expenses upon his return to school within two years.

Money earned is held as a bond for the fulfillment of the purpose of getting an education at this school and can be used only when there and cannot be used for any other purpose. If a student is sent away or leaves without permission these earnings may be used to help needy and worthy students at the discretion of the Faculty of the school.

Accounts are made out and handed to the students about the first of each month; parents should require their children to send their bills home promptly that they may see what is owing to the school.

All bills should be paid in cash and within one week after the accounts are received.

Those failing to pay promptly are liable to suspension from recitation till their bills are paid, but will be required to attend religious services, drill and other exercises at the discretion of the Faculty.

All receipts for money paid the school will be handed to students to be forwarded to their parents.

Clothing

Young ladies are expected to bring rubbers and water proofs or money to purchase them, and are expected to dress plainly and neatly.

Young men are required to wear the navy blue school uniform and cap, which must be worn upon inspection and drill occasions and at all times when off the school grounds.

Every young man must provide himself with a uniform upon entering the school.

The school has arranged to have measures for suits taken and made at a reasonable price. The price will be from $11.50 to $12.50 per suit.

Tuition *without room* or *Board* will be charged at the rate of $2.00 a month, one-half payable in cash, balance in labor. Cash payments must be made invariably in advance.

Students will be required to furnish the following:

1 mattress, 1 pillow, 3 sheets, 3 pillow-slips, and such other bed-covering as will make them comfortable; a broom, a lamp, towels and slop pail.

Course of Study

First Year

Reading, spelling, arithmetic, language lessons, geography, penmanship, drawing, hygiene.
Manual Training: Cooking, sewing, laundering, blacksmithing, woodworking, agriculture.

Second Year

Reading, spelling, arithmetic, grammar and composition, geography, hygiene, United States history, drawing.
Manual Training: Cooking, sewing, laundering, blacksmithing, woodworking, agriculture.

Third Year

English and American classics, spelling, arithmetic, grammar, United states history, history of Virginia, elementary physics, drawing, hygiene.
Manual Training: Cooking, sewing, laundering, blacksmithing, woodworking, agriculture, horticulture.

Fourth Year

English and American classics, spelling, arithmetic, (completed) grammar, civil government, physical geography, elementary chemistry, drawing, hygiene.

Handout 3
The Manassas Industrial School, 1914-1915

Class Schedule

10:05-10:15 Phonics
10:15-10:30 Recess
10:30-10:40 Spelling
10:40-11:15 Arithmetic
11:15-12:00 Agriculture (Tues., Wed., Fri.)
11:15-12:00 Reading and Story Telling (Thurs., Sat.)
12:00- 1:30 Dinner and Recess

1:30- 2:15 Trades
2:15- 2:30 Music
2:30- 3:00 Study
3:00- 3:10 Physical Culture
3:10- 3:45 Virginia History
3:45- 4:00 Penmanship (Wed., Fri.)
3:45- 4:30 Geography (Tues., Thurs.)
4:00- 4:30 Hygiene (Wed., Fri.)

Regular Four-Year Courses Offered

I. Academic-Normal Course.
II. Agricultural Course.
III. Trades Courses in
    1. Blacksmithing
    2. Carpentry and Painting
    3. Shoemaking
    4. Wheelwrighting
IV. Home Economics Course including Sewing, Cooking, Laundering and Housekeeping

Because of a regrading of the work, the classes in the regular courses are now styled First, Second, Third and Fourth Years. The Junior A and Junior B classes are preparatory.

I. Academic-Normal Course

This course aims primarily to prepare teachers who shall be able to teach in the rural school. It is so designed however, that students completing the work shall be able to meet the requirements for admission to schools doing a higher grade of work. A part of the Fourth Year is devoted to practice teaching under the supervision of the instructor in Methods.

All subjects required in this course that are not explained below will be found under the Academic Normal Course.
Agronomy: A study of plants, texture and composition of the soil, preparation of the soil, drainage, etc.
Animal Husbandry: The care of horses, mules, cattle and swine.
Commercial Geography: A study of the human and social factors underlying the commercial and industrial organization, the commercial and industrial life of the rural community, the division of labor, the factory system, transportation and local distribution.
Farm Management: A study of "system" and the factors that enter into the acquiring of executive ability, the advantages of good management.
Land Tenure: A general study of leases, mortgages, contracts, the different systems of "holding" and papers involved in the transfer of land.
Poultry Husbandry: Care of breeding stock and eggs, incubation and care of chickens, marketing.

II. School Gardens

The school garden is a special feature of the agricultural work. Plots are rented to the students for this purpose. They pay for the seeds they use for plowing and harrowing when done by the school and all incidental expenses. A larger part of the profits derived therefrom is given to the student in the event he is able to dispose of the products. Greater than the monetary interest, however, is the development, pleasure and real knowledge that the student gets. The school gardens attracted much attention last year and promise to yield far greater results this season.
Beginning with the school year 1916-17 it is planned to make a one-year course in school gardening compulsory for all students.

III. Trade-School Course

The Trade School offers courses in Blacksmithing, Carpentry and Painting, Shoemaking and Wheelwrighting. It gives a definite, graduated course of instruction which aims to fit each student to be a thorough craftsman. While the students receive credit for productive work, the primary aim is not the financial aid but the educational value that is derived from such commercial work. The completion of Junior B or its equivalent is required.

As students will not be able to do much productive work during the first years of the course, they will need about $80 to pay their expenses each year.

The Abolition of Slavery in the Western Hemisphere: Its Consequences for Africa

Statement of Purpose

This is a two- to three- day teaching unit for inclusion in mainstream American history survey courses. This brief unit may be included in several different places in an American history course. One option is discussing the debate over slavery in the Constitutional Convention of 1787, focusing on the decision to end the slave trade in twenty years (Article 1, section 9). Another place for this topic is in connection with the Emancipation Proclamation and the Thirteenth Amendment at the end of the Civil War. It might also fit into a unit on the institution of slavery and the American abolitionist movement during the years before the Civil War. More time may be spent if the teacher wishes to assign students to further work, reporting to the class on the topics covered here.

Introduction

This teaching unit offers a global perspective on the abolition of slavery for standard high school American history survey courses. Too often students are left with the impression that the passage of the thirteenth Amendment settled the issue of African slavery in the world. In fact abolition was a worldwide historical movement with powerful consequences for all nations and regions of the Atlantic world, especially Africa. With additional curricular support, American History teachers can build this global perspective into their courses without radically altering existing course formats. Teachers can address questions of motivation, perspective and historical significance as they examine this topic. Students can study American history in connection with other world areas and less in isolation from global factors. In particular, students will be reminded of the profound consequences of the abolition movement for Africa itself.

Objectives

- Examine the perception, common in the United States, that slavery ended with the Thirteenth Amendment.
- Connect African and Latin American historical experiences with U.S. history.
- Present the abolition movement in a global context.
- Introduce students to comparative history.
- Introduce the complex factors—economic, humanitarian, and political—behind the abolition movement.
- Examine the relative power of humanitarian, economic, and political motives as forces in history.
- Introduce the consequences for Africa of the abolition of slavery outside of Africa.
- Help students develop the skills to make historical hypotheses from information gathered from various sources. Encourage higher level thinking skills. Introduce complexity and intellectual controversy into the curriculum.

Historical Background

The slave trade was an unmitigated misery—a crime unredeemed by one extenuating circumstance . . . it led to an unpardonable destruction of population. During the whole period of the trade it has been estimated that somewhere between 30 and 40 million souls were lost to Africa. The victims were the most virile and active people of West Africa—the young and healthy men and women.

—Adu Boahen, a Ghanaian scholar

Partly due to the sheer size of the Atlantic slave trade and the enormous volume of capital and human energy expended in maintaining the trade, the abolition movement took over a century to complete. A complex web of humanitarian, economic and political factors, each supporting the others, served to put an end to the slave trade and then to slavery itself outside of Africa by the end of the nineteenth century. Within the first decades of this century, slavery was mostly done away with in Africa too. The industrial revolution with its emphasis on a mobile labor force, technology, and the market potential of free laborers as consumers mounted a powerful case against the use of slave labor. But the relentless logic of free market economics by itself was not enough to secure abolition. Agricultural interests in the New World, dependent on single crops, such as tobacco, sugar, and cotton grown by slave labor, put up a powerful

Abolition of the Slave Trade and the Emancipation of Slaves

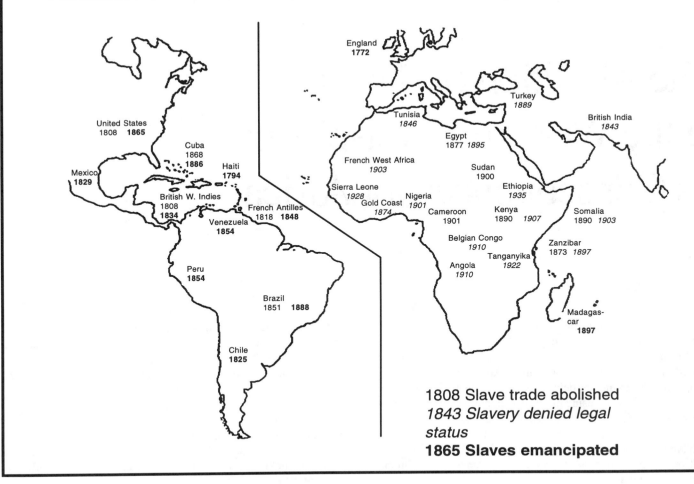

England 1772

United States 1808 1865

Mexico 1829

Cuba 1868 1886

Haiti 1794

British W. Indies 1808 1834

French Antilles 1818 1848

Venezuela 1854

Peru 1854

Chile 1825

Brazil 1851 1888

Turkey *1889*

Tunisia *1846*

British India *1843*

Egypt 1877 *1895*

French West Africa *1903*

Sierra Leone *1928*

Gold Coast *1874*

Nigeria *1901*

Sudan 1900

Ethiopia *1935*

Cameroon 1901

Kenya 1890 *1907*

Somalia 1890 *1903*

Belgian Congo *1910*

Zanzibar 1873 *1897*

Tanganyika *1922*

Angola *1910*

Madagas-car **1897**

1808 Slave trade abolished
1843 Slavery denied legal status
1865 Slaves emancipated

resistance to abolition. In the end, it took the great antislavery crusade, the Abolitionist Movement, allied with economic interests to stir up popular opinion for abolition to a level that forced governments to respond. Slave revolts and slave resistance also played a major role by putting great political pressure on slave societies. By the middle of the eighteenth century an uprising or disturbance in the Caribbean every few years culminated in the great triumph of Toussaint L'Ouverture in Haiti in the 1790s. The humanitarians who led the antislavery crusade—mostly reformers, preachers, writers and politicians—often had Africans working in their movement, sometimes taking leadership roles. By 1800, slavery had become a sin according to some religionists, uneconomical in business and commerce, and contrary to the right of man for those who supported the Enlightenment ideas expressed in the American and French Revolutions. In the West, except for new technological innovations like the cotton gin, it had become a dying institution.

What was the effect of the slave trade era on Africa? This is a difficult question for young students of history. After all, Africans supplied the human cargos to slave traders on the west coast of Africa by bringing captives from the interior to be sold. The same was true for slave traders on the east coast of Africa, on the Indian Ocean. Slavery was practiced in various forms in almost all African societies before the Europeans came. This meant that Africa had the necessary

economic organization to enter the Atlantic slave trade. African simply had to adopt their own systems to the new markets, and then were profits for participants on both sides. In time, the slave trade fueled geopolitical shifts and intrigue in West Africa as nations small and large, jockeyed for position and advantage in the trans Atlantic System. It is possible to blame Africans for complicity i what we now see as a great crime against humanity perpetrated by the west. But it is important to emphasize that little evidence shows th most West Africans knew of or understood the brutal consequence of their actions. Yet the long term effects were devastating. Indee the four centuries of the Atlantic slave trade can be seen as an Africa holocaust.

Inevitably abolition in the west meant many African state hitherto dependent on the slave trade, faced severe economic disrup tion (see handout 3). One result was that slavery in Africa actual increased in the nineteenth century. But, as a result of the industri revolution, Europe and the Americas began seeking "legitimate trade with Africa, and it quickly became clear that before Afri could join the new world markets, the Africans would have to gi up their own system of slavery. There was simply no place for sla labor in the new social and economic institutions, and so the We turned to outright colonization as the only way to force Africa in the new industrial economy. Ironically, however, many Africa would later complain that European patterns of coerced lab resembled slavery in all but the name (see handout 4).

Teaching this unit requires students to address some difficult and fundamental questions about Africa about which scholars still disagree. The first and most important question is how African slavery differed from slavery in the West (see handout 2). There is general agreement that the differences were substantial. Two scholars, Miers and Kopytoff, question whether the word slavery even applies to Africa, and suggest the terms "acquired persons" or "marginalized person," living on the fringes of society, as more accurate. In another publication, Miers and Roberts offer a more thorough explanation of African bondage (see handout 2). It is important to stress that humanitarianism and the concept of personal individual liberty are western ideas. In Africa, having the rights offered by society meant belonging to a group. The lineage or kinship group, the attachment to a tribe or a clan, conferred upon the individual the same advantages as individual liberty did in the West: full membership in society. As to whether the African system was "kinder and gentler," as Equiano suggests, one must emphasize that while there were vast differences in the varieties and thus the harshness of African slavery, there was considerable variation in the Americas as well.

A second question addresses the effects of the abolition of slavery in Africa on African societies. Again the picture is very unclear. At first the European powers were slow to press for abolition, fearing it might cause too much disruption and disorder. But as the European colonization of the continent advanced, so did the laws implementing abolition (See map). Still, it was well into the twentieth century before the last traces of slavery were made illegal. The system of forced labor or contract labor put into effect by the Europeans under the colonial system can be seen as a modernized form of slavery (see handout 4). This is an important question to address.

Historians do agree upon African societies' resiliency and toughness in the face of successive shocks over the centuries of the slave trade and its abolition. The endurance of these societies as they underwent these relentless perpetrations from the west is admirable. Students can reflect on how well Africa survived the disruptions of exploitation during these several centuries.

There are certainly many more questions than answers in this material. The object of the lesson is to get students thinking about a very complicated and morally difficult subject.

Some final reminders: Students often get confused by the distinction between the slave trade and the practice of slavery itself. It is important to keep these distinctions clear as discussion progresses. Also try to make fair and consistent comparisons when teaching about Africa. For example, when discussing African slavery, make comparisons with slave systems in the Americas and elsewhere. Discuss how other societies outside of Africa have treated women and children in the past. Point out that Africans did not enslave their own people. Captives were taken from other tribes and ethnic groups who were seen as different. Is there anything in European and American politics and history that might resemble what might be called tribalism?

Implementing the Lesson

Pass out the handouts and the map to students. Taking each handout in order, have the students respond to the questions. They may work in small groups or individually. For homework, students might look up one or more of the individual topics or events covered here and report them to the class. ❑

Bibliography

Boahen, Adu. *Topics in West African History*. London: Longman, 1979.

Crowder, Michael. *West Africa Under Colonial Rule*. Evanston, Ill.: Northwestern University Press, 1968.

Curtin, Philip. *Africa Remembered: Narratives by West Africans from the Era of the Slave Trade*. Madison, WI: University of Wisconsin, 1967.

Curtin, Philip et. al. *African History*. New York: Longman, 1989.

Davis, David Brion. *The Problem of Slavery in Western Culture*. Ithaca, NY: Cornell University Press, 1966.

Foner, Laura and Eugene D. Genovese, eds. *Slavery in the New World: A Reader in Comparative History*. Englewood Cliffs, NJ: Prentice Hall, 1969.

Gann, Lewis H. and Peter Duignon. *Africa and the World*. New York: Chandler Publishing Company, 1972.

Gates, Henry Lewis. *The Classic Slave Narratives*. New York: Penguin, 1987.

Gide, Andre. *Travels in the Congo*. New York: Alfred A. Knopf, 1957.

Grant, Douglas. *The Fortunate Slave: An Illustration of African Slavery in the Early Eighteenth Century*. New York: Oxford University Press, 1968.

Harris, Joseph. *Africans and Their History*. New York: Penguin, 1987.

Manmning, Patrick. *Slavery and African Life*. New York: Cambridge University Press, 1990.

Miers, Suzanne. *Britain and the End of the Slave Trade*. New York: Longman, 1975.

Miers, Suzanne and Igor Kopytoff, eds. *Slavery in Africa: Historical and Anthropological Perspectives*. Madison, WI: University of Wisconsin Press, 1977.

Miers, Suzanne and Richard Roberts, eds. The End of Slavery in Africa. Madison, WI: University of Wisconsin Press, 1988.

Patterson, Orlando. *Freedom in the Making of Western Culture*. New York: Harper Collins, 1991.

Robinson, David and Douglas Smith. *Sources of the African Past: Case Studies of Five Nineteenth-century African Societies*. New York: Africana, 1979.

Wiley, Bell, ed. *Slaves No More: Letters from Liberia, 1833-1869*. Lexington: University of Kentucky Press, 1980.

Williams, Eric. *From Columbus to Castro: The History of the Caribbean, 1492-1969*. New York: Harper & Row, 1970.

Edward Rossiter is Department Head of History and Social Sciences at Newton North High School, Newton, Massachusetts.

Handout 1
A Chronology of the Abolition of Slavery in the Western World

1732   The Bretheren, a German Evangelical Christian sect, establish the first overseas mission in Africa. They call for an end to slavery.

1733   The British Parliament passes the Molasses Act imposing prohibitive duties on imports of sugar, rum and molasses into British territory from any foreign territory. This is the first sign that the British West Indian sugar colonies, based on slave labor, are hurting economically.

1760   A major slave uprising in Jamaica, called Tacky's Revolt, unsettles the slave owning plantation establishment in the Caribbean.

1772   The Somerset judgment in England, handed down by the Lord Chief Justice, abolishes domestic slavery in England, but not in the colonies. Fourteen thousand slaves are freed.

1772 and 1774 King George of England fails to approve bills in the Jamaican, Massachusetts and Virginia colonial assemblies, seeking to limit or abolish the slave trade.

1774-1783 American Revolution severely hurts British sugar plantations in the Caribbean, further eroding the need for slaves in the sugar colonies and boosting the sugar economies of other European countries especially France, at Britain's expense. Thomas Jefferson's first draft of a Declaration of Independence for the thirteen North American colonies challenges slavery on moral grounds. This portion is omitted in final version.

1787   Publication of *Thoughts and Sentiments on the Evil and Wicked Traffic of Slavery and Commerce of the Human Species* by Ottobah Cugoano, an educated Fanti ex-slave. Formation in London of the Society for Abolition of the Slave Trade by William Wilberforce with the support of Prime Minister of England William Pitt. Sierra Leone founded as British colony by an Abolitionist, Granville Sharp, for purposes of settling freed slaves from England and America. Emphasizing the colony's purpose, the main town is named Freetown which is the capital city of Sierra Leone today.

1788   Formation in England of the Africa Association with the goal of replacing the slave trade with legitimate trade with Africa. An association report states the hope that "the people of the inland regions of Africa may soon be united with Europe in that great bond of commercial fellowship which the mutual wants and different productions of other continents have happily established." An increasing demand for palm oil—both to make soap and to lubricate the new machines of the industrial revolution in Europe—leads to more emphasis on "legitimate trade" as opposed to slave trading. Later railroads will vastly increase a demand for palm oil for lubrication. Exports of palm oil from West Africa increase from 1000 tons in 1810 to 40,000 tons in 1855.

1789   William Wilberforce introduces into the British House of Commons a motion calling for an end to the slave trade. In the debate, an opponent claims abolition "would render the City of London one scene of bankruptcy and ruin." Publication in London of *Equiano's Travels* by Olaudah Euquiano (slave name Gustavus Vasa), a freed slave born an Ibo in Benin (now Nigeria). He was freed in the late 1760s and wrote this story of his life. This publication and that of Cugoano's (above), and the work of their authors travelling and speaking against slavery, form a major African influence on the abolition movement. Both are still in print.

1792 The French Revolution abolishes slavery. It is later reinstated by Napoleon who then abolishes it again during the Hundred Days after he escapes from Elba. Yet again revived after Naopleon, it takes another Revolution, the rising of 1848, before France finally abolishes slavery in all French territory. The French go a step further making all inhabitants of French colonies citizens of France.

1794 Successful slave revolt occurs in the French colony of Haiti; it was led by a slave coachman, Toussaint L'Ouverture. Haiti becomes the first black independent country outside of Africa. Fear grows in England of a similar event in a British Caribbean colony.

1808 Britain and the United States abolish their slave trades. In the U.S., the action was mandated by article 1, section 9 of the Constitution. The British send a naval squadron to West Africa to secure enforcement. Denmark had been the first to abolish its slave trade in 1802.

1815 The Vienna Treaty, marking the end of the Napoleonic wars, condemns the world slave trade. In separate treaties with Portugal, Spain and the Netherlands, in many cases supported by cash payments and financial concessions, Britain secures the abolition of the slave trade in those countries to prevent them from gaining an economic advantage. Britain had already abolished her slave trade. Worldwide enforcement is left almost entirely to the British Navy, and illegal slave trading and smuggling persist. Between 1800 and the late 1870s, over three million Africans were shipped across the Atlantic as slaves.

1822 Republic of Liberia is established for freed American slaves in West Africa by the American Colonization Society. Denmark Vesey leads a slave rising in South Carolina.

1831 Nat Turner's slave insurrection in Virginia.

1833 Britain abolishes slavery in the Empire. Slave owners are compensated for their loss at a cost to the British taxpayer of twenty million pounds.

1852 Legitimate trade grows as Gambia exports 150,000 pounds sterling worth of peanuts (called grounds nuts in Africa).

1865 The Thirteenth Amendment to the Constitution ends slavery in the United States.

1874 Britain abolishes slavery in the Gold Coast of Africa.

1884-1885 The Berlin Conference begins the "Scramble for Africa." Partitioning Africa into "spheres of influence," the European powers begin rapid colonization of the continent, thus ending the "Back to Africa" trends in European and American culture. "Back to Africa" interest was not revived until the 1920s.

1888 Brazil is the last nation in the Western Hemisphere to abolish slavery.

1890 An international conference in Brussels, attended by seventeen western nations, produces a treaty abolishing the slave trade within Africa. No African states are present at the conference; most of the continent has been colonized.

1905 A French government decree makes illegal any measure having as its object "the alienation of a third party" in French West Africa. The French government at that time estimates that up to two million inhabitants of French West Africa were "non libres." France continues to allow Africans loyal to France to take "captifs" from enemy villages.

1925 Thirty eight percent to 12,000 laborers, laying the railways for the British in northern Nigeria, were forcibly recruited by their chiefs. The new League of Nations in Geneva takes up the continuing problem of the persistence of slavery in Africa, the Muslim world and Asia.

1926 The League of Nations implements the Slavery Convention of 1926, which establishes the International Labor Organization to investigate the persistence of slavery and forced labor in the world.

1928 Legal status of slavery in Sierra Leone is abolished by the British colonial government.

1992 *Time* reports on the problem of various forms of domestic slavery, mainly involving women and children, in Asia and the Arab World. In January, 1993, the *Boston Globe* runs an article under the headline: *Report raps Mauritania, Sudan for fostering modern-day slavery*. The report is the work of the International Labor Organization, set up in 1926, and now an agency of the United Nations. It also points to the existence of slave or indentured labor in Pakistan, India, Brazil, Peru and several other nations.

Handout 2
Two Comments on African Slavery

**Olaudah Equiano, an ex-slave educated in the West,
comments on African slavery in the eighteenth century**

From what I can recollect of these battles, they appears to have been irruptions of one little state or district into another, to obtain prisoners or booty. Perhaps they were incited to this by those traders, who brought amongst us the European goods which I mentioned. Such a mode of obtaining slaves in Africa is common; and I believe more are procured in this way, and by kidnapping, than in any other. When a trader wants slaves, he applies to a chief for them, and tempts him with his wares. It is not extraordinary, if on this occasion he yields to the temptation with as little firmness, and accepts the price of his fellow-creature's liberty with as little reluctance as the enlightened merchant. Accordingly he falls on his neighbours, and a desperate battle ensues.

(After battle) The spoils were divided according to the merit of the warriors. Those prisoners which were not sold or redeemed we kept as slaves: but how different was their condition from that of the slaves in the West Indies! With us they do no more work than other members of the community, than even their master; their food, clothing, and lodging, were nearly the same as theirs, except that they were not permitted to eat with those who were free-born; and there was scarcely any other difference between them than a superior degree of importance, which the head of a family possesses in our state, and that authority which, as such, he exercises over every part of his household. Some of these slaves have even slaves under them, as their own property, and for their own use.

Cited in Henry Louis Gates, ed., *The Clasic Slave Narratives* (New York: Penguin, 1987), 18-19.

Two contemporary scholars attempt to define African slavery

Slavery in Africa was a complex system of labor use, of the exercise of rights in persons, and of exploitation and coercion, tempered by negotiation and accommodation. Its form varied over time and place. Slaves might be menial field workers, downtrodden servants, cherished concubines, surrogate kin, trusted trading agents, high officials, army commanders, (or) ostracized social groups dedicated to a deity. . . . Owners might be corporate kin groups or individuals of either sex. A minority of individual owners and a majority of first-generation slaves were women, valued for their productive as well as their reproductive capacities, since women did much of the agricultural work in sub-Saharan Africa. Most slaves had families, and some accumulated possessions, even slaves, of their own. Slavery might involve merely small numbers of slaves, living in or near their owners' households, whose daily lives were virtually indistinguishable from those of the free, or it could be a sophisticated system of labor organization in which slaves and owners were divided by social, economic, political, and legal barriers and sometimes lived in separate settlements. Different forms of slavery could coexist in the same society.

Cited in Suzanne Miers and Richard Roberts, eds., *The End of Slavery in Africa* (Madison, Wis.: University of Wisconsin Press, 1988), 3-5.

Handout 3
Chief Osei Bonsu of the Ashanti Kingdom Comments on Abolition

**Chief Osei Bonsu of the Ashanti Kingdom comments on the
abolition of the slave trade to a British agent, Joseph**

'Now,' said the king, after a pause. 'I have another palaver, and you must help me to talk it. A long time ago the great king liked plenty of trade, more than now; then many ships came, and they bought ivory, gold, and slaves; but now he will not let the ships come as before, and the people buy gold and ivory only. This is what I have in my head, so now tell me truly, like a friend, why does the king do so?' 'His majesty's question,' I replied, 'was connected with a great palaver, which my instructions did not authorise me to discuss. I had nothing to say regarding the slave trade.' 'I know that too, retorted the king; 'because, if my master liked that trade, you would have told me so before. I only want to hear what you think as a friend: this is not like the other palavers.' I was confessedly at a loss for an argument that might pass as a satisfactory reason, and the sequel proved that my doubts were not groundless. The king did not deem it plausible, that this obnoxious traffic should have been abolished from motives of humanity alone; neither would he admit that it lessened the number either of domestic or foreign wars.

Taking up one of my observations, he remarked, 'the white men who go to council with your master, and pray to the great God for him, do not understand my country, or they would not say the slave trade was bad. But if they think it bad now, why did they think it good before. Is not your law an old law, the same as the Crammo law? Do you not both serve the same God, only you have different fashions and customs? Crammos are strong people in fetische, and they say the law is good, because the great God made the book; so they buy slaves, and teach them good things, which they knew not before. This makes every body love the Crammos, and they go every where up and down, and the people give them food when they want it. Then these men come all the way from the great water, and from Manding, and Dagomba, and Killinga; they stop and trade for slaves, and then go home. If the great king would like to restore this trade, it would be good for the white men and for me too, because Ashantee is a country for war, and the people are strong; so if you talk that palaver for me properly, in the white country, if you go there, I will give you plenty of gold, and I will make you richer than all the white men.'

N.B. The author is transcribing English as the chief spoke it.
      Crammo=Muslim, Great King=King of England, Great Water=Niger River.

Cited in David Robinson and Douglas Smith, *Sources of the African Past: Case Studies of Five Nineteenth-century African Societies* (New York: Africana, 1979), 189-190.

The Brussels Conference
General Act for the Repression of the African Slave Trade
Brussels, 2 July 1890

In The Name of God Almighty. . .
Being equally actuated by the firm intention of putting an end to the crimes and devastations engendered by the traffic in African slaves, of efficiently protecting the aboriginal population of Africa, and of securing for that vast continent the benefits of peace and civilization;

Have resolved, in pursuance of the invitation addressed to them by the Government of His Majesty the King of the Belgians, in agreement with the Government of Her Majesty the Queen of Great Britain and Ireland, Empress of India, to convene for this purpose a conference at Brussels, and have named as their plenipotentiaries . . . Who, being furnished with full powers, which have been found to be in good and due form, have adopted the following provisions:

Article I

The powers declare that the most effective means of counteracting the slave-trade in the interior of Africa are the following:

1. Progressive organization for the administrative, judicial, religious, and military services in the African territories placed under the sovereignty or protectorate of civilized nations.
2. The gradual establishment in the interior, by the powers to which the territories are subject, of strongly occupied stations, in such a way as to make their protective or repressive action effectively felt in the territories devastated by slave hunting.
3. The construction of roads, and in particular of railways, connecting the advance stations with the coast, and permitting easy access to the inland waters, and to such of the upper courses of the rivers and streams as are broken by rapids and cataracts, with a view to substituting economical and rapid means of transportation for the present system of carriage by men.
4. Establishment of steam-boats on the inland navigable waters and on the lakes, supported by fortified posts established on the banks.
5. Establishment of telegraph lines, insuring the communication of the posts and of the stations with the coast and with the administrative centers.
6. Organization of expeditions and flying columns, to keep up the communication of the stations with each other and with the coast to support repressive action, and to insure the security of high roads.
7. Restrictions of the importation of fire-arms, at least of those of modern pattern, and of ammunition throughout the entire extent of the territory in which trade is carried on.

Article II

2. To give aid and protection to commercial enterprises; to watch over their legality by especially controlling contracts for service with natives, and to prepare the way for the foundation of permanent centres of cultivation and of commercial settlements. (Numerous additional articles follow).

Handout 5
Andre Gide, on French Equatorial Africa, 1922

Andre Gide, a French writer, visits Africa in 1922

29 October

At Bambio, on September 8, ten rubber-gatherers . . . belonging to the Goundi gang, who work for the Compagnie Forestiere—because they had not brought in any rubber the month before (but this month they brought in double, from 40 to 50 kilogrammes)— were condemned to go round and round the factory under a fierce sun, carrying very heavy wooden beams. If they fell down, they were forced up by guards flogging them with whips.

The "ball" began at eight o'clock and lasted the whole day, with Messrs. Pacha and Maudurier, the company's agent, looking on. At about eleven o'clock a man from Bagouma, called Malongue, fell to get up no more. When M. Pacha was informed of this, he merely replied: 'Je m'enf-' and ordered the "ball" to go on. All this took place in the presence of the assembled inhabitants of Bambio and of all the chiefs who had come from the neighbouring villages to attend the market.

The chief spoke to us also of the conditions reigning in the Boda prison; of the wretched plight of the natives and of how they are fleeing to some less accursed country. My indignation against Pacha is naturally great, but the Compagnie Forestiere plays a part in all this, which seems to be very much graver, though more secret. For, after all, it—its representatives, I mean—knew everything that was going on. It (or its agents) profited by this state of things. Its agents approved Pacha, encouraged him, were his partners. It was at their request that Pacha arbitrarily threw into prison the natives who did not furnish enough stuff: etc . . .

30 October

Impossible to sleep. The Bambio "Ball" haunted my night. I cannot content myself with saying, as so many do, that the natives were still more wretched before the French occupation. We have shouldered responsibilities toward them which we have no right to evade. The immense pity of what I have seen has taken possession of me. I know things to which I cannot reconcile myself. What demon drove me to Africa? What did I come out to find in this country? I was at peace? I know now. I must speak.

Questions

From Handout 1—Chronology and Map
1. Which events in this list can be considered humanitarian, economic or political?
2. How do these events interact and support each other to form a single historical movement?
3. Why do you suppose that, having abolished their own slave trade, the British wanted everyone else to abolish theirs?
4. How do these events draw Africa into the global economy? In what ways is Africa affected today by global economic forces?

From Handout 2—African Slavery
1. Which of these documents is a primary source and which is a secondary source? What is the difference? Does the excerpt from the scholarly work support Equiano's assertions? Are Equiano's comments trustworthy and valid? Why or why not?
2. Are there examples in the treatment of women and children, prisoners of war, migrants and subject peoples in western history which compare to African slavery?
3. What reasons might Equiano have for comparing West Indian and African slavery?
4. Consider a village where ten percent of the inhabitants are enslaved in the various ways described in these comments. Make a list of the ways outside forces might disrupt life by the involuntary ending of this system by outside forces. Compare this situation with the American South in the late 1860s after the Civil War.

From Handout 3—The African response to the abolition of the slave trade
1. What seems to be troubling the king in this reading?
2. Why do neither King Osei Bonsu nor Equiano condemn or seem troubled by the institution of slavery in their societies? How are their respective views of African slavery different?
3. Does the king seem to have a good understanding of the West, particularly England?
4. How does the king try to play off Muslim against Christian? Why does he do this?

From Handout 4—The Brussels Conference of 1890
1. Why are no African states present at this conference?
2. Does it appear that the European powers might have other interests in this treaty besides the abolition of slavery? What specifically do you think the treaty means when it mentions "the benefits of peace and civilization" in the opening statement?
3. Do nations have a right to interfere in each other's affairs for humanitarian reasons? Consider this issue in the case of Somalia today.

From Handout 5—Andre Gide travels to French Equatorial Africa
1. What are the differences between slavery and contract or forced labor? What is meant by the term "wage slavery?" Compare this system of labor with that of migrant farm workers in North America and with factory working conditions in some of the newly emerging countries of South Asia today.
2. How can the abolition of slavery in Africa be seen in the context of the needs of the world economy?
3. What does the description of "the Ball" say about the effectiveness of the Brussels treaty of 1890? How would the French owners of this company have responded to this question?
4. What conclusions might you make from this reading about the consequences for Africa of the abolition of slavery in the western world?

Henry David Thoreau and Martin Luther King, Jr.

Statement of purpose: To teach "Civil Disobedience" and "Letter from Birmingham Jail" both as independent documents and in relation to each other. The first two lessons examine documents independently. Lessons three and four examine the similarities and differences of the two documents. Lesson five relates the ideas in the documents to current reform movements and the tradition of American protest.

Time frame: one week to ten days with modifications possible.

Grade Level: designed for secondary school.

Preparation: Students should understand the setting in which Henry David Thoreau and Martin Luther King Jr. lived. This includes: abolitionism, the Mexican War, Thoreau's disdain for slavery, civil disobedience, the system of segregation in the South, the role Martin Luther King played in Birmingham, and nonviolent protest.

Lesson 1—Analyzing the Individual Documents

Objective: Examine the significant topics in Thoreau's essay and King's letter. These topics might include injustice, equality, violence, and forms of protest.

1. Students should read the essay and letter. For each document they should make a list of the most significant topics.

2. In class and in small groups (works best with three to five groups), students should discuss their individual lists and make two group lists (one for Thoreau, one for King) which combine the individual findings. Each group should try to agree on the one or two most important ideas for each document and should elect a spokesperson prepared to explain these to the class. This explanation should include a definition of the topic, its significance in the text, and its historical context in relation to the author.

3. The spokespeople should present the group lists to form two class lists (one for Thoreau, one for King).

4. Each spokesperson should make a short case for the topics her or his group decided were the most significant. Through discussion, students should prioritize the topics found in the class lists and should

now understand the most significant ideas found in the documents.

Discussion questions:

1. Which document is easier to understand? Why?
2. Which of the topics contained in the documents are discussed today?
3. Which document is more compelling? Why?
4. Do the students agree on the most important topic for each document? If not, have them defend their chosen topic(s) and attempt to convince others.

Lesson 2—Examining Additional Sources (Optional)

Objective: Gain a greater understanding of Henry David Thoreau, Martin Luther King, and their times and ideas.

Activity:

1. Read Thoreau's "Slavery in Massachusetts" and/or "A Plea for Captain John Brown."
2. Read King's "I have a Dream."
3. View *Eyes on the Prize* documentary episodes on Montgomery and Birmingham.
4. View scenes in the movie *Gandhi* which demonstrate civil disobedience and nonviolence.

Discussion questions:

1. What topics found in the documents used in Lesson 1 are found in the above sources?
2. What new topics are introduced in the above sources?
3. How do the images of nonviolence in *Eyes of the Prize* and *Gandhi* make you feel? Was this part of the nonviolent strategy?

Lesson 3—Connecting "Civil Disobedience" and "Letter from Birmingham Jail."

Objective: Compare the two documents. Discover which topics are common to both documents.

Activity:

1. As a class, compare the two class lists which were created in Lesson 1, Activity 3. Create two new lists—one for topics shared by Thoreau and King and one for topics found in only one of the documents.
2. Through class discussion, evaluate the topics shared by Thoreau and King to determine which are the most similar and why.

Discussion questions:

1. Is the message of the documents more similar or more different? Were the authors preaching the same position or a different one?
2. In using similar words and phrases, did the authors mean the same thing? For example, do they mean the same thing when they say "injustice"?
3. Which topics do the students think are most important?
4. Which topics did the authors think were most important?

Lesson 4—Writing about the Topics

Objective: Write analytically or creatively about the topics which Thoreau and King shared. Students should convert the topics learned in lessons 1-3 into a paper (3-7 pages). The paper should be based on either one or two of the quotations found in the quotation section, or based on one or two quotation(s) that the student has discovered on her or his own. The quotation(s) can either be set at the top of the paper and referred to, or placed within the paper.

Activities: Students can pick among the following options or create their own.

1. Write an analytical paper which compares and contrasts one or two of the topics shared by Thoreau and King.
2. Write an abolitionist pamphlet which draws on the topics and language of Thoreau and King.
3. Write a fictitious historical piece in which the participant is a contemporary of either Thoreau or King. The piece should show how Thoreau's and King's ideas were practiced.
4. Write a dialogue between Thoreau and King in which they discuss one or two of the major topics. They could agree or disagree.
5. Write a story which combines the ideas of Thoreau and King.
6. Write a factual personal account in which the ideas of Thoreau and King played a significant role.

Lesson 5—Connections with the Present

Objective: Understand how protest movements since the Civil Rights movement have adhered to, or deviated from, the ideas of Henry David Thoreau and Martin Luther King, Jr. Some of these might include Vietnam draft card burning, Catholic nuns pouring blood on draft records,

the Free Speech Movement in Berkeley, abortion clinic blockading, the murdering of doctors who perform abortions, practitioners of euthanasia, radical environmentalists, or the bombing of the World Trade Center. Students should consider how and why individuals break laws for a "higher purpose."

Activities: Students can pick among the following options or create their own.

1. Gather articles or propaganda which describe or define a current protest movement. Present these findings to the class and point out if the language and ideas are similar to or different from those used by Thoreau and King.
2. Defend or attack a current protest movement by explaining how it remains true to or deviates from Thoreau and King.
3. Debate the validity of a movement or individual action, examining how closely it adheres to the ideas of Thoreau and King. This can be done by individuals or teams.

Discussion questions:

1. Is there an American tradition of protest and reform?
2. Are Thoreau and King relevant today?
3. Are there ideas from Thoreau and King which are detrimental to a democracy?
4. Are there ideas from Thoreau and King which are beneficial to a democracy?
5. How does a society determine when one's "higher purpose" is just or unjust?
6. What are the differences between violent and nonviolent protest? Is one more effective than the other?
7. Does the Constitution protect either type of protestor?
8. Is violent protest necessary for our society to become more just? Is nonviolent protest necessary?
9. Are there ideas or principles for which you would protest? What are they and how would you protest?

Useful Quotations for Lesson 4
I. Quotations by Henry David Thoreau

"Must the citizen ever for a moment, or in the least degree, resign his conscience to the legislator? Why has every man a conscience, then? I think that we should be men first, and subjects afterward. It is not desirable to cultivate a respect for the law, so much as for the right. The only obligation which I have a right to assume, is to do at any time what I think right."
Henry David Thoreau in "Civil Disobedience."

"The fate of the country does not depend on how you vote at the polls—the worst man is as strong as the best at that game; it does not depend on what kind of paper you drop into the ballot box once a year, but on what kind of man you drop from your chamber into the street every morning."
Henry David Thoreau in "Slavery in Massachusetts."

"'The fear of displeasing the world ought not, in the least, to influence my actions.' If we do not listen to our conscience 'the principal avenue to reform would be closed.'"

Thoreau as quoted in Robert D. Richardson Jr., *Henry Thoreau—A Life of the Mind* (Berkeley: University of California Press, 1986), 32.

II. Excerpts concerning Thoreau

"There is a higher law than civil law—the law of conscience—and that when these laws are in conflict, it is the citizen's duty to obey the voice of God within rather than that of the civil authority without."

Explanation of "Civil Disobedience" found in Walter Harding, ed., *The Days of Henry Thoreau* (New York: Dover Publications, 1982), 207.

"Thoreau's chief purpose in Civil Disobedience was to wean men away from their adherence to an insidious relativism and to persuade them to return again to the superior standard of absolute truth."

"As a man of thirty, Thoreau could look forward to the day when governments, as well as men, would put justice above expediency, absolute right above the Constitution. The dictates of the individual conscience would then be accepted as having a validity superior to legislation, and governments themselves would admit as much."

Glick Wendell, "'Civil Disobedience': Thoreau's Attack upon Relativism", *Western Humanities Review* 7 (Winter 1952-53): 37, 41-42.

III. Quotations by Martin Luther King, Jr.

"But they [Birmingham's decent white citizens] remained publicly silent. It was silence born of fear—fear of social, political and economic reprisals. The ultimate tragedy of Birmingham was not the brutality of the bad people, but the silence of the good people."

Martin Luther King Jr., *Why We Can't Wait* (New York: Mentor, 1964), 50.

"We must say to our white brothers all over the South who try to keep us down: We will match your capacity to inflict suffering with our capacity to endure suffering. We will meet your physical force with our soul force. We will not hate you. And yet we cannot in all good conscience obey your evil laws. Do to us what you will. Threaten our children and we will love you.... Say that we're too low, that we're too degraded, yet we will still love you. Bomb our homes and go by our churches early in the morning and bomb them if you please, and we will still love you. We will wear you down by our capacity to suffer. In winning the victory, we will not only win our freedom. We will so appeal to your heart and your conscience that we will win you in the process."

Martin Luther King quoted in Stephen B. Oates, *Let the Trumpet Sound* (Mentor, New York: 1982), 228-9.

"The nonviolent approach does not immediately change the heart of the oppressor. It first does something to the hearts and souls of those committed to it. It gives them new self-respect; it calls up resources of strength and courage that they did not know they had. Finally it reaches the opponent and so stirs his conscience that reconciliation becomes a reality."

Martin Luther King quoted in Flip Schulke and Penelope McPhee, *King Remembered* (New York: Pocket Books, 1986), 93.

"During my early college days I read Thoreau's essay on Civil Disobedience for the first time. Fascinated by the idea of refusing to cooperate with an evil system, I was so deeply moved that I reread the work several times. I became convinced then that non-cooperation with evil is as much a moral obligation as is cooperation with good. No other person has been more eloquent and passionate in getting this idea across than Henry David Thoreau. As a result of his writings and personal witness we are the heirs of a legacy of creative protest. It goes without saying that the teachings of Thoreau are alive today, indeed, they are more alive today than ever before. Whether expressed in a sit-in at lunch counters, a freedom ride into Mississippi, a peaceful protest in Albany, Georgia, a bus boycott in Montgomery, Alabama, it is an outgrowth of Thoreau's insistence that evil must be resisted and no moral man can patiently adjust to injustice."

King quoted in John H. Hicks, ed., *Thoreau in Our Season* (Amherst: University of Massachusetts Press, 1967), 13.

IV. Excerpts which relate to Thoreau and King

"We are confronted primarily with a moral issue. It is as old as the Scriptures and is as clear as the American Constitution. The heart of the question is whether all Americans are to be afforded equal rights and equal opportunities. . . those who do nothing are inviting shame as well as violence. Those who act boldly are recognizing right as well as reality."

John F. Kennedy, 11 June 1963 quoted in King, *Why We Can't Wait*, 32.

"If the end of government is to promote the welfare of its citizens, then a state which undermines the morality of its citizens forfeits its claims to legitimacy."

William A Herr, "A More Perfect State: Thoreau's Concept of Civil Government," *Massachusetts Review* (Summer 1975): 484.

"The American Bill of Rights embodies the modern concept of political liberty—the concept of liberty which centers in the freedom of the moral consciousness from control by the state."

Benjamin Ginsberg, "Rededication to Freedom," found in Willard Uphaus, "Conscience and Disobedience," found in Hicks, 24.

"The right to be let alone is the underlying theme of the Bill of Rights. It has continued to be fertile soil for the cultivation of individual freedom."

Erwin N. Griswold quoted in Uphaus, "Conscience and Disobedience," 24. ❑

Taking A Stand: Lesser-Known Leaders that Helped Launch the Civil Rights Movement

Clayborne Carson, director of the Martin Luther King, Jr. Papers Project, shocked his audience at the 1994 OAH Focus on Teaching Day luncheon by stating that an African-American civil rights movement would have begun even if there was no Reverend King. Carson wanted to remind people that the Civil Rights movement was not created by a single charismatic leader but by thousands of "ordinary" people taking "extraordinary" stands against racial prejudice. This was why, as a consultant to the film series *Eyes on the Prize: America's Civil Rights Years,* Carson insisted that faces of young people who participated in the movement be prominently displayed throughout the series.

Recognizing the contributions of "lesser-known leaders" to the Civil Rights movement is important because today's young people, looking for heroes and role models, might overlook the simple acts of courage and fortitude of their friends, relatives, and community leaders. In addition, a more historically accurate account of the Civil Rights movement emerges with the inclusion of maids and housekeepers walking to and from work rather than riding their city's segregated buses; college students risking beatings and arrests to "sit-in" segregated eating places; and Mississippi sharecroppers risking their jobs, homes, and lives to gain their voting rights. It is difficult to imagine what course the Civil Rights movement would have taken without the monumental contributions of leaders such as Martin Luther King and Malcolm X. In the same light, it is difficult to see how the movement could have begun without the courage and perseverance of its lesser-known leaders.

Objectives

- To learn how "ordinary" people, both black and wh[ite] helped launch the Civil Rights movement with their extraor[di]nary courage and fortitude.

- To see the multiplicity of people and events that contr[ib]uted to the birth of the Civil Rights Movement.

- To establish a chronology of events that led up to [the] Civil Rights movement, giving students an overview of cau[ses] and effects.

- To give students an introductory framework from wh[ich] they can better understand subjects such as segregation, nonv[io]lent civil disobedience, lynchings, African-American nati[on]alism/separatism, and landmark court decisions such as *Ple[ssy] v. Ferguson* and *Brown v. Board of Education.*

Time Period
One to two class periods

Grade Level
High School and Middle School

Activities
Part I

1. Divide the class into groups, each with at least f[ive] students.

2. Pass out one essay to each student, without letting th[em] know that there are five different essays. Be sure that e[ach] group has at least one each of the five: (1) Greensb[oro] Woolworth's "Sit-in," (2) *Brown v. Board of Education,*

ynching of Emmett Till, (4) Voting Rights in Mississippi, d (5) Montgomery Bus Boycott.

3. Have each student read the essay on his/her own, listing main points and summarizing it in two to three sentences.

4. Have each student read his/her summary to the group.

5. When students realize they have different essays, have em discuss what the essays have in common. Hopefully, the le of "ordinary" people will come up in their discussions ithout the teacher having to remind them.

6. Have each group build a time line, using the five fferent essays. This will enable students to see causes and fects. It will also enable them to see the multiplicity of ople and events that launched the Civil Rights movement.

Part II

1. Divide the class into groups, this time bringing together ose who read the same essay. For example, those who read out the Greensboro Woolworth's "Sit-in" will meet as one oup and those who read about the Montgomery Bus Boycott ll meet as another group.

2. Each group will prepare and present group summaries of eir essays to the class.

3. Have a class discussion with students pointing out what ey see as the key factors leading to the Civil Rights movement.

4. (optional) Have students relate accounts where they itnessed "ordinary" people doing extraordinary things on half of other people. The account could be of friends, latives, neighbors, or themselves. Have students discuss w such extraordinary acts affected their family or community.

Part III

This lesson plan is meant to be an introduction to the Civil ights movement. From here, teachers can choose their own rections. Possible themes include:

- Directions that important leaders such as Martin Luther ing and Malcolm X took the Civil Rights movement, now at the role of "lesser-known leaders" have been established. mong other things, King and Malcolm X have been portrayed opposing one another on the issue of violence, although this still debated. For studying the early Civil Rights movement's nphasis on nonviolence, Carol Hunter's lesson plan, "Non-olence in the Civil Rights Movement," in the Spring 1994 sue of the OAH Magazine of History, is very useful.

- Trace the roles played by Civil Rights leaders that did not ake newspaper headlines or find their way into history books nce the period covered in the lesson plan. This is not an easy sk. It will require research, which might include oral stories.

- Study competing ideas and strategies such as accommo-tion/integration vs. nationalism/separatism, starting with e ideas of Booker T. Washington vs. Marcus Garvey. Here,

Rita Koman's lesson plan, "Legacy for Learning: Jennie Dean and the Manassas Industrial School," in the Summer 1993 issue of the OAH Magazine of History, which introduces a counterpart to Washington's more famous Tuskegee Institute, might be useful.

- Look at the role that organizations played in the Civil Rights movement, including the Congress of Racial Equality (CORE), the Southern Christian Leadership Conference (SCLC), the Student Nonviolent Coordinating Committee (SNCC), the Black Muslims, and the Black Panthers.

- Analyze the impact of the Cold War on the direction of the Civil Rights movement.

- Examine roles that whites, women (black and white), music, and religion played in the Civil Rights movement.

- Take up the story where the lesson plan leaves off. Discuss, for example, the difficulties in implementing the Brown v. Board of Education decision (including Central High School in Little Rock, Arkansas). Or examine civil rights cases after Brown, including the claim of "reverse discrimina-tion" as argued in Regents of the University of California v. Bakke (1978).

- Take a look at race relations and efforts to create racial justice today. Then working backwards, trace how the Civil Rights movement has evolved since the period covered by the lesson plan. Discuss what good has come of it. Also discuss what has gone wrong.

Supplemental Books and Films

For the Greensboro Woolworth's "Sit-ins": Miles Wolff, *Lunch at the 5&10* (Chicago: Ivan R. Dee, 1970); and "Ain't Scared of Your Jails," *Eyes on the Prize: America's Civil Rights Years* (Blackside Productions, 1987).

For Brown v. Board of Education: Richard Kluger, *Simple Justice* (New York: Alfred A. Knopf, 1976); and *Separate But Equal* (Republic, 1991).

For the Lynching of Emmett Till: *William Bradford Huie, Three Lives for Mississippi* (New York: WCC Books, 1965); and "Awakenings," *Eyes on the Prize.*

For Voting Rights in Mississippi: Anne Moody, *Coming of Age in Mississippi* (New York: Dell Publishing, 1968); "Mis-sissippi: Is This America?," *Eyes on the Prize*; and *Missis-sippi Burning* (Orion, 1989).

For the Montgomery Bus Boycott: David Garrow, *The Walking City: The Montgomery Bus Boycott, 1955-1956* (Brook-lyn: Carlson Publishing, 1989); "Awakenings," *Eyes on the Prize*; and *Long Walk Home* (Live Home Video, 1990).

Mitch Yamasaki is an associate professor of history at Chaminade University of Honolulu and Chair of the OAH's Committee on Teaching. He is the author of Hawaii's Trade with the People's Republic of China *(1982).*

The Origins of the Civil Rights Movement

It began with a request for a bus. In 1950, black students attending the segregated Clarendon County school system in South Caro[...] outnumbered white students three to one. White schools, however, received over sixty percent of the county's education appropriations. As a re[...] the county spent $179 a year educating one white student and $43 a year educating one black student. Several black schools in the county there[...] had no indoor plumbing. Students used outdoor "earth toilets." The county had thirty school buses—all for white schools. Some black chil[...] walked nine miles to and from school each day. Reverend Joseph DeLaine, teacher and principal of a small black school in the county, asked R[...] Elliot, chairman of the county school board, to provide black schools with one school bus. Elliot told DeLaine, "We ain't got no money to b[...] bus for your nigger children."

DeLaine gathered signatures from parents of black students attending schools in Clarendon County and filed a class-action suit against [...] school board. First name on the alphabetical list was Harry Briggs, a service station attendant, World War II veteran, and the father of five child[...] *Briggs v. Elliot* was heard in federal district court in 1950. In September of that year, Gardner Bishop, a Washington, D.C. barber and commu[...] activist, led eleven black children through brand new John Philip Souza Junior High School. It was a spacious glass and brick structure loc[...] next to a golf course, with 42 brightly-lit classrooms, a 600-seat auditorium, and a double gymnasium. Pointing out that some of the new classro[...] were empty, Bishop asked that the black students he brought with him be admitted to the all-white school. The request was denied. The child[...] including twelve-year-old Spottswood Thomas Bolling, Jr., were therefore forced to attend Shaw Junior High, a dingy and dilapidated 48-year[...] school located next to The Lucky Pawnbroker's Exchange. They subsequently sued the District of Columbia's school board in *Bolling v. Sh[...] (1951)*. Seven-year-old Linda Brown had to cross dangerous railroad tracks to board a bus that took her to an all-black school miles away f[...] her home. In 1951, Linda's father sued the Board of Education of Topeka, Kansas to allow his daughter to attend the all-white school much cl[...] to their home. In the same year, sixteen-year-old Barbara Rose Johns, a junior at the all-black Morton High School in Virginia, led a strike to pr[...] the school's inadequate and unsafe conditions. Fourteen-year-old Dorothy Davis took part in the strike. Getting no response, students filed a cl[...] action suit against their school board in *Davis v. County School of Prince Edward County (1951)*. Ethel Belton and seven other black parents li[...] in Claymont, a suburb of Wilmington, Delaware, wanted their children to attend the all-white Claymont School, rather than have them buse[...] Howard High School in Wilmington. When their children were denied admission, the parents sued the state board of education in *Belton v. Geb[...] (1951)*.

The National Association for the Advancement of Colored People (NAACP) represented the plaintiffs in each of these cases. They [...] eventually combined and heard on appeal by the United States Supreme Court as *Brown v. Board of Education of Topeka* in 1953. With *Br[...] the NAACP hoped to overturn the "separate but equal" doctrine established in *Plessy v. Ferguson (1896)*. When southern states began to estab[...] segregated public schools and transportation systems after the Reconstruction Era, they were accused of violating the Fourteenth Amendmer[...] the United States Constitution (ratified in 1868), which stated that "No State shall . . . deny any person within its jurisdiction the equal protec[...] of the laws." The Supreme Court in *Plessy* ruled that separate public facilities may be maintained so long as they were equal.

Charles Hamilton Houston led the NAACP's assault on *Plessy*. Seeing the "equal" aspect of the *Plessy* doctrine as its weak point, Hou[...] began his work by documenting the inequality that existed between white and black facilities in the South. In 1936, Houston came across L[...] Lionel Gaines, a 25-year-old black man who was denied admission to the all-white University of Missouri law school, the only public law sc[...] in the state. The state did, however, offer to either pay Gaines's out-of-state tuition to an integrated law school in another state or build a law sc[...] on the campus of an all-black college and admit him there. Houston represented Gaines in his suit against the state, arguing that neither alterna[...] satisfied Gaines' right to a separate but equal education. The United States Supreme Court agreed in *Missouri ex rel. Gaines v. Canada (19[...] ordering the law school to admit Gaines. In subsequent cases, the Supreme Court ordered blacks to be admitted to public graduate and professi[...] schools where states failed to provide them separate but equal facilities. Faced with the dilemma, the president of the University of Oklah[...] despairingly stated, "You can't build a cyclotron for one student."

Houston's former law student, Thurgood Marshall, succeeded him as head of the NAACP's legal division. Marshall felt that it was tim[...] show that school segregation, in and of itself, hurts students. In the *Brown* cases, Marshall and his associates introduced as evidence the wor[...] psychologist Kenneth Clark. Clark's experiments showed that segregation made black children feel inferior and convinced them to accept inferi[...] "as part of [their] reality." In his closing statement to the Supreme Court, Marshall argued that the only way the Court could uphold segrega[...] was "to find that for some reason Negroes are inferior to all other human beings." They could not. Speaking for a unanimous Court in 1954, C[...] Justice Earl Warren maintained that "in the field of public education the doctrine of 'separate but equal' has no place. Separate educational facil[...] are inherently unequal." Knowing there would be "massive resistance" to the Court's decision, and rather than assign a specific date, Warren ord[...] that integration begin with "all deliberate speed."

As the *Brown* cases made their way to the Supreme Court, Joseph Delaine, whose request for a school bus helped launch the court fight, [...] fired from the teaching position he held for ten years. His wife, two sisters, and one niece also lost their jobs. Delaine's house was burned to the gr[...] as firemen stood by and watched. His church was burned down a little while later. When Delaine tried to rebuild, every bank in the county denied [...] credit. When he shot back at a drive-by sniper, Delaine was charged with felonious assault with a deadly weapon. Harry Briggs and the other parents [...] signed the original law suit faced similar intimidation. Plaintiffs in the other four cases were likewise harassed, but they did not back down. Their cou[...] and perseverance led to the landmark court decision that eventually made integrated schools a way of life in America. ❑

he Origins of the Civil Rights Movement

On 1 December 1955, Rosa Parks, a 42-year-old African-American seamstress, was arrested for not giving up her bus seat to a white passenger. custom and by law, the front seats of the Montgomery City Bus Lines were reserved for white passengers. Black passengers had to pay their es up front and then enter the bus from the rear door. Black passengers were also expected to give up their seats if a white passenger could not d a seat up front.

That night, black community leaders met and decided to protest the city's segregated bus system with a one-day boycott on 5 December 1955. ick ministers announced the boycott at their Sunday sermons. College instructor Jo Ann Robinson and a few of her students mimeographed and tributed over 35,000 handbills announcing the boycott.

On December 5, over ninety percent of the blacks who regularly rode the buses avoided them. Nearly empty buses drove through the streets Montgomery. Exhilarated by its success, they decided to continue the boycott until three demands were met: (1) that black passengers be treated irteously, (2) that seating should be on a first-come first-served basis, and (3) that black bus drivers be hired for predominantly black routes. w would have thought the boycott would go on for more than a year.

Historians disagree on the origins of racial segregation. In *The Strange Career of Jim Crow* (New York: Oxford University Press, 1955), C. n Woodward notes that southern race relations after the Civil War were relatively fluid. Whites and blacks rode in the same railroad cars and at the same restaurants. Woodward sees the populist movement of the 1890s, which united poor whites and blacks politically, as changing all s. White conservatives, frightened by the class insurgency and the prospect of blacks returning to power (as during Reconstruction), were able convince the majority of whites that "white supremacy" should be the cornerstone of life in the South. Hence southern states, beginning in the)0s, passed laws disenfranchising blacks and separating the races. Joel Williamson disagreed with Woodward. In *After Slavery* (Chapel Hill: iversity of North Carolina Press, 1965), Williamson claimed that southern whites and blacks were already living in separate worlds by the mid- 70s. Furthermore, except as slaves and later as servants, whites were never willing to share their facilities with blacks. The "Jim Crow" laws arating the races merely codified a system that already existed. In *Race Relations in the Urban South* (New York: Oxford University Press, 1978), ward Rabinowitz saw segregation as a product of southern urbanization. New cities construct public facilities, such as schools, parks, streetcars, l waiting rooms. Unwilling to share such facilities with blacks, whites advocated building separate facilities for blacks. In Rabinowitz's view, cks would have had no access to schools, parks, and other public facilities without segregation.

Regardless of its origins, opponents of segregation charged that such systems violated the Fourteenth Amendment to the United States Constitution ified in 1868), which states that "No State shall . . . deny to any person within its jurisdiction the equal protection of the laws." In *Plessy v. Ferguson* '96), a case challenging segregated railroad passenger cars, the United States Supreme Court acknowledged that "the object of the [Fourteenth] iendment was undoubtedly to enforce absolute equality of the two races before the law." The Court concluded, however, that the Amendment "could have been intended to abolish distinctions based on color, or to enforce . . . a commingling of the two races upon terms unsatisfactory to either."

Plessy's "separate but equal" doctrine gave southern states the green light to pass a series of Jim Crow laws in the early-twentieth century. In)5, Georgia passed a law prohibiting blacks and whites from using the same park facilities. In 1915, Oklahoma installed separate telephone booths blacks and whites. A Mississippi ordinance, enacted in 1922, barred blacks and whites from sharing the same taxicab. While segregation did exist only in the South, it became the law of the land there.

Everyone knew that separate facilities in the South were *not* equal. There were sporadic protests against segregation before World War II. None, wever, threatened to bring down Jim Crow. As Americans fought Nazi racism in World War II, Swedish scholar Gunnar Myrdal reminded them that y had a "Negro problem" at home. In *An American Dilemma* (New York: Harper, 1944), Myrdal stated that if America was to become a great nation ad to face up to and correct its own racial policies. Blacks fought in large numbers during World War II, earning citations and positions of leadership. :h individuals would not easily accept second-class citizenship when they returned home. Many of them became civil rights activists in the 1950s.

As the Montgomery bus boycott dragged on, the white community began to feel its effects. Losing its main passengers, the bus company was ced to raise fares and cut back services. Downtown shopkeepers claimed that, as a result of the boycott, they lost over a million dollars of sales black customers by the end of January 1956.

Rather than give in, Mayor W.A. Gayle and Montgomery's white Citizens' Council launched a "get-tough" policy. White people, Gayle stated, ı not care whether the Negroes ever ride a city bus again if it means that the social fabric of our community is to be destroyed." Prominent boycott ders were fired from their jobs. Others were threatened with layoffs. Police harassed car-pools, organized to drive black domestics to white iseholds miles away from their homes. Car-pool drivers were routinely pulled over and cited on trumped-up charges. White women quietly ve their black maids and housekeepers to and from their homes during the boycott. Infuriated by whites "act[ing] as chauffeurs to Negroes /cotting the buses," Mayor Gayle published a list of their names in the local paper. Women on the list received threatening phone calls. Most re ostracized by friends and relatives, but many continued to drive their employees.

The bus boycott came to an end in November of 1956, when the United States Supreme Court ruled that Montgomery's segregated bus system s unconstitutional. Martin Luther King, Jr., a young minister who was jailed and had his house bombed during the boycott, emerged as a leader the Civil Rights movement and the newly formed Southern Christian Leadership Conference. But as King acknowledged, the success of the 'cott was due mainly to the courage and perseverance of the thousands of black boycotters and their white supporters. When asked how she felt ing the boycott, an elderly black woman replied, "My feet is tired, but my soul is rested." ❏

The Origins of the Civil Rights Movement

At 4:30 p.m. on 1 February 1960, Ezell Blair, Jr., Franklin McCain, Joseph McNeil, and David Richmond, four 18-year-old freshmen from the North Carolina Agricultural and Technical College (A&T), sat down at the Greensboro Woolworth's lunch counter. When the waitress came by, one of them told her "I'd like a cup of coffee, please." "I'm sorry," she replied, "We don't serve Negroes here." When the young man reminded the waitress that he had just purchased toothpaste and school supplies "at a counter just two feet away from here," she pointed to the stand-up counter and said, "Negroes eat at the other end." They remained in their seats. Believing that ignoring them was the best policy, store manager C.L. Harris allowed the young men to sit at the counter until closing time.

The next morning, the four returned with fellow students from A&T and female students from nearby Bennett College. Most of them brought their school books and studied at the lunch counter. Every once in a while, a student would ask a waitress, "Miss, may I make an order?" The students were again ignored.

On the third day, A&T and Bennett students were joined by white students from the Women's College of the University of North Carolina. Demonstrators occupied 63 of the 66 seats at the lunch counter. By this time, the Greensboro "sit-in" had become a national news item. Others followed. Within two months, sit-ins were taking place in 54 cities in nine states.

Tensions grew in some southern cities. White hecklers verbally taunted black sit-in students and their white sympathizers. Others threw french fries and gum at them. Still others poured sugar, milk, catsup, and coffee over their heads. On 27 February 1960, white teenagers in Nashville, Tennessee attacked sit-in students, pulling them off their stools, punching and kicking them. None of the demonstrators fought back. When the police arrived, they did not arrest the white teenagers. Instead, they arrested the 81 sit-in students for "disorderly conduct."

As thousands of students began to take part in sit-ins, violent reactions escalated. Seeing a need to coordinate this mass movement, student leaders from southern black colleges held a three-day convention during Easter weekend. The convention stressed nonviolence. Despite beatings from white agitators and local police, demonstrators were told, "Don't strike back or curse back if attacked . . . remember the teachings of Jesus, Gandhi and Martin Luther King." Toward the end of the convention, a student-run organization for continuing the sit-ins was formed—the Student Nonviolent Coordinating Committee (SNCC). A unique feature of early SNCC was its inherent democracy. Its motto was, "If you are looking for a leader, look in a mirror." They did. As scores of SNCC leaders and coordinators were arrested in demonstrations, scores more took their place.

Efforts to grant blacks equality and to integrate them into mainstream white society began almost a century before the sit-ins—during the Reconstruction Era. The Thirteenth Amendment to the United States Constitution, ratified at the end of the Civil War in 1865, freed all slaves. In southern states, however, "Black Codes" were enacted to control former slaves. These codes limited black occupations to farming and domestic service. They also prohibited blacks from bearing firearms. Under the codes, blacks were assessed stiff fines for drunkenness, vagrancy, begging, and "misspend[ing] what they earn." If they could not pay the fines, local authorities auctioned them off to white employers to work off their fines.

The Black Codes outraged northerners, particularly the Radical Republicans in Congress. They drafted the Fourteenth Amendment to the United States Constitution, which stated that "No State shall make or enforce any law which shall abridge the privileges or immunities of citizens of the United States . . . nor deny to any person within its jurisdiction the equal protection of the laws." It was ratified by the states in 1868, after ex-slaves were given suffrage and thousands of ex-Confederates were disenfranchised. Congress then passed the Civil Rights Act of 1875 as enabling legislation for the Fourteenth Amendment. The Act stated that "All persons within the jurisdiction of the United States shall be entitled to the full and equal enjoyment of the accommodations, advantages, facilities, and privileges of inns, public conveyances on land and water, theaters, and other places of public amusement; subject only to the conditions and limitations established by law and applicable alike to citizens of every race and color, regardless of any previous condition of servitude."

Most white Americans, in the North as well as the South, felt that Congress had gone too far with the Civil Rights Act of 1875. While the majority of whites in this period disapproved of slavery, few were ready to integrate with blacks or accept them as their equals. For this reason, there was little public outcry when the United States Supreme Court in the *Civil Rights Cases of 1883* narrowly construed the Fourteenth Amendment so that it only applied to public (state) facilities. In other words, privately owned restaurants and theaters were free to turn away customers on the basis of race and color. Establishments that catered to black customers could segregate them from white patrons. Areas designated for blacks were usually the least desirable, as illustrated by the name given to their section in movie theaters—"nigger heaven."

With legal means of achieving equality and integration deserting them, some African Americans turned to civil disobedience. Black communities, from time to time, used boycotts, picketing, mass marches and sit-ins to protest, among other things, school segregation in the North and segregated streetcars in the South. In the 1930's, for example, black communities across the nation launched "don't buy where you can't work" campaigns.

Seeing such protests as a threat to their way of life, some southern communities struck back with ferocity. Demonstrators were beaten, jailed and sometimes lynched. "Sure we were scared," recalled Franklin McCain, one of the original Greensboro Four, "I suppose if anyone had come up behind me and yelled 'Boo' [on the first day] I think I would have fallen off my seat." But the four stayed. And others followed. Their courage inspired young blacks and whites to take part in the growing Civil Rights movement. It also helped prod Congress into passing the Civil Rights Act of 1964. Shepherded through Congress by President Lyndon B. Johnson, a social crusader intent on securing himself a place in history, the Act made it illegal for privately owned restaurants and theaters to segregate or turn away customers on the basis of race or color. It also prohibited private businesses from hiring and firing employees on the basis of race or color. ❏

The Origins of the Civil Rights Movement

Emmett Till, an African-American teenager from Chicago, went to visit his relatives in Leflore County, Mississippi during the summer of 1955. About a week after he arrived, Till showed off the photograph of a white girl he claimed to be his girlfriend. A couple of boys taunted Till and dared him to ask the white gal working in Bryant's Grocery and Meat Market for a date. He took the dare. Till went inside and talked to Carolyn Bryant, the store owner's wife. As he left the store, Till told her "bye, baby" and whistled at her.

A few nights later, Carolyn's husband Ron Bryant and his brother-in-law J.W. Milam came to the house of 64-year-old Mose Wright, Till's granduncle. Milam told Wright that they came for "the boy who done the talkin'." Wright tried to explain that Till was only fourteen-years-old and that he did not understand local customs. They ignored Wright's pleas and dragged Till off in their truck. "If you cause any trouble," Milam warned Wright, "you'll never live to be 65."

Three days later, Till's body was found in the Tallahatchie River. It was nude and tied by the neck, with barbed wire, to a hundred-pound metal fan. Till had been so badly beaten, before being shot through the head, that he could only be identified by the initialed ring on his finger. Observing the corpse, one policeman said that it was the worst beating he had seen in his career.

Till attended an all-black school in Chicago and knew about segregation. What he did not know was the rigid race rules that existed in the South and the price paid by those who broke them.

Lynching, as a method of enforcing southern racial codes, began during the Reconstruction Era (1865-1877). White masters beat their black slaves before the Civil War. But their violence was tempered by the damage inflicted on their own property. During Reconstruction, southern whites were humiliated by military occupation, mass disenfranchisements, and ex-slaves elected as their public officials. Secret organizations, such as the Ku Klux Klan, retaliated by beating, whipping, and murdering southern blacks and their white supporters. These acts of violence kept many blacks from the polls, enabling southern whites to win back control of state and local governments in elections between 1869 and 1877.

These electoral victories convinced many southern whites that intimidating blacks was the only way to retain political control. Humiliating and degrading blacks, therefore, became a way of life in the South. Blacks, for example, were expected to step to the side when a white person approached them. A black male, regardless of his age or occupation, was called "boy." Blacks were beaten routinely around election time to remind them not to vote. Strictest of the racial codes involved the way black men looked at, talked to, or talked about white women.

Lynching was the ultimate form of intimidation. Lynching was not an exclusively southern practice. Nor was hanging the only form of lynching. Victims were also shot and beaten to death. Sam Hose, a black Georgian, was burned and dismembered before a huge crowd in 1899. Whites as well as blacks were lynched. By the beginning of the twentieth century, however, lynching victims were almost always black. Between 1900 and 1914, over 1,100 blacks were lynched. Lynchers were rarely prosecuted and almost always acquitted.

In the face of this violence and intimidation, Booker T. Washington, founder of the Tuskegee Institute (1881), advised blacks to accept segregation and second-class citizenship for the time being. Washington's school offered blacks vocational training—to become carpenters and brick layers—economic opportunities for those willing to live with social and political inequality. W.E.B. Du Bois, the first African American to earn a Ph.D. from Harvard University, disagreed with Washington. "The way for a people to gain their reasonable rights," Du Bois argued, "is not by voluntarily throwing them away." He believed that voting "is necessary to modern manhood [and that] discrimination is barbarism." Du Bois helped found the National Association for the Advancement of Colored People (NAACP) in 1909. The NAACP's early members were mainly white liberals such as social worker Jane Addams and philosopher John Dewey. Its principal aim was to eradicate racial discrimination.

Some blacks rejected Washington's accommodation strategy *and* the NAACP's goals of equality and integration. For Bishop Henry M. Turner, there was "no manhood future in the United States for the Negro." Beginning in the 1880s, Turner urged blacks to return to Africa, "the land of our ancestors," and "establish our own nation, civilization, laws, [and] styles of manufacture." In the 1920's, flamboyant Marcus Garvey built a steamship company to transport blacks to Africa and founded black-owned factories and businesses to promote economic self-sufficiency. After Garvey's arrest (for fraud), his followers like Earl Little, father of Malcolm X, carried on the nationalist/separatist tradition of Turner and Garvey.

Others blacks chose simply to leave the South. Thousands of blacks migrated to Kansas and the Oklahoma Territory in the 1880s. Between 1910 and 1950, over five million blacks migrated out of the South, the largest migration in American history. Most migrated to northern cities, which provided job opportunities, especially during the two world wars. Chicago, where Emmett Till's relatives moved to, became a Mecca for black migrants. There was prejudice and segregation in the North, but not the constant humiliation and degradation that blacks faced in the deep South.

J.W. Milam and Ron Bryant were put on trial for kidnaping and murdering Emmett Till nearly a month after his body was found. On 21 September 1955, Mose Wright took the stand. When asked by the prosecutor if he could identify the white man who took his grandnephew away on the last night he saw the boy alive, Wright stood up, pointed to Milam and declared, "Thar he" (that is he). Wright then identified Bryant as Milam's accomplice. Milam and Bryant never took the stand. In his closing statement, their defense attorney told the all-white jury, "I'm sure that every last Anglo-Saxon one of you has the courage to free these men." After a five-day trial, it took the jury a little more than an hour to find the two "not guilty."

Regardless of the predictable verdict, the simple courage of Wright and other blacks who testified in the trial helped to bring down the system that degraded and intimidated blacks. There would be more beatings and killings before this was accomplished. But when beatings, cross-burnings, and lynchings no longer intimidated blacks, the race codes that such acts tried to enforce could no longer be maintained. ❑

The Origins of the Civil Rights Movement

In 1962, Fanny Lou Hamer, a 44-year-old sharecropper from Sunflower County, Mississippi attended a mass meeting to increase black vo[te] registration. Struggling in a system designed to keep blacks down, Hamer was inspired by the meeting. She volunteered, along with sevente[en] others, to go to the courthouse in Indianola to register. At the courthouse, the applicants were ordered to give their residence, place of employme[nt] and other information that was later used to identify and intimidate them. After this, they had to take literacy tests—interpreting parts of t[he] Mississippi constitution. Applicants were not told if they passed the test when they left the court house. The authorities intercepted the bus carryi[ng] the applicants out of Indianola and fined the driver $100 for driving a wrong-colored bus.

When she got home, Hamer's boss ordered her to withdraw her voter application. When she refused, Hamer was fired from the job she he[ld] for 18 years and ordered off the plantation. She later found that she had failed the literacy test. Hamer told the registrar that she would return eve[ry] thirty days to take the test until she passed, which she did in January 1963.

For her actions, Hamer and her family faced daily intimidation and harassment. Her husband and daughter were arrested, and both lost the[ir] jobs. The Hamers got a $9,000 water bill for a house that had no running water. Hamer was shot at from a speeding car. She was arrested f[or] encouraging others to register to vote. In jail, she was beaten. "The first Negro began to beat," she recalled, "and I was beat until I was exhauste[d] . . . the State Highway Patrolman ordered the second Negro to take the blackjack. The second Negro began to beat . . . I began to scream, and o[ne] white man got up and began to beat me on my head and tell me to 'hush.'"

African-American voting rights in the South were born out of conflict and controversy about a hundred years before Hamer registered to vo[te.] After the Civil War, northern Republicans were outraged by the election of ex-Confederate generals and cabinet officers to southern state and fede[ral] offices. Most southern blacks were excluded from these elections. Northern Republicans also feared losing control of Congress with the retu[rn] of southern Democrats, absent during the war. A cry among northerners was "who won the war, anyway?"

Determined to "remedy" this situation, Radical Republicans took control of "Reconstructing" the South in 1867. They disenfranchis[ed] thousands of ex-Confederates while securing suffrage for blacks by enacting the Fifteenth Amendment to the United States Constitution (ratifi[ed] in 1870), which stated that "The right of citizens of the United States to vote shall be not denied or abridged by the United States or by any Sta[te] on account of race, color, or previous condition of servitude." Under military occupation, the newly established southern electorate (wi[th] Republican majorities) elected blacks to state and national offices. Many of them turned out to be capable legislators, but some fell under the contr[ol] of unscrupulous "scalawags" (southerners who cooperated with Reconstruction authorities) and "carpetbaggers" (northerners seeking jobs a[nd] economic opportunities in the occupied South).

Northerners soon grew weary of the cost of Reconstruction and the bloodshed caused by its southern opponents, including the Ku Klux Kla[n.] After suppressing the Klan in the early 1870's, they began to withdraw federal troops from the South, the last of them leaving in 1877. Meanwhi[le] southern elites, calling themselves the "Redeemers," guided their Democratic party—"the white man's party"—to victories across the South. The[se] elites, mainly businessmen and plantation owners, faced the most serious challenge to their power from poor southern farmers, many of whom join[ed] the Populist Party in the 1890's. In their political struggle, both Populists and Democrats courted black voters. With their money, power, a[nd] paternalistic influence, conservative Democrats kept most blacks from voting Populist. At the same time, they accused Populists of courting "Neg[ro] domination" by dividing the Democratic Party.

Defeated Populists vented their frustration, not on the Democrats, but on the blacks they had earlier sought as allies. Supported by conservati[ve] Democrats, they moved to disenfranchise southern blacks. The Fifteenth Amendment prohibited states from disenfranchising blacks on accou[nt] of their race. The majority of southern states therefore amended their constitutions, between 1895 and 1910, to include literacy tests and oth[er] devices to prevent blacks from voting. Illiterate whites were usually exempted from literacy tests if their fathers or grandfathers voted in the sta[te] before 1867. Other southern states used poll taxes, which most blacks could not afford, to prevent them from voting. In this way, the focus [of] southern politics shifted back from class to race. Poor whites took comfort in the belief that "the lowest white man counts more than the highe[st] Negro." Conservative Democrats took comfort in the fact that "white supremacy" would keep poor southerners loyal to their Party.

Literacy tests, poll taxes, and methods used since the Reconstruction Era—beatings, public whippings and lynchings— virtually disenfra[n]chised southern blacks. They became so politically impotent that when the Ku Klux Klan was reborn in the 1920s its main targets were Catholi[cs] and immigrants instead of southern blacks.

Strong efforts to revive African-American voting in the South did not begin until the Student Nonviolent Coordinating Committee (SNC[C] and other civil rights organizations founded the Voter Education Project (VEP) in 1962. VEP conducted voter registration drives throughout t[he] South. The project registered over 500,000 new voters by 1964. Breakthroughs were made in every state except Mississippi, which produced le[ss] than 4,000 new voters out of almost 400,000 adult blacks. As in Fanny Lou Hamer's case, Mississippi's white Citizens' Councils were effecti[ve] in identifying and intimidating potential black registrants.

Civil rights groups targeted Mississippi for a voter registration drive during "Freedom Summer," 1964. Hundreds of voter registrati[on] volunteers, mostly middle-class white college students from the North, poured into the state. The drive's leaders included college students and loc[al] residents like Hamer. White Mississippians reacted as if they were being invaded. Homes of those cooperating with the voter drive went up [in] flames. Three volunteers—two white (Andrew Goodman and Michael Schwerner) and one black (James Chaney)—were murdered. But the dri[ve] persisted. Meanwhile, the flagrant brutality of white racists moved the nation to take action. One result was Congress's passage of the Voting Rig[hts] Act of 1965, with which the federal government once again intervened to insure the rights of black voters. ❑

The Declaration of Independence: To What Extent Did It Have Meaning for African Americans?

Editor's note: The next three lesson plans concern various aspects of the of U.S. history–slavery, Indian policy, and foreign policy. The lesson plans are designed to be used in conjunction with the National History Standards.

Era 3: Standard 2

STUDENTS SHOULD UNDERSTAND: HOW THE AMERICAN REVOLUTION INVOLVED MULTIPLE MOVEMENTS AMONG THE NEW NATION'S MANY GROUPS TO REFORM AMERICAN SOCIETY.

Wilson, *History of the American People*, 1902

New York Slave Market, ca. 1730.

Anticipatory Set: With a cooperative learning model, use the document sets to consider the effect of the American Revolution on free and enslaved African Americans. Divide students into five groups of four to five students each. Assign a chairperson and a recorder for each group. Each group should then be assigned one document set and a copy of the Declaration of Independence. They should spend their time discussing the questions provided and any others that might arise. Also use Historical Thinking Standard 3.

R eview the data

E xtract the 'Big Picture'

L ook for specifics

A ssociate specifics by grouping

T est pattern or relationship

E xpress finding

These steps can be followed while using the document sets provided. The steps can also be analyzed by connecting them to the ideas of the Declaration of Independence.

Discuss these "RELATE" steps with the students before handing out the document sets. Explain to them how "RELATE" can help their critical thinking skills.

Source for "RELATE": Robin Fogarty and Jim Bellanca, *Catch Them Thinking: A Handbook of Classroom Strategies* (Palatine, Ill: Skylight Publishing, 1986).

Significant Figures in the Slavery and Liberty Debate, ca. 1776

Wilson, *History of the American People*, 1902

Patrick Henry, an important figure in the American Revolution and a slave holder.

PATRICK HENRY, famous for his call to revolution, "Give me liberty or give me death," lived from 1736 to 1799. He began a long political career as a member of the Virginia House of Burgesses, representing Hanover county of that commonwealth. He gained fame as a leading figure in the opposition to the Stamp Act and other British policies in the colonies after the Great War for Empire (a.k.a., The Seven Years' War, 1756-1763) and was an early advocate of a military defense from the British. Henry served as a delegate to the First Continental Congress (1774-1776). In 1775, he began a two-year term as commander-in-chief of the Virginia revolutionary militia, and the people of Virginia elected him governor from 1776 to 1779, and again from 1784 to 1786. He also served as an Anti-Federalist delegate to the Virginia Convention for the ratification of the Constitution. At first he opposed ratification, but later–realizing the Constitution would in all likelihood be ratified–demanded the inclusion of the first ten amendments. Patrick Henry was also a major planter and a slave holder.

Source: George Thomas Kurian, *Dictionary of Biography* (New York: Laurel, 1980).

THOMAS PAINE, a radical political philosopher and activist, lived from 1737 to 1809. British by birth, Paine immigrated to the American colonies in 1774. Two years later he wrote his famous pamphlet, *Common Sense*, which called for an immediate separation from England. The pamphlet eventually sold between 200,000 and 300,000 copies and greatly precipitated the American Revolution. During the war, Paine both served in the continental army and continued to publish his writings–this time in *Crisis*. In 1787, Paine returned to Europe and became an apologist for the French Revolution, writing *The Rights of Man*, a response to Edmund Burke's (1729-1797) anti-revolutionary *Reflections on the French Revolution* (Burke did, however, support the American Revolution). Paine was tried and convicted of treason in England for his views concerning the French Revolution, but he escaped to France and was elected to the French Convention in 1792, arrested by Robespierre, and later released with the aid of James Madison (1751-1836). Paine remained in France until 1802 and published his two-part work on deism, *The Age of Reason* (1794-1796). He died in 1802 in "relative obscurity."

Source: George Thomas Kurian, *Dictionary of Biography* (New York: Laurel, 1980).

The Life and Works of Thomas Paine, 1925

Thomas Paine, a radical political philospher and activist.

DOCUMENT SET 1
Petition of New Hampshire Slaves, 12 November 1779

The petition campaigns waged by Negroes in Massachusetts were a graphic response to contentions of some proslavery writers that slaves were a contented lot under slavery, accepting their fate and their divinely-ordained position in society. But Massachusetts Negroes were not alone in petitioning state legislatures—on November 12, 1779, 19 slaves from New Hampshire petitioned their own legislature, pleading for the "state of liberty of which we have been so long deprived." The petition was rejected by the legislature on June 9, 1780, a cryptic note in the daily journal indicating that "the House is not ripe for a determination in this matter." Not until June 26, 1857, was a law enacted in the state declaring that no person should be deprived of the right of citizenship because of color. But the legislature was far behind public opinion. The 1790 census recorded fewer than 200 slaves in New Hampshire, less than one-third the number counted in 1767 indicating a decline in the practice of slavery. Evidence of antislavery feeling was clearly expressed when a black runaway from George Washington's estate was sought in Portsmouth in 1796. The furor in the community against this search was so great that the hunt was called off. –Issac W. Hammond, 1889

To the Honorable, the Council and House of Representatives of said state, now sitting at Exeter in and for said state:

The petition of the subscribers, natives of Africa, now forcibly detained in slavery in said state most humbly *sheweth*. That the God of nature gave them life and freedom, upon the terms of the most perfect equality with other men; That freedom is an inherent right of the human species, not to be surrendered, but by consent, for the sake of social life; That private or public tyranny and slavery are alike detestable to minds conscious of the equal dignity of human nature; That in power and authority of individuals, derived solely from a principle of coercion, against the will of individuals, and to dispose of their persons and properties, consists the completest idea of private and political slavery; That all men being amenable to the Deity for the ill-improvement of the blessings of His Providence, they hold themselves in duty bound strenuously to exert every faculty of their minds to obtain that blessing of freedom, which they are justly entitled to from that donation of the beneficent Creator; That through ignorance and brutish violence of their native countrymen, and by the sinister designs of others (who ought to have taught them better), and by the avarice of both, they, while but children, and incapable of self-defence, whose infancy might have prompted protection, were seized, imprisoned, and transported from their native country, where (though ignorance and unchristianity prevailed) they were born free, to a country where (though knowledge, Christianity and freedom are their boast) they are compelled and their posterity to drag on their lives in miserable servitude: Thus, often is the parent's cheek wet for the loss of a child, torn by the cruel hand of violence from her aching bosom; Thus, often and in vain is the infant's sigh for the nurturing care of its bereaved parent, and thus do the ties of nature and blood become victims to cherish the vanity and luxury of a fellow mortal. Can this be right? Forbid it gracious Heaven.

Permit again your humble slaves to lay before this honorable assembly some of those grievances which they daily experience and feel. Though fortune hath dealt out our portion with rugged hand, yet hath she smiled in the disposal of our persons to those who claim us as their property; of them we do not complain, but from what authority they assume the power to dispose of our lives, freedom and property, we would wish to know. Is it from the sacred volume of Christianity? There we believe it is not to be found; but here hath the cruel hand of slavery made us incompetent judges, hence knowledge is hid from our minds. Is it from the volumes of the laws? Of these also slaves cannot be judges, but those we are told are founded on reason and justice; it cannot be found there. Is it from the volumes of nature? No, here we can read with others, of this knowledge, slavery cannot wholly deprive us; here we know that we ought to be free agents; here we feel the dignity of human nature; here we feel the passions and desires of men, though checked by the rod of slavery; here we feel a just equality; here we know that the God of nature made us free. Is their authority assumed from custom? If so let that custom be abolished, which is not founded in nature, reason nor religion. Should the humanity and benevolence of this honorable assembly restore us that state of liberty of which we have been so long deprived, we conceive that those who are our present masters will not be sufferers by our liberation, as we have most of us spent our whole strength and the prime of our lives in their service; and as freedom inspires a noble confidence and gives the mind of emulation to vie in the noblest efforts of enterprise, and as justice and humanity are the result of your deliberations, we fondly hope that the eye of pity and the heart of justice may commiserate our situation, and put us upon the equality of freemen, and give us an opportunity of evincing to the world our love of freedom by exerting ourselves in her cause, in opposing the efforts of tyranny and oppression over the country in which we ourselves have been so long injuriously enslaved.

Therefore, Your humble slaves most devoutly pray for the sake of injured liberty, for the sake of justice, humanity and the rights of mankind, for the honor of religion and by all that is dear, that your honors would graciously interpose in our behalf, and enact such laws and regulations, as you in your wisdom think proper, whereby we may regain our liberty and be ranked in the class of free agents, and that the name of slave may not more be heard in a land gloriously contending for the sweets of freedom. And your humble slaves as in duty bound will ever pray.

Portsmouth Nov. 12, 1779.

Signed: Nero Brewster, Pharaoh Rogers, Romeo Rindge, Seneca Hall, Cate Newmarch, Peter Warner, Cesar Gerrish, Pharaoh Shores, Zebulon Gardner, Winsor Moffatt, Quam Sherburne, Garrett Cotton, Samuel Wentworth, Kittridge Tuckerman, Will Clarkson, Peter Frost, Jack Odiorne, Prince Whipple, Cinio Hubbard.

Source: Issac W. Hammond, ed., "Slavery in New Hampshire," *Magazine of American History* 21 (January 1889): 63-4.

Questions
1. What do the petitioners mean by "the God of nature gave them life and freedom, upon the terms of the most perfect equality with other men"? How does this relate to the preamble of the Declaration of Independence? To whom are they appealing with such language?
2. What do they mean by freedom being an "inherent right?" Is that the same as an inalienable right?
3. Are the petitioners misusing the words of the Declaration of Independence? Why or why not?
4. What is the main point of the petition?
5. What conclusion can one draw about the impact of the Declaration of Independence?

DOCUMENT SET 2
Patrick Henry and Robert Pleasants

From Patrick Henry to Robert Pleasants, Hanover, 18 January 1773.

I take this opportunity to acknowledge the receipt of Anthony Benezet's book against the slave trade. I thank you for it. It is not a little surprising that the professors of Christianity, whose chief excellence consists in softening the human heart and in cherishing and improving its finer feelings, should encourage a practice so totally repugnant to the first impressions of right and wrong. What adds to the wonder is that this abominable practice has been introduced in the most enlightened ages. Times that seem to have pretensions to boast of high improvements in the arts and sciences, and refined morality, have brought into general use, and guarded by many laws, a species of violence and tyranny which our more rude and barbarous, but more honest ancestors detested. Is it not amazing that at a time when the rights of humanity are defined and understood with precision, in a country, above all others, fond of liberty, that in such an age and in such a country we find men professing a religion the most humane, mild, gentle and generous, adopting a principle as repugnant to humanity as it is inconsistent with the Bible, and destructive to liberty? Every thinking, honest man rejects it in speculation; how few in practice from conscientious motives!

Would anyone believe I am the master of slaves of my own purchase I am drawn along by the general inconvenience of living here without them. I will not, I cannot justify it. However culpable my conduct, I will so far pay my devoir to virtue as to own the excellence and rectitude of her precepts, and lament my want of conformity to them.

I believe a time will come when an opportunity will be offered to abolish this lamentable evil. Everything we do is to improve it, if it happens in our day; if not, let us transmit to our descendents, together with our slaves, a pity for their unhappy lot and an abhorrence of slavery. If we cannot reduce this wished-for reformation to practice, let us treat the unhappy victims with lenity. It is the furthest advance we can make toward justice. It is a debt we owe to the purity of our religion, to show that it is at variance with that law which warrants slavery.

I know not when to stop. I could say many things on the subject, a serious view of which gives a gloomy perspective to future times. [Wirt, *Life of Henry*, I, 152-153]

Source: Henry Steele Commager and Richard B. Morris, eds., *The Spirit of 'Seventy-Six: The Story of the American Revolution As Told By Participants* (New York: Harper & Row, 1975), 402.

From Robert Pleasants to Patrick Henry, Curles, 3rd mo. 28, 1777.

[I write to you on a subject of great importance for your consideration.] It is in respect to slavery, of which thou art not altogether a stranger to mine, as well as some others of our friends sentiments, and perhaps too thou may have been informed that some of us from a full conviction of the injustice, and an apprehension of duty, have been induced to embrace the present favorable juncture, when the representatives of the people have nobly declared *all men equally free*, to manumit divers of our Negroes; and propose, without any desire to offend or thereby to injure any person, to invest more of them with the same inestimable priviledge. . . .

Indeed few, very few, are now so insensible of the injustice of holding our fellow men in bondage as to undertake to vindicate it; nor can it be done, in my apprehension, without condemning the present measures in America; for if less injury offered to ourselves from the mother country can justify the expense of so much blood and treasure, how can we impose with propriety absolute slavery on others? It hath often appeared to me as if this very matter was one, if not the principal cause of our present troubles, and that we ought first to have cleansed our own hands before we could consistently oppose the measures of others tending to the same purpose; and I firmly believe the doing this justice to the injured Africans would be an acceptable offering to him who "rules in the Kingdoms of men," and "giveth wisdom to the wise, and knowledge to those who have understanding," and for a purpose too of His own glory; and happy will it be for us if we apply our talents accordingly; for such it is that are often made a blessing to themselves, to their posterity, and to mankind in general. But if on the contrary we seek our own glory and present interest by forbidden means, how can we expect peace here, or happiness hereafter? Or may we, therefore, "break off our sins by righteousness, and our iniquities by showing mercy to the poor, if haply it may be a lengthening of our tranquillity!"

The Declaration of Rights is indeed noble, and I can but wish and hope thy great abilities and interest may be exerted towards a full and clear explanation and confirmation thereof; for, without that, the present struggle for liberty, if successful, would be but partial, and instead of abolishing, might lay the foundation of greater imposition and tyranny to our posterity than any we have yet known; and considering the uncertainty of future events, and all human foresight, the immediate posterity of those now in power might be effected by such partiality, as well as others whose grievances might remain unredressed.

It would therefore become the interest, as well as duty, of a wise and virtuous legislature, in forming a government, to establish a general, uniform and constant liberty, as well civil as religious; for this end, I just propose to drop a hint, which hath appeared to me as likely to accomplish the great and wise end of a general freedom, without the dangers and inconveniences which some apprehend from a present total abolition of slavery, as any thing that hath occurred to me, and perhaps might be as generally approved; which is to enact that all children of slaves to be born in [the] future be absolutely free at the usual ages of 18 and 21, and that such who are convinced of the injustice of keeping slaves, and willing to give up the property which the law hath invested them with, may under certain regulations (so as not at an age to become chargable, or from other impediments obnoxious to the community) have free liberty to do it.

By such a law I apprehend the children would be educated with proper notions of freedom, and be better fitted for the enjoyment of it than many now are; the state secured from intestine enemies and convulsions (which some think would attend a total immediate discharge), its true interest promoted, in proportion to the number of free-men interested in its peace and prosperity, and, above all, to do that justice to others which we contend for and claim as the unalterable birthright of every man. [Wirt, *Life of Henry*, III, 49-51.]

Source: Henry Steele Commager and Richard B. Morris, eds., *The Spirit of 'Seventy-Six: The Story of the American Revolution As Told By Participants* (New York: Harper & Row, 1975), 402-5.

Questions
1. Does Patrick Henry own slaves? Can one tell from his letter and arguments? Why or why not?
2. How does Christianity/the New Testament condone or reject slavery? How does Henry's use of Christianity support or negate his argument?
3. How does Pleasants see manumission as redemptive? How will slavery corrupt the future of liberty and the nation? Why must the end of slavery be absolute?
4. Is Pleasants more concerned with the ideals of liberty and Christianity or with the plight of blacks?

DOCUMENT SET 3
Tom Paine and Lemuel Haynes

From Tom Paine, *Pennsylvania Journal and The Weekly Advertiser*, 8 March 1775.

The chief design of this paper is not to disprove [slavery], which many have sufficiently done; but to entreat Americans to consider:

1. With what consistency or decency they complain so loudly of attempts to enslave them, while they hold so many hundred thousands in slavery; and annually enslave many thousands more, without any pretence of authority, or claim upon them?

2. How just, how suitable to our crime is the punishment with which providence threatens us? We have enslaved multitudes, and shed much innocent blood in doing it; and now we are threatened with the same. And while other evils are confessed and bewailed, why not this especially, and publicly; than which no other vice has brought so much guilt on the land?

3. Whether, then, all ought not immediately to discontinue and renounce it, with grief and abhorrence? Should not every society bear testimony against it, and account obstinate persisters in it bad men, enemies to their country, and exclude them from fellowship; as they often do for much lesser faults?

4. The great question may be—what should be done with those who are enslaved already? To turn the old and infirm free would be injustice and cruelty; they who enjoyed the labors of their better days should keep and treat them humanely. As to the rest, let prudent men, with the assistance of legislatures, determine what is practicable for masters, and best for them. Perhaps some could give them lands upon reasonable rent; some, employing them in their labor still, might give them some reasonable allowances for it; so as all may have some property, and fruits of their labors at their own disposal, and be encouraged to industry; the family may live together, and enjoy the natural satisfaction of exercising relative affections and duties, with civil protection and other advantages, like fellow men. Perhaps they may sometime form useful barrier settlements on the frontiers. Then they may become interested in the public welfare, and assist in promoting it; instead of being dangerous, as now they are, should any enemy promise them a better condition. . . .

These are sentiments of JUSTICE AND HUMANITY [Conway, ed., *The Writings of Paine*, I, 7-9.]

Source: Henry Steele Commager and Richard B. Morris, eds., *The Spirit of 'Seventy-Six: The Story of the American Revolution As Told By Participants* (New York: Harper & Row, 1975), 404.

Questions
1. Why does Paine find the American fear of enslavement hypocritical?
2. Why did Americans conveniently ignore the philosophical contradiction between African slavery and American freedom? Does Paine offer his own reasons, or is he simply chastizing?
3. How would Paine treat slave owners?
4. Why doesn't Paine desire the immediate abolition of slavery? Is he being hypocritical?

From Lemuel Haynes (23-year-old mulatto minuteman from western Massachusetts), 1776.

Liberty Further Extended: Or Free thoughts on the illegality of Slave-keeping; Wherein those arguments that Are used in its vindication Are plainly confuted. Together with an humble Address to such as are Conceaned in the practise.

> *We hold these truths to be self-Evident, that all me are created Equal, that they are Endowed By their Creator with Ceartain unalienable rights, that among these are Life, Liberty, and the pursuit of happiness. –Congress.*

. . . Liberty is a Jewel which was handed Down to man from the cabinet of heaven, and is Coaeval with his Existence. And as it proceed from the Supreme Legislature of the univers, so it is he which hath a sole right to take away; therefore, he that would take away a mans Liberty assumes a prerogative that Belongs to another, and acts out of his own domain.

One man may bost a superorety above another in point of Natural previledge; yet if he can produse no convincive arguments in vindication of this pre-heminence his hypothesis is to Be Suspected. To affirm, that an Englishman has a right to his Liberty, is a truth which has Been so clearly Evinced, Especially of Late, that to spend time in illustrating this, would be But Superfluous tautology. But I query, whether Liberty is so contracted a principle as to be Confin'd to any nation under Heaven; nay, I think it not hyperbolical to affirm, that Even an affrican, has Equally as good a right to his Liberty in common with Englishmen. . . .

It hath pleased god to make of one Blood all nations of men, for to dwell upon the face of the Earth. Acts 17, 26. And as all are of one Species, so there are the same Laws, and aspiring principles placed in all nations; and the effect that these Laws will produce, are Similar to Each other. Consequently we may suppose, that what is precious to one man, is precious to another, and what is irksom, or intolarable to one man, is so to another, consider'd in a Law of Nature. Therefore we may reasonably Conclude, that Liberty is Equally as pre[c]ious to a Black man, as it is to a white one, and Bondage Equally as intolarable to the one as it is to the other: Seeing it Effects the Laws of nature Equally as much as in the one as it Does in the other. But, as I observed Before, those privileges that are granted to us By the Divine Being, no one has the Least right to take them from us without our consen[t]; and there is Not the Least precept, or practise, in the Sacred Scriptures, that constitutes a Black man a Slave, any more than a white one.

Shall a mans Couler Be the Decisive Criterion whereby to Judg of his natural right? or Becaus a man is not of the same couler with his Neighbour, shall he Be Deprived of those things that Distuingsheth [Distinguisheth] him from the Beasts of the field? . . . O Sirs! Let that pity, and compassion, which is peculiar to mankind, Especially to English-men, no Longer Lie Dormant in your Breast: Let it run free thro' Disinterested Benevolence. then how would these iron yoaks Spontaneously fall from the gauled Necks of the oppress'd! And that Disparity, in point of Natural previlege, which is the Bane of Society, would Be Cast upon the utmost coasts of Oblivion. . . . SO when shall America be consistantly Engaged in the Cause of Liberty!" If you have any Love to yourselves, or any Love to this Land, if you have any Love to your fellow-men, Break these intollerable yoaks, and Let their names Be remembered no more, Least they Be retorted on your own necks, and you Sink under them: for god will not hold you guiltless.

Source: Richard D. Brown, ed., *Major Problems in the Era of the American Revolution, 1760-1791: Documents and Essays* (Lexington, Mass. and Toronto: D.C. Heath, 1992), 309-10.

Questions
1. How does Haynes use the word "liberty"? Is there a larger significance to this?
2. How are religious ideas used in the Petition?
3. How does the opening quote of the document relate to the rest of the document?
4. How had the Declaration of Independence affected his view of liberty? Is there an irony in this?

The Declaration of Independence

In Congress, July 4, 1776, A Declaration by the Representatives of the United States of America, in General Congress assembled.

When in the Course of human Events, it becomes necessary for one people to dissolve the Political Bands which have connected them with another, and to assume, among the Powers of the Earth, the separate and equal Station to which the Laws of Nature and of Nature's God entitle them, a decent Respect to the Opinions of Mankind requires that they should declare the causes which impel them to the Separation.

We hold these Truths to be self-evident, that all Men are created equal, that they are endowed by their Creator with certain unalienable Rights, that among these are Life, Liberty, and the pursuit of Happiness. That to secure these Rights, Governments are instituted among Men, deriving their just Powers from the Consent of the Governed, That whenever any Form of Government becomes destructive of these Ends, it is the Right of the People to alter or to abolish it, and to institute new Government, laying its Foundation on such Principles and organizing its Powers in such form, as to them shall seem most likely to effect their Safety and Happiness. Prudence, indeed, will dictate that Governments long established should not be changed for light and transient Causes; and accordingly all Experience hath shown, that Mankind are more disposed to suffer, while Evils are sufferable, than to right themselves by abolishing the Forms to which they are accustomed. But when a long Train of Abuses and Usurpations, pursuing invariably the same Object, evinces a Design to reduce them under absolute Despotism, it is their Right, it is their Duty, to throw off such Government, and to provide new Guards for their future Security. Such has been the patient Sufferance of these Colonies; and such is now the Necessity which constrains them to alter their former Systems of Government. The History of the present King of Great-Britain is a History of repeated Injuries and Usurpations, all having in direct Object the establishment of an absolute Tyranny over these States. To prove this, let Facts be submitted to a candid World.

He has refused his Assent to Laws, the most wholesome and necessary for the public Good.

He has forbidden his Governors to pass Laws of immediate and pressing Importance, unless suspended in their Operation till his Assent should be obtained; and when so suspended, he has utterly neglected to attend to them.

He has refused to pass other Laws for the Accommodation of large districts of People, unless those People would relinquish the Right of Representation in the Legislature, a Right inestimable to them and formidable to Tyrants only.

He has called together Legislative Bodies at Places unusual, uncomfortable, and distant from the Depository of their public Records, for the sole Purpose of fatiguing them into Compliance with his Measures.

He has dissolved Representative Houses repeatedly, for opposing with manly Firmness his Invasions on the Rights of the People.

He has refused for a long Time, after such Dissolutions, to cause others to be elected; whereby the Legislative Powers, incapable of Annihilation, have returned to the People at large for their exercise; the State remaining in the mean time exposed to all the Dangers of Invasion from without, and Convulsions within.

He has endeavoured to prevent the Population of these States; for that Purpose obstructing the Laws of Naturalization of Foreigners; refusing to pass others to encourage their Migrations hither, and raising the Conditions of new Appropriations of Lands.

He has obstructed the Administration of Justice, by refusing his Assent to Laws for establishing Judiciary Powers.

He has made Judges dependent on his Will alone, for the Tenure of their Offices, and the Amount and Payment of their Salaries.

He has erected a Multitude of New Offices, and sent hither Swarms of Officers to harass our People and eat out their Substance.

He has kept among us, in Times of Peace, Standing Armies without the consent of our Legislatures.

He has affected to render the Military independent of and superior to the Civil Power.

He has combined with others to subject us to a Jurisdiction foreign to our Constitution, and unacknowledged by our Laws; giving his Assent to their Acts of pretended Legislation:

For quartering large Bodies of Armed Troops among us:

For protecting them, by a mock Trial, from Punishment for any Murders which they should commit on the Inhabitants of these States:

For cutting off our Trade with all Parts of the World:

For imposing Taxes on us without our Consent:

For depriving us, in many Cases, of the Benefits of Trial by Jury:

For transporting us beyond Seas to be tried for pretended Offences:

For abolishing the free System of English Laws in a neighbouring Province, establishing therein an Arbitrary Government, and enlarging its Boundaries, so as to render it at once an Example and fit Instrument for introducing the same absolute Rule into these Colonies:

For taking away our Charters, abolishing our most valuable Laws, and altering fundamentally the Forms of our Governments:

For suspending our own Legislatures, and declaring themselves invested with Power to legislate for us in all Cases whatsoever.

He has abdicated Government here, by declaring us out of his Protection and waging War against us.

He has plundered our Seas, ravaged our Coasts, burnt our Towns, and destroyed the Lives of our People.

He is, at this Time transporting large Armies of foreign Mercenaries to compleat the Works of Death, Desolation and Tyranny, already begun with circumstances of Cruelty and Perfidy scarcely paralleled in the most barbarous Ages, and totally unworthy the Head of a civilized Nation.

He has constrained our fellow Citizens taken Captive on the high Seas to bear Arms against their Country, to become the Executioners of their Friends and Brethren, or to fall themselves by their Hands.

He has excited domestic Insurrections amongst us, and has endeavoured to bring on the Inhabitants of our Frontiers, the merciless Indian Savages, whose known Rule of Warfare, is an undistinguished Destruction, of all Ages, Sexes and Conditions.

In every stage of these Oppressions we have Petitioned for Redress in the most humble Terms: Our repeated Petitions have been answered only by repeated Injury. A Prince, whose Character is thus marked by every act which may define a Tyrant, is unfit to be the Ruler of a free People.

Nor have we been wanting in Attentions to our British Brethren. We have warned them from Time to Time of Attempts by their Legislature to extend an unwarrantable Jurisdiction over us. We have reminded them of the Circumstances of our Emigration and Settlement here. We have appealed to their native Justice and Magnanimity, and we have conjured them by the Ties of our common Kindred to disavow these Usurpations, which, would inevitably interrupt our Connections and Correspondence. They too have been deaf to the voice of justice and of Consanguinity. We must, therefore, acquiesce in the Necessity, which denounces our Separation, and hold them, as we hold the rest of Mankind, Enemies in War, in Peace, Friends.

We, therefore, the Representatives of the UNITED STATES of AMERICA, in GENERAL CONGRESS, Assembled, appealing to the Supreme Judge of the World for the Rectitude of our Intentions, do, in the Name, and by the Authority of the good People of these Colonies, solemnly Publish and Declare, That these United Colonies are, and of Right ought to be FREE AND INDEPENDENT STATES; that they are absolved from all Allegiance to the British Crown, and that all political Connection between them and the State of Great Britain, is and ought to be totally dissolved; and that as FREE AND INDEPENDENT STATES, they have full Power to levy War, conclude Peace, contract Alliances, establish Commerce, and to do all other Acts and Things which Independent States may of right do. And for the support of this Declaration, with a firm Reliance on the Protection of divine Providence, we mutually pledge to each other our Lives, our Fortunes and our sacred Honor.

Signed by ORDER and in BEHALF of the CONGRESS,
JOHN HANCOCK, PRESIDENT

Beyond Victimization: African Americans

Statement of Purpose

My United States History survey classes at BHS are quite heterogeneous in terms of both ability and ethnic background. Approximately one third of my students are African American. I am constantly seeking ways to make the survey course relevant to their past so as to engage them more fully in their study of American history. A continuing problem has been a tendency on the part of most texts to portray minorities merely as victims, a process that inevitably leads to a not so subtle dehumanization of their role in our history and makes more difficult explanation of the "sudden" outburst of black protest in the so-called "Civil Rights Movement."

My approach in the classroom, therefore, is to portray a long and ongoing black freedom movement, a history of African-American protest that has a long, long history. Until recently, the weakest part of this portrayal has been the colonial and revolutionary period. Two valuable works began to interest me and move me into a search for materials that could more realistically illustrate the actual nature of the African-American experience during this period.

Gary B. Nash's *Red, White, and Black* includes this assessment: "Africans were not merely enslaved. Indians were not merely driven from the land. . . . . To include Africans and Indians in our history in this way, simply as victims of the more powerful Europeans, is hardly better than excluding them altogether. It is to render voiceless, nameless, and faceless people who powerfully affected the course of our historical development as a nation" (Nash, 2-3).

Sidney and Emma Kaplan's *The Black Presence in the Era of the American Revolution* first gave me some tools to provide voices, names, and even faces for the revolutionary period. In the fall of 1989 I began to make use of some petitions for manumission presented in this work. These petitions were offered by New England slaves to their colonial legislatures, and they powerfully point out the paradox of white colonists who were demanding their freedom from England and at the same time continuing to condone slavery.

My brief use of this source consisted merely of my reading some of the petitions aloud and conducting a discussion as to their contents. The discussion was followed by a short writing assignment.

Student Objectives

First, a word about the use of primary sources in the classroom. After twenty one years of teaching history in heterogenous classes, I labor under no illusion of turning most my students into budding historians. Dealing with primary documents is both tedious and time-consuming, particularly in a survey course. At the same time it is most distressing to listen to students who "just want to know the facts"—never mind how the facts were discovered. For such students who seem to think that history is what lies between the covers of their text, I feel a real obligation to give some glimpse of what history

really is—the process of history.

One trick is to include documents of high human interest. I have no doubt that most students will find, for example, Document 29 which focuses on the personal struggle of slave Peter Hawkins more appealing than say Document 4, James Otis' abstract rationale for the supremacy of natural law and liberty for enslaved Africans.

Given the constraints of time in a U.S. History survey course, a lot of trial and error use of these documents will be necessary in order to sort out the documents and discover which are successful for students. In some cases there will be a need to expand context for better understanding or alter the order in which the documents are presented to reduce confusion and clarify insights. A common dilemma ever present in this approach is whether or not to provide long, detailed contexts (as in Document 12) to increase human interest, or whether to provide a shorter context and allow the documents to speak for themselves.

Each of the documents presented should be given to students in the order they appear here and with the accompanying contexts and questions. Some of the more complex documents (difficult in vocabulary and content) should be read and the questions discussed in class before students are asked to provide written answers. You should encourage students to work in study groups of four to compare their written responses once they are completed. Some of the documents should be read and questions answered for homework. Again study groups of four students should enable students to share their written findings, and students should then be permitted to revise their answers before turning them in for teacher evaluation.

Knowledge objectives

Students need to learn:

1. that slaves in New England were openly and articulately asking for their freedom as a direct consequence of the crisis with England in which white colonists were demanding their own freedom.

2. that the paradox of white Americans fighting for their liberty from England, while seeking to continue holding slaves, offered an ideological lever both for New England and Virginia slaves to assert their right to freedom.

3. that slaves in Virginia were also inspired by the American Revolution to ask for their freedom but that repressive impediments erected by slave holders made such expression more difficult in Virginia.

4. that increasingly repressive legal restrictions on blacks in Virginia evolved over a period of time in response to events such as Bacon's Rebellion, the Revolutionary War, and the Gabriel Insurrection.

5. that these repressive measures were related in part to the size of

the Virginia slave population compared with the relatively small slave population of New England.

6. that slave codes in Virginia left slaves virtually defenseless before the arbitrary whims of their masters.

7. that legal restrictions bolstering and defining the institution of slavery in Virginia had the effect of restricting the evolution of civil liberties for whites as well.

8. that separation or return to Africa was a major goal of some blacks even in the Revolutionary era.

9. that some whites supported and took dangerous risks to obtain freedom for blacks.

10. that Christian religious groups such as the Quakers and Methodists made major courageous efforts to weaken or end slavery in Virginia.

11. that part of the black freedom movement in both New England and in Virginia was motivated by the Great Awakening.

12. that the unity between New England and Virginia in resisting England was a key to American success in the Revolution.

13. that there were both humanitarian and non-humanitarian reasons for the ending of the African slave trade in Virginia.

14. that unique geographical and population characteristics of Virginia help to explain the evolution of slavery in Virginia and the response of white Virginian's to Dunmore's Proclamation.

Howard Pyle, *Book of the American Spirit*, 1923

The arrival of the first slaves in the English colonies, 1619.

15. that Dunmore's Proclamation inspired some Virginia slaves t increase their resistance to slavery.

16. that the British did not take full strategic advantage of th presence of huge numbers of blacks in the South by fully offerin and promoting a general emancipation.

17. that blacks fought heroically both on the American and Britis sides during the American Revolution in both New England an Virginia.

18. that during the Revolutionary War some Virginia slave holder would sometimes "free" a slave to serve as a substitute for hir in fighting the war, and that enough of these same slave holder reneged on this arrangement that the Virginia legislature had t pass a special law to attempt to ameliorate the practice.

19. that the Declaration of Independence underwent several draf and that Jefferson was forced to strike his exaggerated assertion about the African slave trade.

20. that after the Revolution, free blacks were increasingly pe ceived by Virginia slave holders as a threat.

21. that the more assimilated to white Virginia culture slave became, the more likely they were to resist the institution c slavery and seek their own freedom.

22. that not only were there fewer slaves in New England compare to Virginia, but New England slaves tended to be proportionall more highly assimilated than blacks in Virginia.

23. that different assimilation levels of New England slaves com pared to Virginia slaves help to account for their greater positiv assertion of a right to freedom compared with Virginia slave

24. that personality as well as personal problems and preoccupa tions (such as Lord Dunmore's pursuit of land in America) ca have a real impact on pivotal historic events (such as Britain' failure to appreciate the rapidity with which Virginia leade were moving toward strategies of cooperation with New Er gland in the pursuit of their own independence).

Skill Objectives

Students should be able to:

1. make use of a dictionary to clarify meanings of words used i primary sources.

2. distinguish between a primary and a secondary source.

3. identify factual patterns drawn from readings of primary source

4. make predictions based upon factual patterns deduced from reading of primary sources.

5. make inferences and draw conclusions from facts presented i primary sources.

6. critically analyze their text (referred to as Jordan) and be able t discover omissions and facts that contradict other source including primary sources.

7. assess the credibility of judgments made by historians and off alternative explanations for historical events.

8. detect a historian's bias.

9. distinguish the *tone* of a written passage in order to appreciat the feelings of the author.

10. improve their own writing by developing well thought o

written responses shared with fellow students in study groups to questions keyed to primary sources.

. distinguish and compare the point of view of individual authors who are describing the same event.

. interpret motive from facts and tone appearing in primary sources.

. develop greater understanding of human motive by writing from a point of view other than their own.

. defend their own opinions using factual evidence obtained from primary sources.

. distinguish fact from opinion by detecting opinion expressed in primary sources.

. compare content of primary sources as to fact and relative persuasiveness.

. understand and appreciate why there exist many unanswered questions in history.

. understand the varied sources of evidence used by historians in conducting their research

. realize and appreciate that historians must often deal with partial, contradictory evidence.

. understand and appreciate why the kinds of evidence that historians have traditionally used tends to provide an abundance of information on more affluent individuals in history in comparison with lower class people.

. realize and appreciate that history is not set and complete, that the search for the past is very much a lively art of historical detection, involving a sometimes tedious but exciting hunt for clues that reveal human motive.

Background
Prior to the introduction of these materials, students should have studied the geography of the New England, Middle, and Southern colonies. A major theme in this study is the unique southern reliance slave labor and a plantation economy that resulted from the special features of southern rivers, soil, climate, and the decision to farm tobacco, rice, and indigo. The New England and Middle colonies are contrasted, and the reasons for the evolution of manufacturing in these colonies is made clear. Students should have completed a survey of the contrasting lifestyles in the New England, Middle, and Southern colonies, including attention to the institution of slavery as practiced in the 17th and 18th century. Students should also have covered the major events leading up to the crisis between England and the American colonies following the French and Indian War, focusing on the resistance to England in Boston, including the "Boston Massacre" and leadership of the Sons of Liberty.

Document Contents
Document 1
A petition to Massachusetts Governor Thomas Gage and the General Court, 25 May 1774, from "a Grate Number of Blackes of the Province . . . held in a state of Slavery within a free and christian country." (Document included as quoted in Kaplan, 13, 15)

Context
Although the petition we are about to examine was rejected without debate by the General Court in September 1774, Abigail Adams, living in Boston, wrote to her husband John (who you will recall was the defense attorney for the troops tried for the "Boston Massacre" four years earlier):

"There has been in town a conspiracy of the negroes. At present it is kept pretty private, and was discovered by one who endeavored to dissuade them from it . . . . They conducted in this way . . . to draw up a petition to the Governor, telling him they would fight for him provided he would arm them, and engage to liberate them if he conquered." She concluded, "I wish most sincerely there was not a slave in the province; it always appeared a most iniquitous scheme to me to fight ourselves for what we are daily robbing and plundering from those who have as good a right to freedom as we have" (as quoted in Kaplan, 15).

Questions
1. Describe the major reasons given by these enslaved Africans for why they should be freed.
2. What words in this petition might have been inspired by the works of Jonathan Edwards and George Whitefield? (Review Jordan, 96-7, on the Great Awakening.)

Document 2
James Otis, *The Rights of the British Colonies Asserted and Proved* [as quoted in Leslie H. Fishel and Benjamin Quarles, eds., *The Negro American: A Documentary History* (Glenview, Ill.: Scott Foresman, 1967), 44.]

Context
We have seen that in their dispute with England, white colonists increasingly relied on arguments that spoke to the notion of freedom as a natural, God-given right and that from their point of view the English Parliament's legislation for the colonies was discriminatory and encroached on their rights as Englishmen. The embarrassing contradiction of claiming liberty while at the same time supporting slavery in the colonies, caused a few New England whites, such as the conscience-stricken proponent of freedom of the press mentioned above, and the worried Abigail Adams, to begin support in the white community for manumission.

One of the first Americans to grasp the full importance of the slavery contradiction in the evolving revolutionary philosophy was James Otis. You will recall that in 1761, as attorney for a group of Boston merchants who objected to the issuance of general search warrants ("writs of assistance") by British officials, James ("A man's house is his castle") Otis argued that a law was invalid if it ran counter to man's natural rights. Two years later in this essay, Otis warns that Negro slavery is just such a violation of natural rights.

Questions
1. Summarize in your own words the major argument (different from any we've seen so far) given by Otis for manumission.

2. Do you think that Otis would have been likely to use the same major argument ten years later after the passage of the Intolerable Acts? Explain why or why not.

3. In what ways might this major argument complicate and make more difficult unity between the New England and Southern colonies in resisting perceived threats to their liberties?

Document 3 and 4

Selections from Thomas Jefferson's *Declaration of Independence*, 4 July 1776.

Context

You have had an opportunity to learn about the direct participation of African Americans in the Battles of Bunker Hill, Lexington, and Concord. (See Kaplan, 16-24; photocopy copies for classroom use and discussion.) As your text reading (Jordan, 123-32) makes clear, events such as these now moved New England representatives to the Second Continental Congress into a position supporting a formal break with England. Yet it was a *Virginian*, Richard Henry Lee who, on 7 June 1776, acting under directions from his own State Convention (which during the revolutionary crisis had replaced the House of Burgesses as Virginia's representative body), formally offered a motion that "these United Colonies are, and of a right ought to be, free and independent States." It was to a Virginian also, to whom the Second Continental Congress turned to draft the formal Declaration of Independence.

Questions

1. Review your text (Jordan, 132-3). What does Winthrop Jordan say about what the words "all men are created equal" meant at the time the Declaration was written?

2. Based on Abigail Adams's letter to her husband quoted in Jordan on page 132, how might she have reacted to the final Declaration of Independence? Write a three paragraph letter to Thomas Jefferson criticizing the Declaration and explaining what is wrong with it from Abigail's point of view.

3. How might illiterate women and blacks have learned what was said in the Declaration? Describe the many ways that these people could have learned what was going on without being able to read or write.

4. Would an illiterate woman or enslaved African's knowledge of current events be greater living in New England compared with living in Virginia? Explain why or why not.

5. Write a three paragraph letter to Thomas Jefferson criticizing the Declaration and explaining what is wrong with it from an enslaved African's point of view.

Document 5

Portion of a Rough Draft of Jefferson's Declaration of Independence [as quoted in James West Davidson and Mark Hamilton Lytle's *After the Fact: the Art of Historical Detection* (New York: Knopf, 1982), 71.]

Context

This attack on the African slave trade is a part of Jefferson's first draft of the Declaration and was to be included in the section describing the many grievances that the colonists had against King

George III. Before we examine the first draft, it may be helpful t read an entry in John Adams's diary for 24 September 1775 [a quoted in Kaplan, 25-6]:

"In the evening . . . two gentlemen from Georgia, came into o room . . . . These gentlemen gave a melancholy account of the Sta of Georgia and South Carolina. They say that if one thousand regula troops should land in Georgia, and their commander be provided wi arms and clothes enough, and proclaim freedom to all the negro who would join his camp, twenty thousand negroes would join from the two Provinces in a fortnight. The negroes have a wonderf art of communicating intelligence among themselves; it will r several hundreds of miles in a week or fortnight. They say their on security is this; that all the king's friends, and tools of governmer have large plantations and property in negroes; so that the slaves the Tories would be lost, as well as those of the Whigs."

Documents 6 and 7

(6) Deed Number 6 of Henrico County, Virginia, 1800. [Sourc as quoted in John Henderson Russell, *The Free Negro in Virgini 1619-1865* (New York: Dover, 1969), 84]. (7) Petition of Saul Virginia State Legislature, 9 October 1792. [source: as quoted James Hugo Johnston, *Race Relations in Virginia and Miscegen tion in the South, 1776-1860* (Amherst: University of Massachuse Press, 1970), 12-3]

Context

Between 1777 and 1785 acts of emancipation either throu courts or legislatures went into effect in Vermont, Pennsylvan Massachusetts, New Hampshire, Connecticut, Rhode Island, a Maryland. The spirit of manumission also got a big boost from t American Revolution in Virginia.

This was particularly true in the piedmont and mountain front regions of western Virginia. Support came also from younger, we educated Virginians such as Thomas Jefferson. The greatest force f emancipation, however, came from Quaker and Methodist church

A partial victory occurred with passage of the manumission la of 1782 which empowered a master to free his slave without fi obtaining legislative permission. This law also required of slav owners who manumitted slaves over forty-five years of age the du to provide for their maintenance, in order that they would not becor burdens to the taxpayer. It was in this same spirit of fairness that 1783 the Virginia legislature had passed a law which protected blac from whites who were abusing the substitute law. At this time t legislature also freed by special act and at the expense of the state a slave who could prove any honorable service rendered by him to t American revolutionary cause.

The free black population at that time was about 3,000. With two years after the 1782 law, this population had doubled. In eig years the free black population was nearly 13,000, by 1800 it w 20,000, and by 1810 it had reached over 30,000. From 1782 to 18 manumission of slaves reached its peak. As troops returned hor and labor shortages eased, many masters made money by granti deeds of manumission paid for by slaves or humanitarian benefact such as Quakers.

These developments touched off a reaction among many slave holders who perceived the free blacks as a growing menace. Efforts began to restrict the free black population or to end private manumission. These efforts, given a great boost by the revelation of the Gabriel Plot, led to legislation enacted in 1806 requiring that all slaves manumitted after 1 May 1806 be required to leave the state. Source for much of this context, including estimates of the free black population in Virginia is Russell, *The Free Negro,* chapter 3.]

Questions

1. In Document 6, who is being freed? Who is the owner?

2. How do you believe the owner was able to gain his own freedom? How did he accumulate enough money to purchase his wife and child? Is there any way of knowing these facts? How would you go about trying to find out? What sorts of sources would be helpful in answering these questions?

3. From all we have studied so far, give as complete an explanation as you can *from the point of view of a Virginia slave holder*, as to why slaves ran away during the Revolution or joined with Dunmore's forces.

4. Notice how frequently Christian religion is mentioned in this petition. Review Document 1. How do you account for the similarities in the arguments being used? Where did the religious content in Document 1 come from?

5. Summarize how *free blacks* are portrayed in these petitions for emancipation.

6. In Document 7, what service did Saul perform in the Revolutionary War? What reasons does he give for being granted his freedom? Who is supporting his petition for manumission?

Documents 8 and 9

(8) St. George Tucker's Letter to a Member of the General Assembly of Virginia on the Subject of the Late Conspiracy of the Slaves, with a Proposal for their Colonization, 1801. [Source: as quoted in Gerald W. Mullin, *Flight and Rebellion: Slave Resistance in Eighteenth Century* (New York: Oxford University Press, 1972), 203.] (9) Petition 6922, Hanover, 2 December 1817. [Source as quoted in Johnston, 17]

Context

St. George Tucker was an aristocratic lawyer and student of the French Enlightenment. Coming to Williamsburg from Bermuda in 1771, he read law with George Wythe, whom he succeeded as professor of law at the College of William and Mary in 1790. Tucker was an amateur astronomer, inventor, and avid gardener. He was also a poet and essayist. The French Revolution and the Gabriel Slave Plot in 1800 must have shaken his Enlightenment faith in human progress and reason, but notice that he continues to be a scientific student of the improvability of humans.

In another part of this report to the Virginia legislature on the Gabriel plot, Tucker comments on the efforts of blacks to join the British in 1775 and argues that the difference between that attempt and the thwarted attempt of Gabriel and his followers was that whereas in 1775 slaves "fought [for] freedom merely as a good; now

they also claim it as a right."

A major effect of the Gabriel Revolt was passage by the Virginia legislature of a new law that required all slaves freed after 1 May 1806 to leave the state within twelve months. It went on to require that, "if any slave hereafter emancipated shall remain within this Commonwealth more than twelve months after his or her right to freedom shall have accrued, he or she shall forfeit all such right and may be apprehended and sold by the overseers of the poor for any county or corporation in which he or she shall be found for the benefit of the poor of such county or corporation."

The law failed to provide for where newly freed slaves might go. Many blacks, including those already free but fearful of getting

Howard Pyle, *Book of the American Spirit*, 1923

A turn-of-the-century view of the colonial slave trade.

caught up in the enforcement of the new law, fled to bordering states. In the years that followed, Maryland, Kentucky, Delaware, Ohio, Indiana, Illinois, Missouri, North Carolina, and Tennessee all passed laws restricting the entrance of free blacks. These events gave impetus to the formation of colonization societies that would organize largely failed efforts to return blacks to Africa (note the full title of Tucker's letter).

The 1806 law also has helped historians to find out more about the lives of slaves and their relationships with their masters. Because of its passage hundreds of petitions were addressed to the legislature to ask for an exception to the penalty provision of the law by showing that the petitioner was not a threat to the state, possessed a positive character, etc. While most of the petitions were written by white lawyers, in many cases they appear to have been written by black petitioners. Document 9 is an example of how revealing to historians these petitions can be. [Source for 1806 law is Russell, 70; Tucker quotes comparing 1775 slave revolts with Gabriel Insurrection are from Mullin, 157.]

Questions

1. Read the selection on the Gabriel Insurrection from Vincent Harding's *There Is A River: The Black Struggle for Freedom in America* (New York: Vintage, 1983), 54-7. What kind of a source is this account? Is there any attempt to be objective in this account? Cite examples from his work to show whose side Harding is on. What sources does Harding use as evidence for what happened in the Gabriel Insurrection?

2. As you read the Harding account, look for any references to free blacks being involved in the plot. Do you think there is sufficient evidence of involvement of free blacks to warrant the new 1806 law? What happened to this plot?

3. What reasons does Tucker give for why slave revolts might occur in Virginia? List examples of his reasons in Harding's account.

4. What does Tucker say was a different reason that some white Virginians gave for the "change in the temper and views of the Negroes?"

5. Do Harding and Tucker agree on what the major inspiration for the Gabriel Insurrection was? For Harding, what was the major inspiration? Give reasons for your answer. For Tucker, what was the major inspiration? Give reasons for your answer.

6. Review Document 6. What special problem was created by the new 1806 law for someone in the same situation as Peter Hawkins was in 1800? Would Peter Hawkins have been as likely to do in 1806 what he did in 1800? Why or why not?

7. What would be your prediction regarding the number of private manumissions that occurred after 1806? Give reasons for your prediction.

8. In Document 9, what did you learn about the slave Amanda?

9. How did Amanda's owner, Mary Austin, feel about her slave? Why did she feel this way?

10. What (not directly mentioned) was Mary Austin asking for in this petition? What did this unmentioned request have to do with Mary's "endeavour to form in the said Amanda till the age of eighteen habits of industry and virtue"? ❏

Bibliography

Brunswick County Papers, 1811-1869, access number 3307-a, Alderman Library, University of Virginia, Charlottesville.

Davidson, James West and Mark Hamilton Lytle. *After the Fact: the Art of Historical Detection*. New York: Knopf, 1982.

Fishel, Leslie H. and Benjamin Quarles, eds. *The Negro American: A Documentary History*. Glenview, Ill.: Scott Foresman, 1967.

Frey, Sylvia R. "Between Slavery and Freedom: Virginia Blacks in the American Revolution." *Journal of Southern History* 49 (August 1983).

Harding, Vincent. *There Is A River: The Black Struggle for Freedom in America*. New York: Vintage, 1983.

Hening, William Waller. *The Statutes at Large, Being a Collection of All the Laws of Virginia*. 13 vols. Richmond, Va., 1809-23.

Isaac, Rhys. *The Transformation of Virginia, 1740-1790*. Chapel Hill: University of North Carolina Press, 1982.

Johnston, J.H. Documents collected and prepared for, *Journal of Negro History* (October, 1927).

Jordan, Winthrop. *The Americans: the History of a People and a Nation*. Evanston, Ill.: McDougal, Littell, 1988).

Kaplan, Sidney and Emma N. Kaplan. *The Black Presence in the Era of the American Revolution*. Amherst: University of Massachusetts Press, 1989.

Morgan, Edmund S. *American Slavery, American Freedom: the Ordeal of Colonial Virginia*. New York: W. W. Norton, 1975.

Mullin, Gerald W. *Flight and Rebellion: Slave Resistance in Eighteenth-Century Virginia*. New York: Oxford University Press, 1972.

Nash, Gary B. *Red, White, and Black: the Peoples of Early America*. Englewood Cliffs, N.J.: Prentice-Hall, 1982)

Palmer, W.P., et al., eds. *Calendar of Virginia State Papers and Other Manuscripts, 1652-1869*. 11 vols. Richmond, Va., 1875-93.

Quarles, Benjamin. *The Negro in the American Revolution*. Chapel Hill: University of North Carolina Press, 1961.

Russell, John Henderson. *The Free Negro in Virginia, 1619-1865*. New York: Dover, 1969.

Selby, Joel E. *The Revolution in Virginia: 1775-1783*. Charlottesville: University of Virginia Press, 1988.

Sobel, Mechal. *The World They Made Together: Black and White Values in Eighteenth Century Virginia*. Princeton, N.J.: Princeton University Press, 1987.

Schwarz, Philip J. *Twice Condemned: Slaves and the Criminal Laws of Virginia, 1705-1865*. Baton Rouge: Louisiana State University Press, 1988.

Van Schreeven, William J., Robert L. Scribner, and Brent Tarter, eds. *Revolutionary Virginia: the Road to Independence, a Documentary Record*. 8 vols. Charlottesville: University of Virginia Press, 1973-1983.

Steven C. Teel teaches history at Berkeley High School, California, and is a member of the OAH Magazine of History Advisory Board.

Document 1

A Petition to Massachusetts Governor Thomas Gage and the General Court, May 25, 1774 from "a Grate Number of Blackes of the Province . . . held in a state of Slavery within a free and christian Country." Source: Petitions quoted in Sidney Kaplan and Emma N. Kaplan, The Black Presence in the Era of the American Revolution (Amherst: University of Massachusetts Press, 1989), 13, 15.

"Your Petitioners apprehind we have in common with all other men a naturel right to our freedoms without Being depriv'd of them by our fellow men as we are a freeborn Pepel and have never forfeited this Blessing by aney compact or agreement whatever. But we were unjustly dragged by the cruel hand of power from our dearest frinds and sum of us stolen from the bosoms of our tender Parents and from a Populous Pleasant and plentiful country and Brought hither to be made slaves for Life in a Christian land. Thus we are deprived of every thing that hath a tendency to make life even tolerable, the endearing ties of husband and wife we are strangers to . . . . Our children are also taken from us by force and sent maney miles from us . . . . Thus our Lives are imbittered . . . . There is a great number of us sencear. . . members of the Church of Christ how can the master and the slave be said to fulfil that command Live in love let Brotherly Love contuner and abound Beare my Borden when he Beares me down with the . . . Chanes of slavery . . . . Nither can we reap an equal benefet from the laws of the Land which doth not justifi but condemns Slavery or if there had bin aney Law to hold us in Bondage . . . there never was aney to inslave our children for life when Born in a free Countrey. We therefore Bage your Excellency and Honours will . . . cause an act of the legislative to be pessed that we may obtain our Natural right our freedoms and our children to be set a lebety at the yeare of twenty one."

When resubmitted in June, 1774, the petitioners added these words: "give and grant to us some part of the unimproved land, belonging to the province, for a settlement, that each of us may there quietly sit down under his own fig tree" and enjoy "the fruits of his labour."

Both petitions were rejected without debate.

Document 2

James Otis, *The Rights of the British Colonies Asserted and Proved* (as quoted in Leslie H. Fishel and Benjamin Quarles, eds., *The Negro American: A Documentary History* (Glenview, Ill.: Scott Foresman, 1967), 44.

"The Colonists are by the law of nature free born, as indeed all men are, white or black. No better reasons can be given, for enslaving those of any colour, than such as baron Montesquieu has humourously given, as the foundation of that cruel slavery excercised over the poor Ethiopians; which threatens one day to reduce both Europe and America to the ignorance and barbarity of the darkest ages. Does it follow that it is right to enslave a man because he is black? Will short curled hair, like wool, instead of Christian hair, as it is called by those whose hearts are as hard as the nether millstone, help the argument? Can any logical inference in favour of slavery, be drawn from a flat nose, a long or a short face? Nothing better can be said in favour of a trade, that is the most shocking violation of the law of nature, has a direct tendency to diminish the idea of the inestimable value of liberty, and makes every dealer in it a tyrant, from the director of an African company to the petty chapman in needles and pins on the unhappy coast. It is a clear truth, that those who every day barter away other mens liberty, will soon care little for their own."

Documents 3 and 4

Selections from The Unanimous Declaration of the Thirteen United States of America, 4 July 1776.

When in the Course of human events, it becomes necessary for one people to dissolve the political bands, which have connected them with another, and to assume among the powers of the earth, the separate and equal station to which the Laws of Nature and of Nature's God entitle them, a decent respect to the opinions of mankind requires that they should declare the causes which impel them to the separation.—We hold these truths to be self-evident, that all men are created equal, that they are endowed by their Creator with certain unalienable Rights, that among these are Life, Liberty and the pursuit of Happiness.—That to secure these rights, Governments are instituted among Men, deriving their just powers from the consent of the governed,—That whenever any Form of Government becomes destructive of these ends, it is the Right of the People to alter or to abolish it, and to institute new Government, laying its foundation on such principles and organizing its powers in such form, as to them shall seem most likely to effect their Safety and Happiness.

He has excited domestic insurrections amongst us, and has endeavoured to bring on the inhabitants of our frontiers, the merciless Indian Savages, whose known rule of warfare, is an undistinguished destruction of all ages, sexes and conditions. In every state of these Oppressions We have Petitioned for Redress in the most humble terms: Our repeated Petitions have been answered only by repeated injury. A Prince whose character is thus marked by every act which may define a Tyrant, is unfit to be the ruler of a free people.

Document 5

A Rough Draft of Jefferson's Declaration of Independence [as quoted in James West Davidson and Mark Hamilton Lytle's *After the Fact: the Art of Historical Detection* (New York: Knopf, 1982), 71).]

He has waged cruel war against human nature itself, violating it's most sacred rights of life and liberty in the persons of a distant people who vever offended him, captivating & carrying them into slavery in another hemisphere or to incur miserable death in their transportation thither. This piratical warfare, the opprobrium of *infidel* powers, is the warfare of the *Christian* king of Great Britain. Determined to keep open a market where *Men* should be bought & sold, he has prostituted his negative [used his veto power] for suppressing every legislative attempt to prohibit or to restrain this execrable commerce. And that this assemblage of horors might want no fact of distinguishing die, he is now exciting those very people to rise in arms among us, and to purchase that liberty of which he has deprived them, by murdering the people on whom he also obtruded them: thus paying off former crimes committed against the *Liberties* of one people, with crimes which he urges them to commit against the *lives* of another.

Document 6

Deed Number 6 of Henrico County, Virginia, 1800 [as quoted in John Henderson Russell, *The Free Negro in Virginia, 1619-1865* (New York: Dover, 1969), 84.]

To all whom these presents may come know ye, that I Peter Hawkins a free black man of the City of Richmond having purchased my wife Rose, a slave about twenty-two years of age and by her have a child called Mary now about 18 mo. old, for the love I bear toward my wife and child have thought proper to emancipate them and for the further consideration of five shillings to me in hand paid . . . I emancipate and set free the said Rose and Mary . . . and relinquish all my right title and interest and claim whatsoever as slaves to the said Rose and Mary.

Peter Hawkins (Seal)

Document 7

Petition of Saul to the Virginia State Legislature, 9 October 1792 [as quoted in James Hugo Johnston, *Race Relations in Virginia and Miscegenation in the South* (Amherst: University of Massachusetts Press, 1979), 12-23.]

"In the beginning of the late war which gave America freedom, your petitioner shouldered his musket and repaired to the American standard, regardless of invitations trumpeted up by British proclamations for the slaves to emancipate themselves by becoming the assassins of their owners. Your petitioner avoided the rock that too many of his colour were shipwrecked on. He was taught that the war was levied on Americans not for the emancipation of the blacks, but for the subjugation of the whites, and he thought that the number of bondsmen ought not to be augmented. Under these impressions he did actually campaign in both armies—in the American army as a soldier, in the British as a spy; which will fully appear reference being had to certificates of officers of respectibility. In this double profession your petitioner flatters himself that he rendered essential service to his country."

A note accompanied this petition:

"Be it known by all to whom it may concern: That Saul, formerly the property of Thomas Mathews, Esquire, during the different invasions of the state by the British army in the late war, left his residence in the city of Norfolk and joined the troups of this state under my command, and when under my authority acted in such a manner as to merit my particular approbation and in my opinion to deserve the applause of his country. In many instances he was more serviceable than if he had been white. From his colour he had the opportunity of visiting the camps of the enemy from which he brought me much valuable information respecting their numbers, and was not only serviceable to me and my command but useful to different officers in the Southern states with whom I had the honor to correspond and from whence they often got information that could not else be so easily assertained. As may be assertained from letters from Gen. Green, the Marquise de la Fayette, Baron Steuben, Gen. Wayne, Gen. Muhlenberg, the last of which was personally acquainted with some of Saul's services. Independent of his service as a spy, when unemployed in that way he was always employed with the flankers in advance with his picquet.

It would be presumptious for me to say how Saul should be rewarded by his country but I can with truth declare that his service was as meritorious and more so than could be expected of a slave, and I venture to say that he who has done so much in the cause of freedom deserves to share a part of it."

"J. Parker"

Mary Newton Stanard, *Colonial Virginia: Its People and Customs*, 1917

An enslaved African female in colonial Virginia.

Document 8

St. George Tucker's Letter to a Member of the General Assembly of Virginia on the Subject of the Late Conspiracy of the Slaves, with a Proposal for their Colonization, 1801. [as quoted in Gerald W. Mullin, *Flight and Rebellion: Slave Resistance in Eighteenth Century* (Oxford University Press, 1972), 203.]

"There is a progress in human affairs which may indeed be retarded, but which nothing can arrest . . .
    Of such sort is the advancement of knowledge among the negroes of this country . . . . Every year adds to the number of those who can read and write; and he who has made any proficiency in letters, becomes a little centre of instruction to others. This increase of knowledge is the principal agent in the spirit we have to fear. The love of freedom, sir, is an inborn sentiment . . . long may it be kept under by the arbitrary institutions of society, but, at the first favorable moment, it springs forth, and flourishes with a vigour that defies all check.
    In our infant country, where population and wealth increase with unexampled rapidity . . . . The growth and multiplication of our towns tend a thousand ways to enlight and inform them. The very nature of our government, which leads us to recur perpetually to the discussion of natural rights, favors speculation and enquiry.
    But many of those, who see and acknowledge this change in the temper and views of the Negroes, ascribe it principally to the mild treatment they have of late years experienced . . . .
    We have hitherto placed much reliance on the difficulty of their acting in concert. Late experience has shewn us . . . they have maintained a correspondence, which, whether we consider its extent, or duration, is truly astonishing . . . Fanaticism is spreading fast among the Negroes of this country, and may form in time the connecting link between black religionists and the white. Do you not, already, sir, discover something like a sympathy between them? It certainly would not be a novelty, in the history of the world, if Religion were made to sanctify plots and conspiracies."

Document 9

Petition 6922, Hanover County, 2 December 1817 [source: as quoted in James Hugo Johnston, *Race Relations in Virginia and Miscegenation in the South, 1776-1860* (University of Massachusetts Press, 1970), 17.]

"Your petitioner, Mary Austin, of Hanover County, begs leave to represent to the General Assembly that she is possessed of a Negro woman aged about fifteen years named Amanda. That the said Amanda, whilst an infant, had her mother taken away from her and was affected with a long and painful illness, during which time your petitioner from motives of duty and humanity nursed her. That your petitioner during her attentions to the said Amanda formed, perhaps unfortunately, a strong and from its continuance, it seems, a lasting attachment for her. And it is now the inclination and intention of your petitioner to endeavour to form in the said Amanda till the age of eighteen habits of industry and virtue. Your petitioner knowing that without interposition of the General Assembly she can make no disposition of the said Amanda, consistently with the laws of the State and impressed with feelings the most abhorrent and distressing of leaving the said Amanda in slavery at the death of your petitioner, therefore, hopes that the General Assembly will see no injury to the State which compares with the happiness of your petitioner in this particular which will forbid the emancipation of the said Amanda."

Twentieth-Century Indian History: Achievements, Needs, and Problems

Donald Parman

I n several important ways, twentieth-century American Indian history anticipated the new western history. Before the 1960s, the few historians who dealt with Indians generally concentrated on military events. Such coverage ended with the Indians' military defeat and assignment to reservations in the nineteenth century. Once this happened, Indians no longer seemed interesting or worthy of further attention. Moreover, the dominant society treated Indians as a kind of appendage to the main story of white frontier settlement or, even worse, a barrier to its "civilizing" impact. Beginning in the 1960s, however, historians became interested in twentieth-century Indian studies, applied a new methodology, and conducted investigations of how this group fit into western regional development.

Several academic trends after World War II stimulated new interest in Indian history. One of the most important developments was the emergence of ethnohistory, an approach that combined historians' critical analysis of documents with anthropologists' interest in such matters as Indian communities' political, social, and religious composition. One of the key goals of ethnohistory was to present a more balanced assessment of Indian life and to end the earlier depictions of Indians as silent pawns in their relations with

whites. Ethnohistory began when Erminie Wheeler-Voegelin, an anthropologist at Indiana University, organized several conferences for historians and anthropologists in the 1950s. These resulted in the formation of the Ohio Valley Historic Indian Conference, later renamed the American Society for Ethnohistory, and the publication of a new journal, *Ethnohistory*. The latter continues, and in 1974 it was supplemented by two other journals, *American Indian Quarterly* and *American Indian Culture and Research Journal*, devoted to Indian studies.

Public interest in Indians also increased greatly during the late 1960s and 1970s. This grew out of the opposition to the Vietnam War, concern over the environment, and the demand for civil rights. During a period of considerable public turmoil and self-examination, many Americans turned to Indian life as an attractive alternative. Hollywood wasted little time in taking advantage of the situation. Three major films released in 1970, *Soldier Blue*, *A Man Named Horse*, and *Little Big Man*, all gave a sympathetic, although often misleading, depiction of Indians. The following year Dee Brown's popular history, *Bury My Heart at Wounded Knee: An Indian History of the American West*, ranked second on the non-fiction best seller list. Although Brown's book

was far less authentic than he claimed, it both reflected and encouraged the public's growing interest in Indians (1).

Although the trends described above fostered scholarly interest in all periods of Indian history, several graduate students completed dissertations on twentieth-century topics during the 1960s. Several of these studies dealt with the Indian New Deal and its chief architect, John Collier. A native of Georgia and a former social worker in both New York City and California, Collier had first become interested in Indians during a visit to Taos Pueblo in late 1920. He became a full-time Indian reformer in 1922 and continued his activism after his appointment as Indian commissioner in 1933. Collier's outspoken advocacy for Indians, his effective although sometimes overdrawn propaganda, and his philosophical stance made him an appealing figure to study. In particular, young scholars at the time were attracted to Collier's "cultural pluralism," which rejected the federal government's long-standing efforts to force Indians to assimilate into white society. Collier demanded that Indian cultures merited preservation because they were valued by Indians and because they could serve as models that could benefit American society in general. As commissioner, Collier won passage of the Indian Reorganization Act

(IRA) in 1934. The new law embodied many of his reform ideas and allowed Indians to form tribal governments that functioned as federal municipalities.

Early studies of the Indian New Deal, however, raised serious questions about Collier's administration of the Bureau of Indian Affairs (BIA). Collier's publicity during the New Deal and his self-serving statements in his later autobiography, *From Every Zenith*, gave the impression that his programs had both vastly improved reservation conditions and raised Indians' morale. He also claimed that his program would have succeeded completely except for the opposition of western congressional leaders and white and Indian assimilationists (2). Scholars who assessed the Indian New Deal, however, found a rather different picture. Some 60 percent of the Indians chose not to form tribal governments under the IRA, mixed-bloods often seized control of the IRA councils and discriminated against full-bloods, and agency superintendents severely restricted self-government. In addition, Collier sometimes seemed as insensitive to Indians' wishes and as arbitrary as had his predecessors (3). Despite the critical assessments of Collier, historians have not reached an interpretative consensus on the Indian New Deal. Even his strongest critics, though, recognize that he reversed the assimilation policy, brought sizable amounts of money from New Deal emergency programs to reservations, and planted the seeds of Indian tribal autonomy that emerged during the past two decades.

Since the initial studies of the Indian New Deal, historians of twentieth-century Native American history have directed most of their attention to the post-World War II era. Interest in the termination policies of the Truman and Eisenhower administrations resulted in Larry J. Hasse's much cited dissertation, "Termination and Assimilation: Federal Indian Policy 1943-1961"; Larry W. Burt's *Tribalism in Crisis: Federal Indian Policy 1953-1961*; and Donald L. Fixico's *Termination and Relocation: Federal Indian Policy, 1945-1960*. Fixico's work was noteworthy because he

E.R. Fryer

Indian Commissioner John Collier, on the right, poses with Henry Taliman, a Navajo leader in 1938.

is one of the very few Indians trained as a historian, and because he was especially sensitive to the human side of termination and the federal policy of relocating Indians to urban areas (4). Although Michael L. Lawson's *Dammed Indians: The Pick-Sloan Plan and the Missouri River Sioux* did not deal with termination directly, it covered much the same time period, and it emphasized the difficulties the Sioux experienced when their best land was flooded by a series of postwar dams that the Corps

of Engineers constructed along the upper Missouri River (5).

Historians have not concentrated on any particular era or topic since termination. Instead, they have addressed a wide range of new subjects and filled gaps in early scholarship. Perhaps a few examples will illustrate the resulting diversity. Peter Iverson's *The Navajo Nation* concentrated on the postwar period as he argued that Navajos had established themselves as a nation. A growing recognition of World

War II's important impact on Indians—both in the military and in their exodus to off-reservation jobs—led to Alison R. Bernstein's *American Indians and World War II: Toward a New Era in Indian Affairs*. Edward Danziger's book on the Indian community in Detroit offers an approach that hopefully others will pursue for western cities. Margaret Connell Szasz's study of Indian education from 1928 to 1974 and Robert Trennert's history of the Phoenix Indian School partly relieved the need for more studies on that badly neglected subject. Another pressing need is for biographies of twentieth-century Indian leaders. Dorothy Parker's recent study of D'Arcy McNickle's varied career as a BIA employee, writer-historian, and reformer provides an excellent model for future treatments of Indian leaders. Indian history continues to attract eager graduate students who are producing dissertations that fill gaps and deal with important subjects that merit study (6).

Without question, the least studied era in twentieth-century Indian history is the period before 1920. Frederick E. Hoxie's *A Final Promise: The Campaign to Assimilate the Indians, 1880-1920*; Hazel W. Hertzberg's *The Search for an Indian Identity: Modern Pan-Movements*; and Janet A. McDonnell's *The Dispossession of the American Indian, 1887-1934* are all important contributions, but the coverage of the first two decades of the century hardly compares to the attention that historians have given to the Indian New Deal. A particular need is to assess the impact that Progressive reforms had upon Indian affairs (7).

Historians have also not given a great deal of attention to the Red Power movement and other events of the past two decades. This is hardly surprising given the restrictions placed on the use of government records and historians' misgivings about "instant history." One exception is Rolland Dewing's *Wounded Knee: The Meaning and Significance of the Second Incident*. After overcoming numerous legal barriers, Dewing gained access to the extensive files the FBI compiled on the 1973 occupation of Wounded Knee and other American Indian Movement (AIM) activities. He not only used the records in writing his book, but edited the collection for a microfilm publication (8). Most writings on the AIM and similar militant groups during the red power period are, unfortunately, polemical in nature.

A greater need is for historians to investigate the profound alterations that have taken place in Indian affairs since the militancy of the 1960s and 1970s. Many of these changes originated during the Johnson and Nixon administrations when the BIA lost its monopoly over providing services to Indians as other federal agencies assumed various responsibilities. Tribal leaders quickly bypassed the BIA and dealt with the outside agencies for education, health, housing, sanitation. and economic development. Through the operation of the Indian Claims Commission Act of 1946, Indians became more sensitive to litigation and began to use federal courts to gain treaty and statutory rights that had been previously ignored. Probably the most famous example of this trend was the *Boldt* decision. In 1974 the federal district court in Tacoma ruled that several Indian tribes in Washington State were entitled to 50 percent of the salmon and steelhead catch because of nineteenth-century treaties. Subsequent litigation in Michigan, Wisconsin, Minnesota, and other states also established Indians' hunting and fishing rights under earlier treaties. The Indians' attempts to obtain water rights in western states have been less decisive, but the issue remains highly important for both Indians and whites (9).

Another important recent development is the passage of legislation affecting American Indians. Indeed, Congress approved more basic measures since 1970 than in any equivalent period of history. Examples include the Indian Civil Rights Act of 1968, which provided legal guarantees to Indians living under tribal governments; the Indian Child Welfare Act of 1978, which gave tribes far greater control over domestic matters, especially the adoption of Indian children; and the Joint Resolution on American Indian Religious Freedom Act of 1978. Indians have always been particularly sensitive about re-

Arizona Historical Society

Thomas Segundo, a Papago veteran, presides over the Papago Tribal Council shortly after World War II.

ligious freedom because of the BIA's strong attempts before 1933 to discourage ceremonials and the problems encountered by peyotists within the Native American Church even after Collier became commissioner. These measures and others that dealt with education and health indirectly resulted from the Red Power protests and also from Indian leaders' lobby activities within the legislative and executive branches.

Finally, recent Indian history offers potential for future studies because tribal governments have finally achieved the kind of authority that Collier envisioned when he secured passage of the Indian Reorganization Act in 1934. A mixture of factors explains this trend. Tribal leaders since World War II have grown increasingly sophisticated and aggressive; recent federal court decisions on taxation powers and other questions have often strengthened tribal authority; and some reservations enjoy sufficient income from natural resources, federal grants, and gaming to fund their own social services and to improve local infrastructures. Many Indians today believe that tribes are sovereign powers or nations with which the federal government and state governments must deal as equals. The strengthening of tribal authority, however, has produced a strong white backlash in many areas. The *Boldt* decision and similar rulings led white sportsmen in Washington state and other states to believe that Indians held unfair advantages because of outmoded treaties. Whites who live and hold property on reservations are equally upset by tribal governments exercising authority over such matters as land use, zoning, sanitation, recreation, hunting, and fishing. Some have formed local protest groups based on specific problems, and these in turn have merged into regional and national organizations. The Citizens Equal Rights Alliance (CERA), formed in 1988, seems to be the most powerful of the current backlash groups because of its widespread membership and comprehensive agenda.

A word of caution is needed in dealing with these recent trends in Indian affairs. Reservations vary tremendously in leadership, historical experiences, resources, and educational levels. Some Indian groups, therefore, have participated fully in recent general trends while others have met repeated failures.

Although Indians have been an important element in American literature since the captivity narratives of the colonial period and James Fenimore Cooper's *Leatherstocking Tales*, Indian authors produced little fiction before the 1960s (10). That situation changed after 1969 when N. Scott Momaday, a Kiowa, won a Pulitzer Prize for *House Made of Dawn* (1968), a novel about a troubled Indian veteran's return from World War II to Jemez Pueblo. Leslie Marmon Silko, a Laguna Pueblo, published *Ceremony* in 1977, which also dealt with a returning veteran's reintegration into an Indian community. James Welch, a Blackfeet-Gros Ventre, wrote two novels, *Winter in the Blood* (1974) and *The Death of Jim Loney* (1979) with contemporary settings. But in *Fools Crow* (1986), his main character was a nineteenth-century Blackfeet warrior. Gerald Vizenor, a Chippewa, has written several novels that embody a baffling mixture of humor, trickster techniques, and current literary theories.

Louise Erdrich's novels have not only gained high marks from literary critics but they brought her the distinction of being the first Indian author to make the best seller lists. *Love Medicine* (1984), *The Beet Queen* (1986), *Tracks* (1988), and *The Bingo Queen* (1994) represent the experiences of Erdrich's own people, the North Dakota Chippewas of the Turtle Mountain reservation. Erdrich credits her husband, Michael Dorris, a Modoc, who formerly directed the Indian studies program at Dartmouth, as her collaborator. Dorris's *A Yellow Raft in Blue Water* (1987), a story of Indian women from three generations established him as a writer of considerable merit (11).

These works and others by recent Indian authors are important historically. Somewhat like ethnohistory, Indians are the protagonists in the stories rather than being relegated to a secondary position.

Pete Price, noted Navajo medicine man, and his colleagues participate in the dedication of a new hospital on the Navajo Reservation in 1938.

The non-Indian reader, indeed, becomes a kind of outsider, observing people and events that are often alien to his or her experience. The Indian novelists frequently use history, albeit a type of personal history, that shows how events profoundly affect individuals. Erdrich's novels, for example, vividly portray the impact of missionaries and white education, the frictions between traditional and progressive Indians, and the dire consequences of treaties and land allotment. Although Indian novelists understand and apply recent literary theory, they frequently incorporate traditional Indian stories, cultural concepts, and oral traditions. Welch obviously schooled himself in history and anthropology and then used *Fools Crow* as a vehicle for conveying a rich understanding of the lifestyle of Plains warriors, their psychology, and their values. Far more readers will derive their understanding of Indians and Indian history from recent Indian authors than they will from the writings of professional historians or anthropologists.

The problems associated with twentieth-century Indian history parallel those facing the field in general. Indian historians, for example, who aspire to write ethnohistory often fail to realize the full potential of that approach. Typically, such scholars present strong prefatory promises that their books will reveal the Indian perspective, disclose the Indian voice, and portray Indians as active participants in the story, but the main bodies of the books deal almost entirely with non-Indian actions and policy matters. Some writers make little attempt to discuss the social, cultural, and religious structures of the tribes involved. In truth, ethnohistory is a difficult approach because the documentation available is almost entirely derived from white sources. Even translations of Indians' statements and descriptions of their behavior are suspect. Moreover, ethnohistory requires a different analytical perspective and a creativity that some scholars have not fully mastered. Finally, ethnohistory is perhaps not suited for broad, general studies that deal with several Indian groups over long periods of time. In

the latter works, policy treatments with greater emphasis on Indians' roles are perhaps the only feasible approach.

A related problem is bias in writing Indian history. Because of its controversial nature, the field seems to attract an inordinate number of writers, both popular and scholarly, who use the field to push their particular agendas or to express their moral outrage at American society. Such activist history can distort events as much as history written to rationalize or to mask the evils done to Indians. Treating Indians as hapless victims robs them of possessing any agency in determining their fate; a view, ironically, that runs counter to activist historians' beliefs. If we are to accomplish greater objectivity, we need, according to one pioneer ethnohistorian, "a better balanced account of Indian-white relations than the 'Indian as savage,' on the one hand, and the unqualified arraignment of whites . . . on the other" (12).

A third major issue is the question of how much of the recent scholarship on Indians has been incorporated into textbooks on general United States history or western history. Frederick E. Hoxie of the Newberry Library, who formerly directed the D'Arcy McNickle Center for the History of the American Indians at that institution, first addressed this issue in an essay nearly a decade ago (13). Hoxie sees some improvement in recent years, but nothing akin to a major breakthrough. Although some of the more recent college texts have included greater coverage of Indians, most of the older standard works still contain photographs of "anonymous Indians," give minimal attention to pre-Columbian societies, and make little attempt to include Indians in subsequent passages. The major stumbling block, according to Hoxie, is that texts are "triumph narratives" that automatically exclude attention to Indians. Hoxie, however, notes that no major textbook project today will fail to include an expert on Indian history among its panel of consultants. "That wouldn't have happened ten years ago," he concludes (14).

The situation in western history texts is much more promising. For example,

Richard White's recent textbook on western history includes far more information on Indians than Ray Billington's and Martin Ridge's *Westward Expansion* and other earlier works that were influenced by Frederick Jackson Turner's "frontier thesis." The same is true of Michael P. Malone's and Richard W. Etulain's text on twentieth-century western history. Donald L. Parman's recent book summarizes twentieth-century Indian history and discusses the subject in the context of regional development. Other general treatments of the twentieth-century West typically include a chapter or chapters on Indians and other ethnic groups in the region (15).

In reviewing the development of twentieth-century Indian history, the achievements over the past three decades are remarkable. The field virtually did not exist before the 1960s. But, since then, scholars have created a sizable body of important studies and has managed to break beyond the "barrier" imposed by Turner's view that the frontier ended in 1890. Indian historians, namely ethnic, racial, and gender specialists, have demonstrated that western regional development was both diverse and complex and that without the story of Indians and other groups, any history of the region would be incomplete. Although twentieth-century Indian history has gained a niche in western regional studies, it remains unclear whether such scholarship will win a place in general history texts and among the educated public. ❑

Endnotes
1. These matters are treated in Donald L. Parman and Catherine Price, "A 'Work in Progress': The Emergence of Indian History as a Professional Field," *Western Historical Quarterly* 20 (May 1989): 185-86.
2. John Collier, *From Every Zenith: A Memoir and Some Essays on Life and Thought* (Denver: Sage Books, 1963).
3. On Collier's commissionership, see Lawrence C. Kelly, *The Navajo Indians and Federal Indian Policy 1900-1935* (Tucson: University of Arizona

Press, 1968); Donald L. Parman, *The Navajos and the New Deal* (New Haven: Yale University Press, 1976); Kenneth R. Philp, *John Collier's Crusade for Indian Reform, 1920-1945* (Tucson: University of Arizona Press, 1977); Graham D. Taylor, *The New Deal and American Indian Tribalism: The Administration of the Indian Reorganization Act, 1934-45* (Lincoln: University of Nebraska Press, 1980); and Laurence S. Hauptman, *The Iroquois and the New Deal* (Syracuse: Syracuse University Press, 1981). Among the more recent publications, Vine Deloria, Jr. and Clifford M. Lytle, *The Nations Within: The Past and Future of American Indian Sovereignty* (New York: Pantheon Books, 1984); and Thomas Biolsi, *Organizing the Lakota: The Political Economy of the New Deal on the Pine Ridge and Rosebud Reservations* (Tucson: University of Arizona Press, 1992) are especially useful.

4. Larry J. Hasse, "Termination and Assimilation: Federal Indian Policy, 1943-1961," Ph.D. diss., Washington State University, 1974; Larry W. Burt, *Tribalism in Crisis: Federal Indian Policy, 1953-1961* (Albuquerque: University of New Mexico Press, 1982); and Donald L. Fixico, *Termination and Relocation: Federal Indian Policies, 1945-1960* (Albuquerque: University of New Mexico Press, 1986).

5. Michael L. Lawson, *Dammed Indians: The Pick-Sloan Plan and the Missouri River Sioux, 1944-1980* (Norman: University of Oklahoma Press, 1982).

6. Peter Iverson, *The Navajo Nation* (Westport, Connecticut: Greenwood Press, 1981); Alison R. Bernstein, *American Indians and World War II: Toward a New Era in Indian Affairs* (Norman: University of Oklahoma Press, 1991); Edward Jefferson Danziger, *Survival and Regeneration: Detroit's American Indian Community* (Detroit: Wayne State University Press, 1991); Margaret Connell Szasz,

Education and the American Indian: The Road to Self-Determination, 1928-1973 (Albuquerque: University of New Mexico Press, 1974); Robert Trennert, *The Phoenix Indian School: Forced Assimilation in Arizona, 1891-1935* (Norman: University of Oklahoma Press, 1988); and Dorothy R. Parker, *Singing an Indian Song: A Biography of D'Arcy McNickle* (Lincoln: University of Nebraska Press, 1993).

7. Frederick E. Hoxie, *A Final Promise: The Campaign to Assimilate the Indians, 1880-1920* (Lincoln: University of Nebraska Press, 1984); Hazel W. Hertzberg, *The Search for an American Indian Identity: Modern Pan-Indian Movements* (Syracuse: Syracuse University Press, 1971); and Janet A. McDonnell, *The Dispossession of the American Indian, 1887-1934* (Bloomington: Indiana University Press, 1989).

8. Rolland Dewing, *Wounded Knee: The Meaning and Significance of the Second Incident* (New York: Irvington Publishers, 1985); and Rolland Dewing, ed., *The FBI Files on the American Indian Movement and Wounded Knee* (Frederick, Maryland: University Publications of America, 1986).

9. For information on Indian water rights, see Lloyd Burton, *American Indian Water Rights and the Limits of the Law* (Lawrence: University Press of Kansas, 1991).

10. Louis Owens, a Choctaw-Cherokee-Irish novelist and a professor of literature, notes that Indians authored only nine novels prior to 1968. See Louis Owens, *Other Destinies: Understanding the American Indian Novel* (Norman: University of Oklahoma Press, 1992), 24.

11. These novels are analyzed in Owens, *Other Destinies* cited above. Owens also discusses works prior to *House Made of Dawn* and presents a bibliography on novels written by Indians.

12. As quoted in Parman and Price, "A 'Work in Progress,'" 194.

13. Frederick E. Hoxie, "The Indians Versus the Textbooks: Is There Any Way Out?" *Perspectives* 23 (April 1985): 18-22.

14. Interview of Frederick E. Hoxie, August 9, 1994.

15. Richard White, *'It's Your Misfortune and None of My Own': A New History of the American West* (Norman: University of Oklahoma Press, 1991); Ray Allen Billington and Martin Ridge, *Westward Expansion: A History of the American Frontier* (New York: Macmillan, 1982); Michael O. Malone and Richard W. Etulain, *The American West: A Twentieth Century History* (Lincoln: University of Nebraska Press, 1989); and Donald L Parman, *Indians and the American West in the Twentieth Century* (Bloomington: Indiana University Press, 1994).

Bibliography

Ambler, Marane. *Breaking the Iron Bonds: Indian Control of Energy Development*. Lawrence: University Press of Kansas, 1990.

Bee, Robert L. *The Politics of American Indian Policy*. Cambridge, Massachusetts: Schenkman Publishing Company, 1982.

Bernstein, Alison R. *American Indians and World War II: Toward a New Era in Indian Affairs*. Norman: University of Oklahoma Press, 1991.

Berthrong, Donald J. *The Cheyenne and Arapaho Ordeal: Reservation and Agency Life in Indian Territory, 1875-1907*. Norman: University of Oklahoma Press, 1976.

Billington, Ray Allen and Martin Ridge. *Westward Expansion: A History of the American Frontier*. New York: Macmillan, 1982.

Biolsi, Thomas. *Organizing the Dakota: The Political Economy of the New Deal on the Pine Ridge and Rosebud Reservations*. Tucson: University of Arizona Press, 1992.

Burt, Larry W. *Tribalism in Crisis: Federal Indian Policy, 1953-1961*. Albuquerque: University of New Mexico

Press, 1982.

Burton, Lloyd. *American Indian Water Rights and the Limits of the Law.* Lawrence: University Press of Kansas, 1991.

Collier, John. *From Every Zenith: A Memoir and Some Essays on Life and Thought.* Denver: Sage Books, 1963.

Cornell, Stephen. *The Return of the Native: American Indian Political Resurgence.* New York: Oxford University Press, 1988.

Danziger, Edward Jefferson. *Survival and Regeneration: Detroit's American Indian Community.* Wayne State University Press, 1991.

Davis, Mary, ed. *Native America in the Twentieth Century: an Encyclopedia.* Hamden, Connecticut: Garland Publishing, Inc., 1994.

Deloria, Vine, Jr. and Clifford M. Lytle. *The Nations Within: The Past an Future of American Sovereignty.* New York: Pantheon Books, 1984.

Dewing, Rolland. *Wounded Knee: The Meaning and Significance of the Second Incident.* New York: Irvington Publishers, 1984.

Dippie, Brian W. *The Vanishing American: White Attitudes and U.S. Indian Policy.* Middletown, Connecticut: Wesleyan University Press, 1982.

Fixico, Donald L. *Termination and Relocation: Federal Indian Policy, 1945-1960.* Albuquerque: University of New Mexico Press, 1986.

Forbes, Jack D. *Native Americans and Nixon: Presidential Politics and Minority Self-Determination.* Los Angeles: American Indian Studies Center (UCLA), 1981.

Hagan, William T. *United States-Comanche Relations: The Reservation Years.* New Haven, Yale University Press, 1976.

Hasse, Larry J. "Termination and Assimilation: Federal Indian Policy, 1943-1961." Ph.D. diss., Washington State University, 1974.

Hertzberg, Hazel W. *The Search for an American Indian Identity: Modern Pan-Indian Movements.* Syracuse: Syracuse University Press, 1971.

Hoxie, Frederick E. *A Final Promise: The Campaign to Assimilate the Indians, 1880-1920.* Lincoln: University of Nebraska Press, 1984.

Iverson, Peter. *The Navaho Nation.* Westport, Connecticut: Greenwood Press, 1981.

Kelly, Lawrence C. *The Assault on Indian Assimilation: John Collier and the Origins of Indian Policy Reform.* Albuquerque: University of New Mexico Press, 1983.

———. *The Navajo Indians and Federal Indian Policy 1900-1935.* Tucson: University of Arizona Press, 1968.

Lawson, Michael L. *Dammed Indians: The Pick-Sloan Plan and the Missouri River Sioux.* Norman: University of Oklahoma Press, 1982.

Limerick, Patricia Nelson. *The Legacy of Conquest: The Unbroken Past of the American West.* New York: Norton, 1987.

Malone, Michael P. and Richard W. Etulain. *The American West: A Twentieth Century History.* Lincoln: University of Nebraska Press, 1989.

McDonnell, Janet A. *The Dispossession of the American Indian, 1887-1934.* Bloomington: Indiana University Press, 1989.

McNickle, D'Arcy. *Native American Tribalism: Indian Survivals and Renewals.* New York: Oxford University Press, 1973.

Nash, Gerald D. *The American West Transformed: The Impact of the Second World War.* Bloomington: Indiana University Press, 1985.

———. *The American West in the Twentieth Century: A Short History of an Urban Oasis.* Englewood Cliffs, New Jersey: Prentice-Hall, 1973.

Olson, James S. and Raymond Wilson. *Native Americans in the Twentieth Century.* Provo, Utah: Brigham Young University Press, 1984.

Owens, Louis. *Other Destinies: Understanding the American Indian Novel.* Norman: University of Oklahoma Press, 1992.

Parker, Dorothy R. *Singing an Indian Song: A Biography of D'Arcy McNickle.*

University of Nebraska Press, 1993.

Parman, Donald L. *Indians and the American West in the Twentieth Century.* Bloomington: Indiana University Press, 1994.

———. *The Navajos and the New Deal.* New Haven: Yale University Press, 1976.

Philip, Kenneth R. *John Collier's Crusade for Indian Reform 1920-1954.* Tucson: University of Arizona Press, 1977.

Prucha, Francis Paul. *The Great Father: The United States Government and the American Indians.* Vol. 2. Lincoln: University of Nebraska Press, 1984.

Sorkin, Alan. *The Urban American Indian.* Lexington: University Press of Kentucky, 1978.

Szasz, Margaret Connell. *Education and the American Indian: The Road to Self-Determination, 1928-1973.* Albuquerque: University of New Mexico Press, 1974.

Taylor, Graham D. *The New Deal and American Indian: The Administration of the Indian Reorganization Act, 1934-45.* Lincoln: University of Nebraska Press, 1980.

Trennert, Robert. *The Phoenix Indian School: Forced Assimilation in Arizona, 1891-1935.* Norman: University of Oklahoma Press, 1988.

Washburn, Wilcomb E. *The Assault on Indian Tribalism: The General Allotment Law (Dawes Act) of 1887.* Philadelphia: Lippincott, 1975.

Wilkinson, Charles F. *American Indians, Time, and the Law: Native Societies in a Modern Constitutional Democracy.* New York: Yale University Press, 1987.

Donald Parman is Professor of History at Purdue University. He is the author of Indians and the Americans West in the Twentieth Century *(1994) and* The Navajos and the New Deal *(1976).*

New Visions, Old Stories: The Emergence of a New Indian History

[U]ntil the late 1960s the history of Native-American people, if taught at all, was a component of frontier history courses in which Indians, like geological barriers, severe climatic conditions, and wild animals were obstacles to the Euro-American settlement.

R. David Edmunds

R. David Edmunds is professor of history at Indiana University-Bloomington. His many books include The Fox Wars: The Mesquakie Challenge to New France, The Shawnee Prophet, *and* The Potawatomis.

I
n February 1969, the "Professional Register" section of the *American Historical Association Newsletter* contained the first job listing for an "American Indian" history position at the University of Wisconsin at Stevens Point. Prior to 1969 no college or university in the United States had ever advertised for a historian specializing in Native-American history; indeed until the late 1960s the history of Native-American people, if taught at all, was a component of frontier history courses in which Indians, like geological barriers, severe climatic conditions, and wild animals were obstacles to the Euro-American settlement. Within this interpretation, lip service was given to Native-American participation in the fur trade, but most teachers and historians focused upon the "Indian wars." Ray Allen Billington's *Westward Expansion*, the most widely used textbook in this period, entitled a chapter describing the western tribes' defense of their homelands as "The Indian Barrier" (1).

By the early 1970s the focus of Native-American history began to change. As the consensus interpretation of American history crumbled and historians reappraised the roles of ethnic minority groups, scholars re-examined the relationship of Native Americans to the non-Indian majority and attempted to create a "new Indian history" which incorporated both history and anthropology. Unlike previ-

ous interpretations which had depicted Indian people only as foils for European activity, the new Indian history was more "Indian centered" and endeavored to present a Native-American perspective of events. Much of this activity emerged from scholars associated with the D'Arcy McNickle Center for the History of the American Indian, at the Newberry Library, in Chicago.

During the past two decades these historians have expanded our understanding of the Native-American experience. Although more traditional historians previously ignored the pre-Columbian period, scholars recently have re-evaluated Native-American societies prior to 1492 and have illustrated that they formed a rich mosaic of cultures with many similarities to contemporary societies in the Old World. Like the cultures which emerged beside the Tigris and Euphrates, the Nile, or the Ganges, the Adena, Hopewell, and Mississippian people of the American interior also were riverine societies which rose, flourished, and eventually declined. Governed by a theocracy, Cahokia, a nascent Mississippian city-state opposite modern St. Louis, boasted a population of over 10,000 in 1100 A.D. Its markets offered products from a region encompassed by the Appalachians, the Great Lakes, the Rocky Mountains, and the Gulf of Mexico. Alvin M. Josephy Jr.'s *America in 1492* features a series of essays surveying preolumbian societies, while Francis ennning's interesting but controversial *The ounders of America* attempts to investigate the relationships between the pro-olumbian societies and historic tribes in the United States. Lynda N. Shaffer's *ative Americans Before 1492* surveys the moundbuilding cultures of the eastern nited States, and offers a concise, readble synopsis designed for a broad, general audience (2).

During the past two decades historins have reassessed their estimates of the re-Columbian populations which comrised these societies. Prior to 1970 most xtbooks stated that before European conct, the Indian population of the United tates numbered somewhere between one nd one-half million people. More recntly, scholars such as Russell Thornton *American Indian Holocaust and Survival*) nd Henry Dobyns (*Their Numbers Beome Thinned*) have illustrated that the opulation was considerably larger, and ow most historians believe that Native mericans numbered at least seven milon. The new assessments are particurly significant, since Charles Hudson as shown that Spanish explorers such as ernando de Soto encountered populous,

complex Mississippian societies in the Southeast as late as 1540-1541, but when Europeans settled permanently along the Atlantic coast in the early-seventeenth century, they encountered far fewer Indians and found the ceremonial centers of the moundbuilders abandoned (3).

Like Cahokia, some of these population centers had declined prior to 1500, but the subsequent destruction of the Mississippians and other Native-American populations was intensified by the introduction of Old World pathogens. Isolated in the Americas, Indian people had developed no natural immunities to the epidemics that plagued Africa and Eurasia, and when these diseases were introduced into the western hemisphere, Native Americans died by the millions. Both Thornton and Dobyns discuss this population decline, but David Stannard's *American Holocaust* examines the combined impact of disease, European colonial policy, and the dissolution of the contemporary native societies. Alfred Crosby also discusses these events in *The Columbian Exchange* and provides a fascinating analysis of how the transmission of plants (especially food crops) and animals between the eastern and western hemispheres altered the sub-

sequent history of both regions (4).

The initial meetings between Indians and Englishmen on the Atlantic coast produced tensions which changed both societies. Historians have illustrated that both sides interpreted the other through a preconceived set of images, and that English colonists attempted to fit Native Americans into a cultural framework imported from Europe. During the 1960s Roy Harvey Pearce analyzed British endeavors to integrate Indians intellectually into European concepts of an "ordered" universe, while more recently James Axtell has illustrated that both sides soon replaced favorable assessments with more negative appraisals. Axtell asserts that Indian reassessments of Europeans resulted from Indian exposure to new diseases and European expansion, while the British adopted negative stereotypes of Native Americans to facilitate their imperialism (5). In a similar vein, Bernard Sheehan argues in *Savagism and Civility* that despite Native-American hospitality, colonists in Virginia were unable to transcend their subscription to stereotypes of "ignoble savages." Focusing upon a later period, James Rawls illustrates that during the nineteenth century Anglo-American settlers in Califor-

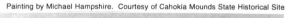

Painting by Michael Hampshire. Courtesy of Cahokia Mounds State Historical Site

Cahokia market. Markets at Cahokia contained products from throughout the eastern two-thirds of the modern United States.

nia continued to manipulate the public image of Native Americans to serve their own political and economic purposes, while Robert Berkhofer's *The White Man's Indian* provides an excellent survey of how changing images of Native Americans have always influenced American science, literature, art, and Indian policy (6).

Modern studies of the American frontier indicate that Native Americans rarely fit such stereotyped images. Although Frederick Jackson Turner once described the frontier as "the meeting point between savagery and civilization," Francis Jenning's *The Invasion of America* points out that such concepts as "savagery" and "civilization" are ethnocentric terms rarely applied equally to both sides (7). More recently, historians such as Richard White, John Mack Farragher, and Daniel Usner have illustrated that until the middle decades of the nineteenth century, the American frontier was a region of "inclusion" rather than "exclusion," and that Native-American, European, and African-American populations and cultures blended together to form multi-cultural societies in which the parameters of ethnic and cultural identity overlapped and were indistinct. In *The Middle Ground*, White

argues that French and Indian peoples in the Great Lakes region created a way of life where European and Indian worlds "melted at the edges and merged" and where it became unclear "whether a particular practice or way of doing things was French or Indian." These mixed-blood, bicultural societies dominated commerce in the Great Lakes and upper Mississippi Valley during the eighteenth and early-nineteenth centuries, and mixed-blood leaders served as important intermediaries between less acculturated tribal communities and European and American governments. Usner's *Indians, Settlers, and Slaves in a Frontier Exchange Economy* illustrates that multi-ethnic societies in the South combined subsistence and barter economies to create a flexible socio-economic environment whose definitions of race and ethnicity were as fluid as its trading patterns. The emergence of plantation agriculture markedly altered this flexibility however, eventually fostering more social stratification and more rigid definitions of race. Richard White's *The Roots of Dependency* traces these changes among the Choctaws and other tribes and analyzes the mechanisms utilized by mixed-blood Choctaw planters to

legitimize their usurpation of leadership Farragher's *Daniel Boone* provides an interesting biographical study of the frontier man, but also illustrates the striking similarities in economic activity, material culture, and gender roles between the Shawnees and white settlers in Kentucky(8

During the nineteenth century, as other Native Americans found themselves overwhelmed by the changes swirling around them, many sought a religious deliverance from the political, social, and economic problems that plagued their communities In *The Death and Rebirth of the Seneca*, model of ethnohistorical inquiry, Anthony F. C. Wallace has traced the decline of the Seneca from a position of political and military dominance over the western Algonquian tribes during the middle-eighteenth century, to the socio-economic dependency of the reservation system in 1800. Describing the Seneca enclaves as "slums in the wilderness," he illustrates how a social pathology of alcoholism, fear of witchcraft, and violence gave rise, in 1799, to a revitalization movement led by the Seneca Prophet, Handsome Lake. Wallace argues that Handsome Lake's new religion provided an effective moral sanction for the Senecas' adaptation to

Community activities. Containing eighty earthen mounds and a population over 10,000, Cahokia was a nascent Mississippian city-state that flourished opposite mode St. Louis in 1100A.D.

new world. By selectively adopting some European cultural patterns, the Senecas retained many facets of their own culture and strengthened their identity and self-respect as Indians (9).

Other revitalization movements were less successful. In *The Shawnee Prophet* and *Tecumseh and the Quest for Indian Leadership*, R. David Edmunds indicates that political fragmentation and socio-economic decline among the Shawnees produced a more militant response. Denouncing Americans as the "spawn of the serpent" (the children of the evil spirit), Tenskwatawa, or the Shawnee Prophet, expounded a doctrine urging his followers to disassociate themselves from their white neighbors and to relinquish many aspects of European culture. Edmunds argues that the Prophet's religious doctrines provided the basis for Tecumseh's efforts to unify politically the tribes in the period before the War of 1812. More recently, Gregory Dowd's *A Spirited Resistance* describes Tecumseh's proposed confederacy as the culmination of pan-tribal alliances which had existed for several decades (10). Joel Martin's *Sacred Revolt* examines similar revitalization movements among the Creeks, while Joseph Herring's *Kennekuk: The Kickapoo Prophet* analyzes a less militant revitalization movement among the Kickapoos in Illinois and Kansas during the 1830s (11). Obviously, the revitalization movements reached their tragic finale in the Ghost Dance, which spread out of the Great Basin and onto the plains in 1890. James Mooney's *The Ghost Dance*, compiled and written shortly after the massacre at Wounded Knee, remains the standard and most authoritative account of Wovoka and his religion, while

Robert Utley's *The Last Days of the Sioux Nation* provides an excellent account of the Lakotas' involvement in the faith. More recently, Jensen, Paul, and Carter's *Eyewitness at Wounded Knee* provides a dramatic, pictorial account of these tragic circumstances (12).

While many Lakota sought a religious deliverance through the mysticism of the Ghost Dance, their children were being

Courtesy of the Tippecanoe County Historical Society

The frock coat and turban of Iowa, a Potawatomi from Wabash, reflects the acculturation typical of many Potawatomi métis.

enrolled, both voluntarily and otherwise, in white men's schools. Intent upon assimilating Native Americans into the Anglo-American mainstream, reformers urged that Indian children be separated from the "savagery" of their families and sent to boarding schools where they could be imbued with "education" and those cultural values deemed necessary for "civi-

lization." As James Axtell and other historians have illustrated this practice emerged during the colonial period, but it reached its height between 1885 and 1930 (13).

Autobiographical accounts such as Francis La Flesche's *The Middle Five*, or Luther Standing Bear's *My People the Sioux* provide insights into the lives of individual Indian students, but recently scholars have assembled and analyzed accounts from large numbers of students, searching for patterns of experience which students shared. Michael Coleman's *American Indian Children at School, 1850-1930* examines autobiographies and reminiscences of over one hundred Indians and illustrates that students seemed rather ambivalent about their boarding school experiences. Most were not surprised that school administrators relied upon student labor for the everyday maintenance of the institutions, and although most students underwent an initial period of homesickness and adjustment, many "willingly accepted useful values, knowledge, and skills of an alien culture." Coleman's volume contains many interesting vignettes illustrating the students' experiences, and his bibliography offers a rich opportunity for additional investigation of this subject (14).

In contrast to Coleman's examination of student experiences at a broad spectrum of institutions, Tsianina Lomawaima's *They Called It Prairie Light: The Story of Chilocco Indian School* provides an in-depth analysis of the experiences of students at Chilocco, a school in northern Oklahoma which emphasized agricultural and vocational education. Based upon careful research and extensive interviews of Chilocco alumni,

Lomawaima indicates that students often formed tribal cliques, and that divisions emerged between students from eastern and western Oklahoma. Like many of the students in Coleman's study, the Chilocco alumni often disliked the regimentation of school life, but they also retained some favorable memories of their Chilocco enrollment. Few, however, enrolled their own children at the institution. Devon Mihesuah's *Cultivating the Rosebuds* provides a good account of the Cherokee Female Seminary, a tribally administered institution modeled after Mount Holyoke College which enrolled primarily mixed-blood students, while Robert Trennert's *The Phoenix Indian School* indicates that this Arizona institution, although dedicated to assimilation, generally failed in its mission and was vulnerable to criticism by reformers during the New Deal era (15). In addition, two films also provide valuable insights into the boarding school experience. "In the White Man's Image," a television documentary produced as part of "The American Experience" critically examines the career of Richard Pratt and the establishment of Carlisle Indian School, while "Where The Spirit Lives" provides a dramatic, if heart-rending dramatization of student experiences in a Canadian boarding school during the 1920s (16).

Since the 1960s, Native Americans in growing numbers have added a new "Indian voice" to the analysis of Native-American history, and the recent Indian commentary has engendered considerable discussion. During the early 1970s Vine Deloria Jr. took non-Indian scholars, politicians, and theologians to task, and although Deloria's comments were not directed specifically at historians, his witty, if sometimes acerbic,

commentary caused many historians and anthropologists to re-examine their motives and methodology (17). More recently, other Indian historians have argued that both the American Revolution and the Constitution were markedly influenced by Native-American concepts of politics and representative government; and although many academic scholars have disagreed, the Native-American assertions have attracted the attention of the general public, including influential members of Congress (18).

Perhaps the most cogent plea for the inclusion of a new Native-American perspective in the writing of Native-American history comes from Donald A. Grinde, a Yamasee historian and a member of the

Courtesy of the Tippecanoe County Historical Society

Jean Baptist Brouillette, a prominent Miami métis, was a prosperous entrepreneur in Indiana during the 1830s.

history faculty at California Polytechnic State University, at San Luis Obispo. In "Teaching American Indian History: A Native American Voice," Grinde argues that the very structure of American history incorporates a series of Euro-American assumptions about change and "progress" in the western hemisphere that imprisons the history of Native-American people within parameters often alien to Native-American cultures. Reflecting perspectives similar to those included in the discussion of African-American or women's history in Peter Novick's *That Noble Dream*, Grinde argues that "the image of the American Indian in history, literature, and art has been largely an 'invented' tradition external to the American Indian experience." Grinde points out that Native-American historians have never championed "essentialism" (that only scholars of Native-American descent can write Native-American history), but that many Indian historians believe that current scholarship often excludes an authentic Native-American voice, and that many non-Indian scholars continue to produce an "American-Indian history" that is "just the history of Indian-white relations (and the colonial conquest perspective at that), or is the history of governmental bureaucracies that have dealt with American Indians." Grinde suggests that historians immerse themselves in Native-American language and culture ("how far, for example, [would] a graduate student in French history . . . get without a knowledge of French and the [opportunity] to go to France to pursue scholarly research as well as to gain an understanding of French life") and includes a good discussion of essays and books which are sensitive to a

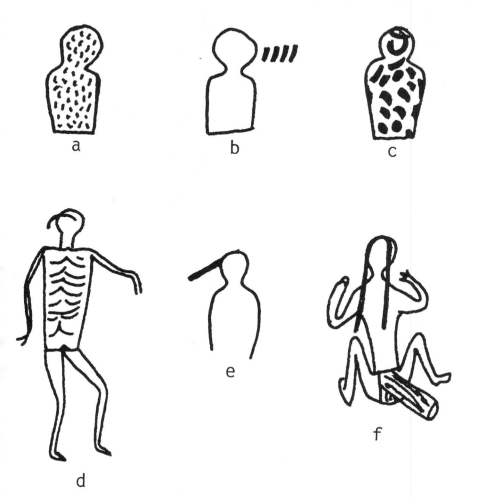

Sioux pictographs from Winter Counts: a) measles; b) whooping cough; c) smallpox; d) starvation; e) dropsy; and f) cholera.

Native-American perspective. Although some historians might challenge some of Grinde's recommendations, almost all would agree with his conclusion that "a critical and potent Native voice . . . will enrich the multivocality of American history and widen our perspectives" (19). ❑

Endnotes

1. *American Historical Association Newsletter* 7 (February, 1969), 17; Ray Allen Billington, *Westward Expansion: A History of the American Frontier* (New York: Macmillan, 1960), 653-72, and passim. In this essay the author has used the terms "Native American" and "Indian" interchangeably. Although "Native American" currently is utilized by academics, "Indian" is used more often within the reservation communities.

2. Alvin M. Josephy Jr., ed., *America in 1492: The World of the Indian Peoples Before the Arrival of Columbus* (New York: Alfred A. Knopf, 1992); Francis Jennings, *The Founders of America* (New York: W.W. Norton, 1993); and Lynda Norene Shaffer, *Native Americans Before 1492: The Moundbuilding Centers of the Eastern Woodlands* (Armonk, N.Y.: M. E. Sharpe, 1992).

3. Russell Thornton, *American Indian Holocaust and Survival: A Population History Since 1492* (Norman: University of Oklahoma Press, 1987); Henry Dobyns, *Their Numbers Be-come Thinned* (Knoxville: University of Tennessee Press, 1973); and Charles Hudson and Carmen Chaves Tesser, eds., *The Forgotten Centuries: Indians and Europeans in the American South, 1521-1704* (Athens: University of Georgia Press, 1994).

4. Thornton, *American Indian Holocaust and Survival*; Dobyns, *Their Numbers Become Thinned*; and Alfred Crosby, *The Columbian Exchange: Biological and Cultural Consequences of 1492* (Westport, Conn.: Greenwood Press, 1971).

5. Roy Harvey Pearce, *Savagism and Civilization: A Study of the Indian and the American Mind* (Baltimore: Johns Hopkins Press, 1967); James Axtell, "Imagining the Other: First Encounters in North America," in Axtell, *Beyond 1492: Encounters in Colonial America* (New York: Oxford University Press, 1992). Also see essays by Axtell in his *The European and the Indian: Essays in the Ethnohistory of Colonial North America* (New York: Oxford University Press, 1981); and in his *After Columbus: Essays in the Ethnohistory of Colonial America* (New York: Oxford University Press, 1988).

6. Bernard Sheehan, *Savagism and Civility: Indians and Englishmen in Colonial Virginia* (Cambridge: Cambridge University Press, 1980); James Rawls, *The Indians of California: The Changing Image* (Norman: University of Oklahoma Press, 1984); and Robert Berkhofer, *The White Man's Indian: Images of the American Indian from Columbus to the Present* (New York: Alfred A. Knopf, 1978).

7. Frederick Jackson Turner, "The Significance of the Frontier in American History," in George Rogers Taylor, ed., *The Turner Thesis: Concerning the Role of the Frontier in American History* rev. ed. (Boston: D. C. Heath, 1956), 2; and Frances Jennings, *The Invasion of America* (New York: Norton, 1975).

8. Richard White, *The Middle Ground: Indians, Empires, and Republics in*

the Great Lakes Region, 1650-1815 (Cambridge: Cambridge University Press, 1991); Daniel Usner, *Indians, Settlers, and Slaves in a Frontier Exchange Economy: The Lower Mississippi Valley Before 1783* (Chapel Hill: University of North Carolina Press, 1992); Richard White, *The Roots of Dependency: Subsistence, Environment, and Social Change Among the Choctaws, Pawnees, and Navajos* (Lincoln: University of Nebraska Press, 1983); and John Mack Farragher, *Daniel Boone: The Life and Times of an American Pioneer* (New York: Henry Holt, 1992).

9. Anthony F. C. Wallace, *The Death and Rebirth of the Seneca* (New York: Alfred A. Knopf, 1970).

10. R. David Edmunds, *The Shawnee Prophet* (Lincoln: University of Nebraska Press, 1983); R. David Edmunds, *Tecumseh and the Quest for Indian Leadership* (Boston: Little, Brown, 1984); and Gregory Dowd, *A Spirited Resistance: The North American Indian Struggle for Unity, 1745-1815* (Baltimore: Johns Hopkins Press, 1992).

11. Joel Martin, *Sacred Revolt: The Muskogee Struggle for a New World* (Boston: Beacon Press, 1991); and Joseph B. Herring, *Kennekuk, the Kickapoo Prophet* (Lawrence: University Press of Kansas, 1988).

12. James Mooney, *The Ghost Dance Religion and the Sioux Outbreak of 1890, Fourteenth Annual Report of the Bureau of American Ethnology* (Washington: U. S. Government Printing Office, 1896); Robert M. Utley, *The Last Days of the Sioux Nation* (New Haven: Yale University Press, 1963); and Richard E. Jensen, R. Eli Paul, and John E. Carter, *Eyewitness at Wounded Knee* (Lincoln: University of Nebraska Press, 1991).

13. James Axtell, "Dr. Wheelock's Little Red School House," in Axtell, ed., *The European and the Indian*, 87-109.

14. Francis La Flesche, *The Middle Five: Indian Schoolboys of the Omaha Tribe*

(Madison: University of Wisconsin Press, 1963); Luther Standing Bear, *My People the Sioux* (Lincoln: University of Nebraska Press, 1975); and Michael C. Coleman, *American Indian Children at School, 1850-1930* (Jackson: University Press of Mississippi, 1993), 194-5.

15. K. Tsianina Lomawaima, *They Called it Prairie Light: The Story of Chilocco Indian School* (Lincoln: University of Nebraska Press, 1994); and Devon A. Mihesuah, *Cultivating the Rosebuds: The Education of Women at the Cherokee Female Seminary, 1851-1909* (Urbana: University of Illinois Press, 1993); and Robert A. Trennert, *The Phoenix Indian School: Forced Assimilation in Arizona, 1891-1935* (Norman: University of Oklahoma Press, 1988).

16. "In the White Man's Image," produced for *The American Experience* (PBS) by Matthew Jones, 1992; "Where the Spirit Lives," produced for *American Playhouse* by Heather Golden, Eric Jordan, and Mary Young Leckie, (Amazing Spirit Productions Ltd.), 1989.

17. Vine Deloria Jr., *Custer Died for Your Sins: An Indian Manifesto* (New York: Macmillan, 1969); and Deloria, *God is Red* (New York: Grosset and Dunlap, 1973).

18. Donald A. Grinde, Jr. and Bruce E. Johansen, *Exemplar of Liberty: Native America and the Evolution of Democracy* (Los Angeles: University of California Regents and the UCLA American Indian Studies Center, 1991); and Oren Lyons and John Mohawk, eds., *Exiled in the Land of the Free: Democracy, Indian Nations, and the U.S. Constitution* (Santa Fe: Clear Light Publishers, 1992).

19. Donald A. Grinde Jr., "Teaching American Indian History: A Native American Voice," *Perspectives* 32 (September 1994): 1, 11-6; Peter Novick, *That Noble Dream: The "Objectivity Question" and the American Historical Profession* (Cambridge: Cambridge University Press, 1988).

Native-American Women in History

Nancy Shoemaker

Ironically, Native-American women figure prominently in traditional narratives of American history, but until recently women's experiences and perspectives have been largely excluded from research in Native-American history. Ask any schoolchild to name famous Native Americans from before 1850, and most likely you will hear of Pocahontas and Sacagawea. But pick up any book surveying American-Indian history, white-Indian relations in the United States, or the history of a particular tribe, and there will be little mention of either specific women or of women in general.

What exactly did Pocahontas and Sacagawea do to earn themselves a place in the pantheon of American-history heroines? Pocahontas was the daughter of the powerful Indian leader Powhatan, whose confederacy of different Indian nations in the Virginia region presented a significant challenge to the English colonists who settled at Jamestown in 1607. Pocahontas is remembered primarily for having saved Captain John Smith's life, an act which was probably part of a native captivity and adoption ritual but which endured in the narrative of American history because it implies that the conquered gladly assisted in their own conquest. Sacagawea became a historical figure for the same reason. As interpreter and guide to Meriwether Lewis and William Clark in their explorations of the Louisiana Purchase from 1804-1806,

Sacagawea opened up the West to American settlement. At least that is how she has often been pictured in American popular culture, one arm extended, graciously directing Lewis and Clark to a landscape green with the promise of wealth. Although one Indian man, Squanto, was cast in that same role in the story of Pilgrim

In the spirit of this uniting of two worlds and two peoples, Pocahontas's and Sacagawea's lives are often distorted to make a better story.

settlement of New England, Indian women seemed to fit this role much better, for the continents were themselves often depicted on maps and in promotional literature as gendered: the woman America, plump and naked except for a few leaves, embraced the iron-clad European conquistador, and the "New World" and "Old World" melded into one.

In the spirit of this uniting of two worlds and two peoples, Pocahontas's and Sacagawea's lives are often distorted to

make a better story. Most people trying to recall who Pocahontas was, want to marry her off to John Smith. In reality, she married another English colonist, John Rolfe, who was instrumental in making tobacco the enormously profitable mainstay of the Chesapeake economy. Similarly, Sacagawea, in a movie from the 1950s starring Donna Reed, falls tragically in love with William Clark, but alas, must give him up because she is an Indian, and he is engaged to marry a white woman. Sacagawea's own story, as recounted in the journals of Lewis and Clark, seems much more tragic. A Shoshoni woman who as a girl had been captured by another Indian tribe, she was one of at least two wives of an abusive French fur trader named Charbonneau, the official guide hired by the exploring party. Popular renditions of these two women's lives get the details wrong, but the underlying reality may not have been all that different. Both Pocahontas and Sacagawea indeed married white men, and for that reason were well-placed to mediate the cultural and economic exchanges between Indians and Euro-Americans. Yet, as historian Clara Sue Kidwell has observed, it is difficult to discern Pocahontas's and Sacagawea's own motives, loyalties, and understandings of the historical events in which they participated.

It is equally difficult to know to what extent the histories of Pocahontas and

Sacagawea can be generalized to shed light on Indian women's experiences in general. In other times and places, Indian women did become important go-betweens in the Indian and Euro-American cross cultural exchange. Sylvia Van Kirk's book, *Many Tender Ties*, a history of women in the beaver fur trade in Canada, showed how crucial Indian women were to the success of the fur trade in its early years. Women processed furs, prepared foods such as pemmican (dried meat mixed with berries), and served as interpreters. And through their marital and sexual relationships with French and British fur traders, they linked their communities to Europeans in ways that both enhanced and complicated economic exchanges and political alliances. In later periods, Indian women continued to be important bicultural mediators, but may have felt increasingly divided by the competing interests of their own people and Euro-Americans. The Paiute woman Sarah Winnemucca, for instance, served as a scout and interpreter for the United States, but later wrote her autobiography and made speaking tours to bring attention to the injustices that had been committed against her people.

Sarah Winnemucca cannot be considered any more representative than Pocahontas or Sacagawea, but currently much of what historians know about Indian women's lives in the past comes from the stories of individual women. Especially useful are autobiographies. Most of these autobiographies of

Indian women were dual-authored, either with anthropologists or with a popular, mainstream writer. Whether the autobiography was part of an anthropologist's attempt to construct a life history that would also inform readers about culture, as in the case of Nancy Lurie's *Mountain Wolf Woman*, or a popular writer's nostalgic rendering of how Indian life used to be, as in Frank Linderman's *Pretty-Shield*, autobiographies can be useful documents for historians interested in understanding the changes in women's lives from their own perspective. Also, some autobiographies, *Pretty-Shield* and Gilbert Wilson's *Waheenee* for example, were originally

Pocahontas, daughter of a powerful Indian leader, in England, 1616.

published with a children's readership in mind, which means that they are very accessible to students.

The production of Indian women's autobiographies continues today. Wilma Mankiller, formerly principal chief of the Cherokee Nation, recently wrote an autobiography. And, Mary Crow Dog (now, Mary Brave Bird) has published two accounts of her life. Her *Lakota Woman* provides a glimpse into women's participation in the restless political struggles of the 1960s and 1970s, focusing on the American Indian Movement and the 1973 militant takeover of the hamlet of Wounded Knee, South Dakota. Despite the tremendous importance of women's autobiographies, historians still face the difficulty of connecting individual experience to the broader issues of native women's changing roles and attitudes.

Other than autobiographies, most of the documents available to historians were written by white men: explorers, government agents, and missionaries. And although these Euro-American recorders of Indian cultures often included some commentary on Indian women, their observations were loaded with assumptions and expectations about what they thought Indians and women were supposed to be. Euro-American accounts of Indian cultures were especially critical of native women's work. Indian women either seemed to work too much or they did work which in Euro-American societies was defined as men's work. At the time of European contact, Indian women in tribes east of the Mississippi were largely responsible for the agricultural fieldwork. They grew the corn, squash, and beans. On the northwest coast, Indian women were active traders, much too shrewd and aggressive than their Euro-American trading partners wanted them to be. And throughout native America, women did much of the carrying. They brought wood and water into the village or camp, and in the case of Plains Indian women had charge of dismantling, packing, transporting, and re-erecting tipis. Euro-American men criticized Indian men for abusing "their women" by treating them like "squaw drudges" or "beasts of burden," a stereotype of Indian women much in contrast with the romanticized, "Indian princess"

portrayals of Pocahontas and Sacagawea.

Euro-American descriptions of Indian politics imposed biases on the documentary record of a different nature. In the often detailed transcripts of Indian councils, why were women rarely mentioned? Is it because they were not there? Or, is it because Euro-American observers of the council did not notice they were there or did not think their presence was worth mentioning? In those cases where women did make their presence known in the political arena, Euro-Americans exaggerated women's political power and derided certain tribes, particularly the Iroquois, for being "petticoat governments" or "matriarchates," disorderly societies in which women ruled over men. While it is true

that among the Iroquois clan mothers had the right to designate a chief's successor and remove or "dehorn" chiefs from office, Iroquois women did not rule over men.

Anthropologists and historians, who must rely greatly on a documentary record which for the most part excludes native women's voices, have been especially suspicious of how Euro-American descriptions of native societies portray them as having separate spheres: a public, male sphere of politics, diplomacy, war, and trade; and a private or domestic female sphere of childbearing, child rearing, food processing, and household management. In reading the historical record, one would learn that women's labor usually took place within the proximity of the village or

Seneca women in cornfields.

camp. While tending to their children, women worked in nearby cornfields or gathered nuts, berries, and other wild foods. They distributed food within the household, and were often said to own the houses. Men's work usually involved dealing with outsiders, and men were most often, but not always, the diplomats, traders, and warriors. Indian women do appear to have been most active in a private or domestic sphere, while men seemed to control the public sphere. But do the documents give this impression of gendered public and private space because Euro-American men imposed their own preferences about distinct male and female worlds on what they saw, heard, and noticed?

Much of the research in Indian women's history thus far has challenged the existence of public/male and private/female spheres in Indian societies by looking for Indian women in the public space and reconstructing a public role for them. Among different tribes in different time periods, there were some women chiefs, some women who spoke in council, some women who went to war, and some women who participated actively in trade with Euro-Americans. However, this literature produced by historians could just as easily be misrepresenting Indian women's experience in its eagerness to find Indian women in places which Euro-Americans defined as the locus of power. One could just as easily criticize the model of male/ public and female/private by asking whether power resided only in the public sphere. Given the significance of the family, or clan, in native political systems, the private or domestic sphere may have been an important site for discussion and decision making about issues such as whether

their people should go to war, move, or make alliances with other nations. In the Iroquois example, the political duties of clan mothers originated in the matrilineal clan structure of Iroquois politics, in which chiefs represented their clans in council. Although few tribes

Nevada Historical Society

Sarah Winnemucca, a Paiute, served as a scout and interpreter for the United States.

had such institutionalized political roles for women, women's significance within the family must have allocated them some influence on decisions affecting the larger community.

Instead of simply highlighting instances

in which native women appeared in a public sphere, historians of Indian women's history and gender history are now bringing a more complex array of questions to their research. Much of this research has focused on the effects of Euro-American contact. Thus, historians researching United States Indian policy have shown how many government programs promoting Indian assimilation saw gender roles as crucially important to transforming Indian cultures. Indian women and men variously responded to these programs, sometimes with open resistance, sometimes by diverting the intent of the policies, and sometimes by selectively accepting certain aspects of the policies to fit more closely their traditional ideas about gender. The impact of missionization on Indian women is similarly being reconsidered. Historians used to believe that Indian women were more likely than men to reject Christianity because missionaries also sought to restructure native families to fit a nuclear, patriarchal model. However, historians are now acknowledging the diversity of women's responses to Christian missions and acknowledge that many Indian women did choose to become Christian. Many even became leaders of women's church groups, and thus helped shape how Christianity became incorporated in native communities.

Few historians have conducted research upon Indian women's history in the twentieth century, even though the political and economic resurgence of native communities in recent decades raises interesting questions about women's participation in tribal government, the post-World War II migration to cities, and economic transitions from farming and ranching to wage labor. In the twentieth

Cherokee Nation Photo by Sammy Still

Wilma Mankiller, former chief of the Cherokee Nation, September 1994.

kind of life to pursue. While the growing interest in American-Indian women's history will make summarizing that history increasingly difficult, it will also bring us closer to understanding what Pocahontas and Sacagawea were really all about. ❏

Bibliography

Albers, Patricia and Beatrice Medicine. *The Hidden Half: Studies of Plains Indian Women.* Lanham, Md.: University Press of America, 1983.

Bataille, Gretchen M. and Kathleen Mullen Sands. *American Indian Women: Telling Their Lives.* Lincoln: University of Nebraska Press, 1984.

Canfield, Gae Whitney. *Sarah Winnemucca of the Northern Paiutes.* Norman: University of Oklahoma Press, 1983.

Crow Dog, Mary, with Richard Erdoes. *Lakota Woman.* New York: Harper Collins, 1990.

Kidwell, Clara Sue. "Indian Women as Cultural Mediators." *Ethnohistory* 39 (Spring 1992): 97-107.

Linderman, Frank B. *Pretty-Shield: Medicine Woman of the Crows.* Lincoln: University of Nebraska Press, 1932.

Lurie, Nancy Oestreich. *Mountain Wolf Woman: Sister of Crashing Thunder, The Autobiography of a Winnebago Indian.* Ann Arbor: University of Michigan Press, 1985.

Mankiller, Wilma and Michael Wallis. *Mankiller: A Chief and Her People.* New York: St. Martin's Press, 1993.

Spittal, W.G. *Iroquois Women: An Anthology.* Ohsweken, Ontario: Iroqrafts, 1990.

Van Kirk, Sylvia. *Many Tender Ties: Women in Fur-Trade Society, 1670-1870.* Norman: University of Oklahoma Press, 1980.

Wilson, Gilbert L. *Waheenee.* Lincoln: University of Nebraska Press, 1981.

Nancy Shoemaker teaches history at the State University of New York at Plattsburgh and is the editor of Negotiators of Change: Historical Perspectives on Native American Women *(New York: Routledge, 1995).*

century, Indian women have been tribal chiefs, political activists, housewives, weavers, educators, provisioners of health care and social services on reservations and in urban communities, nuns, novelists, artists, and ranchers. Of course, they have also been mothers, daughters, wives, grandmothers, and aunts.

Scholars have long recognized the great diversity in the histories of American-Indian tribes and the impossibility of generalizing about Navajos and Cherokees, Menominees and Lakotas. Gender adds another dimension to this diversity. Within tribes, the experiences of men and women differed. Moreover, women within tribal groups may also have had different experiences based on their age, family background, religion, educational and work experiences, and choices they have made about where to live and what

American-Indian Identities
in the Twentieth Century

Wade Davies
and Peter Iverson

When the Navajo poet LuciTapahonso traveled to France, she kept meeting people "who thought I was 'neat'—being a 'real' Indian." They "asked all kinds of questions and wanted to learn Navajo." "It was weird," she remembered, "to be a 'real' Indian." She had grown accustomed to being "just regular, one of the bunch, laughing with relatives and friends, mixing Navajo and English. We were always telling jokes about cowboys, computer warriors and stuff" (1).

All Americans have an immediate image of a "real" Indian. For most of us, the image of Native Americans is based on misrepresentation—in film, advertisements, novels, or curio shops. When Standing Rock Sioux author Vine Deloria, Jr. wrote his classic "Indian manifesto," *Custer Died For Your Sins*, he began it with a chapter on "Indians Today, the Real and the Unreal." "People can just tell by looking at us," Deloria observed, "what we want, what should be done to help us, how we feel, and what a 'real' Indian is really like." After all, he said, "Understanding Indians is not an esoteric art. All it takes is a trip through Arizona or New Mexico, watching a documentary on TV, having known one in the service, or having read a popular book on them" (2).

In the quarter of a century since the publication of *Custer Died For Your Sins*, as Luci Tapahonso reminds us, things may not have improved much. We have moved from lampoons to laments. The most common depictions of Indians today are

---

For most of us, the image of Native Americans is based on misrepresentation—in film, advertisements, novels, or curio shops.

---

of a defeated people whose time has come and gone. Beginning with Dee Brown's *Bury My Heart at Wounded Knee*, a book of the 1960s with enduring influence, to Kevin Costner's *Dances With Wolves*, to Costner's new television series on Native American dispossession, *500 Nations*, contemporary efforts echo a theme raised earlier in the century by James Fraser's statue, "The End of the Trail."

Although more recent attempts to depict Indians are, no doubt, well meaning,

they generally contain at least two fatal flaws. They tend to portray the best years of Indian life as being in the nineteenth century or before. And they usually show Indians only in conjunction with non-Indian aggressions. If the conventional wisdom today has become far more critical of dispossession, it has also focused on the non-Indians as the actors, the winners; Indians inevitably become the acted upon, the losers. Moreover, Indians appear when they figure in a kind of frontier melodrama—which ends tragically.

Indian history, to be sure, properly encompasses the themes of loss and of tragedy. Even so, to use the late-nineteenth century as an example, our story should be more than depicting Custer's defeat as the zenith of Indian experience and the senseless slaughter at Wounded Knee as its nadir. Not all Native Americans fought all white people all the time. The significance of Native-American history cannot be evaluated solely in terms of conflicts with non-Indians. While some Indian communities suffered terrible losses, others did not fight at all. Others still added lands to their domain. Well into the second decade of the twentieth century, new Indian land bases were being established.

Arizona provides a case in point. At

tention is appropriately paid to Geronimo and to the Long Walk of the Navajos. And yet, what about what happened to the Navajos after they returned home following the Treaty of 1868? What about the Hopis, who did not fight the American soldiers? What about the Tohono O'odham, whose "big reservation" was not created until the time of the first world war? What of new reservations, such as Fort McDowell or Ak Chin, not formed until the twentieth century? Such examples underline the fact that Indian history contains gain as well as loss, new beginnings as well as endings.

Nonetheless, in too many of our his-tory books and in the popular imagination, Indians disappear after 1890, perhaps to surface to play a bit part in the Troubled 1960s. The twentieth century, however, reveals a more complicated story. The reality of Indian life is that it is an ongoing series of chapters, with some of the most interesting and important yet to be written. There are more Indians today than there were one hundred years ago. Although some Native languages have been lost, many are still spoken. Although some Native land has been wrested from Indian control, much of the Indian land base remains. Although Indian peoples continue to struggle with poverty, there have been signs of significant economic revitalization. Moreover, Indian poets, painters, novelists, historians, and others are making vital contributions not only to our understanding of Indian individuals and communities, but to our appreciation of the connections between Native Americans and other Americans.

"Real" Indians today work in the same jobs, play the same sports, and hear the same programs and advertisements on the radio as other Americans. They are teachers, ranchers, lawyers, politicians; adults may be devoted to the community high school basketball team while younger folks wear the latest jerseys of the Dallas Cow-

These students from the Lutheran mission school at San Carlos, Arizona, in the 1920s appreciated both ranching and baseball.

boys. Television, pickups, and cars, greater access to colleges and universities, and a significant number of people living off reservations have contributed to a decline in the isolation and insularity which once characterized Indian life. At the same time, despite all the efforts to assimilate Indians into American culture, Native peoples have retained their own identities.

We say identities in the plural because Native Americans come from many cultural backgrounds that make them distinct from each other as well as from non-Indians. But the common grouping of all indigenous Americans as one racial group, whether in federal and state policy or in the popular imagination, has contributed to an Indian identity in conjunction with a tribal identity. One may be thus from a particular local community within a reservation or from a community in an off-reservation town or city, from a tribe or nation, and from a particular region of Native North America. One may be the child of parents from the same tribe or nation, from different tribes or nations, or have one parent who is not an Indian at all. As the twentieth century has progressed, the overall Native-American population has increased. So, too have the numbers of Indians who live in major urban areas where one may be identified initially as an Indian rather than as a member of a specific group of Native Americans.

Other Americans tend to allow for continuity and change in their own families and within the larger society, yet somehow are less flexible in permitting the same for Indians. We see ourselves as no less "real" Americans than Benjamin Franklin or Abraham Lincoln,

even if our housing, transportation, clothing, or entertainment may not be the same. In the same sense, Indians today may live in different homes, use different means of travel, wear different clothes, or be amused by other forms of entertainment than their ancestors. Or they may continue to use some elements of the culture of an earlier

Courtesy of the Heard Museum, Phoenix

Laguna Pueblo woman baking bread. As in all cultures, food is an important ingredient in the workings of Indian community life.

time. All cultures change; Indians never had but one culture and their cultures have always been evolving.

Before the arrival of Europeans, most Native groups associated themselves with their immediate and extended families

and extended kinship networks commonly called clans. More than five hundred years later, family remains important. Family involves generosity and reciprocity—ongoing gifts and obligations that may encourage individuals to return home or never to leave home at all.

That notion of home tends to be tied to a particular place, marked symbolically and otherwise by known markers. Ancient stories may say to a member of a particular community: here is where you and your people belong. This is where we began. Although the reservations created in the late-nineteenth and early-twentieth centuries were imposed creations, Indians have attempted to make these land bases their homes (3). In the generations since, that attachment to reservation has encouraged a kind of allegiance to that particular place. One is not only Lakota or Sioux, but also from Pine Ridge or Rosebud.

Reservation is linked therefore to tribalism, a movement both centuries old and one subject to modification through time. Many Native communities may have been tied together through variations of a common language, stories, and values. But the establishment of reservations as political entities promoted a kind of Native national identity beyond family, clan, or local village or residence. The Navajos in 1969 formally declared their reservation the Navajo Nation. Whether one lives in the part of the Navajo Nation that extends into the states of Arizona, New Mexico, or Utah, one is part of the same political entity (and time zone—the Navajos switch to daylight savings time while the rest of Arizona does not).

The governments which represent the

reservations or nations also were imposed. Acceptance and use of tribal governments vary considerably from one Indian group to another. Nonetheless, on some reservations, tribal politics are very important, regardless of quarrels over origin or form. One ignores the tribal council and the tribal chairperson (or whatever terms are applied) at one's peril. Not unlike Congress, tribal governments may be characterized by factionalism, regionalism, or inefficiency. Yet, such governments have often played central, vital roles in helping Native groups to assert or reassert greater control over their own lives and concerns. This movement has been usually labeled self-determination or sovereignty.

Efforts in this direction have taken a variety of forms: economic, social, and cultural. In many instances, one form cannot be entirely separated from another. For example, attempts to develop cattle ranching on many western Indian reservations clearly represented economic activity. Yet social and cultural priorities were integrated into plans for the use of tribal lands for cattle ranching to assure that such enterprises would be meaningful and productive (4). Most recently, many tribes have turned to gaming as a potent source of new revenue. The Pequots in Connecticut are perhaps the most publicized example. The financial returns, to date, have often been overwhelming. But also important are the changes engendered by this new income. It has permitted more people to remain or return home from residence elsewhere; it has encouraged the building of new museums and other tribal institutions. And if gaming has been perceived as culturally damaging, as was the case on the Navajo Nation, the people have been willing to vote it down, regardless of the money involved.

Another significant instance of tribal self-determination has involved the names

employed for different groups. Many Native groups are designated by names imposed by outsiders, names that they did not choose. As an expression of self-determination, some tribes are insisting on names that are appropriate in their own language. Thus the Papagos of southern Arizona are now officially the Tohono O'odham.

In the early years of this century, another form of identity emerged for many Indians to supplement that of kin and tribe. This form encouraged Native Americans to recognize the things they shared in common with each other. Such an identity, as Indians, of course, had been promoted before. Pontiac, Tecumseh, and

Women students playing basketball at the Phoenix Indian School, 1903. Sports often provided one of the more positive memories of life in boarding schools.

other leaders had tried to get their followers to recognize the advantages of unity and purpose across linguistic and other lines. But the localized nature of tribal life, combined with frequent competition with other Indian communities for land and livelihood had mitigated against such a multitribal understanding (5).

What promoted this kind of Indian— as opposed to tribal—identity? In *The Search for a Modern Indian Identity*, Hazel Hertzberg argued that such institutions as the government boarding schools, ironically, offered a common experience for thousands of Indian youth. Isolated from

home, Indian children learned a language with which they could communicate with each other. Even if English served as that common language, Indians could employ it for their own purposes. The boarding schools helped emphasize the idea that missionaries and federal representatives tended to see the Native peoples as one people. Rather than a prelude to assimilation and disappearance, the boarding school could underscore the need for different peoples to work together in the future. Modern transportation, the postal system, and employment through the Bureau of Indian Affairs also allowed Indians to travel to see each other, write to each other, and work side by side. The schools also proved to be a convenient recruiting ground for the new Native American Church, a religious practice which uses peyote, and which while allowing for variations, encourages a common religious worship (6).

Such unanticipated developments are useful reminders that greater contact with outside forces do not automatically lead to absorption. In fact, to the contrary, such contact may reinforce the value of one's own way of doing things. Or it may allow for a group over time to incorporate some new element into the workings of a particular culture and have it become "traditional," even if it originated elsewhere. The boarding schools may thus, in some instances, have created new American Indian identities. However, as K. Tsianina Lomawaima's study of the Chilocco Indian School, *They Called It Prairie Light*, also contends, students from one tribe often stayed with their peers from home. Tribalism did not exactly disappear in a multitribal setting; contact with students from other tribes frequently reinforced allegiance to one's own people (7).

The Native American Church has been the most important of all national Indian organizations, secular or religious, in the twentieth century, but it has not been by any means the only one. The Society of American Indians (SAI), founded in 1911, offered an early forum for the airing of Native-American grievances and the expression of shared strivings. Primarily supported by well-educated Indians who shared some of the values of other reformers of the Progressive Era, the SAI held annual meetings, published its own journal, and emphasized that the new century meant a new era rather than the disappearance of Indians as identifiable participants in American life.

The National Congress of American Indians (NCAI), formed in Denver, Colorado in 1944, provided a broader and more enduring association, one which contin-ues today. The NCAI helped fight against the efforts of the federal government to eliminate reservations during the so-called termination era from the late 1940s until the beginning of the 1960s. It still serves a valuable role as a means to address major concerns. Rising out of the urban circumstances in which an increasing percentage of Native Americans found themselves, other organizations surfaced in the 1960s. These included the National Indian Youth Council, which enjoyed its greatest strength in the Southwest and southern Plains, and the American Indian Movement, which began in Minneapolis, and flourished primarily in the upper Midwest and northern Plains.

The 1960s also witnessed more mili-tant forms of protest against contempo-rary conditions. In the Pacific Northwest members of many tribal communities joined to advocate Native fishing rights. In the San Francisco area, the occupation of Alcatraz Island in 1969 by the people who termed themselves the "Indians of All Tribes," mirrored both local and national problems. The various demands included in the "Proclamation" from this group reflected, in part, the need for local center for Native American studies and a spiritual center for Indian people. In February 1973, Lakotas and other Indians occupied the village of Wounded Knee on the Pine Ridge reservation in western South Dakota. Sparked primarily by local complaints over the treatment of Indians in

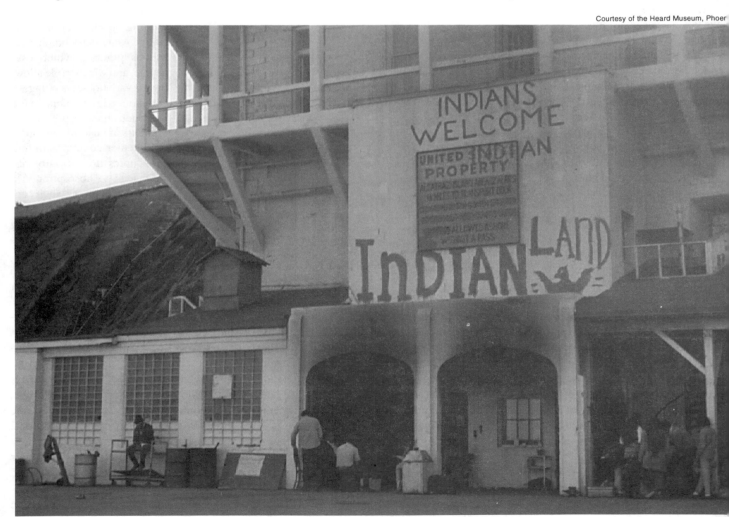

By altering a sign on Alcatraz, "The Indians of All Tribes" proclaimed their occupation of "The Rock" in 1969.

eighboring non-Indian communities, and he status of the tribal government at Pine Ridge, this protest again encompassed ational anger about Native well-being.

More recently, economic and professional organizations have also sought to advance Indian goals and objectives. The Council for Energy Resource Tribes (CERT), created in 1975, brought more han twenty tribes together as a single group to work for more effective use of ribal mineral resources. The Association f American Indian Physicians, founded y San Juan-Laguna physician Beryl Blue pruce gave Indian medical professionals means to communicate and promote Native-American medical education.

Multi-tribal cultural activities have lso been vital in the forging of a new meaning for the old term of Indian. The owwow provides an excellent example f this process. Peoples from various ribes come together, both in urban and ural settings, to take part in an activity nat builds primarily upon Plains-Indian ultural forms to create a shared experience symbolizing pride in heritage and ccomplishment. A film set in Montana,

"I'd Rather Be Powwowing," depicts an Indian man who works for a duplicating company in town, but looks forward to the powwow on the weekend where he can join others in the pleasure of this celebration. On the local, tribal, and regional level, other pastimes such as basketball and rodeo also yield ways in which competition, individual self-expression, and family are reflected. All-Indian basketball tournaments and rodeos may allow for old tribal rivalries not entirely to be put aside. Howard Hunter, from Pine Ridge, an outstanding rodeo cowboy, speaks of enjoying new battles between Lakotas and Crows. As for Navajo rodeos, Hunter suggests, "They don't like to see me come. They know I'll take their money" (8).

American Indians are also Americans. Fifty years ago, a Pima man, Ira Hayes, gained lasting fame when Joe Rosenthal photographed him and other Marines raising the American flag at Iwo Jima. The Navajo Codetalkers, who employed the Dine language in the Pacific campaign, are a source of enduring pride. Tinker Field in Oklahoma is named after General Clarence Tinker, an Osage, who lost his life in the Battle of Midway. Military service contin-

ues to be highlighted in tribal newspapers. The American flag has often been used as a motif in Indian art work. For example, the painting of Bill Rabbit, "In the Land of Milk and Honey," reveals an Indian draped in an American flag, holding an ice cream cone, with "Made in the USA" stamped across the top of the work (9). Regardless of the record of dispossession and the memories of past injustices, Indians remain Americans.

The recent past has witnessed Native Americans entering professions once viewed by many as being closed to Indian participation or antithetical to Indian identity. However, Indians have found that they can combine old and new ways in careers that serve the people. Lori Cupp, a Navajo surgeon, has melded her traditional beliefs with her medical training to meet the needs of her patients. She also saw the importance of being not only an Indian physician, but an Indian woman physician: "I saw early that a woman could work at a job and make a difference in people's lives" (10).

Native involvement in academics and the arts have allowed Indian individuals to take advantage of media that too often in the past stereotyped Native Americans. Indian actors such as Gary Farmer, Graham Greene, and Wes Studi have offered new portrayals of Indian figures in contemporary films. Movies such as "Powwow Highway" yield new understandings of current Indian themes as well as ongoing links with basic values. At colleges and universities, Indian students and faculty members have worked tirelessly to alter old, debilitating images, including the use of Indians as mascots or nicknames for athletic teams. Despite the protests of conservative alumni, Stanford, Dartmouth, and other colleges have abandoned such labels for their squads. In addition, colleges and universities have moved, often only after insistent prompting, to add more Indian students and faculty to their ranks. Such senior scholars as Charlotte Heth, Clara Sue Kidwell, and Alfonso Ortiz have devoted themselves for decades to establishing programs and providing leadership in universities as well as such institutions as the D'Arcy McNickle Center for the History of the American Indian at the Newberry Library in Chicago and the new National Museum of

pache miners at work. Such employment became increasingly important in Indian economies during the ventieth century.

the American Indian in Washington, D.C.

Luci Tapahonso is one of many contemporary Indian voices earning a wide readership. Sherman Alexie, Michael Dorris, Louise Erdrich, Joy Harjo, N. Scott Momaday, Louis Owens, Leslie Marmon Silko, Gerald Vizenor, James Welch, and a host of other poets and novelists offer influential and eloquent interpretations of Indian life. Native-American historians and anthropologists have made important headway in shaping new views of the Indian past. Native painters, sculptors, potters, silversmiths, weavers, musicians, and other artists are participating in perhaps an unprecedented outpouring of inspired and innovative work.

American Indians have also fought to gain control over skeletal remains and cultural property stored in museums and other locations. The Native American Graves Protection and Repatriation Act of 1990 has allowed tribes to take back many cultural artifacts. Museums such as the Heard Museum in Phoenix, under the direction of Martin Sullivan, have helped broker new understandings and accommodations. Such gains have not been achieved without resistance, but they have been most important examples of Native-American sovereignty.

It is imperative that one records such optimistic evidence, because too much of the general public image of Indians remains trapped in negative stereotypes. And, surely, there are major problems that remain in Native communities. Health care, employment, housing, and other continuing dilemmas challenge contemporary leadership. Nonetheless, we would do well to recall the prevailing strengths Native peoples draw from the land, from heritage, from family. For Luci Tapahonso, the powerful identity she drew from her home country, from her family, and from her stories, gave her strength even when she had to be far away from the Navajo Nation. "It was while I stood on top of the Eiffel Tower," she wrote, "that I understood that who I am is my mother, her mother, and my great-grandmother, Kinlichii'nii Bitsi" (11). In that combination of past and present, in that linkage between land, family, and values, "real" Indians are an integral part of American life at the end of the century in which they were

supposed to disappear. ❑

Endnotes

1. Luci Tapahonso, "What I Am," in *Saanii Dahataal The Women Are Singing* (Tucson: University of Arizona Press, 1993), 92.
2. Vine Deloria, Jr., *Custer Died For Your Sins: An Indian Manifesto* (New York: Macmillan, 1969), 1, 5.
3. For example, see Frederick E. Hoxie, "From Prison to Homeland: The Cheyenne River Reservation Before World War I," in *The Plains Indians of the Twentieth Century*, ed. Peter Iverson, (Norman: University of Oklahoma Press, 1985).
4. See Peter Iverson, *When Indians Became Cowboys: Native Peoples and Cattle Ranching in the American West* (Norman: University of Oklahoma Press, 1994).
5. See, for example, R. David Edmunds, *Tecumseh and the Quest for Indian Leadership* (Boston: Little, Brown, 1984).
6. Hazel Hertzberg, *The Search for an American Indian Identity: Modern Pan-lndian Movements* (Syracuse: Syracuse University Press, 1971).
7. K. Tsianina Lomawaima, *They Called It Prairie Light: The Story of Chilocco Indian School* (Lincoln: University of Nebraska Press, 1993).
8. Joan Morrison, "Indian Rodeo," *Native Peoples* 2 (Summer 1989): 22-3.
9. This painting adorns the cover of the University of Oklahoma Press spring 1995 catalogue and is used an illustration for Jack D. Forbes, *Only Approved Indians* (Norman: University of Oklahoma Press, 1995).
10. "Old Ways and New, In Harmony," *New York Times*, 17 February 1994, B1, B4.
11. Tapahonso, *Saanii Dahataal The Women Are Singing*, 92.

Wade Davies earned his B.A. from Indiana University and his M.A. from Arizona State University. He is currently a doctoral student in American-Indian history at Arizona State University. Peter Iverson is Professor of History at Arizona State University.

ORGANIZATION OF AMERICAN HISTORIANS

Future Annual Meetings

•

1996
Chicago

March 28-31
Palmer House
Hilton

•

1997
San Francisco

April 17-20
San Francisco
Hilton

•

1998
Indianapolis

April 2-5
Indiana Convention
Center

•

1999
Toronto, Ontario

April 22-25
Sheraton Centre

Indian Reservation Gaming: Much at Stake

Angela Firkus
and Donald L. Parman

Gaming on Indian reservations is the most important development in Indian affairs during the past two decades. Its economic impacts include bringing large sums of outside money to depressed Indian communities, reducing high unemployment rates, and funding needed social services and public works. Unfortunately, gaming has also produced serious clashes between tribes and states, and allegations about racketeering. And finally, reservation gaming, despite its economic benefits, faces an uncertain future because of numerous unresolved questions.

Although many Indian groups traditionally gambled by playing the stick game, the moccasin game, and wagering on horse races and athletic contests, these activities have little bearing on recent reservation gaming. In reality, bingo halls and casinos are white institutions that Indians appropriated just as they adopted many Euro-American weapons and tools. Gaming, however, carries a special importance because it represents a possible means of ending the desperate poverty on many reservations.

The Florida Seminoles, who live on a reservation in Broward County, Florida, near Ft. Lauderdale, initiated reservation gaming in 1979. This group, with the help of their tribal attorney, negotiated a contract with a management company to allow the construction of a $900,000 bingo hall. The Seminoles were to receive a share of the profits after wages, construction costs, and other expenses were paid from gross receipts. The only asset that the tribe possessed was a *possible* legal immunity from a Florida gambling law that limited jackpots to $100 and restricted games to two days per week. When the

In reality, bingo halls and casinos are white institutions that Indians appropriated just as they adopted many Euro-American weapons and tools.

hall opened in late 1979, it offered jackpots from $12,000 to $60,000, and the games took place daily.

Even before the Seminole bingo started, the local sheriff tried to block it as a violation of state law (1). In *Seminole Tribe of Florida v. Butterworth* (1980), a federal district court prohibited the sheriff from enforcing the Florida gambling stat-

ute. Without examining the intricacies of the case, the ruling agrees with decisions dating back to the 1830s that have denied state jurisdiction over Indian reservations. In the 1980 case, the judge commented that had Florida made bingo a crime, the state could have banned it for the Seminoles. But since Florida permitted bingo, the Seminole games were legal, and the state could not regulate them under its civil authority (2).

A peculiar mix of factors produced the explosion of reservation gaming after the Florida Seminoles' victory. The decision itself provided a more definite immunity against state regulation. In addition, funding for Indians during the first two years of the Reagan administration, 1981-1982, fell from an already inadequate $3.5 billion to $2.5 billion, and tribes badly needed alternative income. The Reagan administration, however, supported Indian self-determination and economic development and helped block a justice department bill that authorized states to regulate reservation gaming.

The arrangements for starting reservation gaming during the 1980s followed two basic patterns. In the first, a tribal government contracted with a management firm to start an operation. Such an agreement stipulated employment preference for tribal members, divided profits (typically around sixty percent to the Indians and forty percent to the company), and specified how long the contract would last. The tribe simply received its share of profits and decided how they would be dispersed. The second pattern involved gaming as a tribal enterprise. Despite a lack of capital and difficulty in gaining loans, more than half of the reservations set up their own operations. Tribally managed gaming operations demonstrated considerable resourcefulness. They reduced start-up costs, for example, by refurbishing abandoned factories or school buildings, secured loans guaranteed by the federal government, and temporarily hired consultants to advise them on such matters as security, training employees, and accounting procedures. The obvious advantage of the second approach was that the tribe received all the profits.

Regardless of which method was used, gaming quickly generated significant funds for many reservations. The Florida Seminoles opened a second highly successful bingo hall near Tampa. The North Carolina Cherokees' bingo games attracted thousands of customers, even in the tourist off-season, by busing people from out of state. High stakes bingo at the tiny Mdewakanton Sioux reservation in Minnesota attracted huge crowds from the nearby Twin Cities area. News stories by the mid-1980s described how tribes were using gambling profits to fund water and sewerage facilities, health clinics, day care centers, college scholarships, and non-gaming enterprises. By 1983 some 130 tribes had bingo operations with twenty to

twenty-five offering high stakes games. Several tribes aggressively expanded into more profitable casino games such as black jack, slot machines, and roulette.

Despite such successes, reservation gaming faced several pitfalls. Some of the contracts with management companies were unfair because of the low percentage awarded the tribes or because the contracts ran too long. Tribes sometimes had no method of monitoring management companies' gross receipts, actual expenses,

Advertisement for Kickapoo Bingo in Kansas.

and true profits. Rumors continued that organized crime had moved into reservation gaming to launder money or to skim profits. The Mdewakanton Sioux ousted their tribal chairman after they discovered that the management company had paid him $80,000 for personal land use for a parking lot and were giving him a monthly payment. A casino at the Lummi reservation in Washington state closed down temporarily when officials learned that two individuals in the management company had felony convictions. The Bureau of

Indian Affairs responded to such problems by developing a set of guidelines in the mid-1980s, but these dealt with contracts and background checks of management company personnel and not with subsequent monitoring.

The most significant problem, however, was the endless litigation that Indians encountered. States initiated most of the cases, although sometimes federal district attorneys brought suits. States continued to try to establish their authority to regulate or prohibit reservation gaming. In other suits, plaintiffs claimed that Indians' gambling violated the Assimilative Crimes Act of 1898 that had extended state criminal laws over federal enclaves such as military bases (3). Other opponents argued that Indian gaming violated the Organized Crime Control Act of 1970. In an important decision, *California v. Cabazon Band*, in early 1987, the U.S. Supreme Court rejected these arguments and ruled that California could not regulate bingo or prohibit draw poker and other card games on the reservation. The decision was even stronger than the 1980 ruling in Florida because California law prohibited casino-type games (4).

The unceasing litigation, constant but unproven rumors about organized crime, and a perceived need to fix regulatory responsibility eventually led to the Indian Gaming Regulatory Act of 1988. Although space does not permit a full legislative history, clearly a central issue was whether the tribes, federal government, or states would exercise authority over reseration gaming. The bills introduced after 1984 until final passage varied greatly in that regard. Some tribal leaders testified that they were already regulating the gambling successfully. Lobbyists from Nevada argued strongly at the hearings for state control, claiming that neither the federal government nor Indians had the expertise needed to keep out organized crime (5). What bothered Nevada spokesmen more than organized crime, however, was the possibility that California reservations might siphon off a portion of the huge customer base in the Golden State.

The final legislation represented a compromise over regulatory power. It divided reservation gaming into three categories and prescribed different regulatory authority for each. Class I included traditional or ceremonial gaming, and this fell totally under tribal control. Class II dealt with bingo, lotto, pull-tabs, and similar games. These operations were subject to tribal control and also to the National Indian Gaming Commission, a group of three appointees who acted as an oversight committee. Class III consisted of all other forms of gambling, especially casino games such as black jack, roulette, and slot machines. To engage in Class III gaming, a tribe had to pass an ordinance and have it approved by the chairperson of the gaming commission. In addition tribes had to negotiate a compact with the government of their state—if it permitted Class III gambling—to establish what types of games would be permitted and what regulatory controls the states and the tribes could exercise. Many Indian leaders viewed the requirement for tribal-state compacts as a serious violation of tribal sovereignty (6).

The passage of the act in 1988 did not end many of the problems that had existed earlier. By August 1993, nineteen different states had concluded compacts with sixty-four tribes. Although governors normally have negotiated with tribes, some state officials have questioned who legally has the power to make the gambling contracts. Some states have refused to bargain with the tribes and have claimed that the Eleventh Amendment protects states from being sued for failing to nego-

Cartoon by Joe Heller, *Green Bay Press-Gazette*, © 1993

political cartoon from 1993. "The Great White Buffalo Hunter Returns."

tiate contracts. Most states, sometimes prompted by a court order, have reached compacts with tribes that divide the power to regulate gambling.

State officials have expressed many concerns during the negotiations. They argued that the compacts infringe on state sovereignty. Some protested that the reservations casinos have an unfair advantage over non-Indian charity bingo operations, which limit prizes. In Wisconsin many non-profit groups have lost revenues when forced into other forms of making money. Churches and other organizations in the state netted $32.4 million in 1989 but only $25.4 million in 1992. Other officials worried about increased crime. Assault, theft, alcoholism, and drug abuse may have increased in some places, but a 1993 study in Wisconsin showed that counties with gambling had a much lower growth of crime than counties without gaming operations. Despite endless rumors, the Federal Justice Department has found no involvement by organized crime. Indian gambling grosses only three percent of the national total and seems an unlikely target for organized crime. Some observers worried that Indian operations would produce compulsive gamblers. Undoubtedly some individuals do fall victim and need help, but most participants gamble for recreation.

Studies indicate that Indian gaming has had a significant impact on several state economies. In 1992, the Wisconsin state government received $49 million from sales, gas, and income taxes from the operation of the Indian casinos. In addition, employment in casinos and bingo operations saved the state $2 million in welfare payments. Wisconsin also benefited from about $80 million spent on construction, goods and services. Out-of-state visitors to Indian gaming facilities spent some $80 million in non-gambling purchases. The Mashantucket

Pequots pay Connecticut $100 million a year to preserve their monopoly on gambling.

The earlier problems with some management companies obviously have continued into recent times. Some tribes entered into unfair management contracts and a few have not been successful with their operations. A 1994 federal investi-

Photo by Jason Tetzloff

St. Croix Casino at Turtle Lake, Wisconsin.

gation of 1986-1992 gaming in the Great Lakes area revealed that management companies had overcharged thirty-seven tribes at least $62 million. Several charged rental fees that exceeded the cost of the machines. Many contracts excluded the tribe from gaining any profit until the debt for the building and consulting fees was paid

to the management company. Seventy of the two hundred tribes that run operations still rely on management companies (7).

Operating costs, which take a large share of the gross revenues, include wages to Indian and non-Indian employees. Most gaming operations attempt to hire as many tribal members as possible but the percentage employed varies. In Minnesota tribal members hold only twenty-five percent of the jobs, while in Wisconsin they hold more than half. Unemployment on reservations in both states has been drastically reduced, however.

The tribes are making money. Total profits for Indian gaming jumped from about a half billion in 1990 to two billion in 1994 (8). Many tribes have used gaming to increase their own budgets. In 1991, the Menominees in Wisconsin made a four million dollar profit from their casino, and for the following year the tribal office had a six million dollar budget. Tribes like the Oneidas of Wisconsin and the Mashantucket Pequots of Connecticut, whose revenues are estimated at more than $375 million and $600 million a year respectively, have completely transformed their communities.

Tribal governments have used much of the profits to expand their gaming facilities, but most leaders have always realized the importance of diversifying their economies. In 1988, about forty of the 310 federally recognized tribes already had economic development plans in place. The more remote reservations will have problems diversifying their economies. Indeed, it was the lack of economic possibilities that prompted them to exploit gaming. With increased amounts of capital, however, some tribes have been more successful in developing their economies than in the past. The Oneidas of Wisconsin have funded a scientific testing laboratory, print shop, retail outlets, a construction company, a hotel, and a plumbing business with gambling revenue. The Prior Lake Mdewakanton Sioux of Minnesota have similarly bought a manufacturing company (9).

Tribes generally have looked to the future as they invested their gaming profits. After decades of inadequate funding, tribal governments are building schools, day care centers, and libraries as well as supporting college students and Head Start programs. Tribal councils are able to show respect to their elders by providing them with housing, recreational centers, transportation, and health care. Some tribes are buying lands that they lost long ago. Many are building cultural centers as well as sponsoring language and cultural heritage programs. A few are making per capita payments even though tribal members have to pay income taxes on such funds.

Although tribes are obviously improving their communities with new revenues, gaming has also aroused misgivings among some Indians. Writer Gerald Vizenor argues that increased profits from gaming will increase competition for tribal leadership positions and thus divide Indian communities. Tribal members do not always agree on how to spend the funds. Unscrupulous managers, Indian and non-Indian, have not only embezzled funds but used some of them to influence tribal members. Other communities have fought, in a few cases violently, over whether they should be operating casinos at all (10).

Concern has also arisen over preserving traditional unity and heritage. Jim Northrup, Jr. of the Fond du Lac Chippewas believes that gambling may accomplish what centuries of assimilation policies have failed to do. He worries that tribal members will no longer look out for the community or its traditions but will be interested in individual profit. Others have noted declines in attendance at ceremonies and community events (11). One scholar writes that gambling has prompted many non-Indians to question the existence of an "Indian identity" and the legitimacy of reservation separatism.

Some whites also mistakenly believe that all Indians have become rich from the operations. A Midwestern governor, for example, recently called for the abrogation of his state's scholarship program for Native Americans because gaming revenues had ended the need for such aid. This type of misconception may hurt the majority of

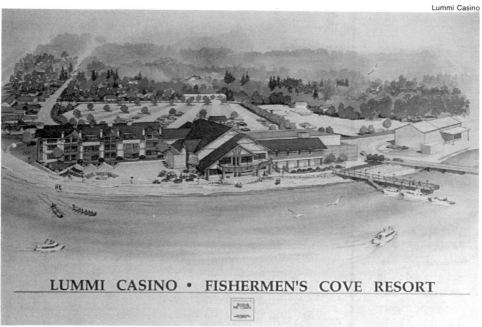

Lummi Casino

LUMMI CASINO • FISHERMEN'S COVE RESORT

The Lummi Nation will soon begin building a new casino and resort complex near the site of their present casino. New gaming compacts with Washington state officials allow for larger betting limits and larger casinos, which should help this vital income source for the Indian tribes expand.

native peoples, two thirds of whom belong to tribes that do not engage in high stakes gambling. For these people, government programs are still crucial to their survival. This fact is emphasized by census figures. From 1980 to 1990, Indian households experienced no gain in income while white and black households increased by twelve percent and eight percent respectively. In 1990, thirty-one percent of Native Americans lived below the poverty line. These figures illustrate that most native peoples are not ben-

efiting from gambling operations. Finally, changes in federal legislation or in judicial rulings could jeopardize the future of Indian gaming.

In assessing the importance of reservation gaming, it is perhaps useful to compare it to past federal policies. In the period before World War II, officials generally encouraged Indians to become farmers. A weak land base and a lack of capital and credit, among other factors, doomed such efforts. After World War II, federal officials encouraged Indians to take urban jobs and subsidized manufacturing on reservations. Although some successes resulted, nearly all the attempts to industrialize reservations failed because of poor infrastructures and remoteness of markets. Although gaming has not been an unqualified success for all reservations, it has overcome serious economic obstacles, improved employment opportunities, boosted morale, and upgraded the living standards of many Indian communities. ❑

Endnotes
1.   *Indianapolis Star*, 14 July 1981.
2.   491 F. Supp. 1015.
3.   For a discussion of this statute, see Vine Deloria, Jr. and Clifford M. Lytle, *American Indians, American Justice* (Austin: University of Texas Press, 1983), 173-4.
4.   The court recognized California's ban on casino gambling, but it maintained that the state itself operated a lottery and permitted bingo. In addition, the ruling noted that the Indians had no natural resources and that federal policies encouraged political self determination and economic self sufficiency. See 480 *U.S. Reports* 202 (1990).
5.   *Las Vegas Review-Journal*, 26 June 1985.
6.   102 STAT. 2476.

7. "Casino Contractors Charge Excessive Fees," *News From Indian Country*, Late January 1994.
8. We have no way of knowing how total profits were divided between management companies and tribes.
9. *Milwaukee Journal*, 20 November 1992.
10. Gerald Vizenor, "Gambling on Sovereignty," *American Indian Quarterly* 16 (Summer 1992): 411-3; Chris Wood, "Gunfire and Gambling: Violence Explodes on a Mohawk Reserve," *Maclean's* 7 May 1990, 22; *Milwaukee Journal*, 25 October 1992; and *Milwaukee Journal*, 2 April 1994.
11. Irl Carter, "Gambling with their Lives: American Indians and the Casinos," *Center for Urban and Regional Affairs Reporter*, August 1992.

Bibliographic Essay

A good source for detailed coverage of specific gaming operations is local newspapers. Many local papers can be accessed through *Newsbank*. Native American newspapers, including *News From Indian Country* and *Indian Country Today*, offer information about a wide variety of reservation economies. Three recent overviews are in the 22 August 1993 *Chicago Tribune Magazine*, *New York Times Magazine* of 27 February 1994, and the Summer 1994 *Critical Inquiry*. For economics, a good background is in Robert H. White, *Tribal Assets: The Rebirth of Native America* (New York: Henry Holt, 1990). To find Congressional testimony by Indians and non-Indians, see Senate Hearing 100-341 (*Gambling: Hearing on S. 555 and S. 1301*, 100th Cong., 1st Sess., 18 June 1987). Roland J. Santoni provides a legal overview in the 26th edition (1993) of the *Creighton Law Review*.

Angela Firkus is a Ph.D. student in history at Purdue University. Donald Parman is a professor of history at Purdue University, author, most recently, of Indians and the American West in the Twentieth Century, *and a frequent contributor to the* Magazine of History.

"The object of the Organization shall be to promote historical study and research in the field of American history and to do all things necessary and proper to accomplish this purpose."

Constitution of the Organization
of American Historians, Article II

Membership in the OAH is your way of actively supporting this simple, straightforward goal . . . to promote historical study and research in American history. As a member of the OAH you'll receive either the *Journal of American History*, the leading publication in the field, or the *Magazine of History*, our publication especially for members in the History Educator program.

You'll also receive the *OAH Newsletter*, with articles, commentary, professional opportunity ads, fellowship announcements, and other valuable information about the organization and the profession, plus a copy of our Annual Meeting *Program* containing a complete list of the sessions planned for the OAH convention.

Join us.

Please start my membership in the Organization of American Historians.

Name_____

Address_____

City_____ State_____ Zip_____

___ Check or money order enclosed (must be drawn in U.S. funds, on U.S. bank)
___ Charge my   ___ Visa   ___ Mastercard   Exp. Date_____
    Card No._____
    Signature_____

Check appropriate income/dues category:

Individual Membership
___ $20, Student (5-year limit; proof of student status required)
___ $35, income under $20,000
___ $50, income $20,000-$29,999
___ $70, income $30,000-$39,000
___ $80, income $40,000-$49,999
___ $90, income $50,000-$59,999
___ $100, income $60,000-$69,999
___ $110, income $70,000-$79,999
___ $120, income $80,000-$89,999

___ $130, income over $90,000
___ $1,200, Life Membership (may be paid in two installments)
___ $1,500, Patron (may be paid in four installments)
___ $45, Associate (not employed as historian)
___ $15, Additional postage outside U.S.
___ $35+, Dual (receive one copy of JAH) Select the appropriate income category for one member; add $35 for the second member.
___ $150, Contributing Member

History Educator Program
___ $35, Primary/Secondary Teacher; members receive the *Magazine of History*, *OAH Newsletter* and Annual Meeting *Program*.

Institutional Subscriptions (may not be in the name of an individual)
___ $140, includes four issues of the *Journal of American History*, the *Magazine of History*, and the *Newsletter*, plus an Annual Meeting *Program*.
___ $15, postage outside the U.S.

Return coupon (photocopy accepted) along with your credit card information or a check or money order made payable to the Organization of American Historians.

Organization of American Historians
112 North Bryan Street, Bloomington, IN 47408-4199

MOH/Sum95

Seeing the People for the Trees: The Promise and Pitfalls of Indian Environmental History

Louis S. Warren

The connection between Indians and the environment seems so obvious as to require no explanation. As a symbolic criticism of European-American insensitivity to the environment, the image of Indians who "lived in harmony with nature" has become a cliché. In addition to the problems of the metaphor—for me, the idea of anyone "living in harmony" suggests they somehow resonated like tuning forks—the reality of American Indian experience is far more complicated. Exploring how Indians perceived the natural systems around them, and how they shaped them to secure their respective versions of "the good life," makes a fascinating study. But of course the story does not end there. Indian uses of the land changed it, and the advent of European and European-American colonists transformed it even more. Indians did not shrink from the challenge of adapting their life ways to these shifting environments. Indians wove old traditions into new environmental conditions; they tried to sustain old lifeways and frequently created new ones. Exploring how they accomplished all this can teach students a great deal about the subtleties of cultural resilience, ecological change, and American history.

In pre-contact America, all Indians relied on mixtures of subsistence activities to make a living from the land, but they differed markedly in emphasis. The various regional environments of the Americas offered distinctive ranges of opportunity for Indians, whose lifeways were never determined by their environment so much as selected from a range of choices within it. Indians of southern New

> *Indians did not shrink from the challenge of adapting their life ways to these shifting environments. Indians wove old traditions into new environmental conditions; they tried to sustain old lifeways and frequently created new ones.*

England, including the Naragansetts, Pequots, and Wampanoags, lived in wood-frame houses covered with grass or bark, grew maize, beans, and squash for over half their food supply, and ventured into the hunting grounds during the winter to secure meat and hides. Catawbas, Choctaws, and other Indians of the South-

east shared similar patterns of seasonal movement and shifting dependence on agriculture, hunting, and gathering. Indians further north, such as the Abenakis and Crees, depended almost entirely on hunting and gathering because the growing season was too short for agriculture. In the Southwest, Acomas, Zunis, and others lived in adobe pueblos, permanent villages where they depended heavily on their farm crops. In the Pacific Northwest, the Tlingits, Kwakiutls, Nootkas, and others built fabulous wooden structures and generally enjoyed a wealthy material culture, supported largely by abundant salmon. In addition to these groups, there were countless others.

Before we explore the ways that Indians responded to disruption of these intimate, localized relationships with the environment, a preliminary warning: there is no quicker way to beggar the richness of Indian environmental history than to cultivate romantic stereotypes of Indians as "primitive ecologists." Such notions are a new twist on the old idea of "noble savagery," and they can—even inadvertently—provide rationalizations for conquest by turning Indians into part of the land, making them candidates for what early colonists called "improvement," and what we know as "development" (1). Aside from that, such notions lost scholarly credibility at least twenty years ago. Their durability among the public makes teaching Indian environmental history all the more important. A primary lesson of any Indian history class must be that Indians were and are real people, and therefore needed (and need) to shape land to make a living from it. We need not, and should not, veer to the opposite extreme and paint Indians as nature wreckers; examples of large-scale environmental destruction among pre-Columbian Indians are the exception, not the rule. But to claim that Indians lived without affecting nature is akin to saying that they lived without touching anything, that they were a people without history. Indians often manipulated their local environments for specific purposes, and while they usually had far less impact on their environments than European colonists would, the idea of "preserving" land in some kind of wilderness state would have struck them as impractical and absurd. More often than not, Indians profoundly shaped the ecosystems around them, as we shall see.

In fact, pre-contact Indians altered the landscape in a host of ways, from extensive networks of trails, roads, and causeways to huge ceremonial mounds, terraced fields, and settlements, in some cases with populations in the tens of thousands. These people did not live off the bounty of an "untouched nature." Indians planted, transplanted, and protected numerous valuable species of plants near village sites and along trails (2). Even more pervasively, from one end of the Americas to the other, Indians shaped the landscape through intentional burning of forests and grasslands. Burning replenished the soil with essential nutrients and speeded up the rate at which they were

recycled, and allowed sunlight to fall on the soil, thereby encouraging vigorous new growth. This was ideal for a new planting of maize, beans, or squash, but a burned area could facilitate Indian survival in other ways. Grasses, shrubs, and nonwoody plants would grow more luxuriously on a burned-over area, promoting

George Wharton James's photo originally entitled, "Man and Boy, Zuni." The Zunis are a southwestern Indian people, tradionally living in Pueblo-style housing.

the increase of elk, deer, beaver, and other wildlife species that depended on such plants and whose abundance astonished early settlers in many parts of America (3). Fire ecology may have played a role in maintaining the Midwestern prairies, preventing reforestation on their eastern perimeter. In other areas, long years of Indian fire management resulted in a mo-

saic pattern of plant and forest stands in varying stages of ecological succession (4). Clearly, Indian America was no "virgin land" of forests primeval. Some scholars have even concluded that virtually all forests in the pre-contact Americas—even the Amazon—were anthropogenic to a considerable degree (5).

Although a scientific understanding of how burning changes an ecosystem is useful for understanding Indian environmental history, Indians themselves did not explain their cultural practices this way. Instead, they relied on rich, complex belief systems to make sense of the natural world, and their cosmology stressed dependence on gracious spirits, who often appeared in the form of animals, to bring game to the hunter, crops to the (usually women) farmers, and salmon to the rivers. Even fire— "Our Grandfather Fire" to many Indians of eastern North America—was a spiritual presence (6).

Propitiating the powerful spirits who controlled crop cycles and the luck of the hunter took a substantial amount of time and effort. Indeed, it seems likely that most Indians would have been reluctant to take sole credit for shaping local ecosystems, deferring instead to the spirits as the true caretakers of the land. The notion that people could control animal populations or plant growth would have struck them as hubris, and in some cases still does (7). Insofar as environmental understandings are informed by spirituality, environmental history can be a valuable window on Indian religion.

Contact with Europeans would strain Indian cosmologies in unprecedented ways. Isolated for millennia from the pathogens of the Old World, Indians fell in vast multitudes to smallpox, chicken pox, measles, and other European illnesses. The extent of the devastation has only been recognized in recent decades. Precision is impossible, but some of the best estimates suggest that Indians in North America (excluding Mexico) declined by 74 percent from 1492 to 1800, from about 4 million to somewhere around 1 million. For the Americas as a whole, Indian populations probably fell 89 percent between 1492 and 1650, from 54 million to 5.6 million (8). In some places Europeans benefitted directly from this calamity: at the Plymouth colony, English colonists moved onto the site of an Indian village destroyed by an epidemic only four years before. They found fertile fields ready for the planting. But usually it would take many years for Europeans and Africans to fill the ecological niche left by this catastrophic mortality; even as late as 1750, there were only 16 million people in the Americas, and most of these lived in coastal areas and along river courses. In the meantime, old Indian fields, villages, and hunting zones in the interior were choked with successful growth. Small wonder that when many Americans first encountered this "widowed land" in the nineteenth century, they thought they were seeing "virgin wilderness" (9).

Students will have no trouble understanding that many undesirable organisms rode along in European baggage, but generally they will be unaware of just how unintentional this process could be. For example, English weeds arrived with English livestock, and colonized New England at least as quickly as the English themselves. Indians had no domesticated livestock, and under the pressure of cattle and sheep grazing, hardy European weeds like the dandelion, stinging nettle, and plantain (which the Indians called "Englishman's Foot," so close did it follow in the steps of the colonizers) frequently replaced native grasses. In some cases, pest plants such as the barberry bush harbored crop-ravaging fungi like black stem rust, which devastated colonists' wheat and rye crops in the 1660s (10). But more often, the transformation of forest and grass communities by European vegetation and livestock meant that Indian lifeways became more difficult than ever before. European pigs destroyed clam banks and wrecked Indian crops, even after New England Indians began erecting fences and taking settlers to the colonial courts for compensation (11).

Given the heterogeneity of Indian cultures and experiences in the period after initial contact, generalizations are difficult. But virtually everywhere, Indians displayed a remarkable ability to innovate and adapt to new conditions. Indian lifeways were no house of cards; they did not collapse upon first contact with white people. Indeed, some groups expanded and grew more powerful than ever. This was particularly true of some nomadic Indians on the Great Plains, such as the western Sioux. In 1492, the Sioux were sedentary horticulturalists in the forests of

Painting by Seth Eastman. In Clement A. Lounsberry, *Early History of North Dakota*, 1919

Painting by Eastman entitled "Ball Play of the Dakota (Sioux) Indians." The Sioux are a northern Great Plains people.

the upper Midwest. They became nomadic buffalo hunters on the Plains after they acquired horses, which spread to the northern plains from the Spanish colonies by the early 1700s. The classic buffalo-hunting cultures of the eighteenth and nineteenth centuries are often esteemed as paragons of "pristine" Indian culture, when in fact they are evidence of the ways that Indians innovated in the face of post-contact environmental change, adopting new animal technologies to improve their conditions (12).

At the same time, it is worth pointing out that not all Indians benefitted equally from the arrival of the horse. The animals' speed and power tended to favor nomadic Indians like the Sioux and Comanche over settled horticultural villagers, such as the Arikaras of the Missouri or the Pueblos of the Rio Grande. Both of these latter groups were powerful entities in the pre-contact period, and both suffered grievously at the hands of mounted nomads after the arrival of Europeans and their horses (13).

Even within Indian communities the acquisition of the horse created new divisions. Among Pawnee men in the area of present-day Nebraska and Kansas, for example, horses became a highly-valued possession. They conveyed greater possibility of success in the annual buffalo hunt, and they became the essential currency of bride price. But Pawnee villagers made their livelihood through a combination of hunting out on the plains and farming the river bottoms of the Platte and Republican rivers. Since they had never domesticated livestock before, their fields had no fences. Horses frequently raided corn fields, trampling beans and squash and greatly increasing the workload of Pawnee women, who were responsible for most horticultural tasks and for looking after the horses. Not surprisingly, horses drove wedges between Pawnee men and Pawnee women. One white observer reported, "There are more broils, jealousy, and family quarrels caused by horses than all other troubles combined. The horse frequently causes separation between man and wife, sometimes for life" (14).

The innovations of horse culture came with other prices too. As Plains Indians came to rely more on horses, their herds competed with buffalo for range and scarce water. To some degree, the swelling numbers of Indian and wild horses—two million of which roamed the Texas Plains in the early 1800s—probably contributed to the declining numbers of bison on the southern Plains in the years before 1850 (15). Shifting patterns of Indian subsistence thereby ramified through local ecosystems, re-shaping Indian social relations, lifeways, and landscapes.

In other places, integration of European biological imports had similarly dramatic consequences for Indians who adopted them. Navajos became powerful sheep herders and traders, and Cherokee women adopted watermelons, sweet potatoes, and peaches with great success. Beginning in the early 1700s, pigs were in ready supply at Cherokee villages, where Cherokee women and children tended the animals in small enclosures. As white settlement and market hunting drained the

Photo by Curtis. In John Burroughs, John Muir, and George Bird Grinnell, *Narrative, Glaciers, Natives*, 1910

Photo of a nineteenth-century Tlinglit (Pacific Northwest) village originally entitled "Deserted Indian Village, Cape Fox, Alaska."

forests of game, Cherokee men found less success on the hunt. Cherokee women filled part of the gap with pork; since pigs were a domestic animal they were integrated into female horticultural responsibilities (16). Indian integration of European-American environmental organisms expanded alongside white colonization, so that Indians on the Great Plains in many cases became cattle raisers, and in the reservation period formed a new identity—and a new livelihood—as Indian cowboys (17). In many cases, Indian subsistence failed even with new innovations, and gradually Indians across the country became more and more dependent on the federal government. But at the same time, Indian adoption of European environmental imports enabled them to retain their independence for longer than would otherwise have been possible. It is difficult to look at the success of the Navajo people, whose sheep economy became their mainstay, and conclude that environmental change uniformly disempowered Indians. Indian cowboys across the West represented the continuing efforts of Indians to create new lifeways out of new tools. How Indians responded to changes in their natural environment is often a story of Indian decline and defeat, but it includes elements of innovation, change, and success.

It is troubling that many Americans interpret Indian innovations—no matter how successful—as evidence of Indian decline. To such minds, Indians with horses are "real" Indians; Indians with pigs and pickup trucks have somehow become "less Indian" than their forebears. By way of contrast, it is worth considering how much Europeans became "Indianized" as they came to depend on plant stocks developed entirely by Indians, especially maize and other New World cultivars like beans, squash, and potatoes. Would we say that white people have become Indians just because they have selectively adopted aspects of Indian culture?

In any case, the notion that Indians must behave in a certain way to be called Indians is badly mistaken. Being Indian depends more on the historical experience

of one's ancestors than on living some idealized, "environmentally-correct" lifeway. Indians did not stop being Indians when they started growing cotton and buying slaves in Georgia—and if they did, why did Americans dispossess them and force them on the Trail of Tears to Oklahoma? Was a Sioux Indian in the pre-contact period any less Indian for not having a horse? Is a Lakota Indian today any less Indian for driving a Volvo? Among other things, Indian history is a tale of constant innovation and change. Indians changed their lifeways prior to the arrival of Europeans; the fact that they have changed them in dramatic ways and perhaps more frequently since 1492 is no proof that Indians have "vanished" or somehow become "less Indian" than they were before. If there is a single, characteristic Indian experience of the environment, perhaps it is the ability to change lifeways in radical fashion to maintain culture and identity. ❑

Endnotes

1. See Richard White, "American Indians and the Environment," *Environmental Review* 9 (Summer, 1985): 101-3; Richard White, "Native Americans and the Environment," in *Scholars and the Indian Experience,* ed. W.R. Swagerty (Bloomington: Indiana University Press, 1984) 181; Richard White, *Roots of Dependency: Subsistence, Environment, and Social Change among the Choctaws, Pawnees, and Navajos* (Lincoln: University of Nebraska Press, 1983), xiii; Richard White and William Cronon, "Ecological Change and Indian-White Relations," in *Handbook of North American Indians,* ed. William C. Sturtevant, vol. 4 (Washington, 1978-1989), 417-29.

2. William Denevan, "The Pristine Myth: The Landscape of the Americas in 1492," *Annals of the Association of American Geographers* 82 (1992): 374.

3. Stephen Pyne, *Fire in America: A Cultural History of Wildland and Rural Fire* (Princeton: Princeton University Press, 1982), 71-83; and William Cronon, *Changes in the Land: Indians, Colonists, and the Ecology of New England* (New York: Hill and Wang, 1983) 51.

4. Cronon, 51.

5. Denevan, 375.

6. Pyne, 71.

7. Robert A. Brightman, "Conservation and Resource Depletion: The Case of the Boreal Forest Algonquians," in *The Question of the Commons: The Culture and Ecology of Communal Resources,* ed. Bonnie J. McCay and James M. Acheson (Tucson: University of Arizona Press, 1987), 132.

8. Denevan, 371. See also Henry Dobyns, *Native American Historical Demography* (Bloomington: Indiana University Press, 1976), and Henry Dobyns, *Their Number Become Thinned: Native American Population Dynamics in Eastern North America* (Knoxville; University of Tennessee Press, 1983).

9. The term "widowed land" is borrowed from Francis Jennings, *The Invasion of America: Indians, Colonists, and the Cant of Conquest* (New York: Norton, 1976).

10. Cronon, 143, 154-5.

11. Cronon, 131.

12. The best discussion of the Sioux experience is Richard White, "The Winning of the West: The Expansion of the Western Sioux in the Eighteenth and Nineteenth Centuries," *Journal of American History* 65 (September 1978): 319-43.

13. Preston Holder, *The Hoe and the Horse on the Plains* (Lincoln: University of Nebraska Press, 1970) is one of the best statements of the phenomenon.

14. Samuel Allis, quoted in Richard White, *The Roots of Dependency,* 181. Similarly, among the Cherokees of the American Southeast, horses belonging to men frequently destroyed women's gardens, even when they were fenced. According to James Adair, a witness to Cherokee village life, women would "scold and give them ill names, calling them ugly mad horses, and bidding them go along, and be sure to keep away." Quoted in Thomas Hatley, "Cherokee Women Farmers Hold Their Ground" 45, in *Appalachian Frontiers: Settlement, Society, and Development in the Preindustrial Era,* ed Robert D. Mitchell (Lexington: University Press of Kentucky, 1991), 45.

15. Dan Flores, "Bison Ecology and Bison Diplomacy: The Southern Plains from 1800 to 1850," *Journal of American History* (September 1991): 465-85. See especially page 481.

16. Thomas Hatley, "Cherokee Women Farmers Hold Their Ground," 44.

17. Peter Iverson, *When Indians Became Cowboys: Native Peoples and Cattle Ranching in the American West* (Norman: University of Oklahoma Press, 1994).

Selected Bibliography

Anyone wishing to familiarize themselves with environmental history is in luck; the field has produced a number of very readable books. Among these:

Cronon, William. *Changes in the Land: Indians, Colonists, and the Ecology of New England.* New York: Hill and Wang, 1983.

Crosby, Alfred W. Jr. *The Columbian Exchange: Biological Consequences of 1492.* Westport, Conn.: Greenwood Press, 1972.

———. *Ecological Imperialism: The Biological Expansion of Europe, 900-1900.* New York: Cambridge University Press, 1986.

White, Richard. *The Roots of Dependency: Subsistence, Environment, and Social Change among the Choctaws, Pawnees, and Navajos.* Lincoln: University of Nebraska Press, 1983.

Indian demography and the impact of virgin soil epidemics is in Henry Dobyns, *Native American Historical Demography* (Bloomington: Indiana University Press, 1976); and Henry Dobyns, *Their Number Become Thinned: Native American Population Dynamics in Eastern North America* (Knoxville: University of Tennessee, 1983).

Indian manipulations of the land have become a popular subject, and a fine summary of recent scholarship is in William Denevan, "The Pristine Myth: The Landscape of the Americas in 1492," *Annals of the Association of American Geographers* 82 (1992): 369-85. The classic work on fire ecology in America is Stephen Pyne, *Fire in America: A Cultural History of Wildland and Rural Fire* (Princeton: Princeton University Press, 1982).

For the mounted buffalo hunters of the Great Plains and their relationship to Great Plains Ecology, see Dan Flores, "Bison Ecology and Bison Diplomacy: The Southern Plains from 1800 to 1850," *Journal of American History* (September 1991): 465-85. Preston Holder, *The Hoe and the Horse on the Plains* (Lincoln: University of Nebraska Press, 1970) is a good treatment of nomadic hunters and sedentary farmers on the Great Plains.

Louis Warren is an assistant professor of history at the University of San Diego, specializing in environmental history and the history of the American West.

"The object of the Organization shall be to promote historical study and research in the field of American history and to do all things necessary and proper to accomplish this purpose."

Membership in the OAH is your way of actively supporting this simple, straightforward goal...to promote historical study and research in American history. As a member of the OAH you will receive either the *Journal of American History,* the leading publication in the field, or the *Magazine of History*, our publication especially for members in the History Educator program. You will also receive the *OAH Newsletter,* with articles, commentary, professional opportunity ads, fellowship announcements, and other valuable information about the organization and the profession, plus a copy of our Annual Meeting *Program* containing a complete list of the sessions planned for the OAH Annual Meeting.

NAME_____

ADDRESS_____

CITY_____STATE_____ZIP CODE_____

❏ Check enclosed (must be drawn in U.S. funds, on U.S. bank)

❏ Charge my _____Visa _____MasterCard **VISA** MasterCard

Card No._____Exp. Date_____

Signature_____

Check appropriate income/dues category:

❏ $35, income under $20,000
❏ $50, income $20,000-29,999
❏ $70, income $30,000-39,999
❏ $80, income $40,000-49,999
❏ $90, income $50,000-59,999
❏ $100, income $60,000-69,999
❏ $110, income $70,000-79,999
❏ $120, income 80,000-89,999
❏ $130, income over $90,000
❏ $150, Contributing Member
❏ $45, Associate

❏ $35+, Dual, receive one copy of JAH (select income category for one member, add $35 for second member)
❏ $20, Student (five-year limit; proof of student status required)
❏ $1,200, Life Membership (may be paid paid in two installments)
❏ $1,500, Patron (may be paid in four installments)
❏ $15, Postage outside U.S.

Magazine of History

❏ $20 per year for members
❏ $25 per year for nonmembers
❏ $35 per year for institutions and libraries

History Educator Program

❏ $35, Primary/Secondary Teacher; members receive the *Magazine of History, OAH Newsletter* and Annual Meeting *Program.*

Institutional Subscribers

❏ $140 Institutional (may not be in the name of an individual)
❏ $15, additional postage outside U.S.

ORGANIZATION OF AMERICAN HISTORIANS
112 NORTH BRYAN STREET
BLOOMINGTON, IN 47408-4199
812-855-7311

MOH/Spr96

Quakers and Indians in Colonial America

Introduction

The record of relations between the Europeans who settled in the American colonies and the indigenous peoples is mixed at best. Through much of the seventeenth century the Puritans of New England enjoyed relatively harmonious relationships with the Indians. Sentiments changed, however, with King Philip's War at the end of the century and with small success in converting or "civilizing" the Indians. The Puritan divine Solomon Stoddard could even call in the early 1700s for "Indians to be hunted by dogs as they do wild animals."

Many religious individuals and organizations were complicit in extinguishing Indian claims to their lands and even in exterminating Indians. One of the exceptions to the generally sorry record of Christendom's response to Indian culture is the Religious Society of Friends (Quakers). This lesson presents their story and offers some of the reasons that Quakers developed a different approach to the natives of the American continent.

Overview/Outcomes

Students are asked to engage in a role play to illustrate an historical event in which Quakers responded to Indian "unrest" in a manner significantly different from their neighbors. The role play should raise questions about why Quakers reacted to the threat of Indian attack in the way they did and it can open up a discussion of the reasons for the Quakers' harmonious relations with Indian people.

Should the teacher desire, parallels can be made to contemporary relationships between dominant and subordinate or hostile elements of society: who are today's "Indians"?

Connections to the Curriculum

This lesson can be used when students are considering the generally sorry track records of European civilization's response to North American Indians, either with exploration in world history or in colonial U.S. history.

Time Period

The role play can be accomplished easily in a forty-minute period. Processing the role play through discussion of standard responses to Indians from Europeans and the different approach of Quakers (and Indian responses to that) could take one or two additional class periods.

Grade Level

High School and Middle School

Activities
Day One

It is recommended that the teacher begin with a role play of the event known in Quaker lore as "Fierce Feathers." See "Teacher's Notes," below.

Days Two and Three

Students might be encouraged to discuss the role play for a while, and then to summarize their assumptions about Quakers, Indians, and conflict. The fuller historical section, "Background on the Response of Eastern Friends," might be introduced either at the end of this day or at the beginning of the next, followed by discussion of earlier student conclusions in the light of this new information.

Assessment

Have the students reflect on why much of Christendom viewed the Indians as savages while the Quakers did not. Are there lessons to be learned from this for today? Who are the alienated people in contemporary society? Who are the misunderstood ones today? Is it wise for people voluntarily to make themselves as vulnerable today as Friends did in the eighteenth century? Would they achieve the same results?

Selected Bibliography

Jones, Rufus. *The Quakers in the American Colonies*. London: Macmillan, 1911.

Kelsey, Rayner. *Friends and the Indians, 1655-1917*. Philadelphia: The Associated Executive Committee of Friends on Indian Affairs, 1917.

Baker, Wanda Coffin and Barbara Mays. *Put Yourself in the Picture*. Richmond, Ind.: Friends United Meeting, 1985.

Quakers and Indians in Colonial America: Teacher's Notes

Role Situation: It is the summer of 1777 in the Upper River Valley community of Easton, NY. Only a few months before the

Revolutionary War battles of Saratoga, settlers around Easton are warned of impending danger. In addition to the threat of an American-British confrontation, raiding parties of Mohawks, allied with the British, are in the area, attacking homesteads and taking scalps.

Many settlers decide to leave the area and wait out the unsettled times with friends and relatives in safer locales. Others retreat to blockhouses built nearby, where thick walls and locally-trained militia offer security. Still others wait it out with stockpiles of weapons behind fortified doors and windows.

The Quaker community at Easton must make a decision about how to respond to the crisis. Typical of Quakers (also known as Friends) of that era, the community must decide on a course of action by gathering a "sense of the Meeting," similar to the process of consensus building. At question are issues of whether to continue the Friends' silent, unprogrammed meetings for worship twice-weekly; whether to remain faithful to the traditional Quaker peace testimony in this dangerous time; or whether to adopt a less traditional course of action to assure safety.

Roles: Distribute statements that reflect possible responses among the Easton Friends to their situation. Have students adopt the attitude reflected by the statement given them.

1. We shouldn't take up weapons, but we can at least secure our homes better by locking doors and windows and boarding up any openings.
2. During this time of unrest on the frontier, we need to alter our customary habits. Let us suspend our meetings for worship, stay in our homes, and not put ourselves in the position of getting caught in dangerous situations.
3. Let us seek an opportunity to meet with the Indians to learn about their side of the issue.
4. God is our security. We should not depend on weapons or military protection.
5. The present crisis offers us the opportunity to test our beliefs and principles. If our principles of peace are true, they will see us through this difficult time.
6. We need to protect ourselves with weapons in this situation. Wartime calls for a different way of thinking and acting.
7. Let us head for the blockhouses until the Indian threat has passed!

Role Play Procedure: Select a "clerk" (facilitator) for the mock Quaker meeting for business. The teacher may want to serve in this capacity. Instruct the students to portray their given roles initially, but advise that as opinions are expressed they may allow themselves to be convinced otherwise.

Allow sufficient time for all points of view to be expressed; see if any consensus emerges as students change their positions. The clerk should draw the role play to a conclusion if a decision is agreed on by all present or end the exercise by recognizing that no decision can be made at present time.

Processing the Role Play: Discuss how people felt about their given positions and about the direction of the meeting for business. Compare the decision (or lack thereof!) with that made by the Easton Quaker community.

Background

The actual response of Easton Friends might surprise students. Faced with a clear and present danger, aware of alternatives to their pacifist position, the Quakers chose to continue their normal routine, taking no particular precautions against possible attack.

On 17 September 1777, the small Friends community gathered unarmed, for their silent meeting for worship. During the meeting, a band of Indians, led by the Mohawk chief Fierce Feathers, came into the meetinghouse. Their weapons were drawn; fresh scalps hung from their belts. Seeing no weapons in the room and the distinctive bonnets and hats of the Quakers, however, the Indians recognized the worshipers as "children of Onas" (an Indian name for William Penn). They lowered their weapons and were invited by the clerk of the meeting to join in worship. For a short time they did and then milled about outside until the Quakers' silent waiting was over.

When the Friends came outside, the clerk of the meeting invited the Indians to his home to share a meal from the family's meager supply of bread and cheese, the family's larders having been depleted by two recent forays of British troops through the area.

Why this unusual response? For Quakers it was not out of the ordinary but typical of an ethic formed by their understanding of truth and a common storehouse of mental images of how Friends respond to crisis and to such "strangers in the land" as the Indians.

Out of their origins as a left-wing Puritan group in the seventeenth century England, the Quakers emphasized that all persons, regardless of creed or race, were enlightened by a divine (inward) light. They shared a belief that the Hebrew prophet Isaiah's vision of a "peaceful kingdom" was possible on earth. They owned an English Revolution radicalism that stressed egalitarianism, and they practiced a restorationist Christianity that raised the example of Jesus' "Sermon on the Mount"—and its teaching of peace, love, and humility—to normative status.

These impulses were incarnated in the actions of Friends in the American colonies who exercised political power or chose to seek relations with Native Americans. Their examples and experiences became models of Quaker behavior for later generations of Friends such as those at Easton, New York.

William Penn, the Quaker proprietor of Pennsylvania, recognized the Indian as the true owner of the land granted him by Charles II. Writing to the Indians in America in 1681, he told them that although the King had given him the great estate in their part of the world, he desired to enjoy it with their love and consent

. . . that we may always live together as neighbors and friends else what would the great God do to us who hath made us not to devour and destroy one another, but to live soberly and kindly together in the world.

Arriving in Philadelphia in 1682, Penn confirmed his peaceable intentions in the famous (and semi-legendary) "Treaty of Shackamaxon," immortalized in numerous "Peaceable Kingdom" prints by primitivist Quaker painter Edward Hicks. The French philosopher Voltaire described Penn's agreement with the Indians as the only treaty never sworn to and never broken.

The "Quaker Peace" remained in Pennsylvania until Friends left the government of the colony in 1756 in protest over bounties placed on Indian lives and the pressure to raise a militia to protect frontier settlements from Indian attack.

Similar peaceable relations were enjoyed in other colonies where Quakers were a significant presence in the government. John Archdale, Quaker governor of the Carolinas in the 1690s, forbade the enslaving of Indians, drafted legislation to prevent the sale of liquor, and assured that legal cases involving Indians and whites would be tried by juries made up of both parties.

Many Quakers on the frontier "left the latch-string out" rather than securing their homes during times of Indian unrest. The best known story involved a Pennsylvania Quaker family at the time of the French and Indian War. Retiring for the night amid reports that Indian raiding parties were in the area, the father decided to draw the latch-string in for security. His conscience bothered by that act and unable to sleep, he went back downstairs and put the latch-string out.

The next morning the family awoke safe and secure even though Indians had, indeed, swept through the area during the night and devastated neighboring homesteads. The Quaker father later met one of the Indian raiders at a peace conference and was told that when the Indians had seen the unsecured home, even though they had intended to destroy the house, they passed it by in the realization that those people posed no threat to them.

Well-known eighteenth century Quaker John Woolman undertook an unarmed journey through two hundred miles of wilderness into central Pennsylvania during the French and Indian War to visit a village of Indians. His motivation? Love and desire to see if they might have something to teach him.

Penn, Archdale, and Woolman served as models for later Quaker relations with the Indians. The actions of frontier Quaker men and women who chose to live unarmed among the Indians provided powerful example of fidelity to the Quaker peace testimony. With all of these mental images firmly planted in the wider Quaker community, it is little surprise that the Easton Friends chose to respond to crisis the way they did.

Quakers continued this pattern of peaceful relations with the Indians through the succeeding century, as well. Friends intervened on their behalf with the government, disciplined fellow Quakers for settling on disputed Indian lands, and wrote tracts and books defending the nobility of Indians in their "natural state."

As Quakers followed the expanding frontier, Indians recognized the "broadbrims" as the children of Onas, William Penn, and weapons were never needed for their safety.

Endnotes

1. The source for the "Fierce Feathers" incident is Wanda Coffin Barker and Barbara Mays, *Put Yourself in the Picture* (Richmond, Ind.: Friends United Meeting, 1985), 14-17.
2. The source of the William Penn quotation is "William Penn's Letter to the Indians," a copy in the handwriting of John Kendall, Quaker Collections, MS Collection #853, Haverford College.

Max L. Carter earned his Ph.D. from Temple University in American Religious History. He is currently director of Friends Center at Guilford College, where he also teaches.

Federal Indian Policy in the Gilded Age

Era 7: Standard 4

STUDENTS SHOULD UNDERSTAND: FEDERAL INDIAN POLICY AND UNITED STATES FOREIGN POLICY AFTER THE CIVIL WAR.

The purpose of this lesson plan is to encourage students to understand federal policy toward the Indians, specifically considering the Dawes Act and the emergence of the Ghost Dance. This lesson plan involves several types of documents, including a painting by Bierstadt. Teachers should pay special attention to the ideas and motivations of the "reformers." Were their goals laudable? Are they that different from "reformers" today? Is it possible that reformers of any era will fail to solve wide-sweeping problems—i.e., they simply cannot transcend the unique knowledge that only the individuals immediately involved understand? Or, can we consider the work of reformers generally positive? Are their concerns legitimate or patronizing?

In conjunction with History Standard 4 from Era 7, teachers should also incorporate Historical Thinking Standards 2 and 3.

HISTORICAL THINKING STANDARD 2: Draw upon visual, literary, and musical sources to clarify, illustrate, or elaborate upon information in the historical narrative.

HISTORICAL THINKING STANDARD 3: Hypothesize the influence of the past, including both the limitations and the opportunities made possible by past decisions. Also, consider multiple perspectives of various peoples in the past by demonstrating their differing motives, beliefs, interests, hopes, and fears.

Opening Activity: Distribute Albert Bierstadt's "The Rocky Mountains, Lander's Peak" to the students. The following questions should be asked about the painting to help them develop visual analysis skills:

1) What details do you see in the painting? What is in the foreground? Middle ground? Background?
2) What is the relationship of the mountains to the village? Why?
3) From where is light emanating? Do you think there is a reason for this?
4) What is the artist's point of view about the future of the Indian village? What clues in the painting help you develop the point of view of the artist?
5) The artist produced a pamphlet about the painting in which he concluded with the hope that upon the painting's foreground

plain, "a city, populated by our decendants, may rise, and its art galleries this picture may eventually find a rest place. . . . He who lays his ear to the wild grass may perh[a]hear the distant tramp, not of the buffalos, but of civilizati[on] coming like an army with banners."

What is the artist's point of view concerning the Ind[ian] village in this picture? Is this the main point of the pictu[re]? Why or why not?

Developing Activity 1: Distribute to the students the se[lec]tions from the Dawes Act, Chester A. Arthur's and Gro[ver] Cleveland's views concerning Indian reform, the Timeline, [and] the selection from Helen Hunt Jackson's *A Century of Dishon[or]*.

To analyze the ideas contained in the Dawes Act, the follo[w]ing questions (plus, of course, any the teacher wishes to add) n[eed] to be considered by the students dealing with all of the docume[nts]. A "Point of View" chart might prove helpful.

A) What events led to the enactment of the Dawes Act?
B) How do these events help to explain the purpose of the Da[wes] Act?
C) How does Chester A. Arthur justify the Dawes Act? Wha[t is] the relationship between justification and point of vie[w?] Does he feel it will help the Indians? Does he think it w[ill] help the United States? In 1882, Congress passed the Chin[ese] Exclusion Act. Is the Dawes Act a similar or dissimilar la[w?]
D) What tone does Cleveland take in his letter to Hoke Smith? [Is] he concerned or patronizing?
E) How do Arthur's and Cleveland's points of view relate to [the] Bierstadt painting? How do they differ from it?
F) Would Helen Hunt Jackson support the Dawes Act? Wha[t is] her point of view about how the United States should d[eal] with Indians?
G) Analyze the text of the act to help determine its purpose. H[ow] is land distributed? Why? What happens to land that is [not] used? Why? How is citizenship conferred? What is [the] relationship between citizenship and ownership of the la[nd?]

Developing Activity 2: To understand the point of view [of] the American Indian concerning the "reform" aims of the Da[wes] Act and other Indian policies, the students should consider [the] "Ghost Dance" movement. Distribute the description of [the] Ghost Dance to students. Ask them what the motivation [and] purpose of the Ghost Dance was. Ask them also what clues t[hey] find that allow them to determine the purpose of the movem[ent]. What is the attitude toward community and culture reflecte[d in] the Ghost Dance? How might Native Americans involved in [the]

Ghost Dance feel about the Dawes Act? Why?

Concluding Activity: Distribute the map of the area in which the Ghost Dance movement took place. Compare the text of the Dawes Act with the spread of the Ghost Dance and note the relationship. Consider how analyzing the points of view of those who supported the Act and those who rejected it–and the historical context of its promulgation–help us to draw conclusions about the nature of "reform." When is an intended reform simply not a reform?

Summary Discussion: What were the ultimate results of the Dawes Act on Native Americans? On westward movement? On reform? Should the Dawes Act be evaluated within the context of its times or by its results?

SIGNIFICANT INDIVIDUALS

HENRY L. DAWES (1816-1903) represented Massachusetts in both the U.S. House and Senate for thirty-six years. During the Civil War, he served on the War Contracts Committee. Though a quiet man, he masterfully led several key pieces of legislation through the two chambers and helped to eliminate war-time fraud. Disturbed by what he considered a brutal removal and reservation process, Dawes–in conjunction with the Indian Rights Association–proposed the ending of the current Indian system, replacing it with severalty. He hoped to turn the Indians into self-sufficient economic individualists.

GROVER CLEVELAND (1837-1908) was the only Democratic president of the United States between 1861 and 1913. He is also the only president to have served two non-consecutive terms (1885-9 and 1893-7). Though he won the popular vote three times, the electoral college voted for Benjamin Harrison in 1888. Known for his unyielding convictions, honesty, and integrity, Cleveland gained a committed following. In 1880, he was elected mayor of Buffalo, New York. In 1882, he won the governor's office of that state, and only two years later the American people chose him as the 22nd president. Cleveland championed many reforms, including a reduced tariff, less government patronage, and the Dawes Act. In fact the latter was a part of a larger package that reduced businesses' control over western lands.

HELEN HUNT JACKSON (1830-1885) was a poet, reformer, and novelist. After the tragic deaths of her husband and two sons, Jackson moved to the American West. In 1881, she published her first work, *A Century of Dishonor*, a non-fictional account of U.S.-Indian relations. In 1884 she published *Ramona*, a novel she hoped would serve as the *Uncle Tom's Cabin* of the Indian reform movement. She supported the goals of the Dawes Act.

CHESTER A. ARTHUR (1830-86) was elected vice president of the United States and became the twenty-first president after the assassination of President Garfield in 1881. Arthur is best remembered for modernizing the navy and the passage of both the Chinese Exclusion Act in 1882 and a civil service reform bill in 1883; his contemporaries, though, saw him as little more than a machine politician before he became a very dignified president.

TIMELINE OF EVENTS

1864/5: The Sand Creek Massacre, Colorado Territory

1867: Report issued on the Condition of the Indian Indian Peace Commission established to end the Sioux war Conference at Medicine Creek, Kansas: Kiowa, Comanche, Arapaho, and Cheyenne accept reservation lands in western Oklahoma

1874/5: Red River War Custer expedition into the Black Hills

1876: Battle of the Little Big Horn; Custer defeated

1877: Chief Joseph and the Nez Perces surrender to General Nelson Miles in Montana

1881: Helen Hunt Jackson publishes *Century of Dishonor*

1882: Chinese Exclusion Act passed

1886: Geronimo captured

1887: Dawes Act enacted

1890: Ghost Dance Death of Sitting Bull Battle at Wounded Knee

1896: *Plessy v. Ferguson* establishing doctrine of "separate but equal"

WOVOKA (ca. 1856-1932), a Paiute messiah commonly known to whites as Jack Wilson. During an eclipse of the sun, Wovoka claimed to have visited the "Supreme Being." During their talks, the Supreme Being told Wovoka to live in peace and teach other Indians a celebratory dance–what would become the Ghost Dance. By dancing, living and dead Indians would inhabit one world, and the whites would disappear. The dance and its ideals spread quickly during 1890.

ALBERT BIERSTADT (1830-1902), a German by birth, was a famous painter in his day. A romanticist, he was fascinated with the dramatic landscapes of the American West.

Sources: *Dictionary of American Biography* (New York: Charles Scribner's Sons, 1928-44); George Kurian, *Dictionary of Biography* (New York: Laurel, 1980); and Howard R. Lamar, ed., *The Reader's Encyclopedia of the American West* (New York: Thomas Y. Crowell, 1977).

Albert Bierstadt's "Lander's Peak."

The Metropolitan Museum of Art, Rogers Fund, 1907

Warren A. Beck and Ynez D. Haase, *Historical Atlas of the American West* (© University of Oklahoma Press, 1989).

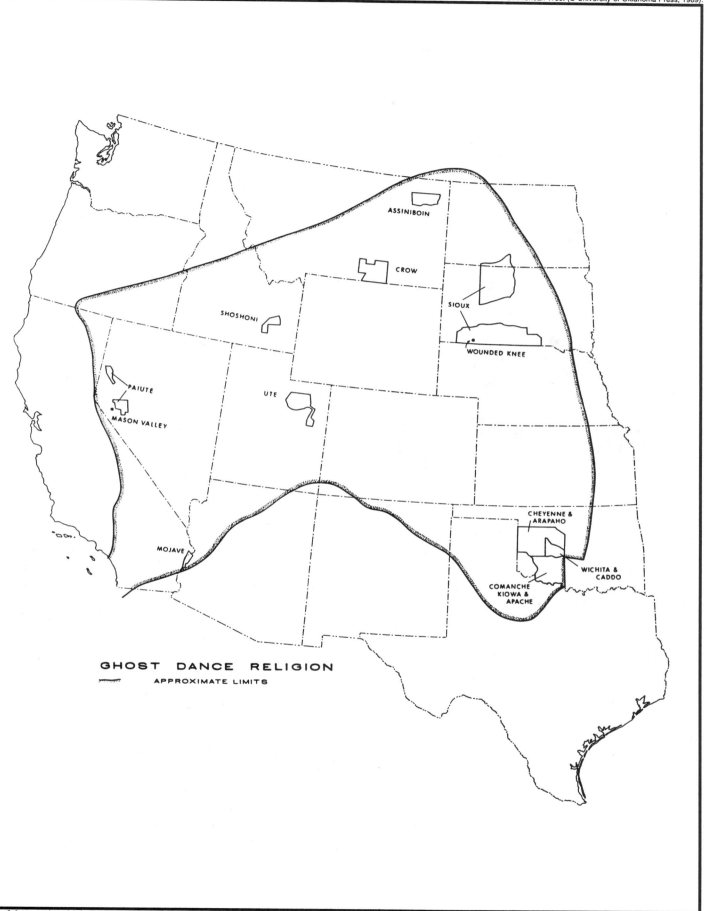

GHOST DANCE RELIGION

APPROXIMATE LIMITS

ASSINIBOIN

CROW

SHOSHONI

SIOUX

WOUNDED KNEE

PAIUTE

MASON VALLEY

UTE

MOJAVE

CHEYENNE & ARAPAHO

WICHITA & CADDO

COMANCHE KIOWA & APACHE

p of the area in which the Ghost Dance occurred.

DOCUMENT 1
General Allotment Act (a.k.a. The Dawes Act) of 1887, excerpted

Senator Henry L. Dawes of Massachusetts, author of the General Allotment Act of 1887.

Be it enacted by the Senate and House of Representatives of the United States of America in Congress assembled, That in all cases where any tribe or band of Indians has been, or shall hereafter be, located upon any reservation created for their use, either by treaty stipulation or by virtue of an act of Congress or executive order setting apart the same for their use, the President of the United States be, and he hereby is, authorized, whenever in his opinion any reservation or any part thereof of such Indians is advantageous for agricultural and grazing purposes, to cause said reservation, or any part thereof, to be surveyed, or resurveyed if necessary, and to allot the lands in said reservation in severalty to any Indian located thereon in quantities as follows:

To each head of a family, one quarter of a section; To each single person over eighteen years of age, one-eighth of a section; To each orphan child under eighteen years of age, one-eighth of a section; and

To each other single person under eighteen years now living, or who may be born prior to the date of the order of the President directing an allotment of the lands embraced in any reservation, one-sixteenth of a section: *Provided*, That in case there is not sufficient land in any of said reservations to allot lands to each individual of the classes above named in quantities as above provided, the lands embraced in such reservation or reservations shall be allotted to each individual of each of said classes pro rate in accordance with the provisions of this act: *And provided further*, That where the treaty or act of Congress setting apart such reservation provides for the allotment of lands in severalty in quantities in excess of those herein provided, the President, in making allotments upon such reservation, shall allot the lands to each individual Indian belonging thereon in quantity as specified in such treaty or act: *And provided further*, That when the lands allotted are only valuable for grazing purposes, an additional allotment of such grazing lands, in quantities as above provided, shall be made to each individual. . . .

Sec. 5. That upon the approval of the allotments provided for in this act by the Secretary of the Interior, he shall cause patents to issue therefor in the name of the allottees, which patents shall be of the legal effect, and declare that the United States does and will hold the land thus allotted, for the period of twenty-five years, in trust for the sole use and benefit of the Indian to whom such allotment shall have been made, or, in case of his decease, of his heirs according to the laws of the State or Territory where such land is located, and that at the expiration of said period the United States will convey the same by patent to said Indian, of his heirs as aforesaid, in fee, discharged of said trust and free of all charge or incumbrance whatsoever. . . .

Sec. 6. That upon the completion of said allotments and the patenting of the lands to said allottees, each and every member of the respective bands or tribes of Indians to whom allotments have been made shall have the benefit of and be subject to the laws, both civil and criminal, of the State or Territory in which they may reside; and no Territory shall pass or enforce any law denying any such Indian within its jurisdiction the equal protection of the law. And every Indian both within the territorial limits of the United States to whom allotments shall have been made under the provisions of this act, or under any law or treaty, and every Indian born within the territorial limits of the United States who has voluntarily taken up, within said limits, his residence separate and apart from any tribe of Indians therein, and has adopted the habits of civilized life, is hereby declared to be a citizen of the United States, and is entitled to all the rights, privileges, and immunities of such citizens, whether said Indian has been or not, by birth or otherwise, a member of any tribe of Indians within the territorial limits of the United States without in any manner, impairing or otherwise affecting the right of any such Indian to tribal or other property. . . .

Sec. 8. That the provision of this act shall not extend to the territory occupied by the Cherokees, Creeks, Choctaws, Chickasaws, Seminoles, and Osage, Miamies and Peorias, and Sacs and Foxes, in the Indian Territory, nor to any of the reservations of the Seneca Nation of New York Indians in the State of New York, nor to that strip of territory in the State of Nebraska adjoining the Sioux Nation on the south added by executive order.

Harper's, 11 February 1882

Distribution of supplies and annuities, 1882. Henry L. Dawes and his supporters believed that such policies destroyed the will and independence of the Indians.

DOCUMENT 2
Reformer Helen Hunt Jackson's Viewpoint

Baggs, *Colorado*, p. 333

Helen Hunt Jackson, an author and pro-Indian reformer.

To assume it would be easy, or by any one sudden stroke of legislative policy possible, to undo the mischief and hurt of the long past, set the Indian policy of the country right for the future, and make the Indians at once safe and happy, is the blunder of a hasty and misinformed judgment. The notion which seems to be growing more prevalent, that simply to make all Indians at once citizens of the United States would be a sovereign and instantaneous panacea for all their ills and all the Government's perplexities, is a very inconsiderate one. To administer complete citizenship of a sudden, all round, to all Indians, barbarous and civilized alike, would be a grotesque blunder as to dose them all around with one medicine. . . . Nevertheless, it is true that. . . . "so long as they are not citizens of the United States, their rights of property must remain insecure against invasion. The doors of the federal tribunals barred against them while wards and dependents." All judicious plans and measures for their safety and salvation must embody provisions for their becoming citizens as fast as they are fit.

Source: Helen Hunt Jackson, *A Century of Dishonor* (Boston: Roberts Brothers, 1881).

DOCUMENT 3
President Chester A. Arthur's Viewpoint

"It has been easier to resort to convenient makeshifts for tiding over temporary difficulties than to grapple with the permanent problem, and accordingly the easier course has been pursued. . . . It was natural, at a time when the national territory seemed almost illimitable and contained many millions of acres far outside the bounds of civilized settlements, that a policy should have been enacted which more than anything else has been the fruitful source of our Indian complications. I refer, of course, to the policy of dealing with the various Indian tribes as separate nationalities, of relegating them by treaty stipulations, to immense reservations in the west, and encouraging them to lead a savage life, undisturbed by any earnest and well directed efforts to bring them under the influences of civilization. The results of this policy are increasingly unsatisfactory. White settlements have crowded the borders of reservations. . . . Indians transferred to new hunting grounds (which have soon become) new homes desired by adventurous settlers. Frequent and disastrous conflicts between the races have resulted. . . thousands of lives have been sacrificed and. . . . millions of dollars expended to solve the Indian problem which exists today as it did half a century ago. The very existence of the Indian prompts us to act now, to introduce among the Indians the customs and pursuits of civilized life and gradually to absorb them into the mass of our citizens, with equal sharing of rights and responsibilities, before the very Indian culture itself evaporates."

Source: James D. Richardson, ed., *A Compilation of the Messages and Papers of the Presidents* (New York: Bureau of National Literature, 1897).

DOCUMENT 4
Letter from President Grover Cleveland to Secretary of the Interior Hoke Smith, 4 May 1895, concerning allotment.

As the commissioners to negotiate and treat with the five civilized tribes of Indians are about to resume their labors, my interest in the subject they have in charge induces me to write you a few words concerning their work. As I said to the commissioners when they were first appointed, I am especially desirous that there shall be no reason in all time to come to charge the commissioners with any unfair dealing with the Indians, and that whatever the results of their efforts may be the Indians will not be led into any action which they do not thoroughly understand or which is not clearly for their benefit.

At the same time I still believe, as I have always believed, that the best interests of the Indians will be found in American citizenship, with all the rights and privileges which belong to that condition. The approach

Wilson, *History of the American People*, 1902

this relation should be carefully made and at every step the good and welfare of the Indian should be constantly kept in view, so that when the end is reached citizenship may be to them a real advantage, instead of an empty name.

I hope the commissioners will inspire such confidence in those Indians with whom they have to deal that they will be listened to and that the Indians will see the wisdom and advantage of moving in the direction I have indicated. If they are unwilling to go immediately so far as we may think desirable, whatever steps are taken should be such as to point out the way and the results of which will encourage these people in future progress. A slow movement of that kind, fully understood and approved by the Indians, is infinitely better than swifter results gained by broken pledges and false promises.

Source: Allan Nevins, ed., *Letters of Grover Cleveland, 1850-1908* (Boston: Houghton Mifflin, 1933).

President Grover Cleveland, an advocate of the Dawes Act.

DOCUMENT 5
"The Ghost Dance Religion" by James Mooney, excerpted

"You must not fight. Do no harm to anyone. Do right always."—Wovoka.

The great underlying principle of the Ghost dance doctrine is that the time will come when the whole Indian race, living and dead, will be reunited upon a regenerated earth, to live a life of aboriginal happiness, forever free from death, disease, and misery. On this foundation each tribe has built a structure from its own mythology, and each apostle and believer has filled in the details according to his own mental capacity or ideas of happiness, with such additions as come to him from the trance. Some changes, also, have undoubtedly resulted from the transmission of the doctrine through the imperfect medium of the sign language. The differences of interpretation are precisely such as we find in Christianity, with its hundreds of sects and innumerable shades of individual opinion. The white race, being alien and secondary and hardly real, has no part in this scheme of aboriginal regeneration, and will be left behind with the other things of earth that have served their temporary purpose, or else will cease entirely to exist.

All this is to be brought about by an overruling spiritual power that needs no assistance from human creatures; and though certain medicine-men were disposed to anticipate the Indian millennium by preaching resistance to the further encroachments of the whites, such teachings form no part of the true doctrine, and it was only where chronic dissatisfaction was aggravated by recent grievances, as among the Sioux, that the movement assumed a hostile expression. On the contrary, all believers were exhorted to make themselves worthy of the predicted happiness by discarding all things warlike and practicing honesty, peace, and good will, not only among themselves, but also toward the whites, so long as they were together. Some apostles have even thought that all race distinctions are to be obliterated, and that the whites are to participate with the Indians in the coming felicity; but it seems unquestionable that this is equally contrary to the doctrine as originally preached.

Different dates have been assigned at various times for the fulfillment of the prophecy. Whatever the year, it has generally been held, for very natural reasons, that the regeneration of the earth and the renewal of all life would occur in the early spring. In some cases July, and particularly the 4th of July, was the expected time. This, it may be noted, was about the season when the great annual ceremony of the sun dance formerly took place among the prairie tribes. The messiah himself has set several dates from time to time, as one prediction after another failed to materialize, and in his message to the Cheyenne and Arapaho, in August, 1891, he leaves the whole matter in open question. The date universally recognized among all the tribes immediately prior to the Sioux outbreak was the spring of 1891. As springtime came and passed, and summer grew and waned, and autumn faded again into winter without the realization of their hopes and longings, the doctrine gradually assumed its present form—that some time in the unknown future the Indian will be united with his friends who have gone before, to be forever supremely happy, and that this happiness may be anticipated in dreams, if not actually hastened in reality, by earnest and frequent attendance on the sacred dance....

One of the first and most prominent of those who brought the doctrine to the prairie tribes was Porcupine, a Cheyenne, who crossed the mountains with several companions in the fall of 1889, visited Wovoka, and attended the dance near Walker lake, Nevada. In his report of his experiences, made some months later to a military officer, he states that Wovoka claimed to be Christ himself who had come back again, many centuries after his first rejection, in pity to teach his children. He quotes

Wilson, *History of the American People*, 1902

the prophet as saying:

"I found my children were bad, so I went back to heaven and left them. I told them that in so many hundred years I would come back to see my children. At the end of this time I was sent back to try to teach them. My father told me the earth was getting old and worn out and the people getting bad, and that I was to renew everything as it used to be and make it better.

He also told us that all our dead were to be resurrected; that they were all to come back to earth, and that, as the earth was too small for them and us, he would do away with heaven and make the earth itself large enough to contain us all; that we must tell all the people we met about these things. He spoke to us about fighting, and said that was bad and we must keep from it; that the earth was to be all good hereafter, and we must all be friends with one another. He said

Sitting Bull, a victim of the Battle of Wounded Knee, 1890.

that in the fall of the year the youth of all good people would be renewed, so that nobody would be more than forty years old, and that if they behaved themselves well after this the youth of everyone would be renewed in the spring. He said if we were all good he would send people among us who could heal all our wounds and sickness by mere touch and that we would live forever. He told us not to quarrel or fight or strike each other, or shoot one another; that the whites and Indians were to be all one people. He said if any man disobeyed what he ordered his tribe would be wiped from the face of the earth; that we must believe everything he said, and we must not doubt him or say he lied; that if we did, he would know it; that he would know our thoughts and actions in no matter what part of the world we might be."

Here we have the statement that both races are to live together as one. We have also the doctrine of healing by touch. Whether or not this is an essential part of the system is questionable, but it is certain that the faithful believe that great physical good comes to them, to their children, and to the sick from the imposition of hands by the priests of the dance, apart from the ability thus conferred to see the things of the spiritual world.

SOURCE: James Mooney, *The Ghost-Dance Religion and the Sioux Outbreak of 1890*, ed. Anthony F.C. Wallace (Chicago: University of Chicago Press, 1965).

Treaty Mistranslations and Diplomatic Dilemmas

Loron Sauguaaram was the spokesman for the Penobscots (and ultimately for all the Abenaki Indians) in a series of negotiations to end Dummer's War which culminated in the Casco Bay Treaty in 1727. Loron became aware of mistranslations of the treaty provisions and dictated a letter detailing exactly how the provisions had been translated to him and in what negotiations and agreements he had participated. This provides the opportunity for an examination of colonial treaty negotiations and a general discussion of cross-cultural understanding and accommodation.

The Abenaki Indians inhabited most of present-day Maine, New Hampshire, and Vermont. During the colonial wars many of these Abenaki migrated north to the French mission villages of St. Francis and Becancour along the St. Lawrence River. The Penobscot and Norridgewock Indians were major Abenaki tribes in central Maine while many other Abenakis lived in small villages throughout western Maine, New Hampshire, and Vermont. The St. Johns and Cape Sable Indians listed in the Casco Bay Treaty were the Maliseet and Micmac Indians who inhabited present-day New Brunswick and Nova Scotia. The term "Eastern Indians" referred to all of these groups.

OBJECTIVES

1. Students will understand the ethnocentric assumptions inherent in the treaty document.

2. Students will recognize the important role of intermediaries in resolving cross-cultural disputes.

3. Students will engage in critical thinking concerning the motivations of the interpreters and the obligations of Loron after he is aware of the mistranslations.

CONDUCT OF CLASS

The instructor should present a brief summary of the historical events leading up to the Casco Bay Treaty and pass out copies of Loron's letter and the treaty text to the students. Students should compile a list of the discrepancies between the treaty text and Loron's version of the negotiations. What were the major issues in dispute and what resolutions of those disputes were advocated by each side? This could be an individual or group homework assignment or a small group in-class activity. Option: Rather than presenting the historical background, see if the students can determine what issues caused Dummer's War by looking at the issues addressed in the two documents.

Class discussion should address the ethnocentric assumption revealed by the various discrepancies between the two document concerning sovereignty, autonomy, submission, alliance land claims ownership, and legal jurisdiction. Students could also ponder the possible motivations for the mistranslations. Are the translator engaged in duplicity and deceit (Massachusetts purposely concealed the extent of its land ownership) or are they merely accommodating irreconcilable viewpoints? How different is this from modern negotiators who achieve settlements by using words which each side can interpret favorably? Would the war have been concluded i accurate translations had been given?

Class discussion could then turn to Loron's obligations to hi tribe since he knows about the mistranslations. What were the various diplomatic and political options for him and his tribe? Wha would have been the likely consequences for his people if he had rejected the treaty? Under what circumstances will the misunder standings created (or perpetuated) by this treaty cause future diplo matic problems? Students should critique Loron's decision to sign the mistranslated treaty to secure peace and dictate a letter to document his understanding of the agreement. The instructor should conclude the class by explaining how most of the differing interpre tations of the treaty provisions were moot points in peace time bu would become crucial issues during frontier tension and warfare ultimately leading to two Massachusetts declarations of war on the Abenakis.

HISTORICAL BACKGROUND

In July 1713, directly after the cessation of hostilities in Europe the Treaty of Portsmouth formally ended Queen Anne's War on the Maine frontier. Anglo-Abenaki relations remained cool because some of the settlements established after the war, particularly those near the Kennebec River, violated the Abenaki understanding of the Portsmouth treaty. Abenaki leaders requested a conference in 1717 but the angry negotiations only served to increase tensions. Massa chusetts Governor Shute repeatedly demanded Abenaki submission to English sovereignty and recognition of English land claims, while Abenaki negotiator Wiwurna outlined the Indian understanding of the treaty. This situation remained unresolved three years later when a band of frustrated Abenakis, attempting to inhibit further settle ment, killed some cattle and burned crops and buildings. Massachu setts retaliated by seizing four Norridgewock Abenakis as hostages, demanding compensation for damages, and then refused to release the Indians when payment was delivered. In 1721, the Massachusetts militia seized Joseph d'Abbadie, son of French Baron St. Castin and his Penobscot wife, Pidianske. The Abenakis retaliated, taking sixty-five captives. They released most of them, however, with an offer to negotiate peace and exchange prisoners. Massachusetts eventually released d'Abbadie, but before this information reached the Indians, some disgruntled Abenakis launched another attack, prompting Massachusetts to declare war.

This conflict, known as Governor Dummer's War, was a disaster for the Abenakis in Maine. French neutrality enabled Massachusetts and New Hampshire to focus their full attention on the Abenakis resulting in aggressive militia patrolling and repeated military expeditions up the Kennebec and Penobscot Rivers. The destruction of Abenaki villages, the disruption of hunting, gathering, and fishing activities and the constant threat of attack caused great hardship for the Indians, eventually driving most of the Abenakis to migrate (many only temporarily) to the Jesuit missions at St. Francis and Becancour, near the St. Lawrence River. Peace negotiations began in 1725 between Massachusetts and representatives of the Penobscot tribe, leading to a peace conference with that tribe in 1726 and ultimately the Casco Bay Treaty in July 1727.

DISPUTED ISSUES

The Casco Bay Treaty confirmed English rights to all land previously purchased, and it called upon the Abenaki to submit to English sovereignty and provide military support against any Indians who broke the peace in the future. However, the implications of the treaty were not clearly spelled out to the Abenaki. A series of letters and Indian actions over the next several years suggest that English interpreters had again mistranslated the provisions during the negotiations. Abenaki submission to English rule, for instance, was translated simply as a salute to the Massachusetts governor. Since the governor responded by saluting the Abenaki leaders, the Indians assumed this indicated equal status and not subjugation. The obligation to provide warrior support was translated as a pledge to attempt to dissuade other Indians from attacking.

Similarly, the provisions concerning Abenaki responsibility for causing the war and their acceptance of Massachusetts law and the jurisdiction of Massachusetts courts over them were not accurately explained. Finally, Massachusetts repeatedly misled the Abenakis concerning the extent of English land claims and ignored Abenaki requests for a definitive boundary.

SUBSEQUENT EVENTS

Dummer's Treaty was followed by seventeen years of peace, during which most of the disputed provisions of the treaty were moot points, although English settlement expansion caused some difficulties. Frontier tensions increased after the outbreak of another Anglo-French war in Europe in March 1744, and the occurrence during the following months of numerous Indian raids from Canada. The Norridgewocks and Penobscots rejected a Massachusetts demand

that they provide military support against these Canadian Indians, but they willingly gave information about Indian activities in the area and sought to dissuade other Indians from attacking. In October 1744, a group of English scalp hunters killed one Penobscot and wounded several others. Massachusetts sent its condolences to the tribe, but at the same time reiterated its demand for warrior support. Diplomacy continued to deteriorate until July 1745, when Canadian Indians attacked the Maine frontier again, prompting Massachusetts to declare war on the Norridgewock and Penobscot Abenakis in August 1745.

The Treaty of Falmouth, in October 1749, concluded this Anglo-Abenaki war with a simple restatement of Dummer's Treaty, (which was again mistranslated) but warfare was renewed during the following two years as the result of the murder of an Abenaki. In 1752 and 1753, the Norridgewocks repeatedly protested a new settlement on the Kennebec River north of Fort Richmond which violated the Abenaki understanding of Dummer's Treaty. Massachusetts officials finally revealed English ownership of land fifty-five miles upriver from Fort Richmond and then mounted a military expedition to construct a new fort, Fort Halifax, to secure their ownership of the territory. This prompted an attack on the new fort on 30 October 1754 and a Massachusetts demand for Penobscot warrior support. Refusing, the Penobscots responded with a series of letters professing peace and outlining their understanding of their treaty commitments. A series of Abenaki raids in early June prompted a renewed demand for Penobscot warrior support and an incident where a band of scalp hunters killed fourteen Penobscot leaders. Massachusetts temporarily withdrew the demand for warrior support and tempers cooled over the next two months, but diplomacy was again interrupted by another Indian attack on the Maine frontier. The Penobscots, fearing reprisals, fled the area, and Massachusetts, assuming this act confirmed the tribe's involvement, declared war on them on 1 November 1755. ❑

BIBLIOGRAPHY

Calloway, Colin G. *Dawnland Encounters: Indians and Europeans in Northern New England*. Hanover, N.H.: University Press of New England, 1991.

Ghere, David L. "Abenaki Factionalism, Emigration and Social Continuity: Indian Society in Northern New England, 1725 to 1765." Ph.D. dissertation, University of Maine, 1988.

———, "Mistranslations and Misinformation: Diplomacy on the Maine Frontier, 1725-1755." *American Indian Culture and Research Journal* 8(1984): 3-26.

Jones, Dorothy V. *License for Empire: Colonialism by Treaty in Early America*. Chicago: University of Chicago Press, 1982.

Morrison, Kenneth M. *The Embattled Northeast: The Elusive Ideal of Alliance in Abenaki-Euramerican Relations*. Los Angeles: University of California Press, 1984.

David L. Ghere is an Assistant Professor of History in the General College at the University of Minnesota. He is the author of six articles concerning the Abenaki Indians.

HANDOUT #1—CASCO BAY TREATY
TREATY MISTRANSLATIONS

The Submission and Agreement of theDelegates of the Eastern Indians

Whereas the several Tribes of the Eastern Indians Viz. The Penobscot, Nerridgawock, St. Johns, Cape Sables, and other Tribes Inhabiting within his Majesties territories of New England and Nova Scotia, who have been engaged in the present War, from whom we, Saguaarum alias Loron, Arexis, Francois Xavier, and Meganumbee, are delegated and fully empowered to enter into articles of pacification with His Majesties Government of the Massachusetts Bay, New Hampshire, and Nova Scotia, have contrary to the several Treaties they have solemnly, entered into the said Governments made an Open Rupture, and have continued some Years in Acts of Hostility against the Subjects of His Majesty King George within the said Governments.

They being now sensible of the Miseries and Troubles they have involved themselves in, and being desirous to be restored to His Majesties Grace and Favor, and to Live in Peace with all His Majesties Subjects of the said Three Governments, and the Provinces of New York and Colonies of Connecticut and Rhode Island and that all former Acts of Injury be forgotten have Concluded to make, and we do by these Presents in the Name and Behalf of the said Tribes make Our Submission unto His Most Excellent Majesty George by the Grace of God of Great Britain, France and Ireland, King Defender of the Faith, & c. in as Full and Ample Manner, as any of our Predecessors have heretofore done. . . .

We the said Delegates for and behalf of the several Tribes above said, Do Promise and Engage, that at all times for Ever, from and after the Date of the presents, We and They will Cease and Forbear all Acts of Hostility, Injuries and Discords towards all the Subjects of the Crown of Great Britain, and not offered the least Hurt, Violence, or Molestation to them or any of them in their Persons or Estates, But will hence forward hold and maintain a firm and constant Amity and Friendship with all the English and will never confederate or combine with any other Nation to their Prejudice. . . .

That His Majesty's Subjects the English shall and may peaceably and quietly enter upon, improve and forever enjoy all and singular their Rights of Land and former Settlements, Properties and Possessions within the Eastern parts of the said Province of the Massachusetts Bay together with all islands, Islets, Shores, Beaches, and Fishery within the same, without any Molestation or Claims by us or any other Indians, and be in no ways Molested, Interrupted, or Disturbed therein. Saving unto the Penobscot, Nerridgawock, and other Tribes within His Majesties Province aforesaid, and their Natural Descendants respectively, and their Lands, Liberties and Properties not by them conveyed or Sold to or Possessed by any of the English Subjects as aforesaid, as also the Privilege of Fishing, Hunting and Fowling as formerly. . . .

If any Controversy or Difference at any time hereafter happen to arise between any time hereafter happen to arise between any of the English and Indians for any real or supposed Wrong or Injury done on either side, no Private Revenge shall be taken for the same but proper Application shall be made to His Majesties Government upon the place for Remedy or Redress thereof in a due course of Justice.

We Submitting Our selves to be Ruled and Governed by His Majesty's Laws, and desiring to have the Benefit of the same. . . We do further in Behalf of the Tribe of the Penobscot Indians, promise and engage, that if any of the other Tribes intended to be Included in this Treaty, shall notwithstanding refuse to Confirm and Ratify this present Treaty entered into on their Behalf and continue or Renew Acts of Hostility against the English, in such case the said Penobscot Tribe shall join their Young Men with the English in reducing them to Reason. . . .

That this present Treaty shall be Accepted Ratified and Confirmed in a Public and Solemn manner by the Chiefs of the several Eastern Tribes of Indians included therein at Falmouth in Casco Bay some time in the Month of May next. In Testimony whereof we have Signed these Presents, and Affixed Our Seals.

Sauguaarum	Arexus	Francois Xavier	Alaganumlee

Done in the presence of the Great and General Court or Assembly of the Province of the Massachusetts Bay aforesaid, being first Read distinctly, and Interpreted by Capt. John Gyles, Capt. Samuel Jordan, and Capt. Joseph Bane, Sworn Interpreters.

Attest J. Willard, Secr.

Source: "Indian Treaties," *Collections of the Maine Historical Society* 4 (1856):118-84. Spelling has been modernized and the document shortened with editing.

HANDOUT #2—LORON SAUGUAARUM'S LETTER
TREATY MISTRANSLATIONS

I . . . do inform you-you who are scattered all over the earth take notice-of what has passed between me and the English in negotiating the peace that I have just concluded with them. It is from the bottom of my heart that I inform you; and, as a proof that I tell you nothing but the truth, I wish to speak to you in my own tongue.

My reason for informing you, myself, is the diversity and contrariety of the interpretations I receive of the English writing in which the articles of peace are drawn up that we have just mutually agreed to. These writings appear to contain things that are not, so that the Englishman himself disavows them in my presence, when he reads and interprets them to me himself. . . .

We were two that went to Boston: I, Loron Sauguaarum, and John Ehennekouite. On arriving there I did indeed salute him in the usual mode at the first interview, but I was not the first to speak to him. I only answered what he said to me, and such was the course I observed throughout the whole of our interview.

He began by asking me, what brought me hither? I did not give him for answer—I am come to ask your pardon; nor, I come to acknowledge you as my conqueror; nor, I come to make my submission to you; nor, I come to receive your commands. All the answer I made was that I was come on his invitation to me to hear the propositions for a settlement that he wished to submit to me.

Wherefore do we kill one another? he again asked me. Its true that, in reply, I said to him—you are right. But I did not say to him, I acknowledge myself the cause of it, nor I condemn myself for having made war on him. . . .

Thereupon, he said to me—Let us observe the treaties concluded by our Fathers, and renew the ancient friendship that existed between us. I made him no answer thereunto. Much less, I repeat, did I, become his subject, or give him my land, or acknowledge his King as my King. This I never did, and he never proposed it to me. I say, he never said to me—Give yourself and your land to me, nor acknowledge my King for your King, as your ancestors formerly did.

He again said to me—But do you not recognize the King of England as King over all his states? To which I answered—yes, I recognize him King of all his land; but I rejoined, do not hence infer that I acknowledge your King as my King, and King of my lands. Here lies my distinction—my Indian distinction. God has willed that I have no King, and that I be master of my lands in common.

He again asked me—Do you not admit that I am at least master of the lands I have purchased? I answered him thereupon, that I admit nothing, and that I knew not what he had referenced to.

He again said to me—If, hereafter, any one desire to disturb the negotiation of the peace we are at present engaged about, we will join together to arrest him. I again consented to that. But I did not say to him, and do not understand that he said to me, that we should go in company to attack such person, or that we should form a joint league, offensive and defensive, or that I should unite my brethren to his. I said to him only, and I understand him to say to me, that if anyone wished to disturb our negotiation of peace, we would both endeavor to pacify him by fair words, and to that end would direct all our efforts.

He again said to me—In order that the peace we would negotiate be permanent, should any private quarrel arise hereafter, between Indians and Englishmen, they must not take justice into their own hands, nor do anything the one unto the other. It shall be the business of us chief to decide. I again agreed with him on that article but I did not understand that he alone should be the judge. I understood only that he should judge his people, and that I would judge mine.

Finally he said to me—There's our peace concluded; we have regulated every thing.

I replied that nothing had been yet concluded, and that it was necessary that our acts should be approved in a general assembly. For the present, an armistice is sufficient. I again said to him—I now go to inform all my relatives of what has passed between us, and will afterwards come and report to you what they will say to me. . . .

These are the principle matters that I wished to communicate to you who are spread all over the earth. What I tell you now is the truth. If, then, any one should produce any writing that makes me speak otherwise, pay no attention to it, for I know not what I am made to say in another language, but I know well what I say is my own. And in testimony that I say things as they are, I have signed the present minutes which I wish to be authentic and to remain for ever.

Source: *Documents Relative to the Colonial History of the State of New York*, E.B. O'Callaghan, ed., 15 vols. (Albany, N.Y.: Weed, Parsons, 1855), 9:966-7. Spelling has been modernized and the document edited.

Indian Removal: Manifest Destiny or Hypocrisy?

The U.S. government policy of Indian Removal in the 1830s provides a focus for the exploration of a variety of related issues in cross-cultural relations during our nation's first half-century of existence. American expansion, in general, and the Indian Removal policy, in particular, were so devastating to the Indians that it prompted spirited opposition from them and necessitated justification by governmental officials. This lesson plan uses quotations from both U.S. government officials and Indian leaders over a half-century to convey the attitudes and assumptions that guided both sides in their interaction.

OBJECTIVES FOR THE STUDENTS

1. To examine the various ethnocentric assumptions and attitudes that enabled U.S. government officials to justify their policies toward Native Americans.

2. To understand the variety of Native-American responses to the encroachments on their land and to the threats to their culture.

3. To experience the imagery and use of metaphor and simile which was so prominent in Native-American oratory.

TEACHING MATERIALS

Handout #1—"Justifications for Conquest" containin quotes from Tennessee Governor John Sevier in 1798, Joh Quincy Adams in 1802, Secretary of War John C. Calhoun i 1818, and Georgia Governor George Gilmer around 1830.

Handout #2—"Native American Responses to Expansion containing single statements by Red Jacket, a Seneca chief i 1792 and by Pushmataha, a Choctaw leader in 1812, as well a two by Tecumseh, a Shawnee chief in 1795 and 1812.

Handout #3—"Indian Removal Policy" containing e× cerpts from speeches by President Andrew Jackson in 1835 an Indian Commissioner William Medill in 1848.

Handout #4—"Native American Responses to Indian R moval" containing quotes from Black Hawk, a chief of th Sauk and Fox in 1833, Speckled Snake, a Creek elder in 182 and George Harkins, a chief of the Choctaws in 1832.

CONDUCT OF CLASS

The first portion of the class should be devoted to fronti relations during the early-nineteenth century which were cha acterized by numerous examples of both confrontation an ccommodation. This part of the class can be concluded in bout twenty-five minutes or expanded to fifty minutes if the nstructor chooses to promote an in-depth analytical discusion of government attitudes and justifications and Native-American responses.

One option would be to begin class by distributing HAND-UT #1 — "Justifications for Conquest" and HANDOUT #2—Native American Responses to Expansion." Students could hen be asked to identify and explain the justifications for onquest in HANDOUT #1 and the solutions to frontier probms proposed in HANDOUT #2. This could be a homework ssignment to prepare for class the next day or an in-class roup activity. The instructor could ask how these views relate o the wars, treaties, and land cessions from 1780 to 1815.

A second option would be to start out by discussing the ree U.S. policy options: destroy the Indians, assimilate the dians, or respect Indian rights and sovereignty. Student leas could be elicited concerning the extent to which the first vo alternatives were pursued and why the third choice was not riously considered. As the discussion develops, the instrucr can read each quotation on HANDOUTS #1 and #2 separtely whenever that specific quote seems most appropriate to e discussion. Students could then discuss which views ould logically lead to policies of confrontation or assimilaon and how they relate to the wars, treaties, and land cessions om 1780 to 1815.

The second portion of the class should focus on the policy f Indian Removal and Native-American reaction to that olicy. This could be concluded in twenty-five minutes if iscussion is limited and the class is primarily conducted in a cture format. A full fifty-minute period would enable much ore discussion and greater analysis of the situation. Also, onducting the first and second portions of the class on onsecutive days (even if each is limited to only twenty-five inutes of class time), allows for homework assignments to epare for the second portion of the class.

The instructor could distribute HANDOUT #3 and ask udents in what ways these quotes portray the Indian Removal olicy as beneficial to the Indians. What assumptions about e adaptability of the Indians lend support to the removal olicy? (They can hunt buffalo; plenty of room so other dians will not object to the newcomers.) Which statements these documents are distortions of the truth? (At the pense of the U.S. government; adopt agriculture in an area en known as "The Great American Desert;" this land forever aaranteed to them.) Compare the favorable options and utonomy for Indians depicted in Jackson's statement with ledill's vision of the inevitable changes that circumstances ill force on the Indians. What other contradictions are there etween the two documents? Additional questions could clude: Do these two officials believe the Indians can ever be similated into society? Is the removal policy based on the sumption that the Indians cannot assimilate or that removal

gives them more time so that they can assimilate?

Another option (or an additional area for discussion) could be pursued by the instructor posing the question: What aspects of white culture were the Indians expected to adopt to assimilate into society? Students could use the Jackson and Medill quotes or their textbook, or they could engage in a brainstorming activity to determine what changes were thought to be necessary for Indians to assimilate. This could be a question for a homework assignment or an in-class group project. The lists could then be discussed and evaluated by exchanging them between the groups or reading them to the whole class. The instructor then could relate the story of the Cherokees who did everything that was demanded (adopted Christianity, representative government, legal system, individual land ownership, and written language as well as white methods of agriculture, education, dress, and mode of living) and still had their land taken and were forced to move to Oklahoma.

The class would conclude with an examination of Native-American responses to Indian Removal. The quotes from Black Hawk, Speckled Snake, and George Harkins could be distributed and discussion could focus on the similarities and differences between these three responses to Indian Removal. What kind of arguments does each use in criticizing the removal policy? What attitudes are revealed about frontier relations in the past and what are the authors' expectations for the future? All six Native-American quotations can be discussed concerning the imagery and the use of metaphor and simile in Native-American orations. The class could conclude with some examples of the tragedies that occurred in the "Trail of Tears." ❏

FURTHER READING

The most useful work for government documents is Francis Paul Prucha, ed., *Documents of United States Indian Policy* (Lincoln: University of Nebraska Press, 1975). Numerous examples of Indian oratory are contained in Peter Nabokov, ed., *Native American Testimony: An Anthology of Indian and White Relations: First Encounter to Dispossession* (New York: Harper and Row, 1978); and T. C. McLuhan, *Touch the Earth: A Self-Portrait of Indian Existence* (New York: Promontary Press, 1971). Jerry R. Baydo, *Readings in American Indian History* (Wheaton, Ill.: Gregory Publishing Company, 1992) contains quotations from both sides.

Students or the instructor desiring more background information about frontier relations during this period could consult three brief books: Jerry R. Baydo, *The History of the American Indian* (Wheaton, Ill.: Gregory Publishing Company, 1992); Theda Perdue and Michael Green, *The Cherokee Removal: A Brief History with Documents* (New York: St. Martin's Press, 1995); and Philip Weeks, *Farewell, My Nation: The American Indian and the United States, 1820-1890* (Arlington Heights, Ill.: Harlan Davidson, 1990).

HANDOUT #1—JUSTIFICATIONS FOR CONQUEST
INDIAN REMOVAL

William H. Seward, *Life of John Quincy Adams*, 1886

John Quincy Adams, an advocate of removal.

Governor John Sevier of Tennessee in 1798

"By the law of nations, it is agreed that no people shall be entitled to more land than they can cultivate. Of course no people will sit and starve for want of land to work, when a neighboring nation has much more than they can make use of."

John Quincy Adams in 1802

"What is the right of the huntsman to the forest of a thousand miles over which he has accidentally ranged in quest of prey? Shall the fields and valleys, which God has formed to teem with life of innumerable multitudes, be condemned to everlasting barrenness?"

Secretary of War John C. Calhoun in 1818

The Indians "neither are, in fact, nor ought to be, considered as independent nations. Our views on their interests, and not their own, ought to govern them. By a proper combination of force and persuasion, of punishments and rewards, they ought to be brought within the pales of law and civilization. Left to themselves, they will never reach that desirable condition. Before the slow operation of reason and experience can convince them of its superior advantages, they must be overwhelmed by the mighty torrent of our population."

Governor George Gilmer of Georgia (ca. 1830)

"Treaties were expedients by which ignorant, intractable, and savage people were induced without bloodshed to yield up what civilized people had the right to possess by virtue of that command of the Creator delivered to man upon his formation—be fruitful, multiply, and replenish the earth, and subdue it."

NOTE: The Calhoun quote is from Francis Paul Prucha, ed., *Documents of United States Indian Policy* (Lincoln: University of Nebraska Press, 1975), 32. The other three quotes are taken from my teaching notes, and I have been unable to determine the original sources.

HANDOUT #2—NATIVE AMERICANS RESPONSES TO EXPANSION INDIAN REMOVAL

Red Jacket, a Seneca chief, in 1792

"We first knew you as a feeble plant which wanted a little earth whereon to grow. We gave it to you; and afterward, when we could have trod you under our feet, we watered and protected you; and now you have grown to be a mighty tree, whose top reaches the clouds, and whose branches overspread the whole land, whilst we, who were the tall pine of the forest, have become a feeble plant and need your protection.

When you first came here, you clung around our knee and called us father; we took you by the hand and called you brothers. You have grown greater than we, so that we can no longer reach your hand; but we wish to cling around your knee and be called your children."

Tecumseh, a Shawnee chief, in 1795

"My heart is a stone: heavy with sadness for my people; cold with the knowledge that no treaty will keep whites out of our lands; hard with the determination to resist as long as I live and breathe. Now we are weak and many of our people are afraid. But hear me: a single twig breaks, but the bundle of twigs is strong. Someday I will embrace our brother tribes and draw them into a bundle and together we will win our country back from the whites."

Tecumseh, a Shawnee chief, in 1811

"Every year our white intruders become more greedy, exacting, oppressive, and overbearing. . . . Wants and oppression are our lot. . . . Are we not being stripped day by day of the little that remains of our ancient liberty? . . . Unless every tribe unanimously combines to give a check to the ambition and avarice of the whites, they will soon conquer us apart and disunited, and we will be driven away from our native country and scattered as autumnal leaves before the wind."

Pushmataha, a Choctaw leader, in 1811

"If Tecumseh's words be true, and we doubt them not, then the Shawnee's experience with the whites has not been the same as that of the Choctaws. These white Americans buy our skins, our corn, our cotton, our surplus game our baskets, and other wares, and they give us in fair exchange their cloth, their guns, their tools, implements, and other things which the Choctaws need but do not make. . . . You all remember the dreadful epidemic visited upon us last winter. During its darkest hours these neighbors whom we are now urged to attack responded generously to our needs. They doctored our sick; they clothed our suffering; they fed our hungry; . . . So, in marked contrast with the experiences of the Shawnees, it will be seen that the whites and Indians in this section are living in friendly and mutually beneficial terms."

NOTE: Quotes from T. C. McLuhan, *Touch the Earth: A Self-Portrait of Indian Existence* (New York: Promontary Press, 1971), 69, 116-7; and Jerry R. Baydo, *Readings in American Indian History* (Wheaton, Ill.: Gregory Publishing, 1992), 52.

HANDOUT #3—INDIAN REMOVAL POLICY

President Andrew Jackson in his annual message to Congress in 1835

John Spencer Bassett, *The Life of Andrew Jackson*, 1911

Andrew Jackson, 1845, symbol of the removal policy of the 1830s.

"All preceding experiments for the improvement of the Indians have failed. It seems now to be an established fact that they can not live in contact with a civilized community and prosper. . . .

The plan for their removal and re-establishment is founded upon the knowledge we have gained of their character and habits, and has been dictated by a spirit of enlarged liberality. A territory exceeding in extent that relinquished has been granted to each tribe. . . . The Indians are removed at the expense of the United States, and with certain supplies of clothing, arms, ammunition, and other indispensable articles; they are also furnished gratuitously with provisions for the period of a year after their arrival at their new homes. In that time, from the nature of the country and by the products raised by them, they can subsist themselves by agricultural labor, if they choose to resort to that mode of life; if they do not they are upon the skirts of the great prairies, where countless herds of buffalo roam, and a short time suffices to adapt their own habits. . . .

The pledge of the United States has been given by Congress that the country destined for the residence of this people shall be forever 'secured and guaranteed to them.' A country west of Missouri and Arkansas has been assigned to them, into which the white settlements are not to be pushed. No political communities can be formed in that extensive region, except those established by the Indians themselves or by the United States for them and with their concurrence."

Indian Commissioner William Medill in 1848

"Apathy, barbarism and heathenism must give way to energy, civilization and Christianity; and so the Indian of this continent has been displaced by the European. . . .

The policy already begun and relied on to accomplish objects so momentous and desirable to every Christian and philanthropist is, as rapidly as it can safely and judiciously be done, to colonize our Indian tribes beyond the reach, for some years, of our white population; confining each within a small district of country, so that as the game decreases and becomes scarce, the adults will gradually be compelled to resort to agriculture and other kinds of labor to obtain a subsistence. . . .

The strongest propensities of an Indian's nature are his desire for war and his love of the chase. . . . But anything like labor is distasteful and utterly repugnant to his feelings and natural prejudices. He considers it a degradation. . . . Nothing can induce him to resort to labor, unless compelled to do so by stern necessity; and it is only then that there is any ground to work upon for civilizing and Christianizing him. But little, if any, good impression can be made upon him in these respects, so long as he is able to roam at large."

NOTE: The quotes are from Francis Paul Prucha, ed., *Documents of United States Indian Policy* (Lincoln: University of Nebraska Press, 1975), 71-2, 77-8.

HANDOUT #4—RESPONSES TO INDIAN REMOVAL

Black Hawk, Chief of the Sauk and Fox, 1833

"We always had plenty; our children never cried from hunger, neither were our people in want. . . . The rapids of Rock River furnished us with an abundance of excellent fish, and the land being very fertile, never failed to produce good crops of corn, beans, pumpkins, and squashes. . . . Our village was healthy and there was no place in the country possessing such advantages, nor hunting grounds better than those we had in our possession. If a prophet had come to our village in those days and told us that the things were to take place which have since come to pass, none of our people would have believed him."

Perry A. Armstrong. *The Sauks and the Black Hawk War*, 1887

Black Hawk, chief of the Sauk and Fox, went to war against Americans in the Old Northwest, 1831-1832.

Speckled Snake, Creek elder (aged 100+), 1829

"Brothers! I have listened to many talks from our Great Father. When he first came over the wide waters, he was but a little man . . . . His legs were cramped by sitting long in his big boat, and he begged for a little land to light his fire. . . But when the white man had warmed himself before the Indians' fire and filled himself with their hominy, he became very large. With a step he bestrode the mountains and his feet covered the plains and the valleys. His hand grasped the eastern and the western sea, and his head rested on the moon. Then he became our Great Father. He loved his red children, and he said, 'Get a little further, lest I tread on thee. . . .' Brother I have listened to a great many talks from our great father. But they always began and ended in this—'Get a little further; you are too near me.'"

George W. Harkins, district chief of the Choctaw Nation, 1832

"We were hedged in by two evils, and we chose that which we thought least. Yet we could not recognize the right that the state of Mississippi had assumed to legislate for us. Although the legislators of the state were qualified to make laws for their own citizens, that did not qualify them to become law makers to a people who were so dissimilar in manners and customs as the Choctaws are to the Mississippians. Admitting that they understood the people, could they remove that mountain of prejudice that has ever obstructed the streams of justice, and prevented their salutary influence from reaching my devoted countrymen? We as Choctaws rather chose to suffer and be free, than live under the degrading influence of laws where our voice could not be heard in their formation.

I could cheerfully hope that those of another age and generation may not feel the effects of those oppressive measures that have been so illiberally dealt out to us. . . . I ask you in the name of justice for repose, for myself and my injured people. Let us alone—we will not harm you, we want rest. We hope, in the name of justice that another outrage may never be committed against us."

NOTE: The quotes are from T. C. McLuhan, *Touch the Earth: A Self-Portrait of Indian Existence* (New York: Promontary Press, 1971), 3, 73, 139.

Struggle for the Continent

This lesson plan is for a classroom simulation designed to simulate the trade, diplomacy, and warfare in eastern North America during the colonial period. The diplomatic and trade relations of the numerous Native-American confederacies, tribes, and tribal factions in this area were far too diverse and complex for the scope of this classroom simulation, so four Native-American groups serve as representatives of the Indian societies of eastern North America. Similarly, the thirteen English colonies are consolidated into two groups to enable the simulation to work effectively while retaining the dynamics of rivalry and autonomy between the English colonies. A stylized map is used to depict the geographic region controlled by each group and restrict trade or warfare to adjacent groups. While the map is generally accurate, it has been simplified for this simulation and should not be considered a precise representation of European claims or of Native-American tribal boundaries. Instructors should use other maps to depict the overlapping European land claims, the location of European forts and/or trading posts, and the multitude of Native-American peoples living throughout the area.

The simplifications described above will enable the simulation to convey effectively the economic, diplomatic, and military rivalries between the colonial powers and the variety of pressures that confronted Native Americans during the period. This simulation would be most effective in a two-hour block or in two one-hour blocks on consecutive days. This assumes ten minutes to pass out materials and explain the conduct of the simulation; about sixty minutes to complete the simulation and twenty minutes for discussion. This would leave an extra ten minutes (assuming two fifty-minute periods) for normal classroom administrative matters or additional discussion. The simulation could be concluded in one hour but only with very limited

discussion and intrusive direction by the instructor to rush students through the simulation.

OBJECTIVES

1. Students will be able to distinguish between the short-term and long-term benefits and difficulties resulting from Native-American alliances with the European powers.

2. Students will understand the interrelationship between trade and diplomatic relations in colonial America.

3. Students will realize how trade dependence and declining resources limited Native-American options in their struggle against the colonial powers.

4. Students will recognize that historical events were not inevitable outcomes but the result of human decisions within limited choices.

5. Students will become curious about the cross-cultural nature of the colonial frontier.

CONDUCT OF SIMULATION

The instructor should divide the class into four colonial and four Native-American groups: Northern English, Southern English, French, Spanish, Abenaki, Iroquois, Shawnee, and Cherokee. Each of the four Native-American groups should receive a copy of HANDOUT #1 containing goals, Native-American victory conditions, a chart of colonial resources, and a score sheet to record military strength, subsistence needs, land transactions, and alliances. Each of the four colonial groups should receive a copy of HANDOUT # 2 containing goals, colonial victory conditions, and a score sheet to record military strength, alliances, land transactions, and the acquisition of furs and deerskins. The instructor could distribute a copy of the map to each group or have transparency of the map made for use on the overhead projector.

The simulation has four turns which could each represent a twenty-five year segment from 1660 to 1760 or each turn could represent one of the four major colonial wars from 1689 to 1763. Each turn has four phases: a Resource and Needs phase, a Trade and Diplomacy phase, a Warfare phase, and a Land and Military Strength phase. During the Resource and Needs phase each group checks their available resources and calculates their needs for that turn. During the Trade and Diplomacy phase each group negotiates with other groups to establish the most advantageous alliance and trade relations. During the Warfare phase, a group or alliance can announce its intention to declare war on another group or alliance, military strengths are compared and the appropriate results assessed. During the Land and Military Strength phase,

each group records land transactions and adjusts its military strength based on the effects of warfare and its success or failure in securing its needs during that turn.

RESOURCES AND NEEDS

The English colonies historically had tremendous advantages over the French, Spanish, or various Indian groups because of their larger population. However, limited cooperation between English colonies, the difficulties of frontier logistics and the relative military effectiveness of the Indians in frontier warfare severely limited the impact of these advantages. While the English had greater access to guns and trade goods (particularly during periods of warfare), the French and Spanish government subsidized these products so that their trade systems could

Elroy McKendree, *A History of the United States and Its People*, 1905

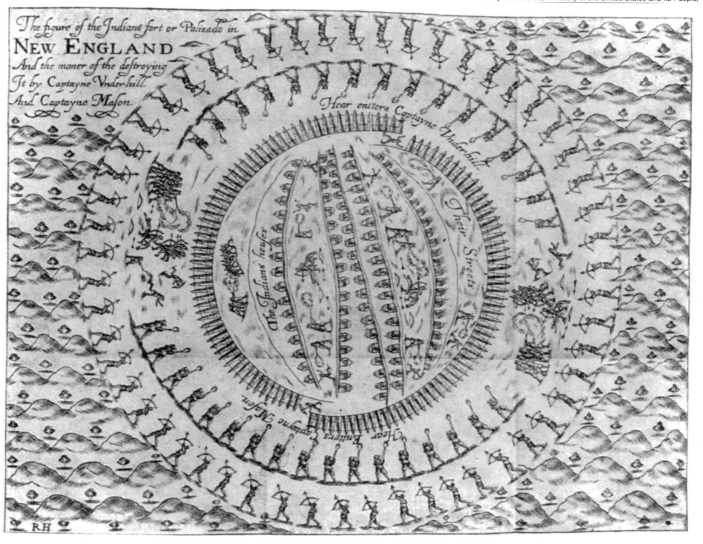

ohn Underhill's Plan of Attack on a Pequot fort in New England, 1637.

operate on roughly even levels with the English in these areas. The simulation reflects this situation by giving all four colonial groups equal amounts of trade goods and guns. On the other hand, the simulation gives both English colonial groups significant advantages in food production and military power but attempts to reflect the actual situation rather than the potential one. Therefore, the English colonial groups have twice the food that the French or Spanish have at their disposal and twice as much military power (soldiers/warriors) as the French or each of the Indian groups. The military weakness of the Spanish (250 soldiers) is evident, but it is significant enough to provide some protection to a Spanish ally (250+500 vs 1000)

Each of the Native-American groups starts the simulation with resources of 500 warriors and 100 fur/deerskins and needs of 50 trade goods, 50 guns, and 50 units of food. During the colonial period, Native Americans became increasingly dependent on European trade goods, finding it easier to exchange beaver pelts and deerskins for their necessities than to produce the necessities themselves. This gradual increase in their dependence was accentuated by the social disruption caused by epidemic diseases, warfare, and migrations. During periods of warfare this depen-

dence even extended to food because hunters were accompanying military campaigns, normal trade relations were disrupted, and normal subsistence areas were unavailable due to migration and militia patrols. Guns were a military necessity and any Native Americans cut off from their supply of guns were at a severe disadvantage.

The resources and needs of the various Native Americans and the resources of the colonial groups during the first turn are reflected on the score sheet. Also indicated is the gradually declining number of furs and deerskins available to each Indian group as their trapping territories become depleted. The number of guns, trade goods, and food units available to the colonial groups each turn remains constant and unused resources cannot be carried over to the next (twenty-five year) turn. The score sheets provide blank spaces for the number of warrior/soldiers and the Native-American needs for turns #2-4 which must be calculated since military strength may have been adjusted during the previous turn. The Indian groups' needs for food, guns, and trade goods are each ten percent of the warrior total.

William Cullen, *A Popular History of the United States*, 1881

Braddock's march against the French and their Indian allies in 1754 ended in a major defeat for the British.

TRADE AND DIPLOMACY

The Native-American groups can join together to resist the European colonists, or they can make alliances with a particular European power as a source of goods and military support against another group. French and Spanish colonies can compete or cooperate in trade and Indian alliances as they choose, but they cannot declare war on each other since their mother countries are on friendly terms. Northern and Southern English colonies can compete in trade and Indian alliances (as individual colonies did historically), but cannot declare war on each other since they have the same mother country.

Native-American groups can ally or trade with any adjacent group. (Exception: The Shawnee are assumed to be adjacent to both the Cherokee and Iroquois despite the intervening strips of French territory depicted on the map.) They can demand diplomatic presents (guns, food, or trade goods) in exchange for their alliance and trade furs/deerskins or units of land for these necessities. The amount of the diplomatic presents, cost of land, and exchange rate for furs/deerskins are all negotiable. Since the number of furs and deerskins available to each Indian group declines, it is important for each Indian group to negotiate the best deals possible. The colonial-group score sheets provide spaces for recording the number of furs/deerskins acquired and the alliances made. The Native-American score sheets also provide blanks for alliances to be recorded and the number of food units, guns, and trade goods acquired can be noted in the open spaces next to the numbers needed.

WARFARE

Warfare is accomplished by comparing the military strength of one group or alliance with the military strength of another group or alliance. If the military strengths are roughly equal, then there are no beneficial or detrimental results from the warfare. If one side has a two to one advantage in military strength, it achieves a marginal victory resulting in the weaker side suffering a ten percent reduction in military strength and a loss of one land area. If one side has a three to one advantage in military strength it achieves a major victory resulting in the weaker side suffering a thirty-percent reduction in military strength and a loss of three land areas. If one side has a four to one advantage in military strength it achieves a total victory, destroying the enemy and taking all of their land. These military strength and land losses are inflicted on each group of a defeated alliance. Option: When calculating military strength for an attack, the instructor could count the full strength of any attackers adjacent to the defender(s) and only half strength for any not adjacent. This would account for the need to retain some military forces to defend one's home territory and for the logistical problems of moving a force to a distant location and maintaining it there.

LAND AND MILITARY STRENGTH

The gain or loss of land through sale or warfare is recorded on the score sheet in this phase. Similarly, military strengths are adjusted and recorded based on the outcome of the warfare phase.

In addition, if an Indian group's needs were not met during a turn, that group's warrior total is reduced by a multiple of two times the shortage. Option: If a Native-American group acquires more than their required needs in a turn, the warrior population could increase by two times the surplus. This would take into account Indian refugees who were driven from their homes and merged into villages that had the resources to accommodate them. While this might be historically accurate for some individual tribes over a short period, it would ignore the general decline in Native-American populations during the entire century that the simulation addresses.

CONCLUSION

The instructor can review the victory conditions, determine how the various groups did in the simulation, and discuss whatever topics were raised by the simulation.

Comparisons could be drawn between the simulation experience and historical events concerning Indian adjustments to trade dependence and declining resources, changes to Indian culture resulting from interaction with Europeans, short-term Indian exploitation of European rivalries, long-term detrimental effects of European rivalries on Indians, and various European or Indian diplomatic/warfare strategies. How successful were multi-Indian alliances, and what difficulties did they have to overcome? How did trade dependence and declining resources limit Indian options? To what extent do European trade relations with Indian groups lead to alliances? To what extent does rivalry over trade with Indians affect relations between Europeans? Did European rivalries in the simulation increase as a result of the declining supply of furs and deerskins? How successful were Indian groups who allied with the English? Spanish? French? For those groups that were successful, would that success have continued in the future? Which historical Indian groups allied with the English, Spanish, or French? How did the historical experience of these Indian groups compare with the simulation? ❑

SUGGESTED READING

Three excellent books with different perspectives on the colonial wars are Francis Jennings, *The Ambiguous Iroquois Empire: The Covenant Chain Confederation of Indian Tribes with English Colonies* (New York: Norton, 1984); Douglas Edward Leach, *Roots of Conflict: British Armed Forces and Colonial Americans, 1677-1763* (Chapel Hill: University of North Carolina Press, 1986); and James H. Merrell, *The Indians New World, Catawbas and their Neighbors from European Contact through the Era of Removal* (Chapel Hill: University of North Carolina Press, 1989). Older studies from a European perspective include Edward P. Hamilton, *The French and Indian Wars: The Story of Battles and Forts in the Wilderness* (New York: Doubleday, 1962); Howard H. Peckham, *The Colonial Wars, 1689-1762* (Chicago: University of Chicago, 1964); and J. K. Steele, *Guerillas and Grenadiers: The Struggle for Canada, 1689-1760* (Toronto: The Ryerson Press, 1969).

HANDOUT #1 - NATIVE AMERICANS/STRUGGLE

ABENAKI, IROQUOIS, SHAWNEE, or CHEROKEE
(Circle your group)

GOALS AND VICTORY CONDITIONS

Indian groups want to maintain population and land while English, French, and Spanish colonies want to defeat their European rivals (or at least prevent victories for their European rivals) while acquiring furs, deerskins and land.

Native American groups

Maintain population and increase land	- Significant Victory
Maintain population and land	- Victory
Lose up to 10% pop. or one land area	- Marginal Victory
Lose up to 20% pop. or two land areas	- Marginal Defeat
Lose up to 30% pop. or three land areas	- Significant Defeat
Lose more than 30% pop. or three land areas	- Devastating Defeat

SCORE SHEET

Resources	#1	#2	#3	#4
furs & deerskins	100	85	70	55
warriors	500	___	___	___
Needs (10% of warriors)				
food	50	___	___	___
guns	50	___	___	___
trade goods	50	___	___	___
Land lost or gained	___	___	___	___
Alliances formed	___	___	___	___
	___	___	___	___

EUROPEAN RESOURCES

Resources	Northern English	Southern English	Spanish	French
soldiers	1000	1000	250	500
food	100	100	50	50
guns	100	100	100	100
trade goods	100	100	100	100

HANDOUT #2 - EUROPEAN COLONIES/STRUGGLE

NORTHERN ENGLISH, SOUTHERN ENGLISH, FRENCH, or SPANISH
(Circle your group)

GOALS AND VICTORY CONDITIONS

Indian groups want to maintain population and land while English, French and Spanish colonies want to defeat their European rivals (or at least prevent victories for their European rivals) while acquiring furs, deerskins and land.

English colonial groups
Gain six land areas and 500 furs or deerskins - Significant Victory
Gain three land areas and 400 furs or deerskins - Victory
Gain one land area and 300 furs or deerskins - Marginal Victory
Maintain land area and gain 200 furs or deerskins - Marginal Defeat
Lose one land area and gain 100 furs or deerskins - Significant Defeat
Lose three land areas and gain no furs or deerskins - Devastating Defeat

French or Spanish colonial groups
Gain three land areas and 400 furs or deerskins - Significant Victory
Gain one land area and 300 furs or deerskins - Victory
Maintain land area and 200 furs or deerskins - Marginal Victory
Maintain land area and 100 furs or deerskins - Marginal Defeat
Lose one land area and gain no furs or deerskins - Significant Defeat
Lose three land areas and gain no furs or deerskins - Devastating Defeat

SCORE SHEET

Resources	Northern English	Southern English	Spanish	French
soldiers	1000	1000	250	500
food	100	100	50	50
guns	100	100	100	100
trade goods	100	100	100	100

(European colony)	Soldiers	Land	Furs & Deerskins	Alliances
Turn #1				
Turn #2				
Turn #3				
Turn #4				
Totals				

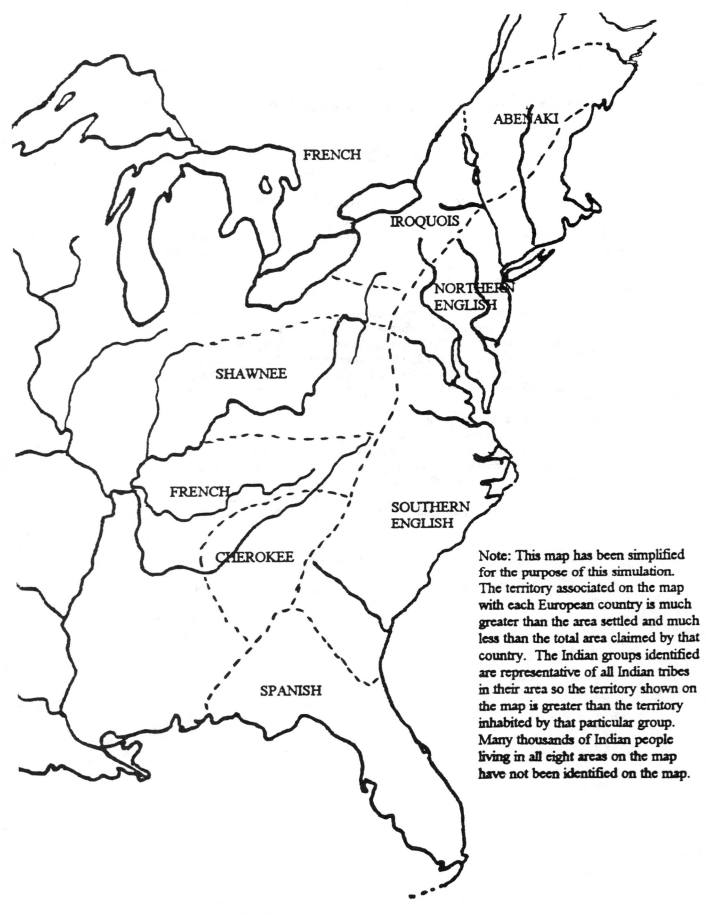

FRENCH

ABENAKI

IROQUOIS

NORTHERN ENGLISH

SHAWNEE

FRENCH

SOUTHERN ENGLISH

CHEROKEE

SPANISH

Note: This map has been simplified for the purpose of this simulation. The territory associated on the map with each European country is much greater than the area settled and much less than the total area claimed by that country. The Indian groups identified are representative of all Indian tribes in their area so the territory shown on the map is greater than the territory inhabited by that particular group. Many thousands of Indian people living in all eight areas on the map have not been identified on the map.

Game map for Lesson Plan 3: "Struggle for the Continent."

Latinos in the United States

Photo by L. Lewis; courtesy of Claremont Graduate School

Bridging the memories told at the table with printed historical narratives fueled my decision to become a historian.

Vicki L. Ruiz

Vicki L. Ruiz is a professor of women's studies and history at Arizona State University. She is the author of Cannery Women, Cannery Lives *(1987) and coeditor with Ellen DuBois of* Unequal Sisters *(2d ed., 1994).*

When I was a child, I learned two types of history—the one at home and the one at school. My mother and grandmother would regale me with stories about their Colorado girlhoods, stories of village life, coal mines, strikes, discrimination, and family lore. At school, scattered references were made to Coronado, Ponce de León, the Alamo, and Pancho Villa. That was the extent of Latino history. Bridging the memories told at the table with printed historical narratives fueled my decision to become a historian.

Almost a decade ago, I wrote an article in which I briefly surveyed the (mis)representations of Latinos in college level U.S. history texts. Out of one 1,343 page synthesis, three paragraphs attempted to detail the history of all Hispanics, and in another, the experiences of Puerto Ricans were set within the context of *West Side Story* (1). Such dismissiveness cannot even qualify as tokenism. Today many textbook writers strive for greater inclusiveness, particularly with regard to Mexican Americans who form approximately two-thirds of Latinos in the United States.

Though coverage varies from text to text, Latino history remains a last minute "add-on," partial and disjointed. Looking toward a more satisfying synthesis, the essays and lesson plans which follow offer points of departure in incorporating Latino voices in U.S. history curricula. This issue highlights historical writings, themes, events, and, of course, people.

In "Origins and Evolution of Latino History," Virginia Sánchez Korrol eloquently outlines interrelated historiographical trajectories as well as provides an extensive bibliography of accessible sources. Emphasizing the interdisciplinary nature of this research, she encourages educators to move beyond the experiences of discrete groups and to grapple with the notion of a shared Latino history and identity rooted in *mestizaje*. Albert Hurtado astutely combines historiography and narrative in his overview of the Spanish Borderlands. Sketching the rich legacies which predate European American settlement, he envisions the region as one of cultural collisions, encounters, and crossroads.

In my essay, I offer a mosaic of the historical experiences of Mexican women in the U.S., emphasizing the ways in which women have frequently relied on their community networks for survival and for social justice. matt garcía illuminates the importance of examining intercultural relations at the local level. His nuanced discussion of the Padua Hills Theatre brings out the roles of Mexican actors as "strategic accomodationists" in their quest to erode prejudice through performance.

I hope that these essays and lesson plans foster an expanded awareness of the Latino presence in U.S. History and encourage teachers to draw upon the resources available in their communities. Connecting the past to the present, I would like to introduce the issue with "University Avenue" by Pat Mora, a poem which resonates among Latinos (myself included) who were and are first generation college-bound.

University Avenue

We are the first
of our people to walk this path.
We move cautiously
unfamiliar with the sounds,
guides for those who follow.
Our people prepared us
with gifts from the land
    fire

      herbs and song
hierbabuena soothes us into morning
rhythms hum in our blood
abrazos linger round our bodies.
cuentos whisper lessons *en español.*
We do not travel alone.
Our people burn deep within us (2). ❏

Endnotes

1. Vicki L. Ruiz, "Teaching Chicano/ Mexican American History: Goals and Methods," *The History Teacher* 20 (February 1987): 167-77. At that time, only one U.S. history text strived to integrate Chicano history in a substantive manner—*America Past and Present*, edited by Rober Devine, et. al.
2. "University Avenue," reprinted from *Borders* by Pat Mora (Houston, Tex. Arte Público Press, 1986), 19.

Acknowledgments

The professional staff at the Organ zation of American Historians, especiall Michael Regoli, provided extraordinar support. I appreciate all of their efforts make this issue a reality. I thank m compadres Esteban y Elia Hernández fo permission to use the wedding photo of Esteban's parents, and I am grateful t ASU history Ph.D. students Christin Marín and Melissa Dyea for their assis tance in locating photographs. Victo Becerra dispensed good advice and goo food. Finally, I would like to acknow edge my contributors who drafted suc thoughtful pieces, particularly Virgini Sánchez Korrol for her vision, commi ment, and *corazón.*

The Origins and Evolution of Latino History

Virginia Sánchez Korrol

I am new. History made me. My first language was spanglish.
I was born at the crossroads and I am whole.

Aurora Levins Morales
"Child of the Americas"(1)

Mexican Americans/Chicanos, Puerto Ricans, Cuban Americans, and their descendants, the oldest and largest sub-groups among a population of some thirty million *Hispanos* in the United States, form the core of a union that matches relatively recent arrivals, predominantly from the Dominican Republic and Central and South America, with long-time U.S. residents; English speaking with Spanish speaking; aliens with citizens; and documented individuals with undocumented immigrants. As the nation's fastest growing "minority," all indicators point to a heightened sense of awareness and receptivity among Latinos across ethnic and national lines, regarding a collective consciousness and historical role in the U.S.

The validation of memory, self-identification, contestation, and affirmation spans centuries as persons of Spanish American heritage have always figured in the making of the United States of America.

Viewed from another perspective, as Native Americans, Latinos were there when Plymouth Rock was just a pebble. As Spanish settlements, *presidios*, villas, pueblos, and missions throughout the Americas pre-date Jamestown by at least

As the nation's fastest growing "minority," all indicators point to a heightened sense of awareness and receptivity among Latinos across ethnic lines and national lines, regarding a collective consciousness and historical role in the U.S.

one hundred years, the origins of a comprehensive Latino/Hispanic entity began well before the massive migrations and immigrations of the present. The forgotten heritage of Hispanics in what is now the United States forms the focus of contemporary historical and literary investigation (2).

Spanish American chronicles, diaries and testimonials, administrative, civil, military, and ecclesiastical records, musical compositions and theatrical works, prose, poetry, travel narratives, and other rich primary sources form the earliest extant literature in what is today the United States. A wealth of materials, including oral traditions, chronicle multifaceted life in colonial settlements from the sixteenth to the nineteenth centuries in what are presently Florida, New Mexico, Georgia, Texas, Arizona, Louisiana, South Carolina, California, Missouri, Mississippi, Kansas, Arkansas, Alabama, and Nebraska, and include as well the Hispanic Caribbean islands. Sources reveal a strong web of regional interconnections that linked the Hispanic Caribbean and South and Central America with U.S. communities, aiding migration from one point to another. The founding of major commercial, religious, and cultural sites—among them the cities of Los Angeles, Santa Fe, St. Augustine, San Antonio, and San Juan—testify to the vitality of a period that set standards for enduring socio-cultural institutions and wove the earliest connecting strands among Spanish Americans.

The nineteenth century brings into focus the formation of peoplehood. This period initiates a rich tapestry of documentation from the regional presses that bridged peripheral northern communities with the southern metropolis in Mexico City, or Havana, or San Juan, to the novels, essays, *testimonios*, and treatises of political exiles. The first historical novel ever written in the United States might well have been *Jicoténcal*, penned by Cuban Felix Varela in Philadelphia in 1826 (3). Along with other literary efforts, Varela's work serves to illustrate the earliest ideas about Latin American nationhood. It is significant also that the first Spanish language newspaper to emerge from U. S. Hispanic communities, *El Misisipí*, published in New Orleans in 1808, initiated a long chain of periodicals that afford the historian intimate glimpses into the ethos of large communities of Americans who happened to speak and write in Spanish (4).

By the time the Treaty of Guadalupe Hidalgo ceded half of the Mexican territory to the United States in 1848, Mexican heritage had become inextricably woven

into the historical fabric of the American Southwest. As they assessed their situation in the "uneasy space that marked the intersection of the cultures of Mexico and the United States," Mexican Americans struggled with issues of identity in the decades following 1848 (5). Their concerns were expressed in writing in dozens of Spanish language newspapers that dotted the Southwest, in folkloric border *corridos* that extolled the virtues of folk heroes like Gregorio Cortez or Juan Chacón, in the actions of rebels like Joaquin Murrieta and Tiburcio Vásquez, and in autobiographies like Mariano Vallejo's that served as a form of cultural resistance. Viewed also through the lens of the landed elite, novels like María Amparo Ruiz de Burton's *The Squatter and the Don* testify to a chaotic world of clashing Anglo and Mexican values as the century neared its conclusion (6).

On the other side of the continent, late-nineteenth and early-twentieth century Cuban and Puerto Rican political

exiles, joined by expatriates from Sout and Central America, articulated an agend of working-class concerns in the Spanis language presses of southern Florida an New York City. Confronting oppressiv colonial structures and the economic dev astation wrought by the ten-year wa Cubans spearheaded extensions of th island's cigar industry in Tampa, Ybo City, and New York City, providing th locus for working-class emigrations tha would continue into the twentieth century Strategies of Antillean independence, radi cal labor organizing, and even the seeds o Puerto Rican feminism were sown; th latter especially with the second editio publication of Luisa Capetillo's *M opinión: Disecatación sobre las libertade de la mujer* in Ybor City (7).

Under leaders like José Martí, Fran cisco González (Pachín) Marin, and Soter Figueroa, "The Bases of the Cuban Revo lutionary Party" were written and ratifie by supportive groups in New York, Ne Orleans, Philadelphia, and other revolu tionary centers throughout the America These ideologies were well known outsid and within exile communities compose predominantly of racially diverse work ing-class men and women. Progressiv views on the social and economic contra dictions found within their communitie appeared in the pages of *Patria*, the revo lutionary organ, and others like *El Latino Americano* or *El Porvenir* (8).

Following the Spanish Cuban Amer can War, focus shifted from independenc to internal community concerns, includ ing the organization of workers in mutua aid societies, unions, and other supportiv associations. Women emerged prom nently among the union ranks, and coul be found at the forefront of workers struggles. In New York, essayists—in cluding Cuban Alberto O'Farrill, editor c the weekly, *Gráfico*; Puerto Rican Artur Alfonso Schomburg, bibliophile of th African experience in the Americas Bernardo Vega, chronicler; and Jesú Colón, columnist for *Justicia*, as well a other papers—defended their communi ties against American foreign and domes tic imperialism (9). In so doing, the

Bronx Hispanic American Registration Committee, November 1956.

followed a tradition set forth by leading nineteenth-century Antillean thinkers who lived and wrote in New York. Included among this group were José Martí, the father of the Cuban independence, and Eugenio María de Hostos, educator of the Americas. These intellectuals, in particular, supported a concept of Hispano-American unity and were acutely aware of their historical place within the Ibero-American family.

Within fifty years, a handful of pioneering intellectuals, writers, and other *pensadores* grappled with the condition and status of Latinos, especially Mexican Americans. Conditioned by the political zone and generation in which they were produced, their contributions proposed to mediate, validate, and, ultimately, redefine the Mexican American, Puerto Rican, or Cuban U.S. experience. In the production of new knowledge, the academics attempted to eradicate debasing stereotypes and to confront racism and discrimination. Among the first scholars to fashion a Mexican American identity were historian Carlos E. Castañeda, sociologist George I. Sánchez, and folklorist Arthur I. Campa. Cultural stirrings concerning self-definition, colonialism, racism, ethnicity, and the sub-altern status of U.S. *Hispanos* surfaced in other camps as well (10).

Identity and affirmation were at the core of literary works written in Latin America, the Hispanic Caribbean, and the United States. In this vein, the works of Octavio Paz delve into the Mexican psyche both north and south of the Rio Grande. The articles of Mario Suarez which establish post World War II concepts of a Mexican American identity are reflected on the East Coast in Puerto Rican Bernardo Vega's memoirs (11). The decade of the sixties witnesses the publications of Guillermo Cotto Thorner's *Trópico en Manhattan*, Piri Thomas's *Down These Mean Streets*, and Jesús Colón's *A Puerto Rican in New York and Other Sketches*. All works describe the migration and harsh conditions in the *barrio hispano* (12). Similar concerns emanated from Chicano writers as they grappled with the bitterness of racism. They strove toward cul-

tural affirmation and bilingual innovation in their creative expression. Listed among this group are Rodolfo "Corky" González's *Yo Soy Joaquin/I Am Joaquin*; Tomás Rivera's epic about Mexican American farm workers, *... y no se lo tragó la tierra/ And the Earth did not Part*; Ernesto Galarza's ethnographic autobiography, *Barrio Boy: The Story of a Boy's Acculturation*; and the classic, *Bless Me Ultima*, Rudolfo Anaya's validation of oral tradition and the transmission of culture (13). It is within this climate of provocative, probing, and often militant activism that Juan Gómez Quiñones issues his influential essay on culture and resistance, "On Culture" (14). Today, these works are viewed as foundational, the first among several building blocks preserving and shaping contemporary Latino ideology.

The onset of the 1970s and 1980s propagated a generation of historians and other academics schooled in the struggles for civil rights in the turbulent 1960s and influenced by the creative expression of their communities. Intent on expanding the boundaries of academic history to in-

clude strong national connections, labor, gender, and ethno-racial perspectives, intergenerational dynamics, interdisciplinary methods, and new categories of analysis, they challenged the demeaning, distorted, and monolithic interpretations of the U.S. Latino experience. Scholars mined the sources documenting the origins and evolutions of Latino communities, unlocking a wide range of materials to new interpretations, sometimes building upon—more often contesting—the intellectual cornerstones of borderlands, frontier, and area studies. Their generation questioned Anglo American hegemony over historical interpretation and their domination of the historical research agenda (15). Not satisfied with merely creating "knowledge for the sake of knowledge," their goals ranged from charting innovative courses and methods that served to "set the record straight," to reconstructing social histories important in and of themselves.

The academic generation of the seventies and eighties sought to reconstruct nineteenth- and twentieth-century diaspora

Courtesy of Hunter College, CUNY

League of Puerto Rican Hispanics, Brooklyn, New York.

communities in all of their ethno-racial, class, and gendered complexities. Incorporating popular culture and written and oral traditions, these academics redefined the parameters of the new social history and, in the process, empowered Latino communities. The result was a historical interpretation that conferred agency on U.S. Latinos, bringing them out of the shadows and on to center stage where their reality contrasted and contested the dominant Anglo experience and where they interacted within and across class lines and ethno-racial barriers, with counterparts across state lines, oceans, and/or national boundaries. The outcome was both U.S. and Latin America drawing strengths from components of both. This harvest of knowledge has proceeded at an impressive pace, yet the corpus of this literature remains peripheral to the core of U.S. history.

Much of the ground-breaking scholarship emanates from academic niches in American, Latin American, cultural, or Hispanic-oriented ethnic studies, or from the earliest departments and programs in Mexican American, Chicano, or Puerto Rican Studies. One need only peruse the bibliographic publi-

cations on Latinos/Hispanos—Albert Camarillo's *Latinos in the United States* is a case in point—to appreciate the scope of

Virgin Mary's float and girls during procession.

the new knowledge (16). Topics range from exploration and settlement of northern New Spain to the work of women in

industry, commercial agriculture, as union organizers and as transmitters of culture from employment and labor history to the politics of language and from the migration/immigration experience to the forging of diverse communities incorporating grass-root leadership and institutional structures.

Examples abound of the seminal work produced by this generation including the frontier studies of David Weber; the intergenerational focus of Mario T. Garcia's study on Mexican American leadership; Ramón Gutiérrez's interdisciplinary analysis of power and sexuality in New Mexico; the family and community studies of Richard Griswold del Castillo and Albert Camarillo; Chicano culture, consciousness, and interrelationship with the non-Hispanic societies by Vicki Ruiz and Sarah Deutsch; studies on race, ethnicity, and identity by Clara E. Rodríguez and Juan Flores; nineteenth-century Cuban community studies of Gerald E. Poyo; the Puerto Rican community by Virginia Sánchez Korrol; the migration/immigration studies of Alejandro Portes and of the Centro de Estudios Puertorriqueños; and bilingualism and pubic education studies of Guadalupe San Miguel, Jr. (17).

Until now, however, historical production has tended to promote primarily the very necessary foundational reconstruction of Latino experiences, viewed predominantly from a North American perspective. In searching for elements of *latinidad*, scholars have tended to explore contemporary U.S. communities excluding the broader Latin American/Caribbean context and neglecting to address Hispanic diversity. Like stepping stones to the past, the collective body of literature encompasses the groundwork for a comprehensive narrative. Current research trends on Latino historiography and literature in the 1990s mark a move toward the premise that Spanish American history legitimately belongs to the Americas—that the concept of borderlands transcends imaginary geo-political or academic boundaries. It argues that the history of Latinos forms an indivisible chapter subject to its own universality and specificity, and integral to our understanding of both U.S. and Latin American history (18).

To speak then in terms of a collective Latino/Hispanic history that posits an integrated consciousness within the broader framework of United States history invites students and scholars alike to conceptualize an area of study in formation. It incorporates multilingual, multicultural, and interdisciplinary perspectives, ethno-racial realities, and analytical categories based on migration experience, labor, social class, gender, and identity. As it seeks to reproduce the past in terms of an Hispanic ethnic and national diversity, it urgently challenges us to search for common ground among groups whose historical entry into what is presently the United States occurred at different times and was conditioned by different circumstances.

Admittedly, the nomenclatures we ascribe to this body of knowledge are paradoxical, imprecise, and politically-laden. The terms Latino, Latina, Hispanic, Hispanic American, Spanish American, or Ibero-Americano seek to embrace the totality of the U.S. experience regardless of class, color, regional variations, national antecedents, gender, or generational differences. Scholar Edna Acosta Belén believes the "shorthand label (Hispanic) is turning into a symbol of cultural affirmation and identity in an alienating society that traditionally has been hostile and prejudicial to cultural and racial differences, and unresponsive to the socioeconomic and educational needs of a large segment of the Hispanic population" (19). Others, however, argue overwhelmingly on the side of difference, citing centuries of regional disconnection and discontinuity among U.S. Latinos, and point to the absence of a common history as a case in point. Still others probe intra-group and generational dimensions challenging static notions of cultural adaptation, contextual dualities, and hence the formation of identity. Referring specifically to cultural evolution among Mexican Americans, who comprise well over a half of the total Latino population, historian George J. Sánchez cautions that a bipolaric model stressing "either cultural continuity or gradual acculturation has short-circuited a full exploration of the complex process of cultural adaptation" (20). Such arguments cannot be ignored, yet in spite of the contradictions, the tide appears to turn increasingly toward endorsement of an overarching Latino/Hispanic ideal. Each group rightfully stakes a nonnegotiable claim to its own past, linguistic variations, creative expression, and overall uniqueness within the broader ethno-racial contours of this nation, but each also proudly appropriates a common historical legacy, shared language, and cultural elements, customs, attitudes, and traditions.

How historians frame the conversation on Latino history is vital. If the danger of assuming affinity within and across this enormously complex population lies in over-generalization, a blurring of distinctions and total homogenization of the groups, the challenge to historians

Confederación General Puertorriqueña.

becomes how best to incorporate and balance the nuances and variegated experiences of all Latinos, particularly of those who figured centrally in the historical enterprise in any given period, without misappropriation, distortion, or omission. According to historian Gerald E. Poyo, grounds indeed exist for collective identity, which he describes as an "evolving phenomenon that by definition thrives on the commonalities within the diverse Latin American background groups." If identity is understood as a continuum of shared experience, then a comprehensive narrative is surely possible. What has been lacking until now is the development of popular consciousness about an integrated past (21).

What then, does it mean to be Latino/ Hispanic in American society at the crossroads of the millennium? How have we persevered and created community in two world contexts? How have we dealt with diversity within and across borders? How, indeed, have we shaped the Americas?

The quest begins with what Genaro M. Padilla refers to as the "Spanish colonial discourse of conquest, exploration, and settlement," that took place between 1492 and the nineteenth century and marks the earliest period in the documentation of Latino history. It concludes with the contemporary issues of the present (22). Undoubtedly, the most pivotal legacy throughout is the process of *Mestizaje*— the blending of Spanish, African, and indigenous American peoples and cultures—so intrinsic, from its beginnings to the present, to the formation of individual identity, national consciousness, and syncretic culture, throughout Latin America and among U.S. Latinos. It holds the key to our understanding of a collective Latino past. ❑

Endnotes

1. Aurora Levins Morales and Rosario Morales, *Getting Home Alive* (Ithaca, N.Y.: Firebrand Books, 1986), 50.
2. Recovering the U.S. Hispanic Literary Heritage is one such project. A ten year enterprise based at the University of Houston, Texas, the project focuses on the implementation of the following programs: (1) an on-line data base; (2) a periodicals recovery program; (3) a consortium of Hispanic Archives; (4) grants-in-aid and fellowships for scholars; (5) a publishing program; (6) a curriculum program; and (7) conferences and disseminations of information.
3. Félix Varela, *Jicoténcal*, Edición de Luis Leal y Rodolfo J. Cortina (Houston, Tex.: Arte Público Press, 1995), xxxv.
4. Nicolás Kanellos, "A Socio-Historic Study of Hispanic Newspapers in the United States," in *Recovering the U. S. Hispanic Literary Heritage*, ed. Ramón Gutiérrez and Genaro Padilla (Houston, Texas: Arte Público Press, 1993), 107.
5. Raymund Paredes, "Mexican American Literature: An Overview," in *Recovering*, 31.
6. María Amparo Ruiz de Burton, *The Squatter and the Don*, ed. Rosaura Sánchez and Beatrice Pita (Houston, Texas: Arte Público Press, 1992); and Genaro Padilla, *My History, Not Yours: The Formation of Mexican American Autobiography*, (Madison: University of Wisconsin Press, 1993). See also, Rosaura Sánchez, "Nineteenth-Century Californio Narratives: The Hubert H. Bancroft Collection," in *Recovering*, 279-92.
7. Nancy A. Hewitt and Ana VandeWater, "La Independencia: Patriotas y Obreras in Cuba, Puerto Rico and the United States, 1898-1921," unpublished paper presented at the Symposium on the History of Latin Workers, the Meany Archives, February 1993. See also, Yamila Azize Vargas, *La Mujer en la Lucha* (Rio Piedras: Editorial Cultural, 1985).
8. Alternative or oppositional presses proliferated throughout the Southwest, particularly as precursors to the downfall of the Porfiriato and the Revolution of 1910. Often, these presses were tied into exile political organizations, but they also informed the community at large on a myriad of issues, including the emancipation of women. *Regeneración*, published by the Flores Magón brothers in 1905, is one example of these presses, which appeared in Laredo, San Antonio, El Paso, Los Angeles, etc. Current research explores the role of women as editors and contributors to these alternative presses. See Clara Lomas, "The Articulation of Gender in the Mexican Borderlands, 1900-1915," in *Recovering*.
9. Nicolás Kanellos, "A Socio-Historic Study of Hispanic Newspapers in the United States," in *Recovering*, 107-28. See also, Virginia Sánchez Korrol, *From Colonia to Community: The History of Puerto Ricans in New York City* (Berkeley: University of California Press, 1994), chapter 5.
10. See Mario T. Garía, *Mexican Americans: Leadership, Ideology, and Identity, 1930-1960* (New Haven: Yale University Press, 1989), for background on Castañeda, Campa, and Sánchez.
11. Mario Suarez's collection of articles appeared in *Arizona Quarterly*, Summer 1947 and Winter 1948. Bernardo Vega, *Memoirs of Bernardo Vega*, ed. César Andreu Iglesias, trans. Juan Flores (New York: Monthly Review Press, 1984).
12. Guillermo Cotto Thorner, *Trópico en Manhattan* (San Juan: Cordillera, 1960); Piri Thomas, *Down These Mean Streets* (New York: Alfred A. Knopf, 1967); and Jesús Colón, *A Puerto Rican in New York and Other Sketches* (New York: International Publishers, 1982). See also Edna Acosta Belén and Virginia Sánchez-Korrol, eds., *The Way It Was and Other Writings* (Houston, Tex.: Arte Público Press, 1994).
13. Rudolfo "Corky" González, *I Am Joaquin/Yo Soy Joaquin: An Epic Poem* (New York: Bantam Books, 1972); Tomás Rivera, ... *y no se lo tragó la tierra/And the Earth did not Part*, trans. Evangelina Vigil-Piñon (Houston: Arte Publico Press, 1987); Rudolfo Anaya, *Bless Me, Ultima* (Berkeley: Tonatiuh/Quinto Sol International, 1972); and Ernesto Galarza, *Barrio Boy: The Story of a Boy's Acculturation* (Notre Dame: University of Notre Dame Press, 1971).
14. Juan Gómez Quiñones, "On Culture," in *Modern Chicano Writers: A Collection of Critical Essays*, ed. Joseph Sommers and Tomás Ybarra Frausto (Englewood Cliffs, N.J.: Prentice Hall, 1979).
15. David G. Gutiérrez, "Significant to Whom? Mexican Americans and the History of the American West," *Western Historical Quarterly* (November 1993): 531.
16. Albert Camarillo, ed., *Latinos in the United States* (Santa Barbara, Calif.: ABC-CLIO, 1986).
17. Sarah Deutsch, *No Separate Refuge: Culture, Class, and Gender on an Anglo Hispanic Frontier in the American Southwest, 1880-1940* (New York: Oxford University Press, 1987); Vicki L. Ruiz, *Cannery Women, Cannery Lives: Mexican Women, Unionization, and the California Food Processing Industry, 1930-1950* (Albuquerque: University of New Mexico Press, 1987); Juan Flores, *Divided Borders: Essays on Puerto Rican Identity* (Houston: Arte Público Press, 1991); Mario T. Garcia, *Mexican Americans: Leadership, Ideology and Identity, 1930-1960* (New Haven: Yale University Press, 1989); Richard Griswold del Castillo, *La Familia: Chicano Families in*

the Urban Southwest, 1948 to the Present (Notre Dame: University of Notre Dame Press, 1984); Ramón Gutiérrez, *When Jesus Came, the Corn Mothers Went Away: Marriage, Sexuality and Power in New Mexico, 1500-1846* (Stanford, Calif.: Stanford University Press, 1991); History Task Force, Centro de Estudios Puertorriqueños, *Migration Under Capitalism: The Puerto Rican Experience* (New York: Monthly Review Press, 1979); Alejandro Portes and Robert L. Bach, *Latino Journey: Cuban and Mexican Immigrants in the United States* (Berkeley: University of California Press, 1985); Gerald E. Poyo, *"With All and For the Good of All": The Emergence of Popular Nationalism in the Cuban Communities of the United States, 1848-1898* (Durham, N.C.: Duke University Press, 1989); Clara E. Rodríguez, *Puerto Ricans: Born in The U.S.A.* (Boston: Unwyn Hyman, 1989); Guadalupe San Miguel, *"Let Them All Take Heed": Mexican Americans and the Campaign for Educational Equality in Texas, 1910-1981* (Austin: University of Texas Press, 1987); and David J. Weber, *The Spanish Frontier in North America* (New Haven: Yale University Press, 1992).

8. See Gerald E. Poyo and Gilberto M. Hinojosa, "Spanish Texas and Borderlands Historiography in Transition: Implications for United States History," *Journal of American History* 75 (September 1988): 393-416; and Gloria Anzaldúa, *Borderlands/La Frontera: The New Mestiza* (San Francisco: Spinster/Aunt Lute, 1987) for conceptual frameworks in this regard.

9. Edna Acosta Belén and Barbara R. Sjostrom, *The Hispanic Experience in the United States* (New York: Praeger, 1988), 84.

10. George J. Sánchez, *Becoming Mexican American: Ethnicity, Culture and Identity in Chicano Los Angeles, 1900-1945* (New York: Oxford University Press, 1993), 13.

11. Gerald E. Poyo, "Thinking About U.S. Latino Identity and History," *Texas Journal of Ideas, History and Culture* 15 (Fall/Winter 1992), 17.

12. Genaro Padilla, "Recovering Mexican American Autobiography," in *Recovering*, 159.

Bibliography

Acuña, Rodolfo. *Occupied America: The Chicanos Struggle toward Liberation*. San Francisco: Canfield, 1972.

Alarcón, Norma. "Chicano Feminism: In the Tracks of 'the' Native Women." *Cultural Studies* 4 (October 1990): 248-56.

Anzaldúa, Gloria. *Borderlands/La Frontera: The New Mestiza*. San Francisco: Spinsters/Aunt Lute, 1987.

Appel, John. "The Unionization of Florida Cigarmakers and the Coring of the War With Spain." *HARR* 36 (February 1956): 38-49.

Arguelles, Lourdes. "Cuban Miami: The Roots, Development and Everyday Life of an Emigre Enclave in the United States National Security State." *Contemporary Marxism* (Summer 1982): 27-43.

Bodnar, John. *The Transplanted: A History of Immigrants in Urban America*. Bloomington: Indiana University Press, 1986.

Camarillo, Albert. *Chicanos in a Changing Society: From Mexican Pueblos to American Barrios in Santa Barbara and Southern California, 1848-1930*. Cambridge, Mass.: Harvard University Press, 1979.

Casals, Lourdes. "Cubans in the United States: Their Impact on U.S.-Cuban Relations." Ed. Martin Weinstein. *Revolutionary Cuba in the World Arena*. Philadelphia: Institute for the Study of Human Issues, 1979.

Colón, Jesús. *The Way It Was and Other Writings*. Ed. Edna Acosta Belén and Virginia Sánchez-Korrol. Houston, Tex.: Arte Público Press, 1993.

———. *A Puerto Rican in New York and Other Sketches*. New York: International Publications, 1982.

Cortada, James W. "Florida's Relations With Cuba During the Civil War." *Florida Historical Quarterly* (July 1980): 42-52.

Deutsch, Sarah. *No Separate Refuge: Culture, Class and Gender on an Anglo-Hispanic Frontier in the American Southwest, 1880-1940*. New York: Oxford University Press, 1987.

Domínguez, Virginia R. *From Neighbor to Stranger: The Dilemma of Caribbean Peoples in the U.S.* New Haven: Yale University Press, 1975.

Duany, Jorge. "Quisqueya on the Hudson: The Transnational Identity of Dominicans in Washington Heights." New York: The CUNY Dominican Studies Institute, Dominican Research Monographs, 1994.

Fagen, Richard R. and Richard A. Brody. "Cubans in Exile: A Demographic Analysis." *Social Problems* 11 (Spring 1964) 389-401.

Gamio, Manuel. *Mexican Immigration to the United States: A Study of Human Migration and Adjustment*. New York: Dover, 1971.

García, Mario T. *Mexican Americans: Leadership, Ideology and Identity, 1930-1960*. New Haven: Yale University Press, 1989.

———. "La Frontera: The Border as Symbol and Reality in Mexican-American Thought." *Mexican Studies/Estudios Mexicanos* 1 (Summer 1985): 195-225.

———. *Dessert Immigrants: The Mexicans of El Paso, 1880-1920*. New Haven: Yale University Press, 1981.

George, Eugenia. *The Making of a Transnational Community: Migration, Development and Cultural Change in the Dominican Republic*. New York: Columbia University Press, 1991.

Gómez Quiñones, Juan. "On Culture." In *Modern Chicano Writers: A Collection of Critical Essays*. Ed. Joseph Sommers and Tomás Ybarra Frausto. Englewood Cliffs, N.J.: Prentice Hall, 1979.

Grasmuck, Sherri and Patricia R. Pessar. *Between Two Islands: Dominican International Migration*. Berkeley: University of California Press, 1991.

Griswold del Castillo, Richard. "Southern California Chicano History: Regional Origins and National Critique." *Aztlán* 19 (Spring 1988-90): 112-3.

———. *The Los Angeles Barrio, 1850-1890: A Social History*. Berkeley: University of California Press, 1979.

Hendricks, Glenn. *The Dominican Diaspora: From the Dominican Republic to New York City: Villages in Transition*. New York: Teachers College Press, 1974.

History Task Force, Centro de Estudios Puertorriqueños. *Labor Migration Under Capitalism: The Puerto Rican Experience*. New York: Monthly Review Press, 1979.

Kanellos, Nicolás. *A History of Hispanic Theatre in the United States: Origins to 1944*. Austin: University of Texas Press, 1990. López, Adalberto and James Petras. *Puerto Rico and Puerto Ricans: Studies in History and Society*. Cambridge, Mass.: Schenkman, 1974.

Limerick, Patricia Nelson. *Legacy of Conquest: The Unbroken Past of The American West*. New York: W. W. Norton, 1987.

Martí, Jose. *Inside the Monster: Writings on the U.S. and American Imperialism*. Philip S. Foner, (ed.) Eleanor Randall, trans. New York: Monthly Review Press, 1975.

Masud-Piloto, Felix. *With Open Arms: Cuban Migration to the United States*. Totowa, N.J.: Rowman and Littlefield, 1988.

Monroy, Douglas. *Thrown Among Strangers: The Making of Mexican Culture in Frontier California*. Berkeley: University of California Press, 1990.

Montejano, David. *Anglos and Mexicans in the Making of Texas, 1836-1986*. Austin: University of Texas Press, 1987.

Morales Carrión, Arturo. *Puerto Rico: A Political and Cultural History*. New York: W. W. Norton, 1974.

Padilla, Felix. *Latino Ethnic Consciousness*. Notre

Dame, Ind.: University of Notre Dame Press, 1985.

Pérez, Louis A., Jr. "Cubans in Tampa: From Exiles to Immigrants, 1892-1901." *Florida Historical Quarterly* 57 (October 1978): 129-40.

Portes, Alejandro and Robert L. Bach. *Latin Journey: Cuban and Mexican Immigrants in the United States.* Berkeley: University of California Press, 1985.

Poyo, Gerald E. *With All and for the Good of All: The Emergence of Popular Nationalism in the Cuban Communities of the U.S., 1848-1898.* Durham, North Carolina: Duke University Press, 1989.

———and Gilberto Hinojosa. "Spanish Texas and Borderlands Historiography in Transition: Implication for United States History." *Journal of American History* 75 (September, 1988).

Rodríguez, Clara E. *Puerto Ricans: Born in the U.S.A.* Boston: Unwyn Hyman, 1989.

Romano, Octavio I. V. "The Anthropology and Sociology of the Mexican-Americans: The Distortion of Mexican-American History." *El Grito* (Fall 1986).

Romo, Ricardo. *East Los Angeles: History of a Barrio* Austin: University of Texas Press, 1983.

Rosaldo, Renato. *Culture and Truth: The Remaking of Social Analysis.* Boston: Beacon Press, 1989.

Ruiz, Vicki L. *Cannery Women/Cannery Lives: Mexican Woman, Unionization and The California Food Processing Industry, 1930-1950.* Albuquerque: University of New Mexico Press, 1987.

Sánchez Korrol, Virginia. *From Colonia to Community: The History of Puerto Ricans in New York City.* Berkeley: University of California Press, 1994.

Saragoza, Alex M. "Recent Chicano Historiography: An Interpretive Essay." *Aztlán* 19 (Spring 1988-90): 1-77.

Vega, Bernardo. *Memoirs of Bernardo Vega.* Ed. César Andreu Iglesias. Trans. Juan Flores. New York: Monthly Review Press, 1984.

Virginia Sánchez Korrol chairs the Department of Puerto Rican Studies at Brooklyn College, City University of New York. She is author of From Colonia to Community: The History of Puerto Ricans in New York City, 1917-1948. *A revised second edition was published by the University of California Press last year.*

THE ORGANIZATION OF AMERICAN HISTORIANS THIRTEENTH ANNUAL FOCUS ON TEACHING DAY

The Organization of American Historians will hold its 1996 Annual Meeting, March 28-31, at the Palmer House Hilton in Chicago, Illinois. An exciting part of the Annual Meeting will be the Thirteenth Annual Focus on Teaching Day, which will include informative sessions on teaching American history at the primary and secondary levels of education. It will be held on Saturday, March 30, 1996. Junior and senior high school teachers will not want to miss this valuable exchange of ideas and information.

March 30, 1996 Focus on Teaching Day Sessions

- Teaching the Vietnam War
- Teacher Professional Development and the Role of College and University Faculty
- "Do a Paper" is Not Enough: The Writing Process in History Courses
- Students as Historians: Teaching Historical Research Skills to Secondary and College Students
- The OAH and the Teaching of History to Undergraduates
- Using Historical Simulations in Secondary and Post-Secondary Classrooms
- A Prototype On-Line Advanced Placement Resource Center in U.S. History

Register early and take advantage of our SPECIAL OFFER

Become a new member of the OAH in the History Educator membership category and you will be admitted into the 1996 Focus on Teaching Day for FREE! Along with becoming a member of the OAH, you will receive our quarterly publications, the *OAH Magazine of History* and the *OAH Newsletter.* You will also receive the Annual Meeting *Program.* History Educator Memberships are $35 per year.

Admission for Focus on Teaching Day is $15 for preregistration and $20 for on-site registration.

Admission includes **all** OAH Annual Meeting sessions on **Saturday**. Focus on Teaching Day registrants are also welcome to take advantage of our exhibit hall on **Saturday**.

If you are unable to attend the 1996 Focus on Teaching Day, be sure to subscribe to the *OAH Magazine of History.* The *Magazine* is a valuable resource for teachers of history. Each issue includes useful lesson plans and informative articles. A one-year subscription to the *Magazine* is $20 for members and $25 for nonmembers.

For more information on the 1996 Focus on Teaching Day, OAH Annual Meeting, or the *OAH Magazine of History*, please print your name and address below and send to: Organization of American Historians, 112 North Bryan Street, Bloomington, IN 47408-4199.

I would like information on: _____

Name: _____

Address: _____

City: _____ State: _____ Zip: _____

MAG/V10N2

The Spanish Borderlands

Albert L. Hurtado

The bare geographical facts of the Spanish Borderlands are enough to establish the importance of the region for the United States. The borderlands encompass the southern tier of states extending from California to the Carolinas, more than one half of the continental U.S. Spain explored and settled parts of this region soon after Columbus made his voyages to the western hemisphere. First in Florida (1565) and then in New Mexico (1598), Spanish conquistadores made permanent settlements in order to defend their productive islands in the Caribbean and the rich mining districts in New Spain (Mexico). Eventually they also settled in what is today southern Arizona and Texas, and along the California coast as well as in French Louisiana which Spain acquired in 1763. The United States acquired this vast area by military conquest and purchase in the first half of the nineteenth century.

Traditionally, the borderlands story has been seen as an episode in the histories of the Spanish, French, and British American empires and as a chapter in the westward expansion of the United States. Such

a view, however, obscures the contemporary importance and continuing relevance of borderlands history. In brief, the region is a sort of laboratory for multiculturalism. Here, the American Indians confronted Spanish intruders and made an uneasy accommodation with them. Unlike the

The borderlands encompass the southern tier of states extending from California to the Carolinas, more than one half of the continental U.S.

British colonists and their Anglo American successors, the Spanish government sought to incorporate Indians in Spanish colonial society. To that end, the crown sent Catholic missionaries to convert the Indians to Christianity and to train them in European trades. The Indians, of course,

had their own strongly held religious traditions and often stoutly resisted missionary efforts and Spanish domination. The Pueblo Indians in New Mexico, where the processes of Indian resistance and accommodation are best understood, outwardly conformed to Catholic norms but continued to practice their own religion in secret. But the exchange of cultural traits was also a two-way affair. Spaniards and Mexicans were influenced by their Indian neighbors as they mingled, traded, and intermarried. Thus, in the southwestern borderlands, distinctive societies emerged that combined aspects of Hispanic, Mexican, and Indian cultures.

Most of the Anglo Americans who began to move into the southwestern borderlands in the 1820s blended into this interesting population. From Texas to California, Anglo men married the daughters of the country, took up the Catholic religion, and swore their allegiance to Mexico. They had many reasons for doing so; marriages and friendships were good foundations for commercial relationships, and new citizens could take advantage of

Mexico's very liberal land laws which provided free grants of thousands of acres on the frontier. Nevertheless, many of these new immigrants were uneasy with Mexican government and society and clung to familiar religious and social practices. Thus, Anglos added a share to the borderlands cultural mix which remains vibrant in many borderlands communities today.

The amalgamation of three cultures has not always been easy or peaceful. The borderlands is not a melting pot, but rather a forge where cultural collisions cause sparks and heat. That process continues today as new immigrants from Mexico and Central America come to the place that by turns has belonged to Indian nations, Spain, Mexico, and the U.S.

This historical drama has taken place on a stage of incomparable beauty and environmental diversity. The desert Southwest is stark and full of surprising contrasts; snowcapped mountains may be seen from sun-baked deserts; and rain in the mountains can bring a torrent hurtling down dry washes in the desert many miles away. Human dwellers have adapted to these conditions for thousands of years. Irrigation was a feature of desert life one thousand years ago, and it is still so today.

The dramatic nature of the borderlands has captured the attention of historians for more than a century. The first Anglo historians were primarily interested in demonstrating the inferiority of Spanish and Mexican institutions and justifying the U.S. conquest of the region. Their biases were influenced by a strong strain of anti-Catholic bigotry which permeated Anglo American society in the nineteenth and early-twentieth centuries. This parochial vision started to change when Herbert E. Bolton (1870-1953) began to investigate the region. Bolton taught at the University of Texas (1901-1909), Stanford University (1909-1911), and the University of California, Berkeley (1911-1943). While not the first historian to study Spain in America, he was arguably the most influential because he wrote dozens of books and trained more than one hundred Ph.D. and three hundred M.A. students, as well as many elementary and high school teachers. Bolton's classic volume, *The Spanish Borderlands*, gave the field its name, and his interpretation dominated the field long after his death. Bolton saw the Spanish settlement in North America as a great saga, a continent peopled with venerable explorer-heroes like Franciso Vasquez de Coronado and Juan Bautista de Anza. He was most impressed with the Catholic missionaries—such as Junipero Serra and Eusebio Kino—who worked among the Indians. Bolton's work went a long way toward muting the religious and cultural bigotry of American historians and gaining a wide popular audience for borderlands history.

Bolton, however, had his faults. While celebrating the missionaries efforts among the Indians, he ignored the negative impact of the Spanish conquest and the missions on them. Nor did he give any attention to Mexico. Bolton was happy to present a distant Spanish colonial past that did not directly challenge Anglo legitimacy. Consequently, in recent years Indian and Mexican scholars have criticized Bolton for presenting a narrow, Hispanophilic view of the borderlands past. These same scholars have done much to correct the distorted picture that Bolton painted. Their work includes imaginative histories of Indian societies, women, and families. They consider not only the Spanish, but the Mexican past as well. Rather than being presented as pioneers with a God-given license to conquer the West, Anglo immigrants are now set in the context of a long and vibrant history.

Once seen as peripheral to American history, the borderlands are now central to our understanding of the multicultural American West. ❑

Bibliography

Bannon, John Francis. *The Spanish Borderland Frontier, 1513-1821*. New York: Holt, Rinehart and Winston, 1970.

Bolton, Herbert E. *The Spanish Borderlands: A Chronicle of Old Florida and the Southwest*. New Haven: Yale University Press, 1921.

Gerhard, Peter. *The North Frontier of New Spain*. Princeton, N.J.: Princeton University Press, 1982.

Gutiérrez, Ramón A. *When Jesus Came, the Corn Mothers Went Away: Marriage, Sexuality, and Power in New Mexico, 1500-1846*. Stanford, Calif.: Stanford University Press, 1991.

Hall, Thomas D. *Social Change in the Southwest, 1350-1880*. Lawrence: University Press of Kansas, 1989.

Jensen, Joan M. and Darlis A. Miller, eds., *New Mexico Women: Intercultural Perspectives*. Albuquerque: University of New Mexico Press, 1986.

John, Elizabeth A. H. *Storms Brewed in Other Men's Worlds: The Confrontation of Indians, Spanish, and French in the Southwest, 1540-1795*. College Station: Texas A & M University Press, 1975.

Spicer, Edward H. *Cycles of Conquest. The Impact of Spain, Mexico and the United States on the Indians of the Southwest, 1533-1960*. Tucson: University of Arizona Press, 1962.

Stoddard, Elwyn R., Richard L. Nostrand, and Jonathan P. West. *Borderlands Sourcebook: A Guide to the Literature on Northern Mexico and the American Southwest*. Norman: University of Oklahoma Press, 1983.

Thomas, David Hurst, ed. *Columbian Consequences*. 3 vols. Washington, D.C.: Smithsonian Institution, 1989-91.

Weber, David J. *The Spanish Frontier in North America*. New Haven: Yale University Press, 1992.

———. *The Mexican Frontier 1821-1846: The American Southwest under Mexico*. Albuquerque: University of New Mexico Press, 1982.

Albert L. Hurtado is a professor of history and departmental director of Graduate Studies at Arizona State University. He is the author of Indian Survival on the California Frontier *(1988) which received the OAH Frederick Jackson Turner Award.*

From Out of the Shadows: Mexican Women in the United States

Vicki L. Ruiz

Beginning with the Coronado expedition of 1540, Spanish-speaking women migrated north decades, even centuries, before their European American counterparts ventured west. The Spanish colonial government, in efforts to secure its territorial claims, offered a number of inducements to those willing to undertake such an arduous journey. Subsidies given to a band of settlers headed for Texas included not only food and livestock, but also petticoats and stockings. Although some settlers would claim "Spanish" blood, the majority of people were *mestizo* (Spanish/Indian), and many colonists were of African descent.

Few women ventured to the Mexican North as widows or orphans; most arrived as the wives or daughters of soldiers, farmers, and artisans. Over the course of three centuries, they raised families on the frontier and worked alongside their fathers or husbands, herding cattle and tending crops. Furthermore, the Franciscans did not act alone in the acculturation and decimation of indigenous peoples, but recruited women into their service as teachers, midwives, doctors, cooks, seamstresses, and supply managers.

Women's networks based on ties of blood and fictive kinship proved central to the settlement of the Spanish/Mexican frontier. At times women settlers acted as midwives to mission Indians, and they baptized sickly or still-born babies. As godmothers for these infants, they established the bonds of *commadrazgo* between

Native American and Spanish/Mexican women. However, exploitation took place *among* women. For those in domestic service, racial and class hierarchies undermined any pretense of sisterhood. In San Anttonio in 1735, Antonía Lusgardia Ernandes, a mulatta, sued her former employer for custody of their son. Admitting

The Spanish . . . offered a number of inducements to those willing to undertake such an arduous journey. Subsidies given to a band of settlers headed for Texas included not only food and livestock, but also petticoats and stockings.

paternity, the man claimed that his former servant had relinquished the child to his wife since his wife had baptized the child. The court, however, granted Ernandes custody. While the godparent relationship could foster ties between colonists and Native Americans, elites used baptism as a venue of social control. Indentured servitude was prevalent on the

colonial frontier persisting well into the nineteenth century.

The history of Spanish/Mexican settlement has been shrouded by myth. Walt Disney's *Zorro*, for example, epitomized the notion of romantic California controlled by fun-loving, swashbuckling rancheros. As only three percent of California's Spanish/Mexican population could be considered rancheros in 1850, most women did not preside over large estates, but helped manage small family farms. In addition to traditional tasks, Mexican women were accomplished *vaqueras* or cowgirls. Spanish-speaking women, like their European American counterparts, encountered a duality in frontier expectations. While placed on a pedestal as delicate "ladies," women were responsible for a variety of strenuous chores.

Married women on the Spanish/Mexican frontier had certain legal advantages not afforded their European American peers. Under English common law, women, when they married, became *feme covert* (or dead in the eyes of the legal system) and thus, they could not own property separate from their husbands. Conversely, Spanish/Mexican women retained control of their land after marriage and held one-half interest in the community property they shared with their spouses. Interestingly, Rancho Rodeo de las Aguas, which María Rita Valdez operated until the 1880s, is now better known as Beverly Hills.

Life for Mexican settlers changed dramatically in 1848 with the conclusion of the U.S.-Mexican War, the discovery of gold in California, and the Treaty of Guadalupe Hidalgo. Mexicans on the U.S. side of the border became second-class citizens, divested of their property and political power. Their world turned upside down. Segregated from the European American population, Mexican Americans in the barrios of the Southwest sustained their sense of identity and cherished their traditions. With little opportunity for advancement, Mexicans were concentrated in lower echelon industrial, service, and agricultural jobs. This period of conquest and marginalization, both physical and ideological, did not occur in a dispassionate environment. Stereotypes affected rich and poor alike with Mexicans commonly described as lazy, sneaky, and greasy. In European American journals, novels, and travelogues, Spanish-speaking women were frequently depicted as flashy, morally deficient sirens.

At times these images had tragic results. On 5 July 1851, a Mexican woman swung from the gallows, the only woman lynched during the California Gold Rush. Josefa Segovia (also known as Juanita of Downieville) was tried, convicted, and hanged the same day she had killed an Anglo miner and popular prize fighter, a man who had assaulted her the day before. Remembering his Texas youth, Gilbert Onderdonk recounted that in proposing to his sweetheart he listed the qualities he felt set him apart from other suitors.

"I told her. . . I did not use profane language, never drank whisky, never gambled, and never killed Mexicans."

Some historians have asserted that elite families believed they had a greater chance of retaining their land if they acquired an Anglo son-in-law. Intermarriage, however, was no insurance policy. In 1849, María Amparo Ruiz married Lieu-

Chicano Research Collection, Arizona State University

"Comadres," Teresa Grijalva de Orosco and Francisca Ocampo Quesada, 1912.

tenant Colonel Henry S. Burton and five years later the couple purchased Rancho Jamul, a sprawling property of over 500,000 acres. When Henry Burton died in 1869, the ownership of Rancho Jamul came into question. After seven years of litigation, the court awarded his widow only 8,926 acres. Even this amount was challenged by squatters, and she would continue to lose acreage in the years ahead. Chronicling her experiences, Ruiz de Burton wrote *The Squatter and the Don* (1885), a fictionalized account of the decline of the ranching class.

Providing insight into community life, nineteenth-century Spanish language newspapers reveal ample information on social mores. Newspaper editors upheld the double standard. Women were to be cloistered and protected to the extent that some residents of New Mexico protested the establishment of coeducational public schools. In 1877 Father Gasparri of *La revista católica* editorialized that women's suffrage would destroy the family. Despite prevailing conventions, Mexican women, due to economic circumstances wrought by political and social disenfranchisement, sought employment for wages. Whether in cities or on farms, family members pooled their earnings to put food on the table. Women worked at home taking in laundry, boarders, and sewing while others worked in the fields, in restaurants and hotels, and in canneries and laundries.

In 1900, over 375,000 to 500,000 Mexicans lived in the Southwest. By 1930 this figure increased ten-fold as over one million Mexicanos—pushed out by revolution and lured in by prospective jobs—came to the United States. They settled into existing barrios and forged new communities both in the Southwest and the Midwest. Like their foremothers, women usually journeyed north as wives and daughters. Some, however, crossed the border alone and as single mothers. As in the past, women's wage earnings proved essential to family survival. Urban daughters (less frequently mothers) worked in canneries and garment plants as well as in the service sector. Entire families labored in the fields and received their wages in a single check made out to the head of household. Grace Luna related how women would scale ladders with one hundred pounds of cotton on their backs and some had to "carry their kids on top of their picking sacks!"

Exploitation in pay and conditions prompted attempts at unionization. Through Mexican mutual aid societies and progressive trade unions, Mexican women proved tenacious activists. In 1933 alone thirty-seven major agricultural strikes occurred in California. The Los Angeles Dressmakers' Strike (1933), the San Antonio Pecan Shellers' Strike (1938), and the California Sanitary Canning Company Strike (1939) provide examples of urban activism.

Like the daughters of European immigrants, young Mexican women experienced the lure of consumer culture. Considerable intergenerational conflict emerged as adolescents wanted to dress and perhaps behave like their European American peers at work or like the heroines they encountered in movies and magazines. Evading traditional chaperonage became a major preoccupation for youth. However, they and their kin faced the specter of deportation. From 1931 to 1934, over one-third of the Mexican population in the United States (over 500,000 people) were deported or repatriated. Discrimination and segregation in housing, employment, schools, and public recreation further served to remind youth of their second-class citizenship. In María Arredondo's words, "I remember. . . signs all over that read 'no Mexicans allowed.'"

Operating small barrio businesses, the Mexican middle-class at times allied themselves with their working-class customers and at times strived for social distance.

The League of United Latin American Citizens (LULAC) represented a group that did both simultaneously. An important civil rights organization, with women's active participation, LULAC confronted segregation through the courts; however, only U.S. citizens could join. Conversely, El Congreso de Pueblos de Hablan Española (Spanish-speaking People's Congress) stressed immigrant rights. Indeed, this 1939 civil rights convention drafted a comprehensive platform which called for an end to segregation in public facilities, housing, education, and employment.

After World War II, Mexican women were involved in a gamut of political organizations from the American G.I. Forum to the Community Service Organization (CSO). An Alinsky-style group, CSO stressed local issues and voter registration. Two CSO leaders, Cesar Chávez and Dolores Huerta, forged the United Farm Workers (UFW) during the early 1960s, he as president, she as vice president. A principal negotiator, lobbyist, and strategist, Huerta relied on extended kin and women friends in the union to care for her eleven children during her absences. Although criticized for putting the union first, Dolores Huerta has had few regrets. As she told historian Margaret Rose,

"But now that I've seen how good [my children] turned out, I don't feel so guilty." Family activism has characterized UFW organizing.

As part of global student movements of the late 1960s, Mexican American youth joined together to address continuing problems of discrimination, particularly in education and political representation. Embracing the mantle of cultural nationalism, they transformed a pejorative barrio term "Chicano" into a symbol of pride. "Chicano/a" implies a commitment to social justice and to social change. A graduate student in history at UCLA, Magdalena Mora, not only wrote about trade union struggles but participated in them as well. She organized cannery workers in Richmond, California and participated in CASA, a national immigrant rights group. An activist since high school, she died in 1981 of a brain tumor at the age of twenty-nine. The informal credo of the Chicano student movement: to return to your community after your college education to help your people. Magdalena Mora never left.

A layering of generations exist among Mexicans in the United States from seventh-generation New Mexicans to recent immigrants. This layering provides a vibrant

Las vaqueras, circa early 1900s.

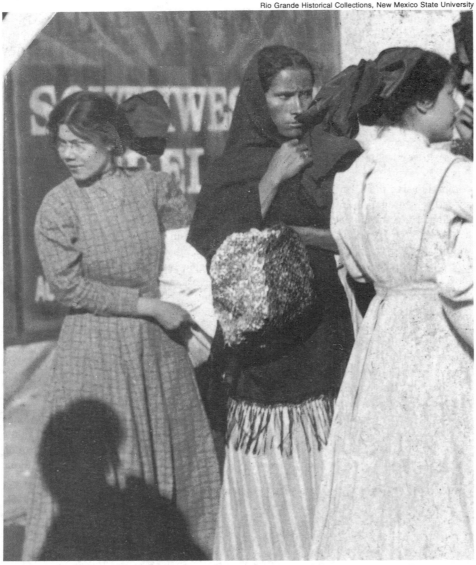

Las solas: Mexican women arriving in El Paso, 1911.

cultural dynamic. Artists Amlia Mesa Bains, Judy Baca, and Yolanda López and writers Sandra Cisneros, Pat Mora, and Cherrie Moraga (to name a few) articulate the multiple identities inhabiting the borderlands of Chicano culture. Across generations, women have come together for collective action. Communities Organized for Public Service (San Antonio) and Mothers of East L.A. exemplify how parish networks become channels for social change. Former student activists María Varela and María Elena Durazo remain committed to issues of economic justice, Varela through a New Mexico rural coop-

erative and Durazo as a union president in Los Angeles. Whether they live in Chicago or El Paso, Mexican women share legacies of resistance. As Varela related, "I learned . . . that it is not enough to pray over an injustice or protest it or research it to death, but that you have to take concrete action to solve it." ❑

Bibliography

de la Torre, Adela and Beatríz M. Pesquera, eds. *Building With Our Hands: New Directions in Chicana Studies.* Berkeley: University of California Press, 1993.

Del Castillo, Adelaida R. ed. *Between Bor-*
ders: Essays on Mexicana/Chicana History. Los Angeles: Floricanto Press, 1990.

Deutsch, Sarah. *No Separate Refuge: Culture, Class, and Gender on the Anglo Hispanic Frontier in the American Southwest, 1880-1940.* New York: Oxford University Press, 1987.

Gutiérrez, Ramón. *When Jesus Came, the Corn Mothers Went Away: Marriage, Sexuality, and Power in New Mexico, 1500-1846.* Stanford: Stanford University Press, 1990.

Martin, Patricia Preciado. *Songs My Mother Sang to Me: An Oral History of Mexican American Women.* Tucson: University of Arizona Press, 1992.

Martínez, Elizabeth. *500 Years of Chicano History in Pictures.* Albuquerque: Southwest Voter Organizing Project, 1991.

Mora, Magdalena and Adelaida R. Del Castillo. *Mexican Women in the United States: Struggles Past and Present.* Los Angeles: UCLA Chicano Studies Research Center, 1980.

Orozco, Cynthia E. "Beyond Machismo, La Familia, and Ladies Auxiliaries: A Historiography of Mexican-Origin Women's Participation in Voluntary Associations and Politics in the United States, 1870-1990." In *Renato Rosaldo Lecture Series Monograph* Vol. 10. Tucson: University of Arizona Mexican American Studies and Research Center, 1992-93.

Ruiz, Vicki L. *Cannery Women, Cannery Lives: Mexican Women, Unionization, and the California Food Processing Industry, 1930-1950.* Albuquerque: University of New Mexico Press, 1987.

———. *From Out of the Shadows: A History of Mexican Women in the United States* (forthcoming)

———. "Mascaras y Muros: Chicana Feminism and the Teaching of U.S. Women's History." In *New Viewpoints in U.S. Women's History.* Ed. Susan Ware. Cambridge: Schlesinger Library Publications, 1994.

Weber, Devra. *Dark Sweat, White Gold: California Farm Workers, Cotton, and the New Deal.* Berkeley: University of California Press, 1994.

Adjusting the Focus: Padua Hills Theatre and Latino History

matt garcía

I n 1991, the year I entered The Claremont Graduate School and began researching the history of Mexican Americans, I became reacquainted with the Padua Hills Theatre. Although three generations of my family had performed at the theater, few images of its past remained in the collective memories of my generation. With the encouragement and support of my community, family, and graduate advisors, I recently published a short history of this institution, the longest-running Mexican American theater in United States history (1). The rediscovery of Padua Hills Theatre, however, reveals more than the forgotten history of a U.S. ethnic group. It also exposes the willful neglect of an important Mexican American institution by a generation of Chicano historians.

From 1931 to 1974, local Mexican American performers presented Spanish-language, Mexican-theme musicals to a mostly English-speaking, white audience. Located in the college town of Claremont, California outside of Los Angeles, the theater attracted the support of many notable patrons, including local professors, artists, and Hollywood stars. The theater's

Consequently, the . . . plays became recognized as much for their ability to defuse prejudice against Mexicans, as for their entertainment quality.

proprietors, Herman and Bess Garner, successfully operated the theater as a non-profit business from 1936 to its close with the expressed intent of forging "intercultural understanding" between European Americans and Mexicans. Consequently, the Mexican Players' plays became recog-

nized as much for their ability to defuse prejudice against Mexicans, as for their entertainment quality.

Admittedly, this intercultural "experiment" had many flaws. Although the Garners intended to present a positive image of Mexican culture, their strict control over scripts (written by Charles Dickenson, a playwright from Pomona College) and their insistence on appealing to the tastes of white audiences resulted in distortions of Mexican and California history. Often, the plays tended to substitute old stereotypes of Mexicans for new ones. Instead of casting Mexicans as thieving, dangerous, or subhuman, the performances depicted them as carefree, docile, or politically benign. Moreover, management-performer relations reflected the social inequalities extant in the larger society. As the following quote demonstrates, the Garners occasionally expressed condescending attitudes which patronized the Paduanos and overemphasized their contributions and those of the theater's trustees:

> For children of Mexican parentage it has been an especially significant, a most wonderful experience, often a veritable turning point in their lives. *Their simple minds*, sometimes tortured with the complexes of a minority group, have suddenly found for themselves an undreamed of background of romance and beauty! Why should they any longer be *apologetic* for their parents and grandparents? Their teachers have told us that this change of outlook has sometimes been little short of marvelous [italics added](2).

Participation in the theater's performances symbolized a "turning point" in the lives of many Paduanos; however, it did not represent the self-discovery expressed by the Garners. For several Mexican Players, Padua Hills provided the opportunity to share with white audiences music and dance commonly experienced

at community festivals and ceremonies within the barrios (3). In addition, encounters with European American managers and audiences familiarized Paduanos with life in a white-dominated society. Some players took away from these interethnic exchanges the knowledge to deflect prejudice and to achieve a degree of prosperity in their careers after their retirements from Padua (4). Last, on a personal level, several Paduanos valued their experiences at the theater for the relationships forged among the players. Casilda Amador Thoreson commented that the group was "like a family," while many Paduanos have credited Padua Hills as the reason for meeting their spouses (5).

The Padua Hills Theatre, therefore, exemplified both the positive and negative aspects of intercultural relations between Mexicans and European Americans in the twentieth century and reflected many of the social conditions of this historical period and place. One would expect an institution such as this to attract a significant amount of scholarly attention and be the source of considerable intellectual debate, particularly among historians of

American culture and entertainmen[t] However, I found very few publication[s] concerning Padua Hills. With the excep[tion] of Pauline Deuel's narrative history[,] *Mexican Serenade*, and a few local a[r]ticles, Padua Hills has received minim[al] attention from scholars of U.S. history (6[).

It seems particularly odd that Chican[o] theater scholars have excluded Padua Hil[ls] Theatre from their studies. The few th[at] treat this history overlook Padua Hills, [or] dismiss the institution as not being repr[e]sentative of the genre. For exampl[e,] Nicolás Kanellos and Jorge Huerta fail [to] make reference to The Mexican Playe[rs] (7). Another scholar, Roberto J. Garz[a] commented specifically on Padua Hil[ls] and its relationship to Chicano theat[er] when he wrote:

> . . . like so many other institutions of this nature which are dedicated to the infusion and diffusion of "culture," such groups did little to represent the actual existence of the Chicano in the American society. Their romantic performances reflected nothing

An informal photo of Bess Garner and the Mexican Players taken in the fall of 1936.

of the harsh realities of the oppressed Chicano population. Worse still, the theater failed to capture and convey that *espiritu* of *La Raza* which was about to manifest itself (8).

Inappropriately comparing the theater and its plays to *Teatro Campesino* (the Chicano activist theater company founded during the 1960s), these scholars held Padua Hills to the standards of an ethnic nationalist politics, and failed to consider the historic period in which the theater and its players developed. Unfortunately, these opinions of Padua Hills Theatre and its legacy have continued to the present (9).

The Paduanos, while not conforming to the tenets of the 1960s political struggles, nevertheless shaped intercultural relations between whites and Mexicans in the United States. Although the Mexican Players may have exercised less autonomy over their productions than other Mexican and Chicano theater groups, their ability to reach thousands of white patrons and alter the prejudices of some audience members deserves recognition. In addition, the owners' investment in the players' development, while less than perfect, reflected a progressive approach to race relations, particularly during the 1930s when the United States repatriated and deported 500,000 Mexican immigrants. In a time of immigrant scapegoating and persecution, Padua Hills offered an alternative vision of Mexican and white relations, an important lesson for today's society. Last, the Padua Hills Theater spawned perhaps the first generation of "Mexican American"

film actors and radio performers, including Mauricio Jara, Natividad Vacio, Manuel Diaz, and Rebecca Romo Wolfe (10). Performing during a period of persistent discrimination in the entertainment

Photo courtesy of Pomona Public Library

The Mexican Players, Casilda Amador, Alfonso Gallado, and Sara Marcias, strike a dramatic pose during spring, 1935.

industry, the success of these artists represents significant accomplishments.

The history of Padua Hills Theater problematizes the nationalist approach of some Chicano scholars, and demands a broadening of the focus of current Latino scholarship to include those groups, like The Mexican Players, which were strategically accomodationist. By including this history, we reflect the more varied nature of the Latino experience which included compromise as well as resistance in confronting discrimination. ❑

Endnotes

1. matt garcía, "'Just Put On That Padua Hills Smile': The Mexican Players and The Padua Hills Theatre, 1931-1974," *California History* (Fall 1995): 244-61.
2. The term "Paduana/o" is used by the Mexican Players to describe themselves. Padua Institute booklet, *A Non-profit Institution Dedicated to Inter-American Friendship: The Educational Phase* (Padua Hills, Claremont, Calif., 1936).
3. Cheva García, interviewed by author, 10 February 1993; Christina Pérez, interviewed by author, 26 April 1993; and Daniel Martínez, Jr., interviewed by author, 16 May 1995.
4. Juan Matute, for example, went on to have a very successful career as an executive for Pan Am Airlines. After their careers at Padua Hills, some Paduanos maintained levels of income that would classify them as part of the "Mexican middle class."
5. Casilda Amador Thoreson, interviewed by the author, 19 May 1995. Many Paduanos met and married as a result of working at Padua Hills. Some of the couples include Alfonso and Conchita Gallardo, Hilda and Mauricio Jara, Porfiria and Enrique Lerma, Juan and Manuela Matute, and José and Ysabel Alba, to name a few.
6. Pauline B. Deuel, *Mexican Serenade:*

The Story of the Mexican Players and the Padua Hills Theatre (Claremont, Calif.: Padua Institute, 1961).

7. Jorge Huerta, *Chicano Theater: Themes and Forms* (Ypsilanti, Michigan: Bilingual Press, 1982); Nicolás Kanellos, *Mexican American Theatre: Legacy and Reality* (Pittsburgh: Latin American Literary Review Press, 1987); and Nicolás Kanellos, ed., *Mexican American Theatre: Then and Now* (Houston, Tex.: Arte Público Press, 1989).

8. Roberto J. Garza, ed., *Contemporary Chicano Theatre* (Notre Dame: University of Notre Dame Press, 1976), 5.

9. For the most recent example of this phenomenon, see Alicia Arrizon, "Contemporizing Performance: Mexican California and the Padua Hills Theatre," in *Mester* 22/23 (Fall 1993/ Spring 1994) [special double issue].

10. Rebecca Romo Wolfe went on from the Padua Hills stage to perform opera on the radio during the 1940s and 1950s. Mauricio Jara, Manuel Diaz, and Natividad Vacio acted in many films, while many other Paduanos performed locally and served as models and spokespeople for the advertisement of Southern California businesses. In addition, Walt Disney, a friend of the Garners, integrated the players into his film *The Three Caballeros*, a Latin American theme movie that combined animated characters with live actors. Rebecca Romo Wolfe, interviewed by the author, 21 June 1994; and Casilda Amador Thoreson, interviewed by the author, 19 May 1995.

matt garcía holds a one year lectureship in Latino History at the University of Illinois, Urbana-Champaign. A Ph.D. candidate at the The Claremont Graduate School, he is completing his dissertation on intercultural relations in the southern California citrus belt. He would like to thank Tavo Olmos for helping with the photographs.

Old Voices, New Voices: Mainland Puerto Rican Perspectives and Experiences

Background Information

A Puerto Rican presence has long existed in the continental United States, reaching back to the final decades of the nineteenth century. It was then that Puerto Rican political exiles opposed to Spanish rule of their homeland took up residence on the mainland, struggling to attain the island's liberation from Spain. With the acquisition of Puerto Rico by the United States in 1898, the numbers of Puerto Ricans migrating in search of economic opportunity began to grow steadily, as landholding changes, accelerated by the influx of large amounts of U.S. capital, resulted in the loss of Puerto Rico's subsistence economy. Some migrants became contract laborers in Hawaii; others moved to the mainland. The 1917 Jones Act, which unilaterally made Puerto Ricans citizens of the United States, served to make movement back and forth between the island and mainland easier.

The sources of information on the everyday struggles and triumphs of these early *pioneros* are limited, but the texts written by two politically active Puerto Ricans of that era, Jesús Colón and Bernard Vega, have provided us with much insight into the early Puerto Rican community that took root in New York. In the foreword to *A Puerto Rican in New York and Other Sketches*, by Jesús Colón, Juan Flores writes:

[These texts] are in fact unique documents of their kind, offering the only sustained glimpses we have of the New York Puerto Rican community during the decades prior to 1950. Here we get a sense of what motivated Puerto Ricans to set out en masse in the first place, who those pioneering families were, and what it was like for them upon landing and seeking out a new life in this bulging

metropolis. We witness first-hand the fantasy-world New York, known to them from illustrated magazines and picture postcards, dashing against the somber reality of the crowded tenements where they came to live, while their prospects for stable employment dwindled the longer they stayed. We also learn how, after the initial fits and starts, the community began forming organizations to provide for the needed cultural cohesion and a political voice in these unfamiliar and often hostile surroundings. And, finally, these documents tell of the Puerto Ricans' initial relations with their newfound neighbors, the multitude of other immigrant nationalities in the touted "melting pot" who, like themselves, had come from foreign shores in search of a brighter future.

Another valuable source of information on the experiences and perspectives of the Puerto Rican migrants is to be found in collected interviews of migrants, gathered by a new mainland-born or raised generation of Puerto Rican scholars intent upon documenting the untold stories of the Puerto Rican migration. These scholars have captured the diversity of the population and its experiences through their interviews of the working class men and women who made up the backbone of the community, as well as through interviews of more well-known Puerto Ricans who left behind a more easily documented record of their struggles and achievements.

Such resources add to a growing body of literature written by Puerto Ricans who draw heavily upon their own personal experiences in constructing their literary works. Taken together, this range of accounts points to similarities in the (in)migrant (immigrant or in-migrant, the latter term applies to Puerto Ricans) experience across ethnic groups and historical eras. These similarities include the struggle to settle and establish themselves in a new land, the painful process of adjusting to a new cultural and linguistic setting, and the intergenerational conflicts that inevitably occur in such contexts. And if read with accounts of other Latino groups in the United States, the common bonds that link Latinos in the U.S., in important respects differentiating them from earlier European immigrant groups, also emerge. But this wealth of resources, carefully read, also vividly illustrates unique aspects of the Puerto Rican experience: coming as citizens, continuing to be involved in a circular migration between island and mainland, entering into a society much more racially

---

NEW YORK STATE CURRICULUM EDITOR'S NOTE: A difference of opinion exists concerning the proper terminology to use in referring to Puerto Rico and the United States. Many writers use *island* and *mainland* as descriptive locators, while others object to these, arguing that "island" diminishes Puerto Rico as compared to the "mainland." We opt, for the sake of variety and succinctness, to use these terms without projecting any superior/inferior meaning in so doing.

OAH EDITOR'S NOTE: While the layout is strictly of our design, the text is reprinted verbatim from the New York State Curriculum.

divided than that of Puerto Rico, settling in urban areas in large numbers at a time when the changing economic structure has made upward mobility for the community as a whole more difficult. Taken together, these sources provide us with invaluable accounts of the voices of a people who have contributed so much to the diversity and strengths of the United States of America and its people. This activity introduces the student to a range of primary source materials that bring to life the history, perspectives, and experiences of Puerto Ricans on the mainland.

Major Ideas

- The Puerto Rican presence on the mainland dates back to the late 1800s; a Puerto Rican community took root in New York City in the early decades of the twentieth century.

- The Jones Act of 1917 made Puerto Ricans U.S. citizens without their consent, served to spur migration (since it was unrestricted), and made Puerto Ricans eligible for the military draft.

- Most Puerto Ricans migrated because of economic factors, including inadequate employment opportunities in Puerto Rico and the lure of better opportunities on the mainland.

- Like other immigrants, Puerto Ricans have had to adjust to a new culture, experiencing hardship and discrimination in the process.

- Many Puerto Ricans have maintained strong ties to Puerto Rico, its culture, and its language; the back-and-forth movement in response to fluctuating economic conditions has strengthened such linkages.

- Many Puerto Ricans have encountered racial prejudice and discrimination on the mainland; their perceived linkages to other people of color have been strengthened as a result.

- Changes in the economic structure of the U.S. have limited opportunities for upward mobility for more recent (in)migrant groups.

- Like the culture of other (in)migrant groups, Puerto Rican culture on the mainland shows evidence of both continuity and change from the home culture.

- Puerto Rican responses to the challenges they face on the mainland have included organizing to: support their political views; improve public education; and build pride in their heritage and language.

- Puerto Ricans' labor has contributed to the economic growth of the United States.

- Puerto Ricans as a group share much with other Latino groups, including close ties with their homeland. This closeness results from greater accessibility to their homeland, economic fluctuations that lead them to move back and forth, and continued reinforcement of their culture and language through contact with new migrants. Puerto Ricans and other Latino groups also share a legacy of sustained racial and ethnic discrimination.

Vocabulary

sweatshops

colonialism

oral history

commonwealth

El Barrio: East Harlem (literally "the neighborhood")

Borinquen: original name for Puerto Rico; name given to the island by the Taíno Indians

boriqueño/boricua: nickname for a Puerto Rican

tabaqueros: cigarmakers

pioneros: pre-World War II members of the Puerto Rican community on the mainland

caracolillo coffee: special high-grade coffee bean

five-peso note: five-dollar bill (Although U.S. dollars are the legal currency in Puerto Rico, many people call dollars *pesos*, [the Spanish currency used on the island before 1898].)

five *centavos*: five cents

patron saints' days: days commemorating Catholic saints. Celebrated like a birthday for children on the day of their namesake; villages and parishes also observe the day of their designated saint.

Vejigante a la bolla, pan y cebolla: Couplet traditionally chanted during Carnival. Its meaning is obscure. *Vejigante* "giant," refers to the masks that are traditional for Carnival.

Rudimentos de América: "American Basics"

pionera: pioneer

needlework: sewing and embroidering by hand

East Harlem: one of the oldest Puerto Rican settlements in New York City

International Ladies' Garment Workers Union: trade union representing workers in the clothing manufacturing industry

undocumented: without legal documents proving one's right to be in the United States

Immigration: the Immigration and Naturalization Service of the U.S. government

Questions

What hardships did the women who were interviewed face in the process of migrating and resettling on the mainland?

What were the strengths of the Puerto Rican community on the island and on the mainland?

How do the women remember Puerto Rico? Have you ever felt nostalgic about an earlier period in your life?

How did the women respond to the difficult conditions they faced? What choices did they have?

What similarities are there between the experiences of the first generation Puerto Rican women and the experiences of their daughters? What conflicts might exist between the generations? Why? Have you ever experienced similar generational conflicts?

Have students in your school whose parents were born outside of the mainland USA had similar experiences or feelings? ❏

MEMORIES OF PUERTO RICO AND NEW YORK

Puerto Ricans who migrated to the United States not only had to leave their homes, families and friends behind. They said farewell to a way of life; one based on a strong sense of community, in which even the poorest people shared the little they had.

Minerva Torres Ríos, 87 years old, came to the United States from Puerto Rico in 1929. For many years she lived in New York City's East Harlem section, one of the oldest Puerto Rican settlements in New York. The people of East Harlem call it simply *El Barrio*, or "the neighborhood."

Ms. Ríos was a member of a popular education and literacy program in El Barrio, organized with the help of the Centro de Estudios Puertorriqueños. She reflects in this essay on her childhood in Puerto Rico and subsequent experiences as a laundry worker in New York City.

To remember is to live. And how well I remember my childhood in the town of Guayanilla, where I was born June 5, 1905. Guayanilla is in the south of Puerto Rico. It's near Ponce, the second largest city in the country. Other towns nearby are Yauco, famous for its *caracolillo* coffee, and Peñuelas, known for its navel oranges and finger bananas. Peñuelas also has the famous Banana Tree Mountain, one of the five highest mountains in Puerto Rico.

One of my most pleasant memories is of my baptism at age seven. I felt so happy, especially when my godparents pinned a five-peso note to my dress. I knew it was money but I had no idea of its value. At that tender age, just like other Puerto Rican children at the time, I thought two or three cents was more than one dollar and that five *centavos* was a lot!

Life there was poor, but it was a happy life. You didn't have the violence you have today. We young girls used to go with the boys down to the river and go swimming together with our old clothes on.

The best times of my childhood were the holidays—the patron saints' days, Three Kings' Day and Carnival. For the patron saints' days we got to celebrate for nine days, winding up with a big party in the town square. We'd have games of chance, children's games and most of all, music. Three Kings' Day, January 6, was a holiday for children, something like the tradition of Santa Claus here in the United States. On that day we would go all around the neighborhood, showing off the presents that the Three Kings had left under our beds. The night before, we would have put a bit of grass under the bed for the kings' camels, who we knew would be tired and would eat the grass hungrily. That's what all Puerto Rican children believed, and I continued to believe in the Three Kings until I was twelve.

Carnival was another time of tremendous enjoyment, especially for children. I remember how we poor people celebrated carnival with water. We'd form groups and throw buckets of water on each other, and we'd put on masks and costumes and dance. We'd parade through the town chanting the famous carnival chant: *Vejigante a la bolla, pan y cebolla!*

In 1914 the First World War broke out. I was nine. That's when my suffering began, because my father had to go to war. How I cried to see my father leave me, my brothers and two sisters. Thank goodness, though, my father did not have to serve much time in the military since he was a school teacher and was soon called back to teach.

In 1918, when I was thirteen, I was in school one morning when the whole building began to shake. I had never felt anything like it, and ran screaming for home. I couldn't even stay standing up, I didn't know what to do; everyone was crying, "My God, it's an earthquake!"

The island was left in ruins by that quake. Every town suffered severe damage. There were deaths, and many people were left homeless: my humble house was damaged. They had to use the schools as temporary hospitals. That was the historic earthquake that destroyed much of Puerto Rico.

In school, we used a textbook called *Rudimentos de América*, because in those days everything in Puerto Rico used to come from here, from the United States. The governor of the island was American, and the laws were made here.

I know the story of Abraham Lincoln, that they taught me in Puerto Rico; the story of George Washington; Benjamin Franklin with a kite . . . They taught some things about Puerto Rico, but there was no textbook on Puerto Rican history. They just taught it orally. They didn't teach us anything about the people of South America. I knew nothing about all that.

I graduated from the eighth grade, which is when you get your first diploma in Puerto Rico. Those who can, go on to study for another four years. But I couldn't continue in school, because there was no high school in my town and I would have had to go to another town and pay. My father and mother had separated by then, and I couldn't afford it.

My mother had to go work in people's houses as a maid, and I worked in a shop embroidering blouses and dresses. The pay was very little. In Puerto Rico at that time poverty was widespread, it was very hard to survive. I decided to come to New York to work in order to help out my mother and siblings. In 1929 I arrived in New York, where the rest of my story takes place.

I left Puerto Rico on a ship called the *Coamo*. There was at that time no other form of transportation between Puerto Rico and the United States. The crossing lasted five days. I spent most of the time up on the deck, in the fresh air to keep from getting seasick. It was quite a pleasant trip and the boat reminded me of a big hotel.

When we reached New York harbor, it was winter and the pier was hidden in fog. We had to wait for two more days outside the port for the weather to clear. Finally the ship sailed into the harbor, and we crossed in front of the Statue of Liberty and you can imagine what an impression that made on me. As the ship passed slowly in front of the statue, I wondered to myself why it was there in the water instead of in a park, where everyone could admire it.

The Statue of Liberty was the first marvel I experienced in the City of Skyscrapers. When we disembarked on the Brooklyn pier it was very cold, and I saw another wonder for the first time: snow. I knew what it was, of course, from studying the history of the United States, but I had never seen it personally and to see the ground all covered in white astonished me.

I moved in with my cousin. His wife soon got me a job in a factory where I worked for about six months. In 1930, a friend of mine got me a job working with her in a laundry on East 94th Street. I started out ironing collars and cuffs in the men's shirt department, using huge machines. We worked Monday through Saturday, from 8 a.m. to 7 at night. My salary was $12 per week. The workers in the laundries weren't unionized and so the bosses could do whatever they liked.

On Mondays and Tuesdays we worked until 8 p.m. On holidays we had to work half-days. The summer was when I really suffered, between the work and the heat. When the temperature outside was 90 degrees, it was more than 100 inside the laundry. I sweated miserably between those two ironing machines but what could I do? Nothing but keep on working in order to keep my job. The Depression was gripping the country and there were no jobs; anyone lucky enough to have one wanted to keep it, no matter how small the salary.

Working in a laundry has always been relatively secure employment, although it's one of the hardest jobs. In the days before the struggle to unionize the laundries, the U.S. president passed the National Recovery Act, prohibiting employers from paying less than $14 per week. I'll always remember that great president, Roosevelt.

We began struggling for a union. It took tremendous effort before the bosses would agree to it. They threatened to take away our jobs, but we workers kept on fighting until we won.

We became unionized in 1936 and things began to go better. But it still wasn't easy because the employers didn't want to give us paid vacations. But after a number of years everything improved. We no longer had to work on holidays or Saturdays, and if we did work those days, we received double pay.

I continued working hard from 1930 until 1970, when I retired. By that time, I earned more than $200 a week with a month of paid vacation. ❑

Abridged from: Minerva Torres Ríos, "Remembranzas," in *Nuestras Vidas: Recordando, Luchando y Transformando*, produced by the El Barrio Popular Education Program, June 1987. Also includes material from an interview with Minerva Torres Ríos by Rina Benmayor of the Centro de Estudios Puertorriqueños, Hunter College. Translated by C. Sunshine.

OUR MOTHER'S STRUGGLE HAS SHOWN US THE WAY

The late 1940s began the period of mass migration from Puerto Rico to the United States under "Operation Bootstrap." Many women who came found work as sewing machine operators in garment factories in New York City, where pay and working conditions were often poor. The women played an important role in the effort to unionize the factories and win better conditions for workers.

Manufacturers, however, soon found it more profitable to move their factories overseas, where they could take advantage of even cheaper, non-union labor. After 20 or 30 years of work, many Puerto Rican women lost their jobs when factories "ran away."

A group of women, some of them the daughters and granddaughters of garment workers, decided to find out more about this part of their community's history. Working with the Oral History Task Force of the Centro de Estudios Puertorriquños, they interviewed former garment workers. From these interviews they produced a radio documentary, "Nosotras Trabajamos en la Costura." They explain:

This program is about our mothers and grandmothers, the thousands of Puerto Rican women who spent their working lives as seamstresses in the garment factories of New York City. These are some of their stories, that we at the Center for Puerto Rican Studies at Hunter College have been collecting. This is an effort to document and explain our history, to ourselves, to our own communities, and to those who may want to share our lives.

My mother is an embroiderer. She does such beautiful, intricate work. She's been doing that for 20 years now, ever since she came to this country. She raised me and my three sisters all by herself. And she doesn't speak English, to this day.

My grandmother learned to sew in Puerto Rico when she was a little girl, sewing and embroidering fancy lingerie for an American company. Then she came to New York in the twenties, and she was a pionera, and she spent all her life in a garment factory.

We came to New York in 1948. My father drove a cab, and my mother worked in a garment factory for 30 years. Just last Christmas she was laid off permanently. And now she has to find a job, at the minimum wage. That's a hard life, and it's happening to a lot of our parents.

When Puerto Rico became a colony of the United States in 1898, American clothing manufacturers didn't waste much time. By 1915, they had set up a whole needlework industry on the island. There they could escape from the unions and make bigger profits by using the labor of women and children.

Lucila Padrón is now in her seventies. She clearly remembers what her childhood was like.

It was awful. I was born in Ponce, Puerto Rico. That's where I was raised and went to school. I started doing needlework when I was a little girl, in order to help my parents, because we were poor. After the housework and school, instead of playing, we had to sew. It was a sacrifice.

Lucila and her sisters started working at home. Local contractors would distribute bundles of fabric already cut and ready to be sewn to women all across the island. The women would return the finished products beautifully sewn and embroidered, all by hand. Then the work was shipped to New York and sold in exclusive department stores like Wanamaker's or B. Altman's.

Our work was really something to see. It was all done by hand— no machines. Tracing, embroidering, assembling, all of it by hand. And do you know what they paid us? For all that intricate work? Later on, when I came to New York, I saw the clothes we made selling in Wanamaker's on 14th Street. Here, those robes or dresses sold for $100 or more. There, they used to pay us for one of those dresses, with all that embroidery—three dollars. So, to earn ten or twelve dollars a week, we had to work day and night.

Lucila was a teenager when she came to New York in 1927. She wanted to continue her education, but instead she had to support herself and then her own family.

When I came to New York, I had a hard time at first, because I couldn't find a sewing job. I used to walk back and forth, across Manhattan, from shop to shop, from one end of the island to the other, until I finally found a job as a seamstress . . . I worked in garment factories for 30 years, working so I could get where I am now and give my children an education. And I'm very proud of that.

Like Lucila, many of our grandparents migrated to New York during these early years looking for work. Some had been driven off the land by American sugar monopolies. Cigarmakers, carpenters and other skilled workers came too.

By 1930 there were over 50,000 Puerto Ricans in the United States. Men, women and entire families came. The journey took five days by boat and most people settled in East Harlem, or along the Brooklyn waterfront.

Luisa López came as a child in 1923 on the steamship *Coamo*.

My mother and father came to get us at the boat, and when I came into the apartment I found my brother at a machine, sewing. What was he doing?

Coffee bags. Everybody used to help my mother; that machine was going on all day long. I was sewing, my sister was sewing, my brother was sewing, everybody to help out.

Sewing meant economic survival for many Puerto Rican families. During the Depression, Luisa and her sister went to work in garment factories. Puerto Rican women were the newcomers, competing for jobs with Italian and Jewish women.

I was working in a shop called Elfran's Dress Company, in El Barrio, on 104th Street. The Italian girls, they wanted to sit down, and the rest of the girls refused to work, because they didn't want to work with Puerto Ricans. When I saw that, I went to the union, and I spoke to the manager, and I told him what had happened. This manager over here was Italian, he was an old-time socialist, the most wonderful person you ever came to know. His name was Joe Piscatello. He called everybody to the union. And I explained to him, "You know, I'm more an American citizen than some of these people are, that don't even know how to speak English." He gave them hell! He gave them hell! So we all went back to work.

By 1937, the International Ladies Garment Workers Union had more than 2,000 Puerto Rican members. Ironically, just a few years later in the early forties, Luisa lost her union job, in a way that forecast what would happen to thousands of garment workers in the seventies and eighties.

His name was Mr. Cohen. And he opened up five shops in Puerto Rico, that's how come I lost my job. We belonged to the union over here, he had to pay us higher wages. While in Puerto Rico at that time, he could pay fifteen and twenty cents an hour.

After World War Two, U.S. manufacturers were offered big tax breaks to set up factories in Puerto Rico. This was part of Operation Bootstrap, the plan to industrialize the island. But these new factories, many of them garment and light industry, never provided enough jobs. So although industry was busy relocating to the island, by the end of the sixties close to a million Puerto Ricans had migrated to New York.

This was our mothers' generation. Our parents settled with family or friends, in furnished rooms or tenement apartments, in East Harlem, the Lower East Side, or the South Bronx . . .

In the 1950s, the garment industry in New York was booming. Puerto Rican women were hired by the thousands as sewing machine operators, one of the lowest paying jobs in the trade. Although many of our mothers were already experienced needleworkers, by this time the garment industry no longer needed such fine skills. Clothing production was changing. Seamstresses used to make whole garments, but now, women were sewing only sections, in assembly-line fashion.

Section work is sewing zippers, or collars. When I first came to this country, I was sewing the whole garment. But later, I found section work. Because working sections, you can make a lot more money. And I was fast.

Section work allowed New York garment manufacturers to increase production. And this new, cheap labor pool meant they could also increase their profits. Thousands of Puerto Rican and black women became low-paid, unskilled section workers—easily exploited, and easily replaced. Because wages were so low, women like María Rodríguez often brought home extra work, even though home work was illegal.

The boss let me take bundles home, and I used to do it at night. I'd work two hours, three hours to make a little more money. And some times weekends I used to take it, and Victor used to help me. I'd teach my husband how to do it, so he used to help me to do the bundles also.

So then, I'd make about $35, sometimes $38.

Many women, like Dolores Juarbe, found themselves working in sweatshops—small, nonunion operations in firetrap buildings which violated minimum wage laws, paid no overtime, sick leave, or vacation.

There was not any union there. In that shop you had to sew, as fast as you could. And everyone smoked. The shop was in a basement. Once in a while the fire department would pay a little visit. The boss told us to stop smoking, that the fire department was on the way. The alerter heard that they were coming, you know, she used to pay them off. So then, they could knock real loud on the door: bam bam bam! And all the cigarettes would disappear.

Not only were our mothers subjected to these poor working conditions, some even had to fight off the boss.

I did not like the boss. The boss could not keep his hands of the girls. He was always walking in and touching them and squeezing them. So one day, he came to me, and like he tried to feel me up, and I told him, "Listen," I said. "I don't like you. I don't like this job, I don't like the way you treat the girls. So you can keep it!" I got ready to leave. "Oh, don't go, don't go." "Oh, no," I said. "You are a pig!"

Many Puerto Rican women looked for union shops where they expected to get protection, benefits and higher wages. During the fifties, labor unions were stepping up their organizing, and many of our mothers and grandmothers led that effort. Some became union chairladies and organizers, and sometimes the chairlady had the power to stop the shop.

Eva Monge remembers how she shut down her housecoat factory to support a dressmakers' strike.

The dresses were going on strike. The boss right away stopped the housecoats and gave us dresses. The first day, I said, "All right, but . . ." I noticed that the strike kept on. So, on the second day I said, "Mrs. Corey, every girl on this shop is going to finish the bundle that they're doing. They're not going to make no more dresses." You know, that boss went to the dressing room and she cried! But it was from anger. She knew that she was wrong—she was breaking the strike.

By the 1960s Puerto Rican women made up over 25 percent of New York sewing machine operators. The rank and file of the garment unions was now overwhelmingly Puerto Rican and Black. But despite their numbers and their histories of activism, few Black or Puerto Rican women find themselves in positions of power. For decades, the top union leaders have been conservative white men.

Gloria Maldonado is a business agent for ILGWU Local 22-89-1. But she is an exception.

I'm the only woman here. The only woman officer, and the only Hispanic business agent. The manager is Puerto Rican, but I'm the only woman. So I'm Puerto Rican, I'm a woman and I'm Black I've got three affirmative action points (laughs).

. . . During the fifties and sixties, our mothers' work gave our families some economic stability. But then, things began to change. Over the last 30 years, well over 200,000 garment jobs have left New York City alone. And so operators have dwindled to a bare minimum in factories like Juanita Erazo's, where older, higher-paid workers are the first to go.

My friend María, she's been working for him for 29 years, just like me. She was the first one he laid off. That's how he discriminates! He gets rid of the one who earns more money, and those are the older and more experienced operators. The boss just spent three weeks in Taiwan, and he came back loaded down. The factory is four stories high, and practically all the floors are filled with that imported work. What he wants to do is turn the factory into a shipping department, and get rid of the operators altogether. Because the work comes already finished, and ready to sell.

Today, garments are cut in New York, sewn in Taiwan, Korea or

Mexico, finished in Puerto Rico, and sent back to New York for distribution. An operator in Haiti is paid 21 cents an hour, for what in New York costs over $3.00.

As they learned with the Puerto Rican model in the thirties and again in the fifties, clothing manufacturers find it even more profitable today to set up shops in Asia, Latin America and the Caribbean. Gloria Maldonado describes just how massive this relocation is.

Some of these countries, they do a lot of needlework. And capital people, they saw the advantage of making good money, at the expense of other people's misery. And at the expense of our people working here. Big firms started going out, and little by little they started expanding, expanding, until before we knew it . . . It used to be maybe two, three garments out of ten that were imported. Now it's five or six out of ten. The shops are not the ones that are running away, it's the manufacturers. For instance, our Joe Namath, you know, big shot Joe Namath, has a line of men's clothes. Where is he getting it done? China. The thing is, that even though they're made there for less money, it's not sold here for less money like years back.

. . . While manufacturers take their capital abroad, our mothers face widespread layoffs, which often deprives them of their pensions. After years at the machines, many of our mothers suffer back and leg pains, or they are crippled by arthritis.

At the same time, thousands of poor women are migrating to the United States, hoping to escape poverty and often, political repression in their countries. They become cheap labor in factories and sweatshops. Many are undocumented and live in fear of deportation. Juanita Erazo was horrified by a recent immigration raid on her factory in Brooklyn.

In the factory there are Dominicans, Ecuadorians, Colombians and Haitians. The last time Immigration raided, they took everyone away. They took Puerto Ricans away too. They handcuffed them, they filled two buses up with people. Then, after they left, the boss went looking around, and there were people hiding in boxes!

As a union official, Gloria Maldonado has seen how all of this has affected our mothers' generation.

People are just not making it. The small shops are closing up, and that's where it affects our people, our generation, of Puerto Rican women who are not old enough to retire, but have put in 20, 30 years. They stay with this one little shop because it was like a family. All of a sudden, the man has to close because there is no work. . . .

These are the women who raised us. The were not only our mothers and grandmothers, but our cousins, aunts, neighbors, friends. They went to the factories early in the morning and sat in front of those machines day after day. They confronted the difficulties of migration, poverty, low pay, discrimination, and unstable jobs. In spite of that, they raised us and kept our families together. They fought for our education, organized in the communities and on the job, and they gave us a legacy of struggle.

My mother's work set the tone in the family, set the tone for hard work and struggle. She never missed a day of work, which used to amaze us. She was there at 8:00 in the morning, she came home at 5, 5:30, by the time she came in from Brooklyn. And what she always said to us was, 'You have to study. You have to study so that you could be a teacher, you could be a nurse.' And we knew what it meant to us, so that we did study. We got somewhere because she worked so hard. Now I know that that's not true for a lot of Puerto Ricans, I know that for the majority of Puerto Ricans, working hard hasn't led to success.

All these stories are a chapter in our history, which for the most part has yet to be told. Our mothers and grandmothers shared their lives with us, so that we could understand more clearly where we are today. ❑

Abridged from Radio documentary: "*Nosotras Trabajamos en la Costura/* Puerto Rican Women in the Garment Industry," produced by Rina Benmayor, Ana Juarbe, Kimberly Safford and Blanca Vázquez Erazo (*Centro de Estudios Puertorriqueños*, Hunter College, 1985). Program funded in part by National Endowment for the Humanities. Bilingual cassette available.

STORIES TO LIVE BY:
CONTINUITY AND CHANGE IN THREE GENERATIONS OF PUERTO RICAN WOMEN

In the following selection, Celia Alvarez, a daughter of Puerto Rican migrants who moved to the mainland in the 1950s, and one of the researchers who collected the women's stories, reflects on her own experiences growing up in New York City. As you read the passage, think about the similarities and differences between her life and the lives of those who came before her.

My mother migrated to New York in the early 1950s during the period of rapid urbanization and industrialization concomitant with Operation Bootstrap on the Island. She was also a seamstress. She married soon after her arrival and subsequently had the three of us, one right after the other.

Raised in the projects of downtown Brooklyn near the Brooklyn Navy Yard I often wondered: What were we doing here? How did we get here? And why? Nobody said too much, however; no one wanted to talk about the poverty and pain, the family truces and secrets which clouded the tremendous upheaval from Ponce to San Juan to New York.

I grew up speaking Spanish, dancing *la pachanga*, *merengue*, and *mambo*, eating *arroz con habichuelas* and drinking *malta y café*. I was smart, and learned to play the chords of the bureaucratic machinery of housing, education, and welfare very well at a very young age. I translated for everyone—my mother, her friends, our neighbors, as well as my teachers. My parents kept us close to home and it was my responsibility to keep my brother and sister in tow.

It was hard to understand it all, to try to make sense of who I was as a Puerto Rican in New York, so I read everything I could get my hands on; watched the games the government would play between Afro-Americans and Puerto Ricans with social service monies; heard the poverty pimps tell their lies; watched the kids die of dope or heard about them getting killed down elevator chutes in the middle of a burglary; noted the high overpriced tags on old food being sold in the only supermarket in the neighborhood; knew of kids being raped and thrown off the roof. And I asked, "Why?"

The socially active local parish church became my

refuge. It was there that I began to make connections with the poor whites, Afro-Americans, and Asians in my community, and said there had to be a better way for us all. I participated in a variety of activities including youth programs, the local food coop, and newsletter, which basically involved me in community organizing, although I didn't know you called it grassroots work then. I got swept up by the energy of the civil rights movement and wanted to go to the march on Washington but my mother said, "No!" She worried about me—didn't like me wearing my Martin Luther King button or getting involved in politics. She was afraid I would get hurt. I always liked being out on the street talking to people, however, and she knew from way back that I was not destined to stay inside.

Tensions flourished when I turned fourteen and told my parents I was going out with a Puerto Rican boy in the neighborhood. Unfortunately, "boyfriend" in America and *novio* in Puerto Rico did not translate to mean the same thing. In 1968 I was chaperoned and followed by my father wherever I went because of that grave mistake. Their biggest fear? That I would get pregnant. They even threatened to send me to Puerto Rico. I had it all planned out that I would run away and stay with my cousin. She was the first to move out and get her own place. At least we could keep each other company. It never happened but we've been close ever since.

During this same period I started high school in a predominantly white school in the heart of Flatbush. I found myself desegregating the Catholic school system, one of five or six *latinas* and Afro-Americans in my class. I was known as one of the girls from the ghetto downtown and was constantly called upon to defend my race. One day it went too far. Someone said my father didn't work and that their parents supported my coming to their school. I "went off"! You just didn't talk about my family!

I never told my parents about the racist slurs—never had the heart. They were breaking their backs to send me to school; my father kept his job at a city hospital for thirty years and took on a second job at the docks. We would all go help him clean offices at night and on weekends after our day outings together. My mother went back to work in a paper factory down the street. Prior to that, she had taken care of the children of women in the neighborhood who worked. I've also worked since about the time I was fourteen.

Anyway, I graduated high school with honors. I had every intention of going to college—I thought it would give me the credentials to be in a position to act on the miseducation that I saw we were getting. Of course I needed money to go, so I went to talk to my guidance counselor. She always prided herself in being able to say a few words in Spanish . . . her way of "relating." I inquired about government grants programs as well as anything else that she could tell me about. All she could say to me was, "Well, you're not the only one who needs money to go to school, dear."

No thanks to her, I managed to get to college with the help of ASPIRA. I marched over to their office on 14th Street—we didn't have a club in our school, there were too few of us—and presented myself to one of the counselors there. I'll always be grateful that he took me under his wing despite the fact he had an overbooked case load. I applied to about ten schools, got into most of them and

decided to go to a new institution in New England that broke away from the traditional, predetermined academic program and was primarily based on a mentoring system between student and teacher.

So I left home and landed in a progressive liberal arts college which looked more like a country club than anything else. It was so quiet I had to study with my radio blasting to concentrate. Ironically, it was there that I found my first Afro-American and Puerto Rican teachers. I was relieved to know someone who understood the reference points in my life without my having to explain. After pursuing some studies on Puerto Rico and the Caribbean—for the only formal mention of Puerto Rico in all my schooling up to that point had been in a geography class in which we had discussed its mineral resources—I studied questions of language planning, bilingualism and education, language, culture, and identity. I thought that knowledge of these areas would be useful to the Puerto Rican community. . . . I was admonished not to study the reality of Puerto Ricans because somehow I would be "getting over" and not doing valid research. Ironically, given my gender, class background, nationality, and race, I was as marginalized as ever in that setting.

Which brings me back to our oral history project. Listening to these women's stories has served as a tremendous source of inspiration and validation of my own experience as a Puerto Rican woman. They captured and brought back to life the struggles of my own socialization during the 1960s. Though born in New York, I grappled with many of the same social issues and problems as Flor, Lucila, and Eulalia. However, it was within the context of the educational opportunities historically afforded me through the civil rights movement, in conjunction with my own parents'

determination, that I was able to actualize myself in higher education and be in a position to help define this project. This oral history project enabled me to integrate all the different parts of myself—my skills as an intellectual, organizer, and nurturer, as well as my experience as a working-class Puerto Rican woman.

Through the public events linked to our research, I have been able to bring this experience back home: *to my own neighborhood* in Brooklyn, which I came to find out was one of the earlier Puerto Rican settlements in New York; and *to my mother* who came to our event on Puerto Rican garment workers and finally understood what it was I did at the university and how it was not a rejection but a continuation of her legacy to me. Our relationship qualitatively changed after that event: there was more honesty between us; we spoke woman to woman. And it is because of this convergence of historical and personal circumstance that I am sharing this collective experience with you the reader. ❑

SOURCE: "Stories to Live By: Continuity and Change In Three Generations of Puerto Rican Women." Excerpts from *Oral History Review*. Rina Benmayor, Ana Juarbe, Blanca Vazquez Erazo, and Celia Alvarez. 16:2 (Fall 1988) pp. 1-46.

Teaching Asian American History

Despite having settled in North America since at least the eighteenth century, Asians have typically been portrayed as immigrants and aliens—perpetual foreigners.

Gary Y. Okihiro

Gary Y. Okihiro is professor of history and Director of the Asian American Studies Program at Cornell University and is the author of Margins and Mainstreams: Asians in American History and Culture.

I ask my students each year in my introductory Asian American history course to survey U.S. history textbooks to note their coverage of Asian Americans. They invariably report that Asians are largely absent from those texts, and when present they appear as the objects of America's foreign relations or domestically as victims and contributors. Among the usual suspects are U.S. expansion into the Philippines in the late-nineteenth century, the Pacific theatre of World War II, and the Korean and Vietnam wars. Notably, all of those topics position Asians in opposition to Americans as both foreigners and the enemy "over there." Despite having settled in North America since at least the eighteenth century, Asians have typically been portrayed as immigrants and aliens—perpetual foreigners.

As victims in textbooks, my students find, Asians commonly appear during discussions of nineteenth-century nativism evidenced in the anti-Chinese movement of that period, and in considerations of the Constitution and its guarantees during times of national emergency as exemplified in the World War II removal and detention of Japanese Americans along the West Coast. Typically, as contributors, Chinese men's labor in the construction of the transcontinental railroad is a favorite, along with the educational and economic achievements of Asian immigrants since the 1960s, an idea that gave rise to the notion of Asians as America's "model minority."

I suppose the authors of U.S. history textbooks are simply reflecting the state of the field in their reliance upon secondary sources. Indeed, most books written about Asian Americans prior to the 1980s stressed those themes of diplomatic and political history that occupy much of the contents of today's textbooks. Still, I retain at least two concerns about my students' findings from their surveys of those texts. There is a remarkable and persistent disinterest in thinking about race and race relations in terms other than black and white, a mind set that is by no means limited to history textbook authors.

My other observation is that the newer, more textured and nuanced accounts of the Asian experience in America published since 1980 have yet to make an impact upon the master narratives of U.S. history. Hopefully, this special issue of the *Magazine of History* will encourage a rethinking about how historians choose to represent Asian Americans, whether absent or present, and their place within the wider American past.

I would be amiss if I failed to justify, however briefly, the inclusion of Asians in our teaching and writing of American history. On the face of it, and because of the limitations of space in textbooks and time in classrooms, many might wonder about considering Asians when they comprise a mere three percent of America's peoples and when a majority of them have arrived in the U.S. only since the liberalizing immigration law of 1965. Including Asian Americans in our teaching and writing appears a luxury that few can afford.

For some, the changing demographies of their classrooms, where increasing numbers of Asian American students are filling the seats, might provide an incentive for including an Asian American component to their courses. Asian American students constitute more than half of the students at several California institutions of higher learning, and they commonly represent over ten percent—and the largest minority group—of students on many campuses across the country. There is, no doubt, much to be said for the notion of educational relevance in that the curriculum should reflect, in part, the social realities and aspirations of students. And Asian American students, along with other students who find themselves marginalized, have demanded services, including courses and administrative structures, responsive to their needs. Those forces have impelled the current, nationwide expansion of Asian American Studies.

Although important, I don't see those factors as compelling educational reasons for including the experiences of Asians in the teaching and writing of U.S. history. Rather, I think, the intellectual necessity of Asian American Studies offers a more convincing reason for its inclusion within the curriculum. I will make the case for

just the most salient aspect of the field's academic merit. Asian American Studies, indeed Ethnic Studies generally, has as its principal object of analysis race. I suppose most will agree that race is an essential unit of study, and has, in fact, comprised a dominant factor in American history. (Surely gender, class, and sexuality are equally important, and we know that these analytic categories are inextricable, but that recognition doesn't negate or diminish the significance of race.) Race within the U.S. has had a long and varied career, but certainly within our present context, race has come to mean "black," and race

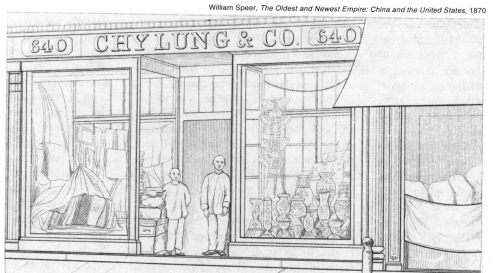

William Speer, *The Oldest and Newest Empire: China and the United States*, 1870

Chinese merchants in San Francisco in the 1860s.

relations, "black" and "white," pivoting upon whiteness and its negation, blackness.

In her *Volatile Bodies: Toward a Corporeal Feminism* (Bloomington: Indiana University Press, 1994), philosopher Elizabeth Grosz argues that "dichotomous thinking necessarily hierarchizes and ranks the two polarized terms so that one becomes the privileged term and the other its suppressed, subordinated, negative counterpart" (p. 3). Thus, for example, white/male/heterosexual constitutes the norm against which black/female/homosexual is defined. Further, notes Grosz, dualisms like mind and body are correlated with other oppositional pairs, such that mind is

reason, reality, depth, active, transcendence—male, and the body, passion, appearance, surface, passive, immanence—female. Binarisms and their correlates, accordingly, structure and maintain privilege and power.

Dualisms, however, cannot account for other positions that complicate their apparently neat and clear-cut definitions and boundaries. Indeed, the ambivalences posed by Asians (and racial others who occupy ambiguous, "middling" positions, like Latinos, American Indians, and biracials) along the borders of race threaten a "category crisis," as termed by Marjorie Garber in her *Vested Interests: Cross-Dressing & Cultural Anxiety* (New York: Routledge, 1992), in which definitional boundaries blur, borderlines become permeable, and the heretofore solid constructs of hierarchies and relations of power become destabilized, calling into question the "naturalisms" of dualisms and of the categories themselves. Asians are neither black nor white, despite attempts to analogize them as in "like black" or "like white," or to negate them as in "nonwhite."

What I am suggesting is that the black-white binarism of race functions in the American experience to sustain white supremacy, or the power of white over black, and that the introduction of a third (or fourth or fifth) position can disrupt (as well as reinforce) the dominant discourse and alter the relations of power. I think, therefore, that the Asian racial subject is indispensable to both an understanding of race and an intervention in the politics of race. Those outcomes, if correct, are forthrightly fundamental and singularly significant.

Asians, the subject matter of this *Magazine*'s issue, are a diverse lot. Asians can be "racially" yellow, black, brown, and white, insofar as those colors constitute discrete phenotypes. Asians derive from West Asia, Central Asia, South Asia, Southeast Asia, and East Asia, but also from Africa, South America, Europe, the Caribbean, Pacific Islands, and North America. Asians not only settled North America before the American Revolution, but they also came just yesterday. The political borders of the U.S. don't contain the boundaries of Asian America because the Asian American identity and position within the American social relations are regional and national but also transnational in compass. Asian American families might be fractured by geo-political alignments, but their identities, constitutive of self, kin, and society, are not necessarily limited by the divide of the nation-state. The foregoing merely hint at the boggling diversity endemic to the group essentialized as "Asian American."

The articles in this issue of the *Magazine* are arranged into three sections: an essay on historiography; five reflections on teaching and studying Asian American history; and five lesson plans. Sucheng Chan, in her sweeping review, "The Writing of Asian American History," divides Asian American historiography into four overlapping periods, beginning with partisan writings (from the 1870s to early 1920s), the period of social scientific studies (from the late 1910s to early 1960s), the revisionist period (from the 1960s to early 1980s), and a coming of age (from the early 1980s to the present). Chan observes that although considerable, the literature on Asian Americans was written mainly by non-historians, including missionaries, diplomats, journalists, polemicists, and social scientists. As a result, historians, who have become the principal architects of Asian American historiography only over the last fifteen years, have had to laboriously search for and sift through fragmentary evidence to correct biased and misinformed interpretations.

Michael Omi reflects upon the never-ending project of teaching Asian Ameri-

can history in his, "Teaching, Situating, and Interrogating Asian American History." He notes the limitations of basing chronology upon the various immigration laws that helped to determine and shape Asian American ethnic groups, and instead proposes that Asian American history must relate to the wider themes of American history, must integrate class and gender in its largely "raced" account, and must respond to the transnational character of post-1965 communities. Omi traces the evolution of his Asian American history course which he has taught for over a decade at the University of California, Berkeley, and how the shifting contexts of student composition and the university's curriculum have affected his course content. "My main intent in the course now is to situate the experience of Asian Americans within the broader historical context of race in the United States," he explains. But he adds that race is structured and in turn structures gender and class, and his course, accordingly, stresses the "intersectionality" of race, gender, and class. Looking back, Omi concludes, the changes in his course suggest that teaching Asian American history is an act of constant negotiation and creativity.

"A minority within a minority, the story of Asian American women has barely begun to be told," Sucheta Mazumdar states in her essay, "Beyond Bound Feet: Relocating Asian American Women." Mazumdar observes that the gender disparity between men and women among Chinese, Japanese, Korean, Filipino, and Asian Indian in America that favored men began with Asian patriarchy and economic necessity, but men in the U.S., she insists, were linked with women in Asia. Further, by thinking of migration not in terms of gender but as the experience of workers, suggests Mazumdar, women become prominent actors in that account. Women worked in Asia and in the U.S., whether as wage workers or within the household, and the centrality of women's labor in the Asian American experience is even more pronounced during the post-1965 period, when unprecedented numbers of women have entered into wage labor.

K. Scott Wong describes a teaching method that allows students to balance scholarly inquiry with personal discovery in his, "Crossing the Borders of the Personal and the Public: Family History and the Teaching of Asian American History." He notes, like Sucheng Chan in her bibliographic essay, that the paucity of historical sources has shaped the direction of research, but, he observes, it has even affected the teaching of Asian American history. In his course at Williams College, Wong asks his students to research and write on family history and to connect that to the wider past. "In most cases," he reports, "the students have embraced this assignment with great enthusiasm." Equally satisfying have been papers from both Asian and non-Asian students, and besides the educational benefits of connecting experience with its context, the exercise allows Wong to work through with his students the notions of historical documents, their production, and their deployments. In classrooms of increasing diversity, this assignment, concludes Wong, provides a common ground and "an avenue for communication" for students, based upon "the shared experience of living as or with Asians in America."

Ji-Yeon Yuh offers a student's perspective in her, "A Graduate Students' Reflection on Studying Asian American History." A doctoral student in history at the University of Pennsylvania when there were limited opportunities in Asian American Studies on that campus, Yuh devised strategies by which to pursue her subject matter, including "to borrow shamelessly from other institutions," "to exhaust all existing resources at Penn," and "to actively work to bring Asian American Studies to Penn." Of great importance to Yuh were her links with the Korean American communities that she studied and with the Asian American Studies field at large, permitting her "to draw strength from the field as a whole rather than from only my particular institution." At the same time, Yuh recognizes that the latitude and support given to her by Penn's non-Asian Americanist mentors have allowed her to concentrate upon her choice of historical research and specialization.

Vivian Wu Wong's essay, "Somewhere Between White and Black: The Chinese in Mississippi," explores the conundrum expressed by a Chinese American in the South, "I guess I was always considered marginal with whites and blacks." That position, as neither white nor black, Wong explains, has played a vital role in the formation of the Chinese American identity in Mississippi. "In the end," she concludes, "the Chinese in Mississippi found that it was to their benefit to reject the black community in order to be accepted however marginally by the white community. The choice has had a price."

The next five selections, presented as teaching units and lesson plans, offer a range of topics within Asian American history. The first two, by Barbara Posadas and Franklin Odo, reveal the diversity of the Asian American experience shaped in part by the particulars of its regional variations.

Barbara Posadas focuses upon Filipino Americans in Chicago during the first half of the twentieth century in her teaching unit designed for inclusion in a U.S. history survey course. Several thousand Filipinos arrived in the Chicago area before 1935 principally as students, unlike the conventional view of Filipinos, generalized from their experiences in Hawaii and the West Coast where they were typically agricultural workers. Most of those students eventually joined Chicago's working-class, a process hastened not by their marriage to Filipinas but overwhelmingly to the American-born daughters of European immigrants. Unlike in California, Washington, and Oregon where anti-miscegenation laws prohibited such unions, Filipinos didn't face that racist barrier in Illinois. Still, as workers, Chicago's Filipinos were largely relegated to service industries and were pitted against African Americans by the Pullman Company in its unsuccessful bid to break the unionization of African American porters. Their dreams of upward mobility in the Philippines, Posadas notes of those former students, were traded for "the

modest comforts of family life and American consumer society."

"Almost everyone in the United States has powerful images of Hawai'i," writes Franklin Odo in his lesson plan, "Asian Americans in Hawai'i." Those images, he states, derive from the media and from tourism. The purpose of his unit, Odo explains, is to help students develop a critical appreciation of those stereotypes and the state's cultural diversity that appear to affirm the caricature. Representations of Hawai'i taken from popular media

---

The political borders of the U.S. don't contain the boundaries of Asian America because the Asian American identity and position within the American social relations are regional and national but also transnational in compass.

---

and the press are subjected to close examination and scrutiny, an exercise that serves to demonstrate the turbulent complexities that lie beneath the surface calm of an apparent simplicity. The Asian American experience in Hawai'i reveals some of that complexity, such as the merits of the "melting pot," the nature of interracial relations and negotiations of ethnic identity, and the myth of the "model minority," thereby allowing an engagement with some of the larger questions that confront contemporary American society.

The remaining three lesson plans deal with particular subjects from World War

II to the present. Arthur A. Hansen, in his "The 1944 Nisei Draft at Heart Mountain, Wyoming," examines the draft and resistance to it among Japanese Americans as a way of introducing to students the changing representations of the past and how they emanate from the social relations. Besides those considerations of the objectivity question, the lesson plan allows students to connect two supposed disparate periods of the Japanese American experience (namely, the periods before and after World War II) and their place within wider U.S. history. Hansen describes the draft resistance movement of 1944 and 1945 and its representation that shifted from disloyalty, criminality, and villainy during the war to patriotism, a struggle for civil rights, and heroism beginning in the late 1980s. Both those who served in the armed forces, the Nisei soldiers, and those who refused to serve, the draft resisters, observes Hansen, "are now styled as being different yet complementary species of praiseworthy Americanism."

Hien Duc Do, in "The New Migrants from Asia," presents a study of Vietnamese in America for inclusion in discussions about trans-Pacific migrations, the Viet Nam war, and the current demographic shifts and their impacts upon U.S. race relations. "Too often," writes Do, "students are left with the impression that Viet Nam was simply a war that the United States was involved in, and not the fact that it is a country and that there are more than one million Vietnamese living in the U.S." His lesson plan, accordingly, encourages students to reexamine the Viet Nam war and its consequences, to apprehend some of the differences between immigrants and refugees, and to understand the formation and development of Vietnamese American communities and their relations with other Asian Americans and racial and ethnic minorities. Despite their relatively recent arrival, Do concludes, Vietnamese have become integral parts of the American mosaic, and their communities are simultaneously insular cultural preserves and trans-border cultural brokers with other communities in America.

"This lesson plan is designed to help students understand the nature of Korean and African American relations in the United States," explains Edward Taehan Chang in his, "Toward Understanding Korean and African American Relations." The 1992 Los Angeles civil unrest and widely publicized boycotts of Korean stores by African Americans during the 1980s and 1990s, notes Chang, have positioned the apparent conflict between Korean and African Americans as "one of the most visible and explosive issues of urban America." Through a study of the respective histories of Korean and African Americans, Chang contrasts those realities against the pervasive myths and misconceptions that have prevailed in the media and that have influenced significantly the mutual perceptions held by Koreans and Africans about one another. Not content with an understanding of the bases for conflict, Chang reflects upon the prospects for coalition-building between Korean and African Americans.

Decidedly a mere beginning, the essays and lesson plans in this *Magazine* reveal some of the intellectual and social benefits that derive from studying and teaching Asian American history, and will hopefully stimulate teachers and students alike to rethink the narratives and silences of American history. ❑

Up and Coming Topics in the
Magazine of History

- Business/Economic History
- Oral History
- Women's Rights
- Literature as History
- Congressional History
- Labor History
- The Presidency
- Imperialism
- Medical History
- Judicial History

STAY TUNED....

The Writing of Asian American History

Sucheng Chan

Asian American historiography is quite peculiar: until the early 1960s, virtually none of the books about Asians in America were written by historians. The sizable literature that exists has been authored, instead, by missionaries, diplomats, politicians, labor leaders, journalists, propagandists, and scholars trained in sociology, economics, social psychology, and political science. Only in the last fifteen years have professional historians moved to center stage in the construction of historical knowledge about Asian Americans. This legacy causes difficulties for historians specializing in Asian American history today: not only must they laboriously excavate widely scattered, fragmentary, "buried" evidence, but must also correct biased interpretations and a great deal of misinformation.

The writing of Asian American history may be divided into four somewhat overlapping periods. The first, characterized by partisanship, lasted from the 1870s to the early 1920s. The second, from the late 1910s to the early 1960s, was

> *This legacy causes difficulties for historians specializing in Asian American history today: not only must they laboriously excavate widely scattered, fragmentary, "buried" evidence, but they must also correct biased interpretations and a great deal of misinformation.*

dominated by social scientists. The third, during which eclectic, revisionist works appeared, extended from the 1960s to the early 1980s. During the fourth (present) stage, which began in the early 1980s, Asian American historiography is finally coming of age.

The first books about Asians in the United States were highly partisan because the immigration of Chinese and Japanese was enormously controversial. The *Oldest and the Newest Empire* (1870), *The Chinese in America* (1877), and *Chinese Immigration: Its Social and Economic Aspects* (1881) written, respectively, by two missionaries, William Speer and Otis Gibson, and a diplomat, George F. Seward, defended Chinese immigration. All three authors had lived and worked in China. Each tried to calm American fears about the growing Chinese presence in the United States by discussing various facets of Chinese civilization and by depicting the Chinese as a hardworking, harmless people. Arrayed against these treatises were such sensationalist accounts as *The Coming Struggle* by M. B. Starr (1873), *Last*

Days of the Republic by Pierton W. Dooner (1880), and *A Short and Truthful History of the Taking of Oregon and California by the Chinese in the Year 1899* by Robert Woltor (1882) that kindled anxieties about a Yellow Peril invasion.

Even the first heavily-footnoted scholarly study in Asian American history, *Chinese Immigration* by Mary Roberts Coolidge (1909), was openly partisan. Coolidge tried to make the Chinese look good by making other groups look bad: she exposed the corruption of European American diplomats and immigration officials, the self-interest of politicians, and the racism of Irish immigrants and Southerners who had migrated to California.

The anti-Chinese clamor became less loud as exclusionary laws began to reduce the number of Chinese in the United States, but it was soon replaced by agitation against Japanese immigration. A second set of authors emerged with pro- and anti-Japanese books. Sidney L. Gulick, a former missionary in Japan and an activist in the peace movement during the World War I era, defended the Japanese influx in *The American Japanese Problem* (1914) and *American Democracy and Asiatic Citizenship* (1918). He was joined in his efforts by several Japanese writers fluent in English. Among the books the latter produced were *Asia at the Door* (1914) and *The Real Japanese Question* (1921) by Kiyoshi Karl Kawakami, a propagandist; *California and the Japanese* by Kiichi Kanzaki (1921), a general secretary of the Japanese Association of America; *Japan and the California Problem* by T. Iyenaga and Kenoske Sato (1921), two political scientists who had taught and studied, respectively, at the University of Chicago; *Japanese-American Relations* by Iichiro Tokutomi (1922), a member of Japan's House of Peers and editor-in-chief of the newspaper, *Kokumin Shimbun*; and *The Unsolved Problem of the Pacific* by Kiyo Sue Inui (1925), lecturer in international relations at Occidental College, the University of Southern California, and Tokyo University and a delegate to the League of Nations. The most scholarly works in this genre are two books by Yamato Ichihashi,

Japanese Immigration (1913) and *Japanese in the United States* (1932), in which he marshaled an impressive amount of information in order to persuade the American public that the Japanese were assimilating (contrary to popular assumptions) and were not causing any problems.

While these well educated and highly placed writers did their best to counter the charges against Japanese immigration in general, they revealed a strong class bias. They tried to smooth the ruffled racial feathers of European Americans by admitting that the behavior of Japanese immigrant laborers might indeed be objectionable but they insisted that "higher class" Japanese were as refined as European Americans and should therefore be welcomed. A similar snobbery can be detected in *The Real Chinese in America* by J. S. Tow (1923), a Chinese consular officer.

Works pitted against continued Japanese immigration came in the form of sociological studies, novels, and propaganda tracts. *The Valor of Ignorance* by Homer Lea (1909), *The Japanese Conquest of American Opinion* by Montaville Flowers (1917), *The Japanese Invasion* by Jesse Steiner (1917), *The Rising Tide of Color Against White World-Supremacy* by Lothrop Stoddard (1920), *Seed of the Sun* by Wallace Irwin (1920), *The Pride of Palomar* by Peter B. Kyne (1921), and *Japanese Immigration and Colonization* by V. S. McClatchy (1921) all articulated a great fear—images of an America overrun, overwhelmed, or overtaken by Japanese, whom the authors recognized were not an inferior race. Precisely because those who opposed Japanese immigration could not be certain whether European Americans or Japanese would win in a "race war," they wanted to make sure that the racial frontier along the Pacific Coast would remain impregnable. Therefore Japanese immigrants, however small their numbers, could not be allowed to establish even the tiniest foothold there.

Whether they defended or attacked Chinese and Japanese immigration, the writings produced during the first historiographical period should be read today not as works of historical scholarship but,

rather, as documents that reveal the temper of the times in which they were produced. For this reason, they still serve a useful purpose.

Books published during the second historiographical period were less impassioned. Written mainly by social scientists, they concentrated on three topics: the assimilation of Asian Americans; the social organization of Asian communities in America; and the incarceration of Japanese Americans during World War II.

The most notable studies on assimilation were done by sociologists affiliated with the University of Chicago. Robert E. Park, the leading light in the sociology department at Chicago, hypothesized that all immigrants passed through a race relations cycle consisting of four stages of interaction with the host society: contact; competition; accommodation; and assimilation. Only two groups did not fit this paradigm—African Americans and Asian Americans. Park and his colleagues thus were intrigued by the "Negro problem" and the "Oriental problem." Their chance to investigate the latter came in late 192 when Park was appointed as the director of research for the Survey of Race Relations on the Pacific Coast. This project was initiated by the Institute of Social and Religious Research, whose officers had an international outlook and practiced the social gospel. They deemed the proposed survey a "great peace promoting task" to improve race relations along the Pacific Coast through the collection of objective empirical data.

The project never achieved its goal due to a shortage of funds and opposition from anti-Asian groups in California, Oregon, Washington, and British Columbia. However, the half dozen sociologists and their graduate assistants assembled for the project did manage to record over six hundred life histories from Chinese, Japanese, Filipinos, and (East or Asian) Indians between 1924 and 1926. They also collected reams of miscellaneous documents. Several books based on this information were published: *The Second Generation Oriental in America* by William C. Smith (1927), *Oriental Exclusion* y Roderic D. McKenzie (1928), *Immigration and Race Attitudes* by Emory Bogardus (1928), and *Americans in Process* by William C. Smith (1937). *Resident Orientals on the American Pacific Coast* by Eliot Grinnel Mears (1928) was also an indirect offshoot of the project. These social scientists were quite sympathetic to the plight of second-generation Asian Americans. As Romanzo Adams put it in the preface he wrote for Smith's 1937 book, "The real question is not one of the capacity of the Orientals, but of our ability to give them a fair opportunity. . . America should understand the young men and women of Oriental ancestry . . . have been born in our own country. . . . These young people are American citizens. . . . (They) are a part of us. . . . Whether they shall make their due contribution to American life or whether they shall be an irritant depends largely on the way Americans of the older stock meet them."

The Chicago School's immense intellectual influence was also felt in dozens of M. A. theses and Ph.D. dissertations written by Filipino graduate students under the mentorship of Emory Bogardus at the University of Southern California. Two books about Filipinos, *Filipino Immigration* by Bruno Lasker (1931) and *The Taxi Dance Hall* by Paul G. Cressey (1932), as well as several studies done in Hawaii, *Interracial Marriages in Hawaii* by Romanzo Adams (1937), *An Island Community: Ecological Succession in Hawaii* by Andrew W. Lind (1938), and a fine Ph.D. dissertation completed by Clarence E. Glick in 1938 but not revised for publication until 1980 under the title, *Sojourners and Settlers: Chinese Migrants in Hawaii*, likewise reflect the Chicago School's theoretical assumptions and fieldwork methods. Another landmark study that originated as a University of Chicago sociology dissertation also took more than three decades to get in print: *The Chinese Laundryman: A Study of Social Isolation* by Paul C. P. Siu (1987). Siu began his research in 1938 but did not submit his completed dissertation until 1953. In it, he modified Georg Simmel's concept of the "sojourner" to organize his rich ethnographic data.

In addition to the sociologists associated with the Survey of Race Relations, educational psychologists at Stanford University also produced several important studies about the adaptation of Asian Americans in the 1930s. *Vocational Aptitude of Second-Generation Japanese in the United States* (1933) and *Japanese in California* by Edward K. Strong, Jr. (1933), and *Public School Education of Second-Generation Japanese in California* by Reginald Bell (1935)—summarized in a single volume, *The Second-Generation Japanese Problem* (1934)—reported that the general abilities of Asian students were not inferior to those of European American students. However, given the prevalence of racial prejudice, Strong and Bell

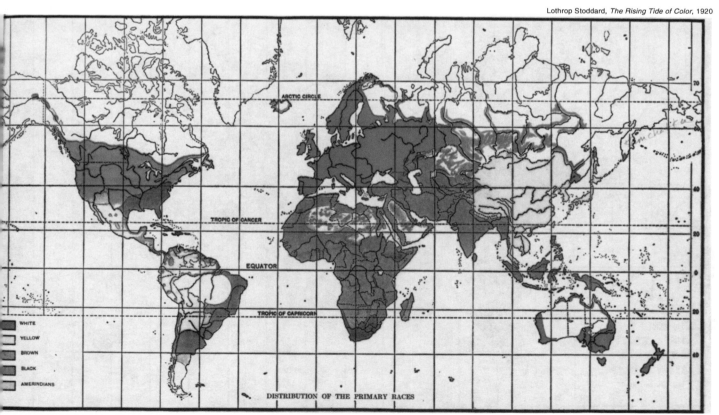

"Distribution of the Primary Races." A white supremacist view from 1920.

advised their "Oriental" students to be realistic in their career choices and to refrain from applying for jobs for which they would not be considered.

A second topic that fascinated social scientists, as well as journalists, from the 1930s through the 1960s was the social organization of Asian communities in America. European American and Asian American writers alike tried to fathom the unique characteristics (more derisively called the "social pathology") of these ethnic ghettos. The publication of books on this topic spanned several decades: *Chinatown Inside Out* by Leong Gor Yun (1936), *San Francisco's Chinatown* by Charles C. Dobie (1936), *Social Solidarity Among the Japanese in Seattle* by S. Frank Miyamoto (1939), *The Growth and Decline of Chinese Communities in the Rocky Mountain Region*, a dissertation completed by Rose Hum Lee in 1947 but not published until 1978, and *The Chinese in the U.S.A.* by Rose Hum Lee (1960). The influence of the Chicago School

is also apparent here: Miyamoto and Lee were among the first Asian American sociologists to be trained at the University of Chicago.

During World War II, several teams of social scientists seized the opportunity provided by the incarceration of 112,000 persons of Japanese ancestry in so-called relocation camps to investigate how people function in confined situations. Sociologists, demographers, political scientists, and anthropologists dutifully recorded the minutiae of life behind barbed wire. Some of the social scientists were employed as resident community analysts by the War Relocation Authority that administered the camps while others worked independently. The literature on this shameful episode in U.S. history is so vast that only a few titles can be mentioned here. *Prejudice: Japanese Americans, Symbol of Racial Intolerance* by Carey McWilliams (1944) and *Americans Betrayed* by Morton Grodzins (1949) were extremely critical

of the internment. The three volumes tha[t] came out of the Japanese Evacuation an[d] Resettlement Study, *The Spoilage* by Dor[-] othy S. Thomas and Richard S. Nishimot[o] (1946), *The Salvage* by Dorothy S. Tho[-] mas (1952), and *Prejudice, War and th[e] Constitution* by Jacobus ten Broek, Ed[-] ward N. Barnhart, and Floyd W. Matso[n] (1954), in contrast, were apologist in thei[r] orientation.

Several books published during th[e] second period do not fit into any of th[e] above three categories. *The Anti-Chines[e] Movement in California* by Elmer [C.] Sandmeyer (1939) has the distinction o[f] being the first major study in Asian Ameri[-] can history written by a professional histo[-] rian. In 1946, Milton R. Konvitz produce[d] the first study of Asian American lega[l] history, *The Alien and the Asiatic in Amer[i-] can Law.* Next, Fred W. Riggs examine[d] the political maneuvers leading to th[e] repeal, in 1943, of the Chinese exclusio[n] laws in *Pressure on Congress* (1950). I[n]

Lothrop Stoddard, *The Rising Tide of Color*, 192[0]

"Categories of white world-supremacy," a map reflecting the white American fear of immigration in the 1920s.

The Japanese Frontier in Hawaii (1953), Hilary Conroy examined how the Japanese government, the Hawaiian government, and American sugar planters negotiated the terms under which tens of thousands of Japanese came to work in Hawaii's sugar plantations.

During both the first and second historiographical periods, regardless of what topic was under investigation, the Asian presence in the United States was almost invariably framed as a "problem." Because they allegedly failed to assimilate, Asian Americans were considered deficient or deviant. In the early 1970s, young Asian American activists on college and university campuses rebelled against such negative portrayals of their forebears and themselves. They rejected the assimilationist paradigm and proposed several alternatives. One was classical Marxist theory, which they extended to encompass Asian Americans as workers exploited by a capitalist system. A second was the internal colonialism model developed by black and Chicano scholars, which allowed them to think of Asian ethnic communities as internal colonies. A third depicted Asian Americans as brothers and sisters of people in Asian nations who had suffered under Western imperialism. The second and third models addressed the same phenomenon at different geographic sites—the European and American colonization of Africa, Latin America, and Asia and their peoples, including those who had been transported to North America as immigrants, indentured migrant laborers, or slaves. According to this view, racial minorities in the United States were "Third World within," whose members shared a common history of oppression with people living in the "Third World without." In their own eyes, the Asian American activists who sought to "decolonize" research and to establish ethnic studies programs during the late 1960s and 1970s were engaged in a struggle that was simultaneously anti-capitalist, anti-racist, and anti-imperialist.

The campus activists produced few book-length studies. The best repositories for their radical perspectives are two anthologies published by the Asian American Studies Center at UCLA: *Roots* edited by Amy Tachiki et al. (1971) and *Counterpoint* edited by Emma Gee et al. (1976). Marxist analysis also permeates the chapters in *Labor Immigration under Capitalism: Asian Workers in the United States before World War II* edited by Lucie Cheng and Edna Bonacich (1984), another UCLA product. *Chinatown, N.Y.* by Peter Kwong (1979) likewise valorizes Asian workers.

More important than the publication of formal books was the proliferation of community-based magazines, journals, newspapers, and anthologies in the 1970s. These publications contained a panoply of Asian American voices, many of them angry and defiant. With the introduction first, of typewriters with changeable fonts, and later, of computers and letter-quality (and eventually laser) printers, Asian American writers no longer had to depend on commercial or academic publishers to disseminate their works. For the first time, desktop-published writings reflecting diverse and uncensored Asian American sensibilities were made widely available at reasonable prices.

However, though the political consciousness of generations of students has been raised through ethnic studies courses and through involvement in community activities, within the academy itself the emerging field known as Asian American studies has made little impact partly because several problems plagued the leftist outpourings of the 1970s. Unsympathetic critics dismissed the bulk of these writings out of hand as "mere rhetoric" and noted the lack of "fit" between the grandiose theories some authors propounded and the meager empirical evidence they used to substantiate their sweeping assertions. A great deal of the analyses of this period was indeed schematic, mechanistic, and deterministic. The emphasis on structural oppression or systemic victimization meant that Asian Americans were seen as mere cogs in a capitalist, racist system. To this day, Asian Americans remain faceless and nameless in most textbooks. When they appear at all, the tidbits of information included about them serve mainly an ornamental function—a token nod toward the nation's "diversity."

In contrast to the militant writings, several surveys or general histories published in the 1970s were more moderate in perspective. Also penned by writers of Asian ancestry, these overviews emphasized the contributions made by Asians to American history and society. *Mountain of Gold* by Betty Lee Sung (1967), *A History of the Chinese in California* by Thomas W. Chinn et al. (1969), *Nisei: The Quiet Americans* by Bill Hosokawa (1969), *Japanese Americans* by Harry H. L. Kitano (1969), *The Challenge of the American Dream* by Francis L. K. Hsu (1971), *A History of Japanese in Hawaii* by the United Japanese Society of Hawaii (1971), and *East to America: A History of the Japanese in the United States* by Robert A. Wilson and Bill Hosokawa (1980) all pleaded for inclusiveness. Their contributionist stance helped to keep old assimilationist assumptions alive.

The assimilation model managed to continue to hold sway even during a time of profound and pervasive social upheaval because it resonates so deeply with the American sense of nationhood. As Philip Gleason has pointed out, America's national identity has been based not so much on such primordial sentiments as a shared ancestry, language, or religion as on a set of political values and practices. It is a peoplehood constructed primarily upon an ideological foundation. Since ideology can be learned and is mutable, native-born Americans assume that immigrants should be able to—indeed are morally obligated to—shed the political beliefs and cultural baggage they bring with them and to adopt the values and behavior befitting Americans.

The facile assumption that *all* immigrants can and should transform themselves overlooks the fact that people of color have encountered enormous hurdles—legal, political, social, and economic—whenever they have tried to enter mainstream society. Thus, before the assimilation model can be dismantled, scholars must demonstrate convincingly that American society has never been the egalitarian paradise it is said to be. A number of European American historians took up that revisionist task in the 1960s and 1970s. In place of broad sociological theories or ardent convictions based on personal experience, these historians assiduously sifted through the available documentary evidence to offer fresh interpretations of why Asians had been so maltreated in America. Roger Daniels, in *The Politics of Prejudice* (1962), emphasized the racist nature of the anti-Japanese movement and showed how even the California Progressives, who were supposed to be liberal and enlightened reformers, did not hesitate to "draw the color line." Stuart Creighton Miller, in *The Unwelcome Immigrant* (1969), argued persuasively that anti-Chinese attitudes had not been confined to California and had, in fact, predated the arrival of Chinese on American soil. Alexander Saxton, in *The Indispensable Enemy* (1971), chronicled how the labor movement relied on anti-Chinese rhetoric and actions to consolidate itself. In *The Heathen Chinese* (1971), Robert McClellan argued that negative images of the Chinese were based on the "private needs" of European Americans and not on the realities of Chinese life. Delber L. McKee analyzed the draconian means used to implement the Chinese exclusion laws in *Chinese Exclusion vs. the Open Door Policy, 1900-1906* (1977). John Modell showed in *The Economics and Politics of Racial Accommodation* (1977) how Japanese in Los Angeles, a city with a weak labor movement, managed to find a niche for themselves.

These studies, while small in number, are nevertheless significant for two reasons. First, with the exception of Sandmeyer's 1939 book and Conroy's 1953 work, they were the very first historical studies of Asians in America done by "real" historians. Second, the authors' fine-grained analyses revealed clearly that the racism and class prejudice shown towards Asian immigrants and their American heirs were not temporary aberrations but were, rather, tendencies deeply embedded in the very social fabric of the United States. One indication of how much scholarly assumptions changed during this period is the fact that only one historical study published in these years, *Bitter Strength*

by Gunther Barth (1964), faulted the Chinese for their own suffering.

Regardless of which conceptual frameworks various authors used, during the first three historiographical periods Asian immigrants and their American-born children were seldom portrayed as individuals with personalities, motives, or agency. To catch glimpses of the humanity of Asian Americans, one must turn to books containing their direct testimonies—primarily autobiographies. Among those available are *When I Was a Boy in China* by Yan Phou Lee (1887), two entries in *The Life Stories of Undistinguished Americans* by Hamilton Holt (1906), *My Life in China and America* by Yung Wing (1909), the first Chinese to graduate from an American university (Yale, 1854), *East Goes West* by Younghill Kang (1937), *Chinaman's Chance: An Autobiography* by No Yong Park (1940), *Father and Glorious Descendant* by Pardee Lowe (1943), *Fifth Chinese Daughter* by Jade Snow Wong (1945), *America Is in the Heart* by Carlos Bulosan (1946), *I Have Lived with the American People* by Manuel Buaken (1948), *Nisei Daughter* by Monica Sone (1953), *My Seventy-Nine Years in Hawaii* by Chung Kim Ai (1960), *Congressman from India* by Dalip Singh Saund (1960), *Journey to Washington* by Daniel K. Inouye (1969), *American in Disguise* by Daniel I. Okimoto (1970), *Farewell to Manzanar* by Jeanne Wakatsuki Houston and James Houston (1973), *Issei: A History of Japanese Immigrants in North*

Sidney Gulick, *The American Japanese Problem*, 1914

The author wanted to emphasize the "respectability" of the Japanese.

America by Kazuo Ito (1973), *And Justice for All: An Oral History of the Japanese American Detention Camps* by John Tateishi (1984), *Hanahana: An Oral History Anthology of Hawaii's Working People* edited by Michi Kodama-Nishimoto et al. (1984), *Voices: A Filipino American Oral History* (1984), *Hearts of Sorrow: Vietnamese-American Lives* by James Freeman (1989), *Quiet Odyssey: A Pioneer Korean Woman in America* by Mary Paik Lee (1990), *Beyond the Killing Fields: Voices of Nine Cambodian Survivors in America* by Wela Usharatna (1993), *Hmong Means Free: Life in Laos and America* edited by Sucheng Chan (1994), and *Filipino American Lives* by Yen Le Espiritu (1995).

Unlike the noisy and combative shift from the assimilationist paradigm to one emphasizing oppression and victimization, the next change in analytical framework that occurred in the early 1980s has elicited little notice. The new element that has crept into historical studies of Asian Americans done in the last decade and a half is the concept of agency—a central idea in the new social history. Although most of the current generation of Asian American historians seldom make such a claim themselves, they are very much a part of the movement to write "history

from below." In the most recent studies,

Mr. Otto Fukushima.   Mrs. Otto Fukushima (American)

The four daughters of Mr. and Mrs. Fukushima: typical American-Japanese children.

A biracial couple and their children in the 1910s—from a pro-Japanese publication.

Asian immigrants (old and new) and their American-born progeny, as individuals

and as members of groups, are depicted as people fully capable of weighing alternatives, making choices, asserting control over the circumstances they face, and helping to change the world in which they live. Like other social historians, the fundamental question that many of today's Asian American historians ask is, "Is human action determined by economic forces and social conditioning or it is the result of human agency and subjectivity?" Most of them have not adopted either of the polar positions implied by this question. Instead, they tend to interpret evidence dialectically: on the one hand, they recognize that structures do limit the ability of individuals to act as subjects or agents in the making of their own history; on the other hand, they recognize that it is human action that creates those structures. Both agency and structure thus must be described and analyzed. Just as earlier studies that highlighted structure and ignored agency told only partial and simplistic stories, so attempts to privilege agency to the neglect of structural constraints are equally unsatisfactory, given the long and complex history of oppression that has haunted the Asian American past.

The best of the historical studies about Asian Americans produced in the last decade and a half are richly textured and subtly nuanced. They address issues in immigration, social, cultural, economic, labor, legal, political, regional/local, women's, and family history. Not only has new evidence been unearthed and imaginatively interpreted, but new questions have also been asked of old evidence and timeworn conclusions. Each work has helped—to borrow the words of the pioneer British social historian, E. P. Thompson—to "rescue" a particular group of Asian Americans from "the enormous condescension of posterity" by restoring to members of that group a sense of their historicity. Slow and tedious as the research may be, today's Asian American historians are finally according various segments of the Asian American population their rightful places in U.S. history. Cumulatively and persistently, the point is being made that the particular historical experiences of Asian Americans, however parochial or trivial they may seem to the academic gatekeepers in the historical profession, did and do matter in the larger story of the nation.

The turn toward social history in Asian American historical scholarship came with the publication of *China and the Overseas Chinese in the United States, 1868-1911* by Shih-shan Henry Tsai (1983). By relying largely on Chinese-language sources, Tsai was able to present the Chinese point of view (or, at least, the point of view of Chinese diplomats and government officials) more cogently than any other scholar had done before or since. So, even though he himself considered his work to be a study of U.S. -Chinese diplomatic relations, his book is also an excellent social history that displays the aggressive efforts made by the Chinese to defend their human rights.

Two other studies also enlarge our understanding of Asian immigration: *Imingaisha: Japanese Emigration Companies and Hawaii, 1894-1908* by Alan T. Moriyama (1985), and *The Korean Frontier in America: Immigration to Hawaii, 1896-1910* by Wayne Patterson (1989). These books show clearly how socioeconomic and political forces interacted with individual ambition to promote the migra-

tion of Japanese and Koreans across the Pacific. An M.A. thesis, "Filipino Immigration to Hawaii" by Mary Dorita, made available in typescript in 1975, chronicled a similar process for Filipinos. Unfortunately, no comparable studies of Chinese or Asian Indian emigration have yet been done, so our knowledge of those two groups continues to be based largely on inference and conjecture. We do have, however, a fine book on how international politics affected the lives of Asian immigrants, *Passage from India: Asian Indian Immigrants in North America* by Joan Jensen (1988). As British colonial subjects, certain Indian immigrants in the United States and Canada who were active in efforts to free their homeland from colonial rule were subjected to extensive surveillance by British intelligence agents who relied on their American counterparts for help.

During the first period of their immigration, Asians entered the United States at multiple localities, and not just at San Francisco or New York, as commonly assumed. In *Chinese in the Post-Civil War South* (1984), Lucy M. Cohen, an anthropologist with a keen eye for historical details, discovered that a small number of Chinese had entered the American South via the Caribbean. These pioneers, along with several hundred Chinese brought to the South to build railroads, ended up working in cotton plantations and eventually dispersed into the local communities. Before they disappeared from the historical record, they left traces of their militance: they went on strike against employers who failed to pay them or to treat them equally as other workers.

Sandy Lydon uncovered yet another point of entry while doing research for *Chinese Gold: The Chinese in the Monterey Bay Area* (1985). He found evidence to suggest that some Chinese may have sailed in their own junks (ships) across the Pacific to Monterey Bay, settling in the region as fishermen specializing in the harvesting of shrimp and abalone. Combining information preserved in local newspapers and myriad other written sources with oral history interviews, Lydon has produced the best local history of a Chi-

nese immigrant community to date.

The next two books to break new ground were written by self-taught historians. In *This Bittersweet Soil: The Chinese in California Agriculture, 1860-1910* (1986), Sucheng Chan, a social scientist turned historian, used information painstakingly collected from the unpublished schedules of several U.S. censuses of population and agriculture and from the archives of over forty counties to recover the long lost story of the crucial role that Chinese played in the development of California agriculture, the state's most important economic enterprise. The methodologies of agricultural economics, economic history, cultural geography, historical anthropology, and historical sociology were used in combination to make this book the first multidisciplinary study in Asian American history.

The Issei: The World of the First Generation Japanese Immigrants, 1885-1924 (1988), by Yuji Ichioka, the most prolific Japanese American historian at work today, shows better than any other study the inner complexities of Asian immigrant communities—communities segmented by class, gender, and political and ideological differences. Using an impressive array of Japanese-language sources, Ichioka reveals how Issei workers not only experienced discrimination at the hands of European American employers and Japanese labor contractors due to their race and class status, but they also suffered from the cynical actions of the Japanese government.

A third self-trained Asian American historian is Him Mark Lai, an engineer by profession. Widely recognized as the dean of Chinese American history, Lai wrote his major work, a magisterial overview of Chinese American history, in Chinese but is presently translating portions of that book into English.

How the inner lives of Asian American communities intersected with the larger host society is covered in several studies. *Making Ethnic Choices: California's Punjabi Mexican Americans* by Karen I. Leonard (1992), *Farming the Home Place: A Japanese American Community in California, 1919-1982* by Valerie Matsumoto

(1993), *Americanization, Acculturation, and Ethnic Identity: The Nisei Generation in Hawaii* by Eileen H. Tamura (1994), and '*For the Sake of our Japanese Brethren': Assimilation, Nationalism, and Protestantism among the Japanese of Los Angeles, 1895-1942* by Brian M. Hayashi (1995). The ethnic identities, assimilation, and acculturation discussed in these books are far more complicated and multidimensional than the monolithic, linear, unidirectional phenomena investigated by social scientists in an earlier era.

Since an overwhelming majority of the Asian immigrants who came in the late-nineteenth and early-twentieth centuries were male workers, labor history is an important component of Asian American history. Edward D. Beechert's *Working in Hawaii: A Labor History* (1985) set the pace with his detailed account of the many strikes—some of them multiethnic—in which Hawaii's sugar plantation workers

engaged. Although *Cane Fires: The Anti-Japanese Movement in Hawaii, 1865-1945* by Gary Y. Okihiro (1991) covers some of the same events as Beechert's book, Okihiro adds a new dimension to the story. He persuasively argues that the anti-Japanese movement in Hawaii and the anti-labor stance of the islands' sugar plantation owners arose from the same source: the desire by Hawaii's ruling oligarchy to preserve its own racial and economic privileges. Moving halfway around the world, Renqiu Yu, in *To Save China, to Save Ourselves: The Chinese Hand Laundry Alliance of New York* (1992), also demonstrates how race and class were intertwined. The traditional leaders of New York's Chinatown did not hesitate to use coercive tactics made available by the Chinese exclusion laws to maintain their own elite position in the face of challenges from certain rebellious members of the community who wished to practice demo-

cratic principles. The most fully developed study in Asian American labor history is Chris Friday's *Organizing Asian American Labor: The Pacific Coast Canned-Salmon Industry, 1870-1942* (1994). With its breathtakingly-wide range of sources, this is the first book that links explicitly Asian American history and U.S. labor history. It demonstrates more clearly than does any other study the multiple, intersecting socioeconomic, interracial, and interethnic hierarchies that circumscribed the lives of Asian American workers while still allowing them some room to maneuver.

Revisionist complexity characterizes recent studies of the World War II incarceration of Japanese Americans as well. *Justice at War: The Story of the Japanese American Internment Cases* by Peter Irons (1983) exposes the hypocrisy of government officials who deliberately concealed pertinent evidence from the U.S. Supreme

Sidney Gulick, *The American Japanese Problem*, 1914

Another pro-Japanese immigration photograph, showing the children as assimilated Americans in the 1910s.

Court. *Keeper of Concentration Camps: Dillon S. Myer and American Racism* by Richard Drinnon (1987) examines the career of the former director of the War Relocation Authority in a most critical (some would say, hostile) manner. *Exile Within: The Schooling of Japanese Americans, 1941-1945* by Thomas James (1987) tells the ironic story of how Japanese American children were taught ideas about democracy while their families were denied the fundamental civil liberties that all Americans are supposed to enjoy; two-thirds of the incarcerated population, for example, were U.S.-born citizens. Sandra Taylor, in *Jewel in the Desert: Japanese American Internment at Topaz* (1993), follows the trail of a group of Japanese Americans from the San Francisco Bay area as they journeyed to the camp established at Topaz, Utah, and eventually back to the "real world." Yasuko I. Takezawa, an anthropologist, in *Breaking the Silence: Redress and Japanese American Ethnicity* (1995), offers an ethnographic account of the redress movement in Seattle and analyzes how that effort affected the ethnic identity of its participants.

Compared to the above topics, Asian American women's history is relatively undeveloped. The first book-length study, *Issei, Nisei, War Bride: Three Centuries of Japanese American Women in Domestic Service* (1986), was written not by an historian but by a sociologist, Evelyn Nakano Glenn. Combining oral history with sociological theory, Glenn places the individual experiences of her interviewees within the conceptual framework of international labor migration in a capitalist world-system. In *Transforming the Past: Tradition and Kinship Among Japanese Americans* (1985), Sylvia J. Yanagisako uses anthropological theory to explain how and why the same family relations can mean quite different things to different generations. Asian American women's history made an important stride with the publication of *Unsubmissive Women: Chinese Prostitutes in Nineteenth-Century San Francisco* by Benson Tong (1994) and *Unbound Feet: A Social History of Chinese American Women in San Francisco* by Judy Yung (1995). Both studies are feminist in orientation. However, Tong, in his eagerness to demonstrate that even the most oppressed individuals possess agency, overstates the extent to which prostitutes were able to overcome the restrictive conditions under which they lived. Yung, meanwhile, deftly weaves vignettes from her own family history with interviews of women unrelated to herself to paint a collective portrait of Chinese American women during the first half of the twentieth century. These books represent the first steps in a long journey to recover the buried history of a "minority within a minority."

Two well-crafted books in Asian American legal history underline the prom-

> *These books represent the first steps in a long journey to recover the buried history of a "minority within a minority."*

ise of this field. *In Search of Equality: The Chinese Struggle Against Discrimination in Nineteenth-Century America* by Charles J. McClain (1994) and *Laws Harsh as Tigers: Chinese Immigrants and the Shaping of Modern Immigration Law* by Lucy E. Salyer (1995) both skillfully mine the voluminous legal records available to reveal the extraordinary sophistication with which the Chinese contested the exclusion laws over several decades. These studies in legal history, along with those in labor history, recuperate the history of Asian immigrants' persistent resistance to oppression, in the process proving how well assimilated they in fact were, in terms of their understanding of democratic rights, their unchangeable physical features notwithstanding.

From the above review, it is obvious that many important gaps remain. The most glaring is the complete absence of any in-depth studies about the historical and current experiences of Filipino Americans. The first theoretical analysis of certain aspects of Filipino American history, *The Philippine Temptation* (1996), was written by a literary scholar, Epifanio San Juan, Jr. In contrast several significant books have been written by sociologists about post-1965 Korean immigration and the tendency of Koreans to engage in small business: *New Urban Immigrants: The Korean Community in New York City* by Illsoo Kim (1981), *Korean Immigrants in America: A Structural Analysis of Ethnic Confinement and Adhesive Adaptation* by Won Moo Hurh and Kwang Chung Kim (1984), *Immigrant Entrepreneurs: Koreans in Los Angeles, 1965-1982* by Ivan Light and Edna Bonacich (1988), and *On My Own: Korean Immigrants, Entrepreneurship, and Korean-Black Relations in Chicago and Los Angeles* by In-Jin Yoo (1996). Studies about the refugees from Vietnam, Laos, and Cambodia greatly outnumber those on contemporary immigration from China, Taiwan, South Korea, the Philippines, India, Pakistan, and other Asian countries. Space limitations prevents me from discussing any of these works, most of them written by social scientists.

Finally, those who do not have the time or desire to read the books discussed in this essay can always peruse several works of synthesis: *Asian America: Chinese and Japanese in the United States Since 1850* by Roger Daniels (1988), *Strangers from a Different Shore: A History of Asian Americans* by Ronald Takaki (1989), *Asian Americans: An Interpretive History* by Sucheng Chan (1991), and *Margins and Mainstreams: Asians in American History and Culture* by Gary Y. Okihiro (1994). While each offers a shortcut to knowledge, readers who rely only on such overviews will miss tasting the veritable intellectual feast that Asian American history can now claim to offer. ❏

*Sucheng Chan is social scientist and self-trained historian at the University of California-Berkeley. She is author of many books including*This Bittersweet Soil *(1986*

Teaching, Situating, and Interrogating Asian American History

Michael Omi

It is tempting to simply frame Asian American history as a chronology of immigration laws and their effects on the volume and composition of Asian immigrants. Specific Asian ethnic groups could be examined in a serial fashion with the Immigration Act of 1965 constituting the key legislative reform which neatly periodizes Asian American history into two broad eras. In the pre-1965 period, distinct groups (principally Chinese, Japanese, Filipinos, Koreans, and South Asians) were subjected to exclusionary laws which dramatically affected their location in the labor market, their political rights, and their prospects for the formation of stable communities. The post-1965 period, by contrast, is characterized by the lifting of prior restrictions and the dramatic influx of new Asian immigrants coming as refugees (Vietnamese, Laotian, Cambodian), as relatives under "family reunification," and as professionals seeking better economic opportunities. Such diversity increasingly renders problematic any notion of a shared Asian American experience in the broader economy, polity, and culture.

The above framework and presentation is not "wrong," but it elides a number of compelling themes and issues: ones which speak directly to how we relate specific "ethnic" histories to the larger American historical narrative; how we integrate concepts of class and gender in these histories; and how we respond to the growing transnational character of immigrant communities.

A Shifting Context

For over a decade, I have taught an introductory Asian American history course, with an enrollment of about 250 students, at the University of California at

> *Such diversity increasingly renders problematic any notion of a shared Asian American experience in the broader economy, polity, and culture.*

Berkeley. Every year it has become an increasingly difficult course to teach. Part of the problem stems from the shifting demographic composition of the students who take the class. When I started in the early-1980s, the class was overwhelmingly made up of freshman students, principally majoring in science, engineering, and math. Now all class levels are evenly represented and more humanities and so-

cial science majors are enrolled. This distribution has made it difficult to know where to "pitch" the class when students clearly display different, and uneven, levels of reading, writing, and analytic skills.

The diversity of Asian ethnic groups which the students represent has grown and correspondingly influenced the themes and issues presented. Initially the class was predominately composed of American-born Chinese, Japanese, Korean, and Filipinos. Now the clear majority are foreign-born with South Asian and Southeast Asian students comprising a growing presence. This has shifted the interest of students from the pre-1965 to the post-1965 period, and focused attention on Asian ethnic groups which have been traditionally marginalized in Asian American Studies.

The relationship of the course to the broader curriculum of the university has changed over time, and with it my sense of what the course was about. Initially the course satisfied the university's general requirement in American history. Meeting the guidelines of this requirement helped to structure the themes for the course. My syllabus reflected an attempt to situate Asian American history within the broader context of U.S. history. My topics and the periodization I deployed—the transformation of the West, the Great Depression, World War II—conveyed the contours of American history, and examined how large-scale economic, political, and cultural transformations affected Asian American immigration and community formation.

The American history requirement was subsequently revised, abolished in fact since and most students entering as freshman after 1983 could fulfill the requirement through high school courses. Freed from specifically addressing the requirement, I began to focus more on how Asian American individuals and collectivities responded to the conditions of their existence and how they challenged and coped with the dominant social order. This was a self-conscious reaction to how I had previously structured the course. I realized that I had focused almost exclusively on macro-level transformations and their impact *on* Asian Americans. The top-down framework emphasized what happened to Asian Americans, not how Asian Americans organized their lives and lived in dynamic engagement with the broader economy, polity, and culture. This change, however, did not involve as dramatic a break with my prior course outline as it would suggest. The extremely poor sense of history which undergraduate students possess still necessitates my describing broad periods in American history at length prior to locating how Asians have been shaped by, and in turn have shaped, this history.

The passage of Berkeley's American Cultures breadth requirement provoked another "identity crisis" for the course, and with it a chance to rethink its focus. The requirement, which is fulfilled by taking an approved course on comparative race and ethnicity in the U.S., was passed by the Academic Senate in 1989 and took effect with the entering class of 1991. The courses are meant to be "integrative and comparative" in nature, and need to take "substantial account" of at least three of the following designated groups: "African Americans, indigenous peoples of the United States, Asian Americans, Chicano/Latino Americans, and European Americans."

My course would not fulfill the requirement as stated, nor was it my intention to substantively transform the class to meet it. What the requirement did was

make me think about how to integrate the experiences of other groups—particularly other racialized minorities—into the history of Asians in the United States. I realized that my presentation had been framed solely as a history of white/Asian encounters, omitting other relationships. Locating the experiences of other groups, in relation to the historical experiences of Asian Americans, allowed me to sharpen the current themes I utilize in the course.

Challenging Paradigms

My main intent in the course now is to situate the experience of Asian Americans within the broader historical context of race in the United States. I start out by challenging three prevailing paradigmatic assumptions which have severely limited an examination and interrogation of the history of Asian Americans. The first is the manner in which race relations in the United States are reduced to relations between "blacks and whites." Historical narratives of racialized minorities in the United States are consequently cast in the shadows of the black/white encounter. Historian Gary Okihiro compellingly poses the question "Is Yellow Black or White?" (1). Implicit in this construction, Okihiro argues, is a bipolar perspective which locates Asians, depending on the historical period in question, to one side or the other of the racial equation. Tomás Almaguer, in his study of race in nineteenth-century California, breaks from the dominant mode of biracial theorizing by illustrating how Native Americans, Mexicans, Chinese, and Japanese are racialized and positioned in relation to one another by the dominant Anglo elite (2). Drawing on this work, I argue that the Asian American historical experience is essential to understanding the racial dynamics which unfolded in the West.

My intent in critiquing the bipolar model of race is not to wholly decenter black/white relations. Certainly racial slavery inordinately shaped the subsequent history of U.S. race relations (as did the genocidal experiences of Native Americans). Rather, my intent is to question whether all racisms are alike in their origins and consequences. Etienne Balibar,

in a discussion of racism and nationalism, makes a distinction between "an *internal* racism (directed against a population regarded as a 'minority' within the national space) and an *external* racism (considered as an extreme form of xenophobia)" (3). The hostilities directed against Asians, beginning in the mid-nineteenth century and resulting in a series of exclusionary measures, can be read as an expression of the latter form of racism, one which is inextricably bound up with the creation, and definition, of the American West.

A second paradigmatic assumption I challenge is the conflation of race and culture. Groups we consider a "race" such as Asian Americans are made of distinct ethnic cultures which are by no means "internally" homogeneous. I take seriously historian David Hollinger's claim that we have reified, to a great extent, what he terms the American *ethno-racial pentagon* (4). African American, Latina/o, Native American, Asian Americans, and European American are now seen as the five basic demographic blocs we treat as the subjects of multiculturalism. The problem is that these groups do not represent distinct and mutually exclusive "cultures." Thus we need to present critically what we mean by "race" and "culture" and the manner in which we articulate the connection between the two.

Related to this is the manner in which "culture" is deployed, particularly in the social science literature, to explain the historical experiences and sensibilities of Asian Americans. Depending on the historical period in question, cultural arguments are used as proof that Asians are a distinct and inassimilable race, or to argue that a strong compatibility between Asian culture and a presumed white, middle-class "American culture" accounts for Asian American mobility and success. Such approaches are both reductionist and determinist, and fail to identity the range of political, economic, and social factors which help us "locate" Asian Americans in particular historical moments.

The third dominant conception which I critique is that of assimilation. A central race relations paradigm, it has influenced the popular discourse of immigrant incorporation. Many share in the belief that different racial/ethnic groups over time would lose their cultural distinctiveness, that structural boundaries would recede, and groups would cease to be segregated in various institutional arenas. The assimilationist framework has been the dominant paradigm in interpreting the historical experiences of Asian Americans. But the manner in which it was deployed, and the "political" implications of it, has varied dramatically. At the turn of the century, it was used as a justification for Asian exclusion; the rationale being that Asians were unassimilable and a significant racial threat to the white population on the West Coast (5). In the 1950s, assimilation was used as a gauge by which to measure the degree of "separateness" of Chinese Americans and as a plea for the shedding of "difference" (6). In the late 1960s, in the midst of ghetto rebellions and the emergence of Asian American consciousness, the assimilationist paradigm was used to illustrate the successful integration of Japanese Americans into the mainstream of American life (7).

There are significant problems with this perspective. Among other things, the assimilationist perspective has assumed a zero-sum relationship between assimilation and the retention of ethnicity. To become more "Americanized," therefore, meant that one was less "Asian." By contrast, recent scholarship on Japanese Americans has suggested that they have been able to maintain high levels of ethnic consciousness and ethnic community involvement, while simultaneously becoming structurally assimilated into the dominant society (8).

Another challenge to the assimilationist framework is the fact that the new wave of post-1965 Asian immigrants have had an unprecedented opportunity to develop "private cultures" within the broader American culture. In sharp contrast to the pre-1965 immigrants, they have been able to maintain more comprehensive links with their respective homelands. The dramatic growth of Asian

American "majorities" in several urban and suburban settings also serves to challenge the easy incorporation of Asians into the "mainstream" of American life. In Monterey Park, California, for example, where Asians comprise over 60 percent of the city's population, it is not clear *who* is assimilating into *what*.

I raise these issues in class to interrogate the assimilationist paradigm and to suggest its limits in comprehending and explaining the historical and contemporary experiences of Asian Americans. Building on this critique, I argue that an alternative perspective would have to ac-

---

I argue that an alternative perspective would have to account for distinct trajectories of incorporation, exclusion, and social/cultural autonomy, and not take assimilation as an inevitable outcome or desirable goal.

---

count for distinct trajectories of incorporation, exclusion, and social/cultural autonomy, and not take assimilation as an inevitable outcome or desirable goal.

The Racialization of Asian Americans

I currently organize my course around the theory of *racial formation* (9). By racial formation, I mean the sociohistorical process by which racial categories are created, inhabited, transformed, and destroyed, a process in which race is a matter of both social structure and cultural representation. Utilizing this paradigm, I look at the shifting construction of Asian Americans and how they have been racialized over time. The class explores how distinct Asian ethnic groups entered this country,

where they ended up in the labor market, how they were viewed in popular culture, and how they were treated by legal and political institutions. It simultaneously looks at how Asian Americans viewed themselves, responded to the situations they encountered, and in so doing, challenged and transformed their structural location and their representations.

At the outset of the course, I present a number of related premises. First, I argue that the history of the United States is truly a multiracial, multicultural one—a history which has been shaped by a complex pattern of conflict and cooperation between, and within, groups. Unfortunately, most historical narratives have tended to marginalize non-white, non-European groups and/or minimize the dynamic manner in which we are all shaped by the prevailing pattern of social relations. Second, I note that the Asian American "experience" is neither a single nor a uniform one. Asian Americans are neither a homogeneous nor a monolithic group, and significant differences exist between, and among, different Asian ethnic groups. Third, I stress that the history of Asian Americans is one which reveals intriguing aspects of the broader patterns of race, class, and gender in the United States. Throughout the course, I try to highlight the meaning of these axes of stratification and difference in the Asian American experience.

Bringing Class and Gender Back In

Elizabeth Higginbotham has noted that scholars employ the concepts of race, gender, and class only when specifically looking at groups which are disadvantaged with regards to these axes of stratification: "Race *only* comes up when we talk about African American and other people of color, gender *only* comes up when we talk about women, and class *only* comes up when we talk about the poor and working class" (10). Analyses which grapple with more than one variable frequently reveal a crisis of imagination. Much of the race/class debate for example, inspired by the work of William Julius Wilson, suffers from the imposition of rigid categories and analyses which degenerate into dogmatic assertions of the primacy of one category over the other.

The experience of Asian Americans is not simply a "racial" one, but one which is structured by class divisions and inequalities. The anti-Chinese movement of the nineteenth century, for example, is inextricably bound to the intense conflict of the period between capital and labor (11). Contemporary Korean-African American conflict in Los Angeles and other urban settings cannot be neatly framed in either purely class or racial terms, but is over-determined by an ensemble of factors involving the ghetto economy, patterns of small entrepreneurship, access to resources, and racial ideology in the United States and South Korea (12). An appreciation of class dynamics is crucial to understanding the nature of race and racism. While racial discrimination in a number of institutional arenas continue to plague Asian Americans, its effects vary widely by class strata (13). The problems encountered by a rich entrepreneur from Hong Kong and a recently arrived Hmong refugee are obviously distinct. The sites and types of discriminatory acts each is likely to encounter, and the range of available responses to them, differ by class location.

With respect to gender, narratives focusing on the initial wave of Asian immigrants have tended to marginalize the significance of gender relations. While partially attributable to the predominantly male composition of the initial wave of Asian immigration, it also reflects a masculinist reading of Asian American history (14). An alternative account can be constructed which "recenters" gender. A survey of immigration laws and the practices surrounding their enforcement reveal the gender biases of exclusionary legislation. The Page Law of 1875 which forbade the entry of prostitutes, for example, was selectively enforced to reduce the influx of Asian women. Under the 1922 Cable Act, American-born Asian women forfeited their U.S. citizenship if they married Asian men "ineligible for citizenship" (15). The possibilities for economic mobility among early Asian immigrants was entirely dependent on the presence, and labor, of women who could help establish and maintain a small enterprise or family farm (16). And in the realm of ideology, the popular images of Asian gendered subjects reveal interesting dimensions about sexuality and race (17).

A useful corrective to rigid "categorization" is scholarship which emphasizes the "intersectionality" of race, gender, and class. Evelyn Nakano Glenn's work on the historical and contemporary racialization of domestic and service work, for example, reveals that race is gendered and gender is racialized (18). Historically, and in contemporary life, any clear demarcation of specific forms of oppression and difference is constantly being disrupted. That said, it remains extremely difficult to weave a coherent historical narrative integrating race, class, and gender. I often find myself isolating one category as the subject for particular scrutiny (e.g., the phenomenon of Japanese "picture brides") and failing to provide a way of integrating the various categories into a satisfying account.

Panethnicity and Transnational Consciousness

I currently organize the concluding part of the class around two themes. One is the nature of contemporary panethnic consciousness and organization among Asian Americans (19). It is indeed ironic that the term Asian Americans came into vogue, in the late-1960s, at precisely the moment when new Asian groups were entering the U.S. who would render the term problematic. Ethnicity, class, nativity, and generational differences have manifested themselves in distinct political agendas. Many foreign-born Asians desperately seek programs such as English-acquisition and job-training programs which can ease their transition into the mainstream of American life. By contrast, more "established" and resource-rich groups are less concerned with basic "survival issues" and instead emphasize mobility ones such as the "glass ceiling" in professional employment. Nonethe-less, issues such as redistricting and reapportionment, Asian American admissions in higher education, and anti-Asian violence cut across different Asian American ethnic groups and offer the potential for panethnic organization and consciousness. What I suggest is that panethnicity is situationally defined, strategically deployed for political ends, and subject to competing influences. As such, the future viability of the term Asian American remains open.

The second concluding theme concerns the character of new Asian immigrant experiences and the conceptual frames we adopt to understand them. Trans-Pacific air travel is now quick and relatively affordable, making the borders and boundaries which separate Asia and the mainland U.S. more fluid. New Asian American immigrants frequently go back-and-forth to meet family obligations, vacation, or allow children a periodic immersion into their respective language and culture. Upper-class professionals who continually shuttle between residences and economic activities in Asia, Canada, and the United States are referred to in Chinese as "trapeze artists" or "astronauts." These experiences pose an intriguing question to our presentation of Asian American history: How do we describe and represent the "new" Asian American immigrants in an era characterized by the increasing transnational flow and circulation of capital, labor, culture, and ideas?

One point of departure is to examine how capitalist restructuring and political transformations in the United States and Asia have contributed to a "dual stream" of Asian immigration—a professional and managerial stratum along with semi-skilled and unskilled labor (20). Another is to examine how the new Asian immigrants retain comprehensive links to the homeland through business transactions, the flow of cultural commodities (e.g., videotapes, CDs), remittances, and frequent trips back "home." I encourage comparative analysis between these new immigrants and the waves of immigrants who came prior to 1965. The point is to assess the impact of transnationalism on economic activities, cultural flows, and group/individual identity—and, in so doing, speculate on the future fate of Asian American communities.

What these emergent themes suggest is that the teaching of Asian American history is always unfinished. The dramatic changes in *Asian America* that I have confronted, and attempted to integrate into the teaching of this introductory course, have made this perfectly clear. ❏

Endnotes

1. Gary Y. Okihiro, *Margins and Mainstreams: Asians in American History and Culture* (Seattle and London: University of Washington Press, 1994), chapter 2.
2. Tomás Almaguer, *Racial Fault Lines: The Historical Origins of White Supremacy in California* (Berkeley and Los Angeles: University of California Press, 1994).
3. Etienne Balibar and Immanuel Wallerstein, *Race, Nation, Class: Ambiguous Identities* (London and New York: Verso, 1991), 38-9.
4. David A. Hollinger, *Postethnic America: Beyond Multiculturalism* (New York: Basic Books, 1995).
5. See Paul Takagi, "The Myth of 'Assimilation in American Life,'" *Amerasia Journal* 2 (1973): 149-58.
6. Rose Hum Lee, *The Chinese in the United States of America* (Hong Kong: Hong Kong University Press, 1960).
7. Harry H.L. Kitano, *Japanese Americans: The Evolution of a Subculture* (Englewood Cliffs, N.J.: Prentice-Hall, 1969).
8. Stephen S. Fugita and David J. O'Brien, *Japanese American Ethnicity: The Persistence of Community* (Seattle: University of Washington Press, 1991),
9. Michael Omi and Howard Winant, *Racial Formation in the United States: From the 1960s to the 1990s*, 2d ed. (New York: Routledge, 1994).
10. Elizabeth Higginbotham, "Sociology and the Multicultural Curriculum: The Challenges of the 1990s and Beyond," *Race, Sex, and Class* 1 (Fall 1993): 14.
11. Alexander Saxton, *The Indispensable Enemy: Labor and the Anti-Chinese Movement in California* (Berkeley and Los Angeles: University of California Press, 1971).
12. Nancy Abelmann and John Lie, *Blue Dreams: Korean Americans and the Los Angeles Riots* (Cambridge: Harvard University Press, 1995).
13. U.S. Commission on Civil Rights, *Civil Rights Issues Facing Asian Americans in the 1990s* (Washington, D.C., February 1992).
14. Sylvia Yanagisako, "Transforming Orientalism: Gender, Nationality, and Class in Asian American Studies" in Sylvia Yanagisako and Carol Delaney, eds., *Naturalizing Power: Essays in Feminist Cultural Analysis* (New York: Routledge, 1994).
15. Sucheng Chan, *Asian Americans: An Interpretive History* (Boston: Twayne Publishers, 1991).
16. Edna Bonacich and John Modell, *The Economic Basis of Ethnic Solidarity: Small Business in the Japanese American Community* (Berkeley and Los Angeles, University of California Press, 1981).
17. Gina Marchetti, *Romance and the "Yellow Peril": Race, Sex, and Discursive Strategies in Hollywood Fiction* (Berkeley and Los Angeles: University of California Press, 1993).
18. Evelyn Nakano Glenn, *Issei, Nisei, War Bride: Three Generations of Japanese American Women in Domestic Service* (Philadelphia: Temple University Press, 1986) and "From Servitude to Service Work: Historical Continuities in the Racial Division of Paid Reproductive Labor," *Signs: Journal of Women in Culture and Society* 18 (Autumn 1992).
19. Yen Le Espiritu, *Asian American Panethnicity: Bridging Institutions and Identities* (Philadelphia: Temple University Press, 1992).
20. Paul Ong, Edna Bonacich, and Lucie Cheng, eds., *The New Asian Immigration in Los Angeles and Global Restructuring* (Philadelphia: Temple University Press, 1994).

Michael Omi is an associate professor of Ethnic Studies at the University of California-Berkeley. He is co-author (with Howard Winant) of Racial Formation in the United States *(2d. ed., 1994). In 1990, he was the recipient of Berkeley's Distinguished Teaching Award.*

Plan Ahead

Future OAH Annual Meetings

•

1997
San Francisco

April 17-20
San Francisco
Hilton

•

1998
Indianapolis

April 2-5
Indiana Convention
Center

•

1999
Toronto, Ontario

April 22-25
Sheraton Centre

•

2000
St. Louis, Missouri

March 30-April 2
Adam's Mark

Beyond Bound Feet:
Relocating Asian American Women

Sucheta Mazumdar

Sometimes I stare at Chinese grandmothers
Getting on the 30 Stockton with
       shopping bags
Japanese women tourists in European hats
Middle-aged mothers with laundry carts
Young wives holding hands with their
       husbands
Lesbian women holding hands in coffee-
       houses
Smiling debutantes with bouquets of yellow
       daffodils
. . . . I look at them and wonder if
They are a part of me . . . . (1)

Genny Lim ends with a paean to the diverse origins but shared experiences of women, in "Samarkand, in San Francisco/ Along the Mekong." But the question lingers. Are these Chinese grandmothers part of me? Are all these women a part of every American woman's history? Where are the histories of grandmothers, of their mothers and sisters and friends? Or have they all been lost because nobody thought of them as part of their own histories?

The history of those who are not rich and famous often gets written by the numbers. Library shelves groan under the weight of books on European migration to the United States. Until very recently, there were no more than a handful of books about Asian immigrants to the U.S. A minority within a minority, the story of Asian American women has barely begun to be told. For the almost two hundred years that have lapsed since Asians first came to the United States, women have come in large numbers only in the last fifty

years. Nineteenth-century Asian immigration was primarily Chinese and predominantly male. As Judy Yung's major new study points out, by 1900 there were just around 4,500 women as compared to almost 90,000 Chinese men on the mainland (2). In Hawaii in 1900, the ratio of men to women was only slightly better; of the 25,767 Chinese, 3,471 or 13.5 percent were women (3). Were there few women emigrating because anti-Chinese prejudice and violence—combined with discriminatory laws proliferating from the 1850s onwards—curtailed both male and female Chinese immigration to the United States? The 1882 Chinese Exclusion Act allowed only merchants, their wives and daughters, students, and diplomats to enter the country; laborers were excluded. Chinese immigrants, like other Asian immigrants after them, were also denied rights to citizenship through naturalization. Those ineligible for citizenship could not legally own land. To what extent did these measures passed by the U.S. federal government, indicative of the hostility with which Asian immigration was received, encourage men not to bring their families?

For the first half of the twentieth century, immigrants from Japan were the largest group among the Asians. Japanese women accounted for only 4 percent of the Japanese population on the U.S. mainland in 1900 and 12.6 percent in 1910 (4). Though the number of Japanese women

emigrating was to rise after this—and by 1920, 35 percent of the Japanese population on the mainland consisted of women, a percentage similar to that of the Korean community—in other Asian immigrant communities like the Filipino and the Asian Indian, the numbers of women emigrating remained few and far between. The writing of Asian American history has focused on those who were here: the "bachelor communities" of Chinatowns; the Punjabi farmworkers from India; and the pinoy [Filipino immigrants] working in salmon canning industries of the Northwest. Why did so few women emigrate from Asian countries? Let us begin with the question of whether the limited migration of Asian women prior to World War II was a particular and unique feature of Asian immigration to the United States, or whether it was due to Asian social and cultural practices that women stayed at home?

A pattern emerges when we look at Asia and the regions from which the immigrants came. Asian out-migration during the nineteenth and early-twentieth centuries was regionally specific. For example, Chinese migrants going overseas overwhelmingly came from a group of counties clustered around the Pearl River in the southern Chinese province of Guangdong. The vast majority of immigrants from Japan came from only four counties in southwestern Japan. The immigrants from India came from the northwestern provce of Punjab. The immigrants from the Philippines came from northwestern corner of Luzon, the Ilocos. These regions, scattered through the vast continent of Asia, had some features in common. All these areas were densely populated, peasant-holdings were reduced to minuscule plots of land, and the regional agrarian economy was undergoing a rapid transformation (5). Sending young men abroad, to earn and send back remittances to supplement the meager resources of the family, while allowing the family to hold on to their land, was one strategy adopted by these communities in their quest for survival. And what better way of ensuring that the young man sent a portion of his income back than having him leave his wife behind? Patriarchal ideology and concepts of marriage, that did not preclude romantic love but considered the interests of the patriliny more important than the individual interests of a man and wife, did not make these arrangements for long separation seem extraordinary.

Whenever Chan Sam wrote to his wife [Huangbo], he had but one thought in his mind: to bridge the distance between himself and the village. He asked after her and his kinfolk, about the house, about the security of the village. Had the bandits been kept away? How much grain did she have in reserve? Has water been draining from the dirt floor? Had termites come back into the house? . . .

Her letters would append at most a line or two to the receipt [for money] she sent back. She'd tell him she was fine, that he shouldn't worry about her, and then pass on news of any births or deaths or marriages in the village (6).

The relationship between the men who came to America and the women who stayed behind was complex. The many songs and poems of the young brides left behind in the villages of Guangdong tell of dust covering one side of the conjugal bed, the loneliness of cold pillows, and of longing for their husbands. Songs from Punjab echo these sentiments. This was one part of the lives of women left behind. But as wives of men who were abroad, the women

Harper's, 1 April 1882

E PLURIBUS UNUM (EXCEPT THE CHINESE).

A pro-Chinese immigration cartoon by Thomas Nast in the early 1880s.

also had higher social status in the village. They enjoyed a modicum of economic security compared to their neighbors. For within the range of limited possibilities and options available to rural women in particular, marrying a man going abroad was not the worst scenario. Rape, enserfment, robbery, kidnaping, and sale into prostitution were very real, everyday dangers facing women as the dual thrust of colonialism and capitalism ripped asunder pre-industrial social and economic modalities.

History often gets written not only by numbers but also by conventions of national mythologies. One of the basic myths of American immigration history is that those who came never went back. "America was believed to be the haven for Europe's oppressed; immigrants were expected to stay once they arrived. To leave again implied that the migrant came only for money; was too crass to appreciate America as a noble experiment in democracy; and spurned American good will and helping hands. . . . [There was] 'scornful denunciation' of migrants for accumulating American money for the subsequent consumption of 'porridge, bloaters, maccaroni [sic] and sauerkraut' on the other side of the Atlantic" (7). One can add rice and noodles and chapatis to this list for many Chinese, Indians, and Filipinos—like many Italians, Greeks, Croatians, Serbians, Slovenians, Hungarians, Poles, Finns, and Canadians—who came to work, returned home. For the Europeans, who did have rights to naturalized citizenship and who faced far fewer discriminatory measures, in 1908, a randomly chosen year, the return rate ranged between twenty to sixty percent (8). Insisting on writing the history of only those who continued to live within the territorial boundaries of the U.S. tells only half the story. Migration and remigration are part of a global process that began with the advent of the steamship and has continued apace with the transportation revolution of the twentieth century. Rather than cutting off Asian American history from its roots in Asia, a global perspective which links the men and women on both sides of the Pacific allows us to reclaim histories of those women who never managed to cross the seas.

When these migrant husbands returned, they took back a bit of America with them and transformed their own cultural and social worlds. When Chan Sam went back to the village in Guangdong, Huangbo, who had never been to North America, opened a can of sweetened condensed milk and a box of crackers. The meal celebrating his return ended with a sweet soup of steaming milk with saltine crackers floating on top (9). In the dream house Chan Sam built in his village for his family, the main sitting room was decorated by local craftsmen with scenes of the Golden Gate Bridge and life in Gold Mountain: a couple in a roadster, its top folded down, motoring by a coral mansion on a wide, palm tree-lined boulevard (10). The money for the house came from the wages of Chan Sam's second wife (concubine) earned in Vancouver by waitressing and sex-work. This brings us to the other side of the story.

The extensive literature about Chinese women with bound feet has obscured our understanding of the extent to which daily life in the Chinese countryside involved hard physical labor and the extent to which Chinese women contributed to the family economy (11). Apart from the very wealthy, most women worked. The daily chores of hauling water, cutting and gathering fuel, threshing grain, feeding the pigs and chickens, raising vegetables, cooking, and taking care of the feeding, clothing, and laundry for the family defined a woman's everyday life in all peasant societies. In South China many women worked in the fields planting and harvesting rice and sweet-potatoes. Yet others worked raising silkworms and spinning silk. Redefining the immigrant experience not in terms of male or female, but in terms of the experience of workers would allow us to centrally relocate women. For above all Asian immigrant women worked in t[he] U.S. Even Great-Grandmother Leo[ng] Shee, married to Chin Lung, one of t[he] richest Chinese men in t[he] U.S., who had bound f[eet] and arrived in San Francis[co] in 1893, worked. "Yin[g]," she told her daughter, "wh[en] you go to America, don't [be] lazy. Work hard and y[ou] will become rich. Yo[ur] grandfather grew potato[es] and although I was busy [at] home, I sewed on foot-trea[dle] machine, made buttons, a[nd] weaved loose threads [or finishing work]" (12).

For nineteenth-centu[ry] Chinese women immigran[ts] there were few opportunit[ies] for wage work. Some work[ed] as fisher women in Monter[ey] Bay in California, a hand[ful] as miners and railroad wo[rk]ers. But the vast majority [of] Chinese women immigra[nts] in the nineteenth centu[ry] were sex-workers. Much h[as] been written about the h[is]tory of prostitution in ni[ne]teenth-century America, b[ut] the focus has been on issu[es] of crime, morality, victi[m]ization, and Christian m[is]sionary rescue (13). But [the] political economy of se[x] work under capitalism, [in]volving women globally, h[as] received much less attenti[on] (14). Asian women se[x] workers were an integral p[art] of this expanding nexus b[e]tween urbanization, indust[ri]alization, and male migrati[on] on the one hand and mili[ta]rism and tourism on the oth[er].

Other women, arrivi[ng] in the U.S. after the turn [of] the century, found work in the cane fie[lds] of Hawai'i, and in the fields of Californ[ia,] Oregon, and Washington. In the su[gar] plantations of Hawai'i, work began at

Franklin Odo and Kazuko Sinoto, *A Pictorial History of the Japanese in Hawai'i, 1885-1924,* 1985

Japanese woman irrigator, Pu'unene, Maui, c. 1912

William Speer, *The Oldest and Newest Empire: China and the United States*, 1870

An idealized drawing of Chinese miners in California in the 1860s.

rly age. The plantation foremen gave no eaks; they hired teenagers like thirteen-ar old Haruno Sato to deliver water and ach to hundreds of workers in the fields 5). The mothers raised children, did the andry, cooked, sewed, and worked in the lds. Others took in laundry, cooked, d ran boarding houses for unmarried ricultural workers. Mrs. Tai Yoo Kim, to had just turned eighteen in 1905, ran lantation boarding house at Honokaa d prepared three meals a day for twenty-e men, including her husband (16). hers, living in urban centers, ran gro-ry stores and fruit and vegetable stands, d worked as domestic servants and fac-y workers. The divide between public d private, between housekeeping and ge-work, so neatly laying out a para-m for women's lives prior to World ar II, does not apply to the lives of men of color who have always worked. rmal definitions of work have however

often left out these activities in the enu-meration of census categories of work.

The centrality of women's work as the defining core of the Asian American expe-rience is even more evident in the history of the post-1965 period. Well over sixty-percent of the Asian American popula-tion, with the exception of the Japanese Americans, continues to be foreign born, the immigrant family starting all over again in a new country typically relies on at least two adult wage-workers to make ends meet. Asian American women are going to work in unprecedented numbers. In some communities, such as the Filipino community, female immigration has out-numbered male immigration and already by 1980 close to 70 percent of Filipinas were part of the labor force (17). At one end of the scale, the emphasis of U.S. immigration legislation favoring those with professional degrees has resulted in a highly qualified cohort of Asian American women

who work as doctors, lawyers, and busi-nesswomen. Some 3.9 percent of Asian American women earn more than $75,000 a year. But almost nine percent of Asian American women working full-time make less than $10,000 per year, and another 28 percent of the Asian American women working full-time make only between $10,000-$20,000 per year (18). The vast majority of them work in restaurants and garment factories and in the hotel-motel service sector. Many work 15 hour days. Over 20,000 Chinese women work in the garment industry of New York. Of the estimated 120,000 garment workers in Los Angeles, well over 20 percent are Chinese, Korean, Vietnamese, Thai, and Cambodian (19).

The women seated at the table are all veterans of garment factories so-called sweatshops in Oakland's Chinatown. They will gladly tell you how it is to work in places without minimum wage or overtime or any other numerous workplace protections American workers take for granted.

They form a group portrait of a grand American institution, one grander to contemplate than actually to experience. They are pioneer women. Instead of investing money they are investing suffering (20). ❏

Endnotes

1. Genny Lim, "Wonder Woman," in *This Bridge Called My Back: Writings by Radical Women of Color*, ed. Cherrie Moraga and Gloria Anzaldua (Watertown: Persephone Press, 1981), 25-6.
2. Judy Yung, *Unbound Feet* (Berkeley: University of California Press, 1995), 243.
3. Ronald Takaki, "They Also Came: The Migration of Chinese and Japanese Women to Hawaii and the Continental United States," *Chinese America: History and Perspectives 1990*, 3.
4. Gary Y. Okihiro, *Margins and Mainstreams: Asians in American History and Culture* (Seattle: University of Washington Press, 1994), 67.
5. These case studies are detailed in Lucie Cheng and Edna Bonacich, eds., *Labor Immigration Under Capitalism* (Berkeley, University of California Press, 1984).
6. Denise Chong, *The Concubine's Children* (New York: Penguin Books, 1994), 38.
7. Walter Nugent, *Crossings: The Great Transatlantic Migrations, 1870-1914* (Bloomington: Indiana University Press, 1995), 158-60.
8. Nugent, *Crossings*, 160.
9. Chong, *Concubine's*, 68.
10. Chong, *Concubine's*, 86.
11. A number of essays in Maria Jaschok and Suzanne Miers, eds., *Women and Chinese Patriarchy* (Hong Kong: Zed Books, 1994) give background information on women's work in the Pearl River Delta.
12. Yung, *Unbound*, 16.
13. See, for example, Peggy Pascoe, *Relations of Rescue* (New York: Oxford University Press, 1990); and Anne M. Butler, *Daughters of Joy, Sisters of Misery: Prostitutes in the American West, 1865-90* (Urbana: University of Illinois Press, 1985).
14. Thanh-dam Truong, *Sex, Money and Morality* (New York: Zed Books, 1990) looks at Asian prostitution and tourism, particularly in the contemporary period, but does not discuss sex-work as part of the development of capitalism.
15. Gary Y. Okihiro, *Cane Fires* (Philadelphia: Temple University Press, 1991), 3.
16. Brett Melendy, *Asians in America: Filipinos, Koreans and East Indians* (Boston: Twayne Publishers, 1981), 162.
17. Teresa Amott and Julie Matthaei, eds., *Race, Gender and Work* (Boston: South End Press, 1991), 305.
18. Susan B. Gall and Timothy Gall, eds., *Statistical Record of Asian Americans* (Detroit: Gale Research Center, 199), 501.
19. Edna Bonacich et al., eds., *Global Production* (Philadelphia: Temple University Press, 1994), 346.
20. Michael Robertson, "Empowering the Women of the Sweatshops," *San Francisco Chronicle*, 24 April 1990.

Sucheta Mazumdar is a professor of history at Duke University.

Crossing the Borders of the Personal and the Public: Family History and the Teaching of Asian American History

K. Scott Wong

In the nearly three decades during which Asian American studies has been evolving, historians in our field have had to confront the problem of locating appropriate sources for research and teaching. Unlike other fields of American history, there are few archives devoted to Asian American history and for a number of reasons, the primary sources needed for certain types of historical research are either scattered across the United States and Asia or simply do not exist. This paucity of sources in some areas of our field has not only shaped the direction of our research and how we are able to go about recovering, reconstructing, and interpreting our past, it has also affected what and how we are able to teach and the nature of the assignments we give our students. In this essay, I would like to offer some thoughts on the use of family history and autobiography assignments in the teaching of Asian American history, drawing primarily on my experience of teaching at Williams College (1).

Although the intellectual quality of the students at Williams College allows me to assign sophisticated readings and require substantial research papers, I have found that many undergraduates are not interested in historiography or the minutiae of Asian American history. Instead, they are more interested in gaining a broad understanding of the topic, and most important, how it affects them personally. Therefore, I have found that the most successful and meaningful assignments

> *Therefore, I have found that the most successful and meaningful assignments are personal or family histories. This allows for a balance between scholarly inquiry and personal discovery.*

are personal or family histories. This allows for a balance between scholarly inquiry and personal discovery. I have the students get in touch with their parents or grandparents and instruct them to start asking about their immigration experiences, their adjustment to American life,

their hopes for their children, and so on. The main guideline is to blend the structural components of immigration with the personal experiences of the immigrant(s) being interviewed. As the semester progresses many of the students begin to come to me with probing questions arising from their research. They ask me if it is possible that their great-grandfathers could have been "paper sons," if their mothers or grandmothers could have been affected by anti-miscegenation laws, or how to best describe their experiences as a "boat person." Suddenly, they begin to realize that they have not heard all there is to hear about the family, that they might not even know why they are in the United States rather than in Korea or Taiwan. In other words, they hit upon events and trends in their families' histories that have had a profound impact on the direction their lives have taken. Both the events and the realization of these events (termed "epiphanies" by one scholar) provide the students with insights that enable them to make connections between their personal lives and the "public record" of written history (2).

Another form of this assignment is to concentrate on themselves, to write their autobiographies as Asian Americans.

Focusing on themselves, new realizations surface in their attempts to place their lives in the broader historical picture. Those who believe that they have never experienced racism finally recall those ugly moments in their childhood when they tried to understand the meaning of being called "Chink" or "Gook," or why they were not invited to parties with their all-white classmates. Despite this focus on themselves, the students become "historians of the present," a process which allows them to contextualize their lives in the broader Asian American experience (3).

At Williams College, I have given this assignment in both my contemporary Asian American history class and my course on comparative American immigration history. In most cases, the students have embraced this assignment with great enthusiasm. Whereas some students once scoffed at the idea of a family history when I first tried the assignment, they now tell me that they are taking the class *because* of the assignment. One senior told me, "I want to graduate with something meaningful in my hand, such as the family history I'll write in this class" (4). In addition, because of the generational and socioeconomic demographics of Williams College, I have a number of students who are very interested in carrying out this assignment in forms other than the standard narrative employed in most family histories and autobiographies. Influenced by a lifetime of watching modern television graphics (from Sesame Street to MTV) and an intellectual attraction to contemporary theory, the students are now producing autobiographies and family histories in the form of videos, photographic essays, extended verse, and physical artifacts. In this last case, the student presented me with passports, clothing, and toys, all carefully wrapped in an archives storage box accompanied by a text which instructed me when to unwrap each object and described each artifact and how it fit into the history of the family's immigration to America. In recent years, my students have also used this assignment to articulate their identities that extend beyond their sense of being Asian Americans. I

have received a number of projects that detail their developing awareness of their sexuality, their bouts with severe depression, their history of domestic abuse, and their acceptance of their bi-racial heritage. To be sure, their Asian American identities and upbringing are vitally connected to these aspects of their lives, but these projects point out very clearly that they do not always privilege ethnicity when coming to terms with their life histories.

I always have a number of non-Asian American students in my Asian American history class and the assignment mandates that they interview an Asian American and record and reflect upon their lives. In many of these cases, the papers are equally revealing as they disclose previous stereotypes they held about Asian Americans which were dispelled after spending time with their informants. For some, this is the first time in their lives they have had direct contact with an Asian American. Previous

to the assignment, their relationship to Asian Americans was either in passing or through the distorted lens of the mass media. For others, this project allowed them to ask their Asian American friends questions they've held in for years out of fear of treading into sensitive areas. If Asian American Studies is to contribute to the "opening" of American society to acknowledge and appreciate its multicultural heritage, perhaps this assignment is the first step for some of our students.

While I have great faith in this assignment, I am well aware that there are a number of problems with using oral history and autobiography to teach and write history. As we try to uncover and reconstruct our historical past, we have to be alert to the politics of using oral history and autobiography as historical documents. They are, of course, gendered and class-based productions of subjective interpretation, mediated by the historical and social factors of the environment in which they

Jeff Gillenkirk and James Motlow, *Bitter Melon*, 198

Wong Yow family, Wedding Day, 1935.

are produced and influenced by the selective process of an individual's or group's historical and collective memory in order to present a picture of the past that serves the objectives of the author(s). Therefore, when used as primary historical sources, one must always be aware of the nature of their cultural production. However, these problems can also be used to great pedagogical benefit when assigning the writing and/or collection of autobiography and family histories. By pointing out to students that in writing their autobiographies and/or family histories, they will be creating historical documents, not unlike the ones they encounter in their assigned readings, their awareness and understanding of the constructed nature of historical evidence can be greatly enhanced. For example, when assigning readings such as sections of the 1876 hearings on Chinese immigration, testimonies from the Commission on the Wartime Relocation and Internment of Civilians, *Quiet Odyssey*, *Hearts of Sorrow*, or *Strangers From a Different Shore*, their experience in constructing their own historical narratives can provide important insights to their understanding of how these texts are collected, organized, and written. Once they become aware of how they can control how their histories are written, they can better appreciate how other histories are constructed and presented to the reader or listener. With this in mind, I devote a class period to discussing theoretical readings about autobiography and oral history and another class session, usually near the date when their assignments are due, in which the students discuss the methodological issues they confronted as they wrote their family histories (5). In this manner, they are encouraged to articulate their understanding of their role as historians and agents of their own historical circumstances. Furthermore, when they come to apprehend the importance of what they have accomplished in this project, they come to understand the power of the construction of history and the importance of claiming their own stories and voices. They now realize that if they do not represent their lives and histories on their own

terms, it will be done by someone else on someone else's terms, if at all. And, placed against the broader backdrop of Asian American history, they will come to a better understanding that without honest and careful representation, peoples' whole histories and cultures can be rendered silent, invisible, and therefore, non-existent. Thus by crossing the borders of the personal and letting it manifest in public, our students partake in the political act of claiming their own histories.

To conclude, I have come to believe strongly in the efficacy of this assignment. It opens up students to new insights about themselves, their families, their friends, and their society. It can give them a sense of historical connection to their own ethnic group and to the lives of those around them. As our classrooms become increasingly diverse in terms of race, ethnicity, gender, class, and sexual orientation, it is essential that we encourage our students to appreciate these differences while trying to locate some area of commonality among them so there is an avenue for communication. In this case, that commonality is based on the shared experience of living as or with Asians in America. Their research will hopefully show them how stereotypes serve only to reduce, falsify, and invalidate real human lives. We owe our students this much.

As scholars and educators, we spend so much time with texts and ideas, creating paradigms and looking for meaning, we often assume that our students live in the same intellectual environment that we do. More often, they do not. They usually have a set of concerns that do not correspond to our daily lives. In many ways this project helps bridge the distance between "professor" and "student" and "writer" from "reader." It has often been as rewarding for me as it has for many of my students. Through their experiences of self-discovery, I learn not only about the specifics of their lives, but I get a glimpse of Asian American history in the making. Their stories are what the scholarship of a few years hence will focus on. By seeing what experiences these students have endured and what concerns them now, I have

found specific parallels and contrasts to earlier periods of Asian American history. When shown this, the students are more apt to appreciate the lives of those long gone because they have come to understand their own lives as history. I, too, have come to a better understanding of the patterns of Asian American history by placing my own life in relation to theirs. So long as we acknowledge the value of our students' lives, I believe we can be honest historians and teachers in our research and in the classroom. ❏

Endnotes

1. Portions of this essay were originally in K. Scott Wong, "Our Lives, Our Histories," in *Multicultural Teaching in the University*, ed. David Schoem et al. (Westport, Conn.: Praeger Publishers, 1993), 87-94. I first developed this assignment when I began teaching Asian American studies as a graduate student at the University of Michigan. When I went to the University of California, Santa Barbara, as a Dissertation Fellow, I was pleased to discover that the director of the Asian American Studies Program, Sucheng Chan, used a very similar assignment in her Asian American history survey courses. Since coming to Williams College, I continue to develop this assignment as I come to better understand the intricacies, limitations, and advantages of using and assigning oral histories as both texts and assignments.

2. Norman K. Denzin, *Interpretive Biography* (Newbury Park, N.Y.: Sage Publications, 1989), 70. Denzin writes, "Epiphanies are interactional moments and experiences which leave marks on people's lives. In them, personal character is manifested. They are often moments of crisis. They alter the fundamental meaning structures in a person's life." I am grateful to Lane Hirabayashi for introducing me to this essay.

3. This phrase is borrowed from the Popular Memory Group, "Popular Memory: Theory, Politics, Method," ed. Rich-

ard Johnson et al. (London Hutchinson, in association with the Centre for Contemporary Cultural Studies, University of Birmingham, 1982), 205.

4. Students in most of the classes in which I give this assignment have made similar comments. Quite a few have informed me that their families help with and read these papers with greater interest than any other they have written in college, the papers often passed from one set of relatives to another. I have even received letters from students a number of years after graduation informing me that the person about whom they wrote had just passed away and how grateful the family was for having a record of their life.

5. There are now a number of texts that are based on or are collections of Asian Americans' oral histories and autobiographies. Some examples include *Hmong Means Free: Life in Laos and America* edited and with an introduction by Sucheng Chan (Philadelphia: Temple University Press, 1994); *Asians in America: A Reader*, Malcolm Collier, ed. (Dubuque, Iowa: Kendall/Hunt, 1993); James M. Freeman, *Hearts of Sorrow: Vietnamese-American Lives* (Stanford: Stanford University Press, 1989); *Growing Up Asian American*, edited with an introduction by Maria Hong, (New York: Avon Books, 1993); *Under Western Eyes: Personal Essays From Asian America*, edited with an introduction by Garrett Hongo, (New York: Anchor Books, 1995); Joann Faung Jean Lee, *Asian American Experiences in the United States* (Jefferson, N.C.: McFarland and Company, 1991); Mary Paik Lee, *Quiet Odyssey: A Pioneer Korean Woman in America* (Seattle: University of Washington Press, 1990); Lydia Minatoya, *Talking to High Monks in the Snow: An Asian American Odyssey* (New York: Harper Collins, 1993); *The Far East Comes Near: Autobiographical Accounts of Southeast Asian Students in*

America, ed. Lucy Nguyen-Hong-Nhiem and Joel Martin Halpern (Amherst: University of Massachusetts Press, 1989); John Tenhula, *Voices from Southeast Asia: The Refugee Experience in the United States* (New York: Holmes and Meier, 1991); and Usha Welaratna, *Beyond the Killing Fields: Voices of Nine Cambodian Survivors in America* (Stanford: Stanford University Press, 1993). Aside from the Norman Denzin essay and the piece by the Popular Memory Group cited above, other helpful writings on oral history, family history, and autobiography include *Autobiography and Postmodernism*, eds. Kathleen Ashley, Leigh Gilmore, and Gerald Peters (Amherst: University of Massachusetts Press, 1994); Herbert Leibowitz, *Fabricating Lives: Explorations in American Autobiography* (New York: Alfred A. Knopf, 1989); Joan W. Scott, "The Evidence of Experience," *Critical Inquiry* 17 (Summer 1991): 733-97; Sau-ling Cynthia Wong, "Immigrant Autobiography: Some Questions of Definition and Approach," *American Autobiography: Retrospect and Prospect*, Paul John Eakin, ed. (Madison: University of Wisconsin Press, 1991), 142-70; and Virginia Yans-McLaughlin, "Metaphors of Self in History: Subjectivity, Oral Narrative, and Immigration Studies," in *Immigration Reconsidered: History, Sociology, and Politics*, ed. Virginia Yans-McLaughlin (New York: Oxford University Press, 1990), 254-90.

K. Scott Wong is an assistant professor of history at Williams College. His articles have appeared in the Journal of American Ethnic History, MELUS, American Quarterly, *and* Amerasia Journal. *He is currently writing a book on the impact of the Second World War on Chinese Americans.*

A Graduate Student's Reflection on Studying Asian American History

Ji-Yeon Yuh

The most common reaction when my graduate student peers hear that I specialize in Asian Americanstudies at the University of Pennsylvania is a pitying shake of the head. Penn does not have a program in Asian American studies, and currently it scrapes along from semester to semester with a few undergraduate courses taught by adjuncts or visiting professors. How, my peers wonder, does a graduate student work on a doctorate in the field when there are no professors at her home institution with whom to work?

The issue here is to work around the absence of Asian American studies, and I've stumbled onto three practical strategies. One is to borrow shamelessly from other institutions. Two of my three dissertation committee members, for example, are professors at other universities. The second strategy is to exhaust all existing resources at Penn. And the third is to actively work to bring Asian American studies to Penn. These three strategies work in part because, despite the lack of Asian American studies, Penn and my department, history, in particular, are not overtly hostile to the field. My advisor, for example, is a strong supporter of my work, and I have the opportunity, through my department, to teach my own course in Asian Americanstudies.

Let me first explain that when I entered graduate school, my intended field of study was immigration and U.S. social history, fields in which Penn has some fine professors. It quickly became clear to me, however, that Asian immigration didn't fit comfortably within the theoretical frameworks set up in the immigration field, and within the first semester I was turning to Asian American studies and its more hospitable framework. That first year of graduate study, however, I was quite alone. Without any classes that included even one article on Asian immigration or Asian Americans, I scoured the library for texts on Asian immigration. There I stumbled onto *Amerasia Journal* and first came upon the names of scholars I would later learn were pioneers in the field. With those names, I sent letters to faculty members in fertile California requesting syllabi and reading lists. And then I found, through a mutual acquaintance, the one person in the area who was teaching an Asian American studies course, a dean at a nearby liberal arts college who has since moved to another institution.

Two years later, when I returned from a leave of absence studying Korean history at a university in Seoul, Penn's situation had improved somewhat. We now had a few courses taught by adjuncts, and that year even had a visiting professor in Asian American studies. That professor is now a valued mentor. Penn also had formed, through student pressure, a search committee for a full-time faculty member in the field. Through the recommendation of my advisor I was made a member of that search committee. After three years of searching, we hired two junior faculty this spring, one in literature and one in sociology. My involvement in the field began in earnest that year as I studied for oral examinations, engaged in the faculty search, and put together a dissertation proposal.

My ties to Penn now mainly revolve around the struggle for an Asian American studies program. As a graduate student who works closely with undergraduates, as a member of the Asian American studies faculty search committee, and as the main organizer for last year's Asian American studies conference held at Penn, I've been witness to an ongoing struggle, a participant in the art of academic hiring, and a cheerleader of sorts for the field as a whole.

My own research and intellectual development, however, lie largely outside Penn and within the Korean communities of which I am a part and which provide the rational for an Asian American studies program, for I am a strong believer in an academics that is rooted in communities and responsive to community needs. Thus, I locate my intellectual home base within the Korean communities where I live and work. This is a return to the roots of Asian American studies, a field originally committed to Asian American communities and their struggles for liberation, struggles which gave birth to the field itself.

Working in Asian American studies at a school where the concept itself is alien to most faculty is not necessarily to be recommended. My solution has been to locate myself firmly within my specific community and to become directly involved in the struggle for Asian American studies programs. Thus, I've been able to draw strength from the field as a whole rather than from only my particular institution. The experience has been rewarding in providing me with a sense of participation, however meager, in the growth of an academic field that is still concerned with justice, liberation, and the betterment of our human condition. ❏

Ji-Yeon Yuh studies the Korean diaspora, Asian American history, and U.S. history at the University of Pennsylvania. She is writing a doctoral dissertation on Korean military brides and their lives as immigrant women.

Somewhere Between White and Black: The Chinese in Mississippi

Vivian Wu Wong

There is this shot in the opening scene of the movie, Mississippi Burning, *where you see two water fountains. One is broken, and chipped, and water is dripping from it. The other is modern, and shining. A white guy goes up to the nice one, and the black kid goes up to the old one. I remember saying to myself, "If I was in the scene, where would I drink?"*

As a kid, I remember going to the theater and not knowing where I was supposed to sit. Blacks were segregated then. Colored people had to sit upstairs, and white people sat downstairs. . . . I guess I was always considered marginal with whites and blacks (1).

Reared in Clarksdale, Mississippi, Chinese American Sam Sue has bitter memories about growing up not knowing how or where to fit in. Since their arrival in the American South over three hundred years ago, Asians have encountered an invisible racial barrier. Neither white nor black, Americans of Asian descent were somewhere in between with no fixed "place in society."

Finding a Place

The majority of the Chinese who settled in the Mississippi Delta arrived between the years 1910 and 1930. However, questions concerning the social, economic, and political future of the Chinese in Mississippi began much earlier, starting in the mid-1800s when a number of Chinese "coolies" (indentured laborers) from Cuba were brought to the American South as a substitute for black labor.

A vast social and economic gulf yawns between the dominant white and subordinate black. Yet one group in Mississippi, a "third race," the Chinese, has managed to leap that chasm. Negroes do not consider them exactly white; Caucasians do not consider them black. They are privileged and burdened with an ambiguous racial identity (2).

This unique situation gave the Chinese in Mississippi the opportunity to "switch" from one racial group to another, while at the same time, remaining "in-between" the white and black communities.

Creating a Community

By comparing the immigration, settlement, and working experiences of the Chinese in California with those in Mississippi one can see the unique position of the Chinese in Mississippi. The most significant differences between the Chinese in Mississippi and the Chinese in California can be seen in terms of social mobility, with respect to class and racial affiliation, and ethnic identity, with respect to the establishment of Chinatowns. The public image of the Chinese who immigrated to the American West differed dramatically with that of the Chinese who immigrated to the American South, although both groups had a profound social impact upon the communities they entered. Since the Chinese workers from Cuba could speak Spanish, they were somewhat respected (3). However, the Chinese laborers in California had to deal with intense anti-immigrant sentiment. Elmer C. Sandmeyer believes that economic forces were most important in fostering anti-immigrant feeling, "because Chinese laborers became unwitting pawns in American labor-management disputes" (4). In Mississippi, the Chinese entered a racial system in which there already existed an "inferior" race. However, in California, the Chinese worked in industries which were the lowest paying and had to face the harshest working conditions. In the eyes of the white community, the Chinese were the "inferior" class.

The main difference in community development was the absence of Chinatowns in the Mississippi Delta (5). San Francisco Chinatown is an example of a community which was created in order to defend the Chinese people socially, economically, and politically. With the Exclusion Act of 1882 and the disenfranchisement of Chinese from the political process, the Chinese communities were left utterly defenseless. They therefore established their own temples and secret societies. In Mississippi, on the other hand, the development of the Chinese Baptist Church, the presence of women in the Chinese community, and the absence of clans made the Chinese more acceptable to the white community. Without traditional Chinese American institutions in the community, the Mississippi Chinese needed alternatives. They created what Loewen calls "parallel institutions," social organizations which were structured to replicate their white counterparts. These institutions, such as Chinese Christian churches, showed the white community that the Chinese "was already perhaps beginning to believe that American ways are better" (6). The Chinese in Mississippi appeared to Whites to be less hostile and more willing to assimilate than the Chinese in California.

A Politicized Economy

Central to this development of the Chinese community in Mississippi was the social and economic relationship which grew between the Chinese and blacks. Many among the southern elite attempted to replace black labor with Chinese coolies, so as to undermine the growing political power of freed blacks (7). Loewen argues that Chinese immigration was encouraged in order to increase "white political power by displacing voting Negroes; for the Chinese. . . would not vote" (8). At the time, Powell Clayton, Reconstruction Governor of Arkansas, believed that

the underlying motive for this effort to bring in Chinese laborers was to punish the Negro [sic] for having abandoned the control of the old master, and to regulate the condition of his employment and the scale of wages to be paid him (9).

Both the Chinese in California, as well as the Chinese in Mississippi, played significant roles in the economic development of American capitalism. One distinct difference however was the fact that Chinese in the South were specifically brought in, as Loewen describes, to displace black labor. One must therefore examine the role that the Chinese played in industries which relied heavily upon black labor, to understand the ways in which the Chinese contributed to the southern economy.

The railroads and cotton and rice fields, for instance, depended upon an abundant supply of cheap labor (10). After the emancipation of black slaves, several southern plantation owners suggested that they find another source of labor. Reasons which favored the importation of Chinese workers, as well as those which objected to such a measure, were many in number. On the one hand, General William H. Chase in 1857 argued that renewing the African slave trade was preferable to introducing Chinese contract laborers and that "this was the only solution for the problem of the labor shortage" (11). However, southern industrialists favored the importation of Chinese, for they, in Cuba and Peru, were reported to be highly industrious and well-behaved. Moreover, using Chinese did not prove to be cheaper than using free black labor. Planters preferred black labor to any other kind, since they "worked harder, could be fired or disciplined with greater ease, and could be taken advantage of, financially, with little fear of retribution" (12). Ultimately, the high cost of transporting workers from China and economic competition with industries on the West Coast prevented large numbers of them from coming to the American South.

The Chinese who were brought to the South either from Cuba or China or who migrated from the West Coast found themselves in a unique social structure which placed them in-between the white and the black communities. At first, the Chinese were treated as if they were "colored." That is, "the call for Chinese as replacements for Negro sharecroppers meant that they would be defined as the equals in status of the race they were to displace" (13). However, the Chinese entered the grocery business, which enabled them to attain relative financial success. The black community's failure to have done this can be explained in several ways. Slavery destroyed the social skills and economic foundation that Blacks needed to establish their own businesses. Loewen also points out the stereotypes that pursued the black businessman. Wholesalers refused to give

---

At first, the Chinese were treated as if they were "colored."

---

him credit, while, at the same time, many blacks shopped at white stores as an attempt to improve their social status (14). More important, a friendly relationship developed between the Chinese and blacks, stemming from more than economic necessity. Not only did Chinese grocers do business in the black community, but they also lived there; and were thus "subject to the same discrimination and prejudice" that the blacks received from the whites (15). The Chinese grocer consequently acted friendlier toward the black customer than did the white grocer. For instance, most Chinese grocers "did not require the deferential courtesy forms customarily demanded by whites" (16). In this way, the Chinese grocers were able to monopolize a portion of the market in the black community to which the white community did not have access. Over time, most of the businesses in the Delta, if they were

not owned by whites, were controlled by the Chinese (17). Their ability to succeed in developing groceries gave the Chinese in Mississippi the opportunity to become socially and economically independent from the white community. The financial success of Chinese businesses placed the Chinese somewhere between "white and black": not quite white due to their racial differences, and yet more than black as a result of their economic status.

Wanting More

Occupying this position of "in-between" white and black was quite satisfying for the Chinese grocer, initially. "These ties were therefore not discouraged until they hindered the advancement of the group into white institutions" (18). The Chinese tried to send their children to white schools, and according to one woman, the white community would let the Chinese go to their school "'cause they don't know no better" (19). Since some of the Chinese families had white friends, the Chinese children were permitted to attend white schools until someone objected on legal grounds.

In 1909, the state Supreme Court of Mississippi decided that "it has been at all times the policy of lawmakers of Mississippi to preserve white schools for members of the Caucasian race alone" (20). The Chinese were technically categorized as a "colored race." Thus Chinese children were denied access to white schools. Disregarding any economic advantages that they may have had in their relationship with the black community, the Chinese, at this point, decided to completely reject their being labeled "colored." They were now more concerned with properly educating their children than with achieving economic success. Because blacks were seen as inferior, Chinese parents did not want their children to attend black schools, they did not want to be considered "colored," and they did not want to assimilate into black culture (21).

The U. S. Supreme Court case of *Rice vs. Gong Lum* is an example of this dilemma and the ambiguity that surrounded the "racial status" of the Chinese community. Mrs. Gong Lum, a resident of considerable standing in the white community of Rosedale, Mississippi, "got very angry with the Rosedale school Board because they kicked her children. . . out of the [white] school" (22). Her argument was that the Lum children were not members of the "colored" race, and that they had a right to receive a "proper" education. They therefore should be allowed to attend white schools. However the Mississippi Supreme Court maintained that white children must be segregated from all other races. Although this appeared to be in contradiction with the Fourteenth Amendment, Chinese children were refused access to white schools. Loewen contends that the white upper class in Mississippi had "no economic 'self-interest' at stake in keeping the Chinese down" (23). However, Cohn points out that the "condition" that was attached to the admission of Chinese children to white schools, reveals the underlying fear that the white community had with admitting Chinese children into white schools. Stating that the Chinese "themselves must see to it that no children of Chinese-Negro blood apply through their community" suggests that Whites were not so much worried about admitting Chinese children into white schools as they were in admitting black children (24). C. Vann Woodward, suggests that the South, or the southern way of life, only allowed the existence of two groups, white and black, no mulattos and certainly no Chinese. A person must be either white or black. The social and political system did not accommodate anyone "in-between." Thus, the incorporation of Chinese into the Mississippi Delta community fundamentally challenged the white community's views about race and white supremacy.

The Chinese in Mississippi tried to resolve this dilemma by turning "into Christian grocers and business people, and, after being for a time neither black nor white, found a new niche as a 'white.' There was no other category in southern experience in which they could be put" (25). However, the white community did not readily accept that transition. As Cohn

describes, whites feared that "if Chinese children were permitted to attend the public schools these Chinese-Negro halfbreeds would go along" (26). The white community in this case was well aware of the fact that they could not make any decision which would eventually lead to the acceptance and integration of blacks into their community. "'Aren't Chinese colored,' they asked. 'If we let them in, won't Negroes want to integrate?'" (27). The question therefore was not whether Chinese children should be allowed to attend white schools, but rather how could they prevent Chinese-African children and possibly black children from attending white schools along with the Chinese.

In reality, the percentage of Chinese men who lived with or married black women amounted to "perhaps twenty percent at its peak" (28). The number of Chinese-African children produced was also relatively few in number. Yet realizing that whites firmly held to a stereotypical view of their community, Chinese leaders determined that, regardless of their individual practices, the white community considered the Chinese people to be a monolithic group. Thus, changing the image of the Chinese community in this respect was crucial. Their acceptance in white society hinged upon the behavior of those among them who lived with Africans. In order to do this, the Chinese community needed to reject their relationship with blacks on a social level. As soon as they could prove to the "satisfaction of the white community that the children whom they present for admittance to the white schools are racially pure Chinese," then whites would be more willing to reevaluate their racial status and place in their community (29).

Making a Choice

To accomplish this task of assimilating with whites, the Chinese attempted to eliminate all Chinese-African relationships within their community. By influencing Chinese males to end African relationships and to abandon their Chinese-African kin, or by forcing those families to leave the community, they set out to "eradi-

cate the Chinese-Negro minority" (30). The Chinese were "insisting that their men shall refrain from having Negro mistresses, and no half-breed children" (31). Interracial marriages between Chinese and blacks were intensely criticized and severely discouraged by the Chinese community as a whole (32). This desire to assimilate forced the Chinese community to avoid any social interaction with the black community.

As a result, the image of the Chinese American community in Mississippi slowly changed and by the 1940s, as Americans started seeing the Chinese as wartime allies, Chinese American children started attending white schools legally. In fact, in 1945, school board president Henry Starling stated that "children of native Chinese strain are pupils of high scholastic and character standards" (33). Contrary to their aforementioned similarities with blacks, the Chinese were no longer seen as a racial threat. Interestingly enough, this new stereotype became an underlying reason for the continued oppression of blacks. The refusal on the part of the white community to allow blacks into the social system was rationalized by their acceptance of the Chinese and their alleged extraordinary abilities. In this way, whites were reassured that "their oppression of Negroes was called forth by that race's particular and peculiar lack of capacity" (34).

In Between and Invisible

Throughout history, the legal status of Chinese in Mississippi changed often. Southern society had no place for the Chinese. "Considered neither white nor black. . . the segregation system attempted to deal with them as exceptions" (35). This dilemma played a vital role in the formation of an ethnic identity in the Chinese community in Mississippi. In the end, it failed, and they had to choose. To be in between was to be invisible.

The choice that the Chinese in Mississippi made nearly sixty years ago to be white rather than black has had profound implications for our society today. Are we two nations as the Kerner Report claims? Are we either white or black? In the end, the Chinese in Mississippi found that it was to their benefit to reject the black community to be accepted however marginally by the white community. The choice has had a price. ❑

Endnotes

1. Sam Sue, interview by Joann Faung Jean Lee, in *Oral Histories of First to Fourth Generation Americans from China, the Philippines, Japan, India, the Pacific Islands, Vietnam and Cambodia* (New York: New York Press, 1991), 3.
2. James W. Loewen, *The Mississippi Chinese: Between Black and White* (London: Oxford University Press, 1971), 2.
3. Lucy M. Cohen, *Chinese in the Post-Civil War South* (Baton Rouge: Louisiana State University, 1984), 57.
4. Shih-shan Henry Tsai, *The Chinese Experience in America* (Indianapolis: Indiana University Press, 1986), 56.
5. Robert Seto Quan, *Lotus Among Magnolias: The Mississippi Chinese* (Jackson: University Press of Mississippi, 1982), x.
6. Loewen, *Mississippi Chinese*, 84.
7. Tsai, *The Chinese Experience*, 8.
8. Loewen, *Mississippi Chinese*, 23.
9. *Ibid.*
10. Quan, *Lotus Among Magnolias*, 5.
11. Cohen, *Chinese*, 26.
12. Loewen, *Mississippi Chinese*, 26.
13. Loewen, *Mississippi Chinese*, 24.
14. Loewen, *Mississippi Chinese*, 46.
15. Loewen, *Mississippi Chinese*, 64.
16. *Ibid.*
17. David L Cohn, *Where I was Born and Raised* (Notre Dame: University of Notre Dame Press, 1967), 189.
18. Loewen, *Mississippi Chinese*, 64.
19. Quan, *Lotus Among Magnolias*, 46.
20. Quan, *Lotus Among Magnolias*, 14.
21. Quan, *Lotus Among Magnolias*, 45.
22. Quan, *Lotus Among Magnolias*, 46.
23. Loewen, *Mississippi Chinese*, 98.
24. Cohen, *Chinese*, 235.
25. Jack Chen, *The Chinese of America* (San Francisco: Harper and Row, 1981), 131.
26. Cohen, *Chinese*, 156.
27. Loewen, *Mississippi Chinese*, 74.
28. *Ibid.*
29. Cohn, *Where I was Born and Raised*, 57.
30. Loewen, *Mississippi Chinese*, 76.
31. Cohn, *Where I was Born and Raised*, 157.
32. Loewen, *Mississippi Chinese*, 76.
33. Loewen, *Mississippi Chinese*, 98.
34. Loewen, *Mississippi Chinese*, 99.
35. Loewen, *Mississippi Chinese*, 2.

Teaching About Chicago's Filipino Americans

Statement of Purpose

Focusing on the Filipino American experience in Chicago during the first half of the twentieth century, this two- to three-day teaching unit is designed for inclusion in a basic United States history survey course. It can be used in its entirety in a longer unit discussing immigration and ethnic community formation, or it can be divided for incorporation in separate segments of the course emphasizing imperialism, schooling and work, race and interracial interaction, and/or the Second World War. Teachers may also ask students to compare and contrast the experiences of Filipino Americans in Chicago with those of ethnic and racial groups in different geographical settings during the same time period.

Introduction

This teaching unit examines the collective life experiences of the several thousand Filipinos who arrived in the Chicago area before 1935. Early twentieth-century immigration by Filipinos to the United States is typically viewed as the movement of un-skilled laborers from the Philippines to Hawai'i and the Pacific Coast states where they became an important ethnic segment in agriculture and cannery work. By contrast, Filipinos more typically came to the Chicago area as students, first as govern-ment scholarship (pensionado) or family-supported students, and later as self-supporting students who expected to combine attend-ing classes with employment. While some succeeded in attaining their educational goals and returned to the Philippines, other Filipinos remained to live and work in Chicago into the post-World War II years, long after their schooling had ceased. Emphasizing the significance of both national patterns and local context in historical development, this unit examines: (1) the reasons which encouraged Filipinos to leave the Philippines and come to Chicago; (2) the strategies which they employed in pursuing and modifying their original goals; (3) the opportunities and constraints which they encountered and the choices which they made as Second City residents; (4) the means by which they sought cohesion and self-definition as an ethnic community; and (5) the nature of their ethnic community experiences.

Objectives

To connect the United States imperial venture in the Philip-pines (and, by implication, in other overseas areas of American territorial acquisition) with the movement of colonials to the United States. To examine the impact of regional context on both the legal status and the social and economic experiences of the newcomers. To assess the relative force of individual agency, ethnic group solidarity, and majority group attitudes and actions in immigrant community building. To scrutinize the heterogene-ity within an ethnic group perceived as homogeneous by those not part of the group. To examine the extent to which United States citizenship by naturalization was available to immigrants from different parts of the world during the twentieth century. To de-velop student abilities in critical thinking and argument.

Historical Background

Although a few Filipinos came to what is now the United States during three centuries of Spanish rule (1571-1898), sub-stantial Filipino immigration began only after the United States acquired the Philippines following the Spanish-American War and its bloody aftermath, the Philippine-American War of 1900-1902, during which American military forces defeated Filipinos seeking independence. American colonial officials inaugurated an extensive program of road-building, disease-fighting, and school-construction in the Philippines. Young Filipinos who successfully made their way through the English-language edu-cational system during the opening years of the century hoped for employment in the professions, in teaching, and in the Philippine civil service. At its best, American imperialism offered these Filipinos inclusion in an emerging world of great promise in the Philippines. Many early students saw themselves as successors to Filipinos who had studied abroad in Europe during the last years of Spanish rule. Their great role model was Dr. Jose P. Rizal, a European-trained ophthalmologist, poet, novelist, and critic of colonialism executed by the Spanish in Manila in 1896. Rizal's achievements, almost unknown in the United States, had little in common with the American image of "uncivilized" and non-Christian Filipinos popularized at the St. Louis World's Fair of 1904 and in other "native village" exhibitions. Filipino students in the United States aimed at combating this negative image and promoting respect for their homeland and its people as a nation worthy of independence. The first students included several hundred Philippine government-sponsored pensionado students placed in carefully selected American high schools, colleges, and universities during the 1900s and 1910s. Their financial support assured, these students generally completed their degrees on schedule and returned home to achieve high rank as teachers, doctors, lawyers, and engineers, or in government service. Their success encouraged many others who, lacking family money or government scholarships, confidently expected to earn living expenses and tuition by working while going to school.

Much more than their countrymen who came to work on the West Coast and in Hawai'i, the Chicago Filipinos were a fairly diverse group who had already succeeded in equipping themselves with ten to twelve years of English-language instruction. Some had already left home in the Philippines years earlier for work or schooling in a provincial center or in Manila. The many, diverse institutions of higher education located in and near Chicago drew Filipinos to the nation's industrial heartland. By 1920, the United States census recorded 154 Filipinos in Chicago. These Filipinos possessed several years more schooling than the average Chicago immigrant of eastern and southern European origin, English language skills, and the educational dreams which they would pursue at Chicago's elite universities, Northwestern and the University of Chicago; at Midwest public universities—Wisconsin, Indiana, and Illinois; at nearby normal schools for teacher education; at liberal arts colleges run by religious denominations; and at Chicago's tuition-free Crane Junior College and other night engineering and accounting programs. During the 1920s, more than two thousand Filipino students moved back and forth from college to full-time work and from college to college. Patterns of chain migration brought brothers, cousins, and townmates, assuring a steady flow of newcomers. Unlike other Asians barred from entry into the United States during the first half of the century, Filipinos faced no restrictions in coming to the United States before 1935. Because the Philippines was a colony, Filipinos, although not eligible for citizenship, were classified as "nationals." In the mid-1930s, this changed, essentially cutting off Filipino immigration for a generation. The Tydings-McDuffie Act of 1934 promised the Philippines independence after ten years but limited Filipino immigration to a fifty-per-year quota during that period. After independence, Filipinos would join other Asians in being totally prohibited from entering the United States.

Over time, complex, varied reasons transformed sojourning Filipino foreign students into working-class immigrants. As chances for economic success decreased in the Philippines in the 1920s, the pull to return diminished. The struggle for day-to-day survival forced many to devote more effort to work than to school. After work, city night life called to some more loudly than books and assignments. Marriage to an American woman could hasten a shift out of school that had already begun. Many of Chicago's Filipinos entered a long transition, which led to abandoning one's studies, seeking a steady job, and becoming working-class settlers in Depression-era Chicago. After the Tydings-McDuffie Act, Filipinos in the United States could not go home, even for a visit, without losing their right to return—to their jobs and to the families which many had begun. By 1940, although only sixty Filipinas over the age of twenty lived in Chicago, 532 of 1,298 Filipino men over the age of twenty had married, ninety percent of these to non-Filipino women, generally the American-born daughters of European immigrant parents. Unlike Filipinos in California, Oregon, and Washington who were barred from marriage to white women by anti-miscegenation laws, Chicago's

Filipinos faced no such legal barrier, yet nonetheless encountered social disapproval of racially "mixed" marriages and discrimination in housing and recreation. Filipino men of this generation rarely achieved professional status in Chicago. A few worked in offices, as accountants, or made use of their almost-completed engineering training, but most remained busboys, waiters, cooks, and chauffeurs—low-ranking service workers with a high level of formal education, 12.2 years on average in 1940. Their most secure jobs were with the U. S. Post Office and with the Pullman Company as attendants on railway club and dining cars. Starting in 1925, Pullman hired Filipinos in an unsuccessful attempt to prevent African American porters from unionizing. A job with Pullman, whose Chicago Commissary Division at one time employed as many as 300 Filipinos, usually meant forsaking educational goals because of being on the road as long as seven days at a time. By the time of American entry into World War II, most Filipinos who had remained in Chicago had settled into available occupations and had traded in their dreams of social mobility in the Philippines for the modest comforts of family life and American consumer society—automobile ownership, picnics organized by Filipino clubs, and the annual celebration of Rizal Day which continues as a major event for Filipinos throughout the United States.

World War II altered life for Chicago's Filipinos. Simultaneous with the 7 December 1941 raid on Pearl Harbor, the Philippines had also come under attack and by mid-1942 was under Japanese rule. The war linked Filipinos and Americans in the patriotic cause—to defeat the enemy, to secure democracy, and to liberate the Philippines. Those Filipinos still young enough to enlist in the armed forces enthusiastically joined up, while others remained with Pullman, in essential wartime work. At the same time—as Japanese Americans along the West Coast endured incarceration—this joint pursuit of common goals diminished, but failed to eliminate, legal discrimination against Filipinos as well as other non-Japanese Asians. At war's end, the Philippines became independent on 4 July 1946, and the new nation's immigrant quota was raised symbolically from 50- to 100-per-year. China and India also received quotas of at least 100-per-year. And Filipinos in the United States, most of whom had come to the United States as young men and were now middle-aged, became eligible for naturalized citizenship, as did Asians from China and India.

Implementing the Lesson

Review United States acquisition of the Philippines in 1898. Discuss the establishment of an educational system in the Philippines modeled on that in existence in the United States during the opening years of the twentieth century. Distribute the handouts and the questions to the students to read and answer. Small groups might each be given two or three handouts and corresponding questions to work on separately with a recorder later reporting the group's findings to the whole class. Students might also be asked to discuss the meaning of ethnicity in immigrants' lives, the role played by race in the lives of non-white immigrants, and the process of becoming American. To extend the unit, students might be assigned written or oral reports comparing and contrasting Filipino American experiences in Chicago with those of ethnic and racial groups in other geographical locations in the United States during the first half of the century.

Bibliography

Alcantara, Ruben R. *Sakada: Filipino Adaptation in Hawaii.* Washington, D.C.: University Press of America, 1981.

Almirol, Edwin B. *Ethnic Identity and Social Negotiation: A Study of a Filipino Community in California.* New York: AMS Press, 1985.

Buaken, Manuel. *I Have Lived with the American People.* Caldwell, Idaho: Caxton Printers, 1948.

Bulosan, Carlos. *America Is in the Heart.* 1943; Seattle: University of Washington Press, 1973.

Chan, Sucheng. *Asian Americans: An Interpretive History.* Boston: Twayne Publishers, 1991.

Cordova, Fred. *Filipinos: Forgotten Asian Americans—A Pictorial Essay/ 1763- Circa-1963.* Dubuque, Iowa: Kendall/Hunt Publishing Company, 1983.

Crouchett, Lorraine Jacobs. *Filipinos in California: From the Days of the Galleons to the Present.* El Cerrito, Calif.: Downey Place Publishing House, 1982.

Daniels, Roger. *Coming to America: A History of Immigration and Ethnicity in American Life.* New York: Harper Collins, 1990.

Doeppers, Daniel F. *Manila, 1900-1941: Social Change in a Late Colonial Metropolis.* New Haven: Yale University, 1984.

Espina, Marina E. *Filipinos in Louisiana.* New Orleans: A. F. Laborde & Sons, 1988.

Espiritu, Yen Le. *Filipino American Lives.* Philadelphia: Temple University Press, 1995.

Friday, Chris. *Organizing Asian American Labor: The Pacific Coast Canned-Salmon Industry, 1870-1942.* Philadelphia: Temple University Press, 1994.

Guyotte, Roland L. and Barbara M. Posadas. "Celebrating Rizal Day: The Emergence of a Filipino Tradition in Twentieth-Century Chicago." In *Feasts and Celebrations in North American Ethnic Communities,* 111-127. Edited by Ramon A. Gutiérrez and Geneviève Fabre. Albuquerque: University of New Mexico Press, 1995.

Karnow, Stanley, *In Our Image: America's Empire in the Philippines.* New York: Ballantine Books, 1989.

Kitano, Harry H. L. and Roger Daniels. *Asian Americans: Emerging Minorities.* 2d ed. Englewood Cliffs, N.J.: Prentice Hall, 1995.

Mason, Sarah R. "The Filipinos." In *They Chose Minnesota: A Survey of the State's Ethnic Groups,* 546-59. Edited by June D. Holmquist. St. Paul: Minnesota Historical Society Press, 1981.

May, Glenn Anthony. *Social Engineering in the Philippines: The Aims, Execution, and Impact of American Colonial Policy, 1900-1913.* Westport, Conn.: Greenwood Press, 1980.

Melendy, H. Brett. *Asians in America: Filipinos, Koreans, and East Asians.* Boston: Twayne Publishers, 1977.

Pido, Antonio J. A. *The Pilipinos in America: Macro/Micro Dimensions of Immigration.* New York: Center for Migration Studies 1986.

Posadas, Barbara M. "At a Crossroad: Filipino American History and the Old-Timers' Generation." *Amerasia Journal* 13 (1986-7): 85-97.

———. "Crossed Boundaries in Interracial Chicago: Pilipino American Families since 1925." *Amerasia Journal* 8 (Fall/Winter 1981): 31-52. Reprinted in *Unequal Sisters: A Multi-Cultural Reader in U.S. Women's History,* 316-29. Edited by Ellen Carol DuBois and Vicki L. Ruiz. 2d ed. New York: Routledge, 1994.

———. "The Hierarchy of Color and Psychological Adjustment in an Industrial Environment: Filipinos, the Pullman Company, and the Brotherhood of Sleeping Car Porters." *Labor History* 23 (Summer 1982): 349-73.

———. "Ethnic Life and Labor in Chicago's Pre-World War II Filipino Community." In *Labor Divided: Race and Ethnicity in United States Labor Struggles, 1840-1970,* 63-80. Edited by Robert Asher and Charles Stephenson. Albany: SUNY Press, 1988.

———. "Mestiza Girlhood: Interracial Families in Chicago's Filipino American Community Since 1930." In *Making Waves: Writings By and About Asian American Women,* 273-82. Edited by Asian Women United of California. Boston: Beacon Press, 1989.

———. and Roland L. Guyotte. "Aspiration and Reality: Occupational and Educational Choice among Filipino Migrants to Chicago, 1900-1935." *Illinois Historical Journal* 85 (Summer 1992): 89-104.

———. "Unintentional Immigrants: Chicago's Filipino Foreign Students Become Settlers, 1900-1941." *Journal of American Ethnic History* 9 (Spring 1990): 26-48.

Reimers, David M. *Still the Golden Door: The Third World Comes to America.* New York: Columbia University Press, 1985.

Sharma, Miriam. "Labor Migration and Class Formation Among the Filipinos in Hawaii, 1906-1946." In *Labor Immigration under Capitalism: Asian Workers in the United States Before World War II,* 579-615. Edited by Lucie Cheng and Edna Bonacich. Berkeley: University of California Press, 1984.

———. "The Philippines A Case of Migration to Hawaii, 1906-1946." In *Labor Immigration under Capitalism: Asian Workers in the United States Before World War II,* 337-358. Edited by Lucie Cheng and Edna Bonacich. Berkeley: University of California Press, 1984.

Stanley, Peter W. *A Nation in the Making: The Philippines and the United States, 1899-1921.* Cambridge: Harvard University Press, 1974.

Sutherland, William Alexander. *Not By Might: The Epic of the Philippines.* Las Cruces, N.M.: Southwest Publishing, 1953.

Takaki, Ronald. *Pau Hana: Plantation Life and Labor in Hawaii, 1835-1920.* Honolulu: University of Hawaii Press, 1983.

———. *Strangers from a Different Shore: A History of Asian Americans.* Boston: Little, Brown and Company, 1989.

Vallangca, Roberto B. *Pinoy: The First Wave (1898-1941).* San Francisco: Strawberry Hill Press, 1977.

Barbara M. Posadas is an associate professor of history and Director of the M.A. Opion in Historical Administration at Northern Illinois University, DeKalb, Illinois, and a member of the OAH Committee on the Status of Minority History and Minority Historians.

Handout 1
Filipinos in Chicago Associate to Meet Their Needs, 1913-1921

[Antonio A. Gonzalez, a Filipino student, discusses the founding and the activities of the Filipino Association of Chicago.]

In 1913 many events, significant in character because of their bearing on the Philippine independence question were taking place in Chicago. Of these, the most important was the intentional and malicious misrepresentation of our country and people in a local theatre by the enemies of our national aspirations. Exhibitions of the "head hunters" and other mountain people of the Philippines with lectures by a certain self-styled authority on Philippine conditions naturally gave the American audience the impression that those were the Filipinos for whom Ex-President Wilson has recommended complete independence. Their pride and their patriotism aroused twenty-three Filipino students in the city to band themselves together into an association which now bears the name given above, chiefly to effectively combat the injustice that was being done the Filipinos, and secondly to promote particularly their common interests and that of their country and people. In that same year the F.A.C. commemorated the death of our most revered patriot [Dr. Jose P. Rizal] at the Reynolds Theatre of the University of Chicago by a literary and musical program. Shortly afterward, the F.A.C. published 400 pamphlets entitled "The Truth About the Philippines," which were distributed to the audience where the aforementioned Filipino misrepresentation was taking place. . . . The F.A.C. grows with time, in membership, activities and importance. At present there are more than 150 members. It was incorporated under the laws of the State of Illinois in 1917, thus giving it a legal existence. . . . It has an effective social committee which sends out good speakers to speak in theatres, colleges, Y.M.C.A.'s and churches; it occasionally holds banquets, dances and receptions in honor of prominent Filipinos and many Americans are always present. [On] the last Rizal Day [December 30, 1920]. . . about 1,000 people listened to Ex-Governor Dunne of Illinois . . . upholding the Filipino plea for independence. . . . The F.A.C. has a relief fund that gives out loans to members who are in need of financial aid; an employment bureau to aid members seeking employment; and permanent committees that take charge of athletics, discussions and social activities. . . .

Source: Antonio A. Gonzalez, "The Filipino Association of Chicago, Inc.," *The Philippine Herald: Official Organ of the Filipino Students' Federation of America* 1 (May 1921): 3-4.

Handout 2
"The Nation's Builders of the Past and the Future," 1929

Filipino Student Bulletin 4 (January 1929)

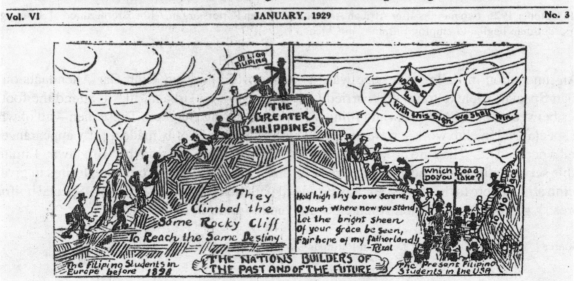

The YMCA's Filipino Student Christian Movement encourages Filipinos in American to keep their goals in sight.

Handout 3
Crane College, Filipino Club, Annual Spring Dance, Hotel Sherman, May 1930

Filipino students at a Chicago junior college hold a dance.

Handout 4
"Filipinos Make Their Debut in Pullman Cars," October 1925

[In October 1925, two months after African American Pullman Porters organize the Brotherhood of Sleeping Car Porters, Pullman begins to employ Filipinos in Chicago.]

An innovation in Pullman Service was the using of Filipinos as Club Car Attendants on the "Cuban Special," deluxe train, that carried Chicago crowds to Urbana, Ill., to attend the football games between Illinois-Nebraska and Illinois-Michigan during October. These men—all of whom have specialized in club work—were uniformed in white and not only made a natty appearance but scored a decided hit. They are now being used as Club Car Attendants on the "Broadway Limited," and this service will be extended to other regular lines, as the Pullman Company desires to give the real club atmosphere to these cars, already provided with luxurious conveniences. Special uniforms in forestry green will be seen on Attendants assigned to Club or other service.

Source: "Filipinos Make Their Debut in Pullman Cars," *Pullman News*, November 1925, 221.

Handout 5

A. Philip Randolph, President of the Brotherhood of Sleeping Car Porters, Addresses African American Pullman Company Porters in *The Messenger: The World's Greatest Negro Monthly*, 1925-26

[A. Philip Randolph criticizes the hiring of Filipinos by the Pullman Company.]

October-November 1925.

But suppose the Pullman Company should threaten to put Filipinos or white men in the Pullman cars as porters, because the Negroes organized to demand a living wage and manhood rights. The only manly and effective answer to that threat would be to tell them that if they want to put Filipinos or white men on the cars because Negro Pullman porters, like white men, are organizing to demand more pay, better hours and better working conditions, to put them on. It is better to maintain your manhood and get off the Pullman cars than to kow tow and lick the boots of the Pullman Company for a few crumbs which any other group of self-respecting men would reject. Negroes in the Pullman service had jobs before they went into the service and they can get jobs if they leave it.

March 1926.

The Company has attempted to break your spirit by putting some Filipinos on a few club cars in utter and flagrant violation of the seniority principle, by herding men from the South around the yards as a threat to the porters, by holding up your check, by framing you up as tho you were bootlegging, through spies who hound and pester you on your runs.

Source: *The Messenger: The World's Greatest Negro Monthly* (October-November 1925): 352, and (March 1926): 68.

Handout 6
"In the Mire of Chicago," 1932

Luis S. Quianio, "In the Mire in Chicago," *Graphic*, 22 June 1932

In a Philippine magazine article, reporter Luis S. Quianio bemoans the dangers ensnaring his countrymen in Chicago, 1932.

Handout 7
"Badge of Loyalty," 1942

"Filipinos on Pullman—No Japs," *Pullman News*, January 1942, 88

[The Pullman Company Issues a Badge of Loyalty to Its Filipino Employees in January 1942.]

TO ALL PULLMAN PASSENGERS: The neat, efficient attendant who waits upon you in club and lounge cars is not a Japanese, since there is none of that nationality in Pullman service. He is a Filipino, of undoubted, intense loyalty to Uncle Sam, . . . Although to most American eyes there is a distinct difference between the physiognomy of the Filipino and the Japanese, there are many who cannot see it. For their eyes the Pullman Filipino employees wear a button [as shown in the cut] as a matter of racial and national pride. Let no American patriot be in doubt when traveling Pullman, as in no case will there be a Japanese—even in simulated Filipino manners. The button—"U.S.A.-Philippines," and respective flags—will be seen under the badges of Pullman employees, whether on blue uniform coat or on white service jacket.

Handout 8
Male Occupation and Education, Chicago, 1940

OCCUPATION	Filipino%	White%	African American%
Professional/Semi-Professional	3.8	7.0	3.3
Farmer/Farm Manager	---	.1	.1
Proprietor/Manager	1.0	10.7	2.7
Clerical/Sales	11.5	22.3	10.1
Craftsman/Foreman	3.2	20.3	9.2
Operative	10.5	22.2	20.1
Domestic Service	4.6	.1	1.4
Service	59.1	8.8	32.8
Farmer Laborer	---	.1	.1
Non-farm Laborer	6.2	8.1	20.1
No Occupation Reported	.2	.5	.4
MEDIAN YEARS SCHOOLING	12.2	7.5 (foreign born) 9.4 (non-foreign born)	7.7

Source: U.S. Bureau of the Census, *1950 Census of Population: Characteristics of the Non-white Population by Race*, 111-2; *ibid.*, vol. 2, "Characteristics of the Population," 642; *ibid.*, vol. 3, "The Labor Force," 874-5, 898.

Questions

From Handout 1—The Filipino Association of Chicago

1. When and why, according to Antonio Gonzalez, did Chicago Filipinos organize the Filipino Association of Chicago?
2. Why did Filipinos believe that the 1913 exhibition of Filipino mountain people misled American audiences? How might this sort of entertainment affect the lives of Filipinos in Chicago? In the Philippines?
3. How many Filipinos belonged to the Association in 1913? In 1921? If you were a Filipino in Chicago during these years, would you have joined the Association? Why? Do you think that most Filipinos joined the F.A.C.?
4. Consider the programs and activities of the Filipino Association of Chicago which are mentioned in this handout. How are Filipinos working to assist each other? How are they working to promote a more positive impression of Filipinos among Chicagoans?

From Handout 2—"The Nation's Builder"

1. According to the illustrator, what goal have Filipino foreign students past and present shared?
2. Filipino students in America are asked, "Which Road Do You Take"? What are their choices, and what does each alternative mean for themselves and for their nation? What might cause them to go down the road labeled "To No Place" by the illustrator?

Handout 3—The Crane College Spring Dance

1. How many men posed in the picture taken at the May 1930 dance sponsored by the Crane College Filipino Club? How many women? Are the women white or Filipina? What do the numbers and the picture tell you about Filipino social life in Chicago?
2. Before the city of Chicago closed Crane Junior College during the Depression, Chicagoans had access to tuition-free higher education. After the school was closed, what factors would have made it difficult for Filipinos to continue their schooling? Is it difficult to go to school and work today?

Handout 4—Filipinos Make Their Pullman Debut

1. Why, according to the *Pullman News*, did the Pullman Company begin hiring Filipinos?
2. Describe the work that Filipinos were assigned. What qualifications did they bring to Pullman work? Are any of today's jobs comparable to Pullman employment? What skills are similar?

Handout 5—A. Philip Randolph Criticizes Pullman's Hiring of Filipinos

1. Why, according to A. Philip Randolph, did the Pullman Company begin hiring Filipinos? Compare this reason with the reason offered in Handout 4. How might race have been a factor in the hiring of Filipinos?
2. What other actions did Pullman take to discourage unionization among its African American porters? Why did companies oppose the unionization of their employees? Why did employees support or fail to support unionization? Then? Today?
3. Contrast the audiences being addressed in Handouts 4 and 5. Who read the *Pullman News* and the *Messenger*?

Handout 6—In the Mire

1. What forces are identified as pulling the Filipino down into the mud? What forces are pulling him up and out?
2. How does the "message" in Handout 6 compare with the "message" in Handout 2?

Handout 7—Badge of Loyalty

1. What event prompted the Pullman Company to issue a "badge of loyalty" to its Filipino workers? Why would Filipinos not want to be mistaken for Japanese?
2. How was the Philippines involved in World War II?

Handout 8—Male Occupation and Education in 1940

1. What were the three most important occupational categories for Filipinos in Chicago in 1940? For whites? For African Americans?
2. Which group had the highest median years of schooling? Which had the lowest? What gave Filipinos in Chicago an educational advantage?
3. What conclusions about occupation, schooling, and race can be drawn from this table?

Asian Americans in Hawai'i

Introduction

Almost everyone in the United States has powerful images of "Hawai'i." But few people know that the current governor's parents came from the Philippines; the lieutenant governor's from Japan; a state supreme court justice's from Korea; a leading businessman's from California. Most of the images are from Hollywood, travel ads, and other media sources or, for the more fortunate ones, the direct view from the tourists' perspective. But even among people who have visited Hawai'i, the images are too often misleading or false. The goal of this lesson is to help students develop the critical faculties needed to detect stereotyping and bias and to form independent and responsible judgments by studying Asian Americans in Hawai'i.

Objectives

To appreciate diversity. Hawai'i is a wonderful site for teaching about the diversity of peoples and cultures within the United States. While there are ethnic and racial problems as everywhere, people tend to "get along" rather better than in other places. How does this work? Do some groups benefit or suffer more as a result?

To detect bias and stereotyping. Hawai'i is also an ideal subject to demonstrate to students that much of what we see in the media or elsewhere is oversimplified and/or distorted. In this lesson, however, the fact that Hawai'i has been so hyped and glamorized makes it easier to see the distinction between stereotype and reality.

To show how Hawai'i can become part of a useful teaching strategy for students to learn about their own "local" region and culture. Moving from the outside-exotic to the inside-familiar will help students understand that the world is tied together in many ways. Wherever you are, the local, regional, and national media (TV, magazines, MTV, films, newspapers) will have a "shorthand" means of informing their clientele that your "place" is to be featured—in music, costume, landscape, etc. What is the message being transmitted about your "home"? And how can you influence that message to make it more authentic?

Methodologies

There are as many methodologies as there are skilled teachers. But we have some assistance here. In 1992 and 1995, the National Endowment for the Humanities, a federal agency, cooperated with the Historic Hawai'i Foundation and the Ethnic Studies Department of the University of Hawai'i at Manoa, to sponsor a summer workshop on Hawai'i's history for secondary teachers. Each partici pant was required to create several lesson plans and these ar available through ERIC and, in hard copy, from the Historic Hawai' Foundation. Most are very detailed because they are done for semester-long course and contain valuable information, perspec tives, and resources. The following format is for a much shorte period of study and would allow students to focus on Hawai'i fc several weeks while continuing to read their textbooks or othe assignments covering the broader range of your curriculum. In th meantime, various skills will be enhanced: reading for comprehen sion and with critical ability; collaborative group work; research planning and implementing projects; use of computers; use of loca resources; and designing finished products to persuade peers of "message."

1. Provide a deceptively "easy" and entertaining method of entr into the lesson. Form groups assigned to produce images c Hawai'i. Depending on technologies available, students migh use a bulletin board collage, slide show, videotape, or CD Rom Provide little assistance except to suggest families, magazine: travel agencies, video rentals, etc., for general access to image of people, places, and events. This phase is designed to show th dangers of swift, subjective, and shallow judgments. Have the begin the research for phase two so they may write or call fc more information but give them a minimum amount of time t complete this phase so that their completed projects reflec existing impressions of Hawai'i. Have the groups preser findings to the class and provide time for discussion of eac presentation.

2. After the initial presentations, at least some students wi recognize or can be prompted to recognize that these image may not be complete or sensitive. As a next assignment, forr groups to research and report on Hawai'i from the "insider perspectives. These might be occupational such as journalist or refuse workers or politicians or teachers (in Hawai'i, teacher are predominantly Japanese American females while universit professors are largely white males) or ethnic groups such as th indigenous Native Hawaiians, European Americans callec "haoles," or larger groups of people descended from Asians Filipinos, Japanese, Chinese, and/or Koreans. These ethni groups have books and documentaries recording their historie

Most communities have ethnic or racial groups associated, whether in reality or as images or both, with particular jobs or economic class. Hawai'i is no different. This phase of the lesson will require more time for in-depth research. Group presentations should be much more sophisticated than the first set, in terms of complexity of issues and diversity of the "real" Hawai'i.

. Finally, have them assess and report on your own community/ "local" issues using the insights gained from the previous assignments. This last section will do two things: first, reinforce the point that ethnic and other groups do have different cultures and histories but are dealing with similar issues like jobs, discrimination, traditional values, the environment, politics, international pressures, etc; and second, it will demonstrate that all communities are subject to oversimplification and stereotyping and that we can be trained to detect these problems.

Evaluation

Have students write, individually, a personal reflection of the activities and significance of the lesson. It may be useful to require daily journal, even if some entries are minimal, to assist in the final evaluation.

Resources

Consult, first, the ERIC entries for the NEH Summer Institute. The Wong Audiovisual Center in Sinclair Library at the University of Hawai'i at Manoa has an extensive list of films and videos dealing with Hawai'i and its groups. Individual faculty of the Ethnic Studies Department research and write about the various groups including Japanese, Chinese, Filipino, African American, European American, Native Hawaiian, and other Pacific Islander communities. The Hawaiian Studies Center focuses on Native Hawaiians. The Geography Department has references to maps of the region. The address for the University of Hawai'i at Manoa is: Honolulu, Hawai'i 96822. For general visitor information, contact a local travel agency or the Hawaii Visitors Bureau. Two general histories, outdated but still the best available, are Gavan Daws, *Shoal of Time*, and Lawrence Fuchs, *Hawaii Pono*. For literature, contact Bamboo Ridge Press, Box 1781, Honolulu, Hawai'i 96839. The address of the Historic Hawaii Foundation is Box 1658, Honolulu, Hawai'i 96806.

Asian Americans in Hawai'i: Are There Any?

This essay provides background information for anyone interested in learning or teaching about the experiences of Asian Americans in Hawai'i. The subtitle of this essay calls attention to the fact that, in Hawai'i, most people descended from Asian immigrants do not use the term "Asian American." Instead, many refer to their specific ethnic "nationality" backgrounds, such as "I am Korean" or "I am Chinese-Hawaiian." Or they use the term "local" to designate those who are descended from the Native or Asian immigrant working class to mark them off from the Caucasian elite (haole) who owned or managed the plantations of old. This is noticeable in situations ranging from everyday conversation to political discussions regarding public policy and to literary criticism of poetry, novels, and plays written in the islands.

At the same time that Hawai'i is interesting for its unique characteristics, it is important to all Asian Americans for several reasons. Since the 1850s and for over a century, more Asian Americans have lived there than in the rest of the United States. As a result, some of that history has set the pace for the rest of the nation. For example, Hawai'i is the only state that has never had a majority of whites. Is it one model for the future in many parts of the country? The total population is about one million people. The largest single group is Caucasian—about one-third of the total population. Japanese Americans make up another one-fourth. Native Hawaiians (overwhelmingly part-Hawaiian) are just under 20 percent while Filipinos are about 12 percent and Chinese about 5 percent of the total. There is a sizable military population, primarily white and African American although with important numbers of Latinos.

The Native population is descended from Polynesian voyagers who settled in Hawai'i in at least two separate major waves beginning almost two millennia ago. They developed a complex society sustaining a large population, variously estimated as between 300,000 to 800,000, before being "discovered" by the English explorer, James Cook, in 1778. Hawai'i thus became one of the numerous indigenous peoples to fall under European and, then, American, control. By the mid-nineteenth century, the Hawaiian leaders were largely under the influence of foreign elements and their numbers as well as ability to assert self-determination rapidly declined. Sugar production became the dominant economic activity between the mid-nineteenth and mid-twentieth centuries. The dramatic increase in need for cheap labor led to the importation of thousands from China, Japan, the Philippines, Korea, Puerto Rico, Portugal and a few other parts of Europe, and sections of the United States, creating a multi-ethnic working class that eventually had tremendous influence over Hawaii's future—hence the importance of the concept of "local."

Hawai'i logically becomes the site of debating the merits of a "melting pot society." Why do we want one? How would that happen? Is this a desirable goal? It is also the home of intermarriage, where more people marry outside of their ethnic group than with each other. How does this affect inter-racial relations? What happens to ethnic identity? Hawai'i helped give birth to the notion of Asian Americans as the myth of the "model minority"—a minority group once oppressed that succeeded in assimilating into mainstream America through its own efforts. Thus, there are a variety of larger issues confronting the United States that may be usefully engaged through the study of Asian Americans in Hawai'i. ❑

Franklin Odo is chair of the Ethnic Studies Department at the University of Hawai'i, Manoa. He is assistant to the provost for Asian Pacific American Research and Public Programming at the Smithsonian Institution and, in 1995-1996, visiting professor of history at Columbia University.

The 1944 Nisei Draft at Heart Mountain, Wyoming: Its Relationship to the Historical Representation of the World War II Japanese American Evacuation

Statement of Purpose

By examining a controversial aspect of the World War II eviction and detention experience of Americans of Japanese ancestry—the drafting of U.S. citizen Nisei from behind barbed wires at a federal internment facility in Wyoming administered by the War Relocation Authority—this brief unit of several-days duration is designed to introduce students to two controversial historiographical issues. The first one involves the changing representation of past reality. The second, and closely related, issue pertains to how historical truths and value judgments are reflective of a society's circumstances and power relations. Since the situation under examination occurred in 1944 during the Japanese American Evacuation—yet achieved renewed prominence within the movement for Japanese American redress between the late 1960s and the present—this unit may be taught profitably in conjunction with either World War II or recent U.S. history.

Introduction

The teaching unit offers a means of studying a major event in Asian American and U.S. history, the World War II Japanese American Evacuation, that not only invites an investigation into its causes, developments, and consequences, but also induces an appreciation for how the past as a whole is constructed, communicated, and used as a source of identity and empowerment. Too often, students are taught about the details of events like the Japanese American Evacuation without comparable classroom time devoted to placing them into a meaningful historical context and situating them within an appropriate historiographical frame of analysis. While discharging this dual burden, the teaching unit ideally should capitalize on the contested response to the draft at the Heart Mountain center—compliance and dissent—to prod student exploration of the problematic nature of such concepts as loyalty, patriotism, and heroism. In this connection, the roles played at Heart Mountain in 1944 by three "representative" Nisei (Frank Emi, Ben Kuroki, and James Omura) should be catechized.

Objectives

To examine the perception, widespread within the America public even after the passage of the Civil Rights Act of 1988 that the Japanese American Evacuation was justified on th grounds of wartime security, generally humane in its imple mentation, passively conformed to by Americans of Japanes ancestry, and limited in significance to the period of U.S participation in World War II;

to correlate Asian American historical experiences with U.S history;

to connect the Japanese American Evacuation to the pre- an post-World War II experience of Asian Americans, in gen eral, and Japanese Americans, in particular;

to introduce the phenomenon of intracultural variation and dem onstrate its significance in terms of a highly stereotype ethnic community in an acute crisis situation;

to sensitize students to a prominent historiographical questio (objectivity versus subjectivity), non-traditional forms o evidence (photographs and oral histories), and innovativ historical concepts (hegemony/counterhegemony oppres sion/resistance, history/memory); and

to assist students in appreciating that historical study, to be tru to the complexity of the past, must embrace such dualities a change and continuity, generalities and particularities, an consensus and conflict.

Historical Narrative

On 2 November 1944, in the Federal District Court i Cheyenne, Wyoming, Judge Eugene Rice sentenced the seve leaders of the Heart Mountain Fair Play Committee (FPC) to fou years at Leavenworth Federal Penitentiary in Kansas for conspir ing to violate the Selective Service Act and for counseling othe draft-age Nisei (U.S. citizens of Japanese ancestry) at the Hear Mountain Relocation Center to resist military induction. Th moving spirit among these convicted men was Frank Seishi Em a twenty-year-old Nisei grocer from Los Angeles, California, who was married and the father of two small children.

After a four-month internment at California's Pomona Assembly Center, the Emi family transferred to Heart Mountain in northwestern Wyoming in September 1942. One of ten detention camps in desolate western and southern areas administered by the War Relocation Center (WRA) for evicted West Coast Americans of Japanese ancestry during World War II, Heart Mountain reached its peak population of 10,767 by January 1943. The next month, Emi was obliged, like all adults in WRA camps, to fill out a "loyalty" questionnaire. Dismayed by its two most controversial questions—one of which asked: "Are you willing to serve in the armed forces of the United States wherever ordered?"—and by news that a segregated army unit of Nisei volunteers was being formed to showcase Japanese American loyalty, Emi responded that "under the present conditions I am unable to answer these questions." He then advised other confused Heart Mountain Nisei to answer likewise. In December, Emi heard an older camp Nisei well versed in the U.S. Constitution proclaim that the government had abridged Nisei rights without due process of law and, therefore, they should cease pursuing appeasement. Consequently, Emi and several other Nisei joined with this spokesman to create the Heart Mountain Fair Play Committee.

The FPC did not galvanize into a viable organization, however, until 20 January 1944. On that date Secretary of War Henry L. Stimson announced that the army, which in early 1942 declared American Japanese undraftable because of ancestry, had reinstated normal selective service for Nisei as a step toward their regaining full citizenship. By mid-February the FPC was holding regular meetings and by month's end had 275 dues-paying members. Frank Emi (whose domestic situation exempted him from being drafted) and the FPCers reacted to the resumption of the draft by noting, suspiciously, that Nisei were treated as citizens only when it was to the government's advantage. They maintained that if the government restored their full citizenship rights they would gladly comply with selective service requirements. Toward this end, the FPC first consulted an attorney about pursuing a test case challenging the application of selective service law to men interned behind barbed wire, and then petitioned President Franklin Roosevelt to clarify their citizenship status.

In March-April 1944 the FPC's influence peaked. Not only did the organization gain widespread support for its position, but sixty-four Heart Mountain Nisei refused their preinduction physicals. In early May a federal grand jury indicted all but one of these resisters. Tried as a group in Wyoming's largest mass trial, the sixty-three men were found guilty on June 26 and sentenced to three years in a federal penitentiary. A month later, Frank Emi and the other six FPC leaders were secretly indicted by the same grand jury. Although not waiving their right to a jury trial, like the resisters had, their plight (as indicated earlier) was virtually the same.

The day before the Wyoming court convicted the FPC steering committee, it acquitted yet another Nisei on trial for being a party to the alleged conspiracy, thirty-one year old journalist James Matsumoto

Omura. Born near Seattle, Washington, Omura served in the 1930s as English-language editor for a string of Japanese vernacular newspapers in Los Angeles and San Francisco. In this capacity, he earned the enmity of the Japanese American Citizens League (JACL) leadership, whom he assailed as frivolous, obsequious flag-wavers and castigated for presuming to speak for all Nisei in spite of their organization's comparatively scanty membership. The bad blood between the JACLers and Omura curdled when he launched the first Nisei magazine of politics and culture, Current Life, in October 1940. In featured editorials for his progressive monthly, Omura berated them regularly through the final published issue of January 1942. By then, owing to the Japanese attack on Pearl Harbor on 7 December 1941, the U.S. declared war on Japan, and this situation set the stage for a showdown between the JACL leadership and James Omura.

On 19 February 1942, President Roosevelt, capitulating to pressure by politicians, nativist groups, and influential media figures, signed Executive Order 9066—purportedly for "military necessity." This document, which authorized the secretary of war to establish military areas "from which any or all persons may be excluded as deemed necessary or desirable," was the instrument by which 120,000 Americans of Japanese ancestry, two-thirds of them U.S. citizens, were incarcerated for up to four years in concentration camps like Heart Mountain. Four days after its issuance, James Omura and Fumiko Okuma (the business manager of Current Life to whom Omura was secretly married) appeared in San Francisco at hearings sponsored by a House of Representatives select committee chaired by Congressman John Tolan of California to investigate "national defense migration." Earlier a parade of JACL leaders had informed the Tolan Committee that the government could count on their complete support should mass eviction and detention of their entire ethnic population be viewed as imperative for prosecuting the war. To this position, whereby loyalty was equated with the sacrifice of rights and accommodation to authority, Omura and Okuma flatly dissented. While the fiercely patriotic Omura agreed with JACLers that subversive actions within the Japanese American community should be reported to government officials, he denigrated their notion that mass evacuation was a necessary evil and disparaged their chauvinistic policy of "constructive cooperation." "I would like," intoned an indignant Omura, "to ask the committee: Has the Gestapo come to America? Have we not risen in righteous anger at Hitler's mistreatment of Jews? Then is it not incongruous that citizen Americans of Japanese descent should be mistreated and persecuted?"

On 27 March 1942, the army issued a proclamation declaring that in two days the free movement of Japanese Americans out of the strategic defense areas of the West Coast would be frozen and their enforced movement into assembly centers begun. Omura, who had determined not to linger in San Francisco for internment, fled to the "free zone" of Denver, Colorado, where his wife had already rented space to house Current Life. Unable to continue the magazine's publication, Omura started an employment placement bureau. In addition to assisting Denver's burgeoning war refugee population

(Colorado's Ralph Carr was the only Western governor to welcome Japanese Americans) find jobs free of charge, Omura filed several racially discriminatory cases through the War Manpower Commission that led to Nisei defense jobs. To pay his bills, Omura took gardening jobs, worked in a munitions factory, and wrote free-lance articles for Denver's several Japanese vernacular newspapers. On 28 January 1944, he accepted the position of English-language editor for one of them, the *Rocky Shimpo*.

Almost a year prior to editing the *Rocky Shimpo*, Omura had contested the JACL supported Nisei combat unit because it was segregated and, therefore, a symbol of racism. Omura's appointment to his new post closely followed Secretary of War Stimson's announcement about Nisei draft resumption, another policy that Omura knew the JACL had urged upon the government. When this measure caused the Heart Mountain Fair Play Committee to mushroom, Omura opened the *Rocky Shimpo*'s pages to that organization for news releases. Then, on 28 February 1944, Omura wrote his first editorial about draft reinstitution and the reaction to it by those detained in WRA camps. His concern at this point was not Heart Mountain, but the actions taken at the Granada, Colorado, and Minidoka, Idaho, centers. There draft resistance had been sporadic and punctuated with denunciations of democracy and avowals of expatriation to Japan. Whereas Omura believed that the government should restore a large share of the Nisei's rights before asking them to sacrifice their lives on the battlefield, he could not condone impulsive, reckless, and irresponsible draft resistance.

It soon became plain to Omura that the Fair Play Committee represented an organized draft resistance movement dedicated to the principle that citizen Japanese should do their duty as Americans, equally, but not before being treated equally by the U.S. government. Thereafter in his *Rocky Shimpo* editorials he supported the FPC, not as an organization but solely on the issue of restoration as a prelude to induction. That the *Heart Mountain Sentinel*, the camp newspaper, was staunchly pro-JACL (and, as such, censorious of the FPC for placing Japanese American loyalty and patriotism at risk) assuredly added fuel to Omura's fiery editorials. These gained members for the FPC and dramatically increased *Rocky Shimpo* sales in Heart Mountain and the other camps (where, opined Omura, "at least 90 percent of the people . . . are opposed to the JACL"). But Omura's hard-hitting editorials also caused the government to sever his connection with the paper in mid-April 1944 and then, two months later, prompted the Wyoming grand jury to indict him plus the seven FPC leaders.

At the Cheyenne trial involving Frank Emi and James Omura (who was acquitted under the First Amendment constitutional right of "freedom of the press") a third Nisei, Ben Kuroki, was in attendance as a potential government witness. Although not called to testify, Kuroki was interviewed by a *Wyoming Tribune* reporter at the trial's closing. In the resulting article he branded Emi and his cohorts as "fascists," blasted their activities as "a stab in the back," and bewailed that "they have torn down all [that] the rest of us [Nisei] have tried to do." Considering what Ben Kuroki had accomplished in the war, these words carried great weight.

Born and raised in Nebraska, the twenty-five year old Kuroki and his farming family had not been subject like most Japanese Americans to mass eviction and detention. One of a handful of Nisei the Army Air Corps accepted for service, Kuroki overcame immense prejudice against him to become a gunner in thirty perilous bombing missions over Axis North Africa and Europe. Rotated back to the U.S. as the first bona fide Nisei war hero in early 1944, Sergeant Kuroki's canceled appearance on a hit radio show in southern California triggered a cause célèbre. Annoyed that this cruel slight had occurred because the network feared the highly decorated Kuroki's ancestry might offend West Coast residents, the elite Commonwealth Club invited him to address them in San Francisco on February 4. Much of Kuroki's talk covered his wartime experiences and how they had deepened his respect for democracy. But before concluding he alluded ruefully to the prejudice he had met in California upon his return from battle: "I don't know for sure that it is safe for me to walk the streets of my own country." Capstoning his oration, Kuroki echoed the JACL Creed—"Though some individuals may discriminate against me, I shall never become bitter or lose faith, for I know that such persons are not representative of the majority of the American people"—and reminded his listeners that Nisei soldiers were proving their loyalty to the United States on the bloody battlefield of Italy. When Kuroki sat down, the 600-plus audience gave him a ten-minute standing ovation.

The combat Nisei to whom Kuroki referred were in the 100th Infantry Battalion. Rooted in prewar Japanese American volunteers and draftees in Hawaii, the 100th was activated as a special battalion in mid-June 1942 upon being sent to the mainland for training. Not until late September of the next year, however, did the 100th see duty on the Italian front and suffer its first casualties. In January 1944, the battalion gained a glowing reputation for its stouthearted performance in the Battle of Cassino. This battle and others decimated the battalion's original 1,300 soldiers, and replacements and reinforcements were badly needed. Eventually these troops would be supplied by the all-Nisei 442nd Regimental Combat Team, which arrived in Europe in June 1942 and thereafter incorporated the battle-tested 100th as its 1st Battalion.

The 442nd, destined to become the most decorated unit for its size and length of service in American military history, was comprised initially of Hawaiian and mainland Nisei who had volunteered for service when the government announced its formation on 1 February 1943. The expectation was that Hawaiian Nisei volunteers would number 1,500 and their mainland counterparts twice that figure. Almost the reverse occurred. In Hawaii, where there was no mass wartime eviction of Japanese Americans, more than 2,600 were inducted (out of the nearly 10,000 who volunteered); on the mainland, only around 800 volunteers were inducted (from the total volunteer pool of approximately 1,250 Nisei in the WRA camps).

That so few of the eligible 23,600 draft-age Nisei in the camps had volunteered—at Heart Mountain out of 2,300 eligible men a mere 38 were volunteers—was of dire concern to the War Department, the WRA, and the JACL. Therefore, when the Nisei draft resumed in January 1944, they hoped that those eligible would readily comply with selective service regulations and, if necessary, fight and even die for their country. In April of that year, while FPC draft resistance was still intense at Heart Mountain, the army encouraged by the WRA and the JACL decided to send Kuroki on a morale building tour of three WRA camps, beginning with turbulent Heart Mountain.

The partisan *Heart Mountain Sentinel* paved the way for Kuroki's visit. In its April 8 issue it printed two letters from "outsiders" side by side: the first was from a Caucasian member of Kuroki's bomber team saluting him as a person who had "proved himself as loyal an American as any man who had ever crossed the ocean"; the second letter was from Nisei George Nomura attacking the FPC for its "diabolical plan to evade their undeniable obligation to serve this state [USA]." The front page of the *Sentinel's* April 22 issue juxtaposed its lead story about the war hero's imminent visit with a smaller item announcing James Omura's ouster as *Rocky Shimpo* editor; also on this page was a reprinted letter from seven Caucasian members of the Iowa National Guard acclaiming the valor and patriotism of Nisei soldiers from Heart Mountain with whom they had shared the fight against fascist forces in Italy.

Kuroki's week-long, end-of-April excursion to Heart Mountain was chronicled in printed accounts and photographs by the *Sentinel* in its April 29 and May 6 editions as being an unblemished triumph: "Kuroki 'Takes' Heart Mountain." But two private accounts of the Nisei sergeant's visit, even though deriving from a stridently pro-Kuroki and anti-FPC perspective, tell a rather different tale.

On May 1, Heart Mountain's director, Guy Robertson, informed WRA Director Dillon Myer by post that "Sergeant Kuroki was dined and danced and spoke before many different groups, including members of the so-called Fair Play Committee," yet felt compelled to add that on Kuroki's departure day, six more Nisei refused their preinduction examinations. The weekly reports by the camp's community analyst, Asael Hansen, are still more revealing. They indicate that the shy five feet, nine inch, 145-pound airman's reception at Heart Mountain was a decidedly mixed one. Whereas 3,000 camp residents greeted him, the crowd at a scheduled mid-week address was much smaller than anticipated and hardly anybody gathered for his sendoff. Then, too, while Kuroki's speeches were applauded and he was swarmed over by the camp's adoring children and teenagers, their Japanese alien parents were offended by his completely American ways and point of view on the war (such as his emphatic prediction that "we" will soon bomb Japan). His encounters with Nisei draft resisters, moreover, did not proceed smoothly. Four of them allegedly had a session with him punctuated by this exchange: "What would you do if you were us?" "I'd volunteer for induction." "So you think it is all right for us to be evacuated and locked up here." On another occasion, following a "quite heated" session between Kuroki and the FPC membership, "a few of the men expressed a strong desire to beat him up."

When Kuroki granted the aforementioned interview to the *Wyoming Tribune* in the wake of the November trial of the FPC leaders and James Omura, he told the reporter about the two sessions that Asael Hansen had documented a half year earlier. On the first occasion the resisters had rationalized their not showing for their draft physicals by quoting laws and the Constitution, though he could tell that "they didn't really understand what they were talking about but had been influenced by others." Convinced that the FPC was the influencing agent, he met with that organization and registered his strong disapproval of their actions. However, they persisted along the same course, culminating in the trial of their "key leaders" that had brought him to Cheyenne as a government witness against them.

Before Heart Mountain's November 1945 closure, 85 men were imprisoned for draft law violations, while for all ten WRA camps the total was 315. Averaging twenty-five years in age, the resisters typically served two years in federal prisons before President Harry Truman issued them a blanket postwar pardon. As for the FPC leaders, their verdict and sentencing was overturned on appeal after eighteen months of imprisonment. Not all WRA camp draft resisters were given the same treatment, for it depended on what judge heard their case. For example, Judge Louis Goodman dismissed the indictments against seven Tule Lake, California, draft resisters. "It is shocking to the conscience," he declared, "that an American citizen be confined on the ground of disloyalty and then, while so under duress and restraint, be compelled to served in the armed forces or be prosecuted for not yielding to such compulsion."

In spite of substantial draft resistance, the great majority of eligible Nisei men in the WRA camps complied with their orders. Even at Heart Mountain, 700 men reported for their selective service physicals; of these, 385 were inducted, of whom eleven were killed and fifty-two wounded in battle. Totally some 13,500 Nisei men from the ten camps entered the U.S. Army. More than 75 percent of them—or put another way, more than 50 percent of all eligible Nisei males—saw army service in the 442nd Regimental Combat Team during its 225 days of heavy combat in Italy and France in 1944-45. This represented the highest percentage of eligible males of any racial or ethnic group assigned to a World War II combat unit, and this situation resulted in more than 700 deaths and 9,486 casualties. When President Truman received the 442nd on the White House lawn on 15 July 1946, he told them, "You fought not only the enemy but you fought prejudice—and you have won."

Ben Kuroki, whose fame was overshadowed by the collective exploits of the "Go For Broke" 442nd, nonetheless stayed in the limelight for several years after his sojourn at Heart Mountain. While there he had announced his intention to fight in Asia—and before long he did. In 1945, he overcame a War Department regulation to become the first and only Nisei to serve in active combat with the Army Air Force in the Pacific theater, participating as a turret gunner on a B-29 in twenty-eight bombing missions over Tokyo and other Japanese cities. When he returned to the United States in early 1946, he was booked into the palatial Waldorf Astoria Hotel and asked to take part with celebrated generals and political leaders in a *New York Herald Tribune* forum on the war, and his remarks were then published in the *Reader's Digest* ("The War Isn't Over at Home"). Kuroki also was the subject of a 1946 biography entitled *Boy From Nebraska*. After traveling around the country on a JACL-endorsed speaking tour, Kuroki married, attended college, and became, in his home state, the first Japanese American editor of a general newspaper. Later he won awards for journalistic excellence when editing a suburban Michigan newspaper before continuing (and ending) his career in southern California. Although not a public figure for most of the postwar years, Kuroki was the invited keynote speaker and honored guest at the December 6, 1991, opening of the Museum of Nebraska's exhibit on Nebraska and World War II. The very next day, the *New York Times*, in its lead editorial commemorating the fiftieth anniversary of Pearl Harbor, acclaimed Ben Kuroki as an "authentic hero" and linked his wartime accomplishments with those of the legendary 442nd.

For resisters like Frank Emi and their supporter James Omura there was no public applause, leastwise not until recently. The JACL's wartime position that the sole way for Nisei to prove their loyalty was through military service, coupled with the extraordinary postwar publicity given the 442nd and the concurrent image construction of Japanese Americans as a model minority, made these men anonymous in mainstream America and social outcasts among their coethnics. Insofar as draft resistance was heard of in the Japanese American community, it was in derogatory terms: "draft dodgers," "pro-Japan," "hot heads," "trouble-makers," and "traitors." Omura's situation was still worse. His "crime" of defending the FPC's position was compounded by his opposition to the JACL's leadership and public policy. Branded a pariah, he was harassed by members of his own community to the point where his employment opportunities dried up and his marriage ended in divorce. Remaining in Denver, he switched from journalism to landscape gardening, remarried, raised a family, and turned his back on other Japanese Americans and their concerns.

In the 1970s two University of Wyoming-based professional historians (Roger Daniels and Douglas Nelson) published books based strictly on written public records that dramatized the draft resistance movement at Heart Mountain and treated sympathetically the roles played by the FPC membership and Omura. But it was not until the next decade and the climax of the movement for Japanese American redress and reparations, according to Frank Emi, that their reputation as "demented ogres" was recast within (and even beyond) their community. After Congress established the Commission on Wartime Relocation and Internment of Civilians (CWRIC) in 1980, that body held hearings in six major U.S. cities during 1981-82 to investigate matters surrounding the wartime camps and to recommend appropriate remedies.

At these hearings, resisters told their stories. In New York, for example, FPC member Jack Tono testified first that the JACL had abandoned the resisters during the war and made their lives miserable thereafter, and then rebuked Ben Kuroki, "our great war hero," for having labeled Frank Emi and the other FPC leaders "fascists" at their 1944 trial.

At CWRIC's Seattle hearing, redress activists (most notably, the renowned Chinese American playwright Frank Chin), were surprised to discover James Omura (who they believed dead) not only in attendance but testifying and apparently anxious both to enter the redress fray and to refurbish his and the FPC's reputation. By the time CWRIC had issued its report, *Personal Justice Denied*, in early 1983, Chin and his Japanese American cohorts had begun exhuming the resisters' buried past by taping oral history interviews with them and by systematically researching pertinent documents both in their personal collections and at institutional archives. Moreover, this same group of activists were primarily responsible for the participation of Omura, Emi and numerous other resisters in academic symposia and community forums that spotlighted their wartime experiences.

Whereas CWRIC judged that the Japanese American evacuation was unjustified (caused not by military necessity, but by race prejudice, war hysteria, and a failure of political leadership, and recommended a formal apology by Congress to Japanese Americans along with $20,000 payments to each camp survivor) Chin and his widening band of allies were anxious to go beyond the commission's investigation and explore the machinations of the JACL leadership vis-a-vis Omura and the resisters. This task they began in earnest once President Ronald Reagan signed the Civil Rights Act of 1988, which enacted into law the CWRIC recommendations.

In the interval between 1988 and the present, the draft resisters and James Omura have secured their place in the sun in Japanese American and United States history. Although there continues to be opposition to this historical revisionism, particularly from "old guard" JACL leaders and reactionary patriots whether or not of Japanese ancestry, the trend is unmistakable. Before his death in 1994 James Omura had been deluged with community, national, and international honors, and proclaimed an American hero in the tradition of Thomas Paine, Henry David Thoreau, Martin Luther King, and Caesar Chavez. Additionally, Frank Emi (the sole surviving FPC leader) and the resisters from Heart Mountain and the other WRA camps have been memorialized for their wartime role through a profusion of academic and commercial publications, documentary films, and imaginary literature. Their act of civil disobedience, twenty years before the 1960s civil rights movement, is now recognized as a historic benchmark in the U.S. civil rights chronology. Instead of invidious distinctions being made, as before, between the wartime behavior of the members of the 442nd Regimental Combat Team and the Heart Mountain Fair Play Committee, they are now styled as being different yet complementary species of praiseworthy Americanism.

Implementing the Lesson

Prior to teaching this unit, have students read the section in their U.S. history survey textbook devoted to the Japanese American Evacuation. If at all possible, assign Roger Daniels's brief but comprehensive 1993 study, *Prisoners Without Trial: Japanese Americans in World War II*, as collateral reading. It would also be useful to show one or more relevant documentary films. Stephen Okazaki's *Years of Waiting*, which is set largely at the Heart Mountain camp, is particularly effective because it deals with the plight of an interned Caucasian woman artist married to a Nisei, and hence speaks to Asian American and non-Asian American students alike. Another good documentary film to use is Rae Tajiri's *History and Memory*, since it communicates how memory preserves the wartime experience of Japanese Americans and can be used to supplement and challenge the historical representation of it in mainstream cultural constructions. A third documentary, Robert Nakamura's *Something Strong Within*, is good to use because its footage on camp life at Heart Mountain includes Ben Kuroki's 1944 visit there. First, pass out to students copies of the above "Historical Narrative." Then, after they have read this narrative, divide the class into small groups and have them discuss it briefly in general terms. Next, distribute the six handouts to the students and have them review their contents. Finally, as a class, discuss the questions on each of the handouts in sequential order.

Bibliography

Anderson, Jeffrey W. "Military Heroism: An Occupational [Operational] Definition." *Armed Forces and Society* 12 (Summer 1986): 591-606.

Appleby, Joyce, Lynn Hunt, and Margaret Jacob. *Telling the Truth About History*. New York: W.W. Norton, 1994.

Bodnar, John. *Remaking America: Public Memory, Commemoration, and Patriotism in the Twentieth Century*. Princeton: Princeton University Press, 1992.

Chan, Sucheng. *Asian Americans: An Interpretive History*. Boston: Twayne Publishers, 1991.

Chin, Frank. "Come All Ye Asian American Writers of the Real and the Fake." In Jeffery Paul Chan et al, eds., *The Big Aiiieeeee! An Anthology of Chinese American and Japanese American Literature*. New York: Meridian, 1991.

Daniels, Roger. *Concentration Camps USA: Japanese Americans and World War II*. New York: Holt, Rinehart and Winston, 1971.

———. *Prisoners Without Trial: Japanese Americans in World War II*. New York: Hill and Wang, 1993.

———, Sandra C. Taylor, and Harry H. L. Kitano, eds. *Japanese Americans: From Relocation to Redress*. Salt Lake City: University of Utah Press, 1986.

Drinnon, Richard. *Keeper of Concentration Camps: Dillon S. Myer and American Racism*. Berkeley: University of California Press, 1987.

Ehrlich, Gretel. *Heart Mountain* [novel]. New York: Viking, 1988.

Espiritu, Yen Le. *Asian American Panethnicity: Bridging Institutions and Identities*. Philadelphia: Temple University Press, 1992.

Hansen, Arthur A. *Japanese American World War II Evacuation Oral History Project: Part IV: Resisters*. Munich: K.G. Saur, 1995.

———. "Oral History and the Japanese American Evacuation." *Journal of American History* 81 (September 1995): 625-39.

———. "A Riot of Voices: Racial and Ethnic Variables in Interactive Oral History Interviewing." In Eva M. McMahan and Kim Lacy Rogers, eds., *Interactive Oral History Interviewing*. Hillsdale, N.J.: Lawrence Erlbaum, 1994.

Hosokawa, Bill. *JACL in Quest of Justice: The History of the Japanese American Citizens League*. New York: William Morrow, 1982.

———. *Nisei: The Quiet Americans*. New York, William Morrow, 1969.

Ishigo, Estelle [Peck]. *Lone Heart Mountain*. Los Angeles: Hollywood Chapter of the Japanese American Citizens League, 1972.

Larson, T. A. *Wyoming's War Years, 1941-1945*. Laramie: University of Wyoming Press, 1954.

Lears, T. J. Jackson. "The Concept of Cultural Hegemony: Problems and Possibilities." *American Historical Review* 90 (June 1985): 567-93.

Lee, Joann Faung Jean. *Asian Americans: Oral Histories of First to Fourth Generation Americans from China, the Philippines, Japan, India, the Pacific Islands, Vietnam and Cambodia*. New York: The New Press, 1991.

Mackey, Mike. "Heart Mountain Relocation Center: Both Sides of the Fence." M.A. Thesis, University of Wyoming, 1994.

Martin, Ralph G. *Boy From Nebraska: The Story of Ben Kuroki*. New York: Harper & Brothers, 1946.

Nelson, Douglas W. *Heart Mountain: The History of An American Concentration Camp*. Madison: The State Historical Society of Wisconsin, 1976.

Niiya, Brian, ed. *Japanese American History: An A-to-Z Reference from 1868 to the Present*. New York: Facts on File, 1993.

Nomura, Gail, et al., eds. *Frontiers of Asian American Studies: Writing, Research, and Commentary*. Pullman: Washington State University Press, 1989.

Norkunas, Martha. *The Politics of Public Memory: Tourism, History, and Ethnicity in Monterey, California*. Albany: SUNY Press, 1993.

Novick, Peter. *That Noble Dream: The "Objectivity Question" and the American Historical Profession*. Cambridge: Cambridge University Press, 1988.

Okihiro, Gary Y. *Margins and Mainstream: Asians in American History and Culture*. Seattle: University of Washington Press, 1994.

Stanford, Michael. *A Companion to the Study of History*. Cambridge: Blackwell, 1994.

Takaki, Ronald T. *Strangers from a Different Shore: A History of Asian Americans*. Boston: Little, Brown, 1989.

Takezawa, Yasuko I. *Breaking the Silence: Redress and Japanese American Ethnicity*. Ithaca: Cornell University Press, 1995.

Taplin, Ian M. "Why We Need Heroes to be Heroic." *Journal of Popular Culture* 22 (Fall 1988): 133-42.

Tateishi, John. *And Justice For All: An Oral History of the Japanese American Detention Camps*. New York: Random House, 1984.

Thelen, David, ed. *Memory and American History*. Bloomington: Indiana University Press, 1990.

Weglyn, Michi [Nishiura]. *Years of Infamy: The Untold Story of America's Concentration Camps*. New York: William Morrow, 1976.

Wilson, Robert A. and Bill Hosokawa. *East to America: A History of the Japanese in the United States*. New York: William Morrow, 1980.

Arthur A. Hansen is professor of history and director of the Oral History Program and its Japanese American Project at California State University, Fullerton. A specialist on the World War II eviction and detention experience of Americans of Japanese ancestry, his most recent publication is "Oral History and the Japanese American Evacuation," Journal of American History *(September 1995).*

Handout 1
Chronology of the Heart Mountain Draft Controversy
in the Context of the Japanese American Evacuation Experience

September 1940 Congress approves the first-ever U.S. peacetime draft of personnel for the armed forces. Under the Selective Service Act every U.S. male citizen aged between 21 and 36 is required to register. The act prohibits racial discrimination in drafting recruits. Approximately 3,500 Nisei (native-born U.S. citizens of Japanese ancestry) are drafted within the first year of the act's operation. At the time of the act's passage, the census shows 126,947 Japanese in the U.S., of whom 79,642 (62.7%) are American citizens.

December 1941 On December 7, Japan attacks U.S. Navy base at Pearl Harbor, and the following day the U.S. declares war on Japan. On December 11, the Federal Bureau of Investigation (FBI), under authorization of a presidential warrant, detains 1,370 Issei (Japan-born U.S. residents) classified as "dangerous enemy aliens."

January 1942 On January 5, all Japanese American selective service registrants are placed in Class IV-C along with enemy aliens. Many Japanese Americans already in military service are discharged or put on "kitchen police" or other military tasks. The next day California Congressman Leland Ford urges the removal of all Japanese from the West Coast. On January 29 U.S. Attorney General Francis Biddle issues a series of orders establishing prohibited zones to be cleared of all enemy aliens.

February 1942 On February 13, the West Coast congressional delegation urges the removal of alien and citizen Japanese alike from the strategic areas of California, Oregon, and Washington, while the following day the Native Sons of the Golden West urge the evacuation of all Japanese, regardless of citizenship status. On February 16, FBI arrest and detention of Japanese aliens is reported to be 2,192. Three days later, President Franklin Roosevelt signs Executive Order 9066, which authorizes the secretary of war to establish military areas "from which any or all persons may be excluded as deemed necessary or desirable." On February 20, Secretary of War Henry L. Stimson appoints Lieutenant General John L. DeWitt as the military commander responsible for executing Executive Order 9066, and on the next day hearings by the House Select Committee Investigating National Defense Migration (Tolan Committee) begin on the West Coast to investigate problems of enemy aliens and others living along the Pacific shore.

March 1942 On March 18, President Roosevelt creates the War Relocation Authority (WRA). On March 21, the initial group of Japanese Americans "volunteers" arrive at the Manzanar Assembly Center in California, the first of sixteen such temporary detention centers. On March 27, the period of voluntary evacuation out of designated West Coast military exclusion areas ends. On March 30, the War Department discontinues induction of Nisei into armed services.

June 1942 On June 17, the War Department announces that it will no longer "accept for service with the armed forces Japanese or persons of Japanese extraction, regardless of citizenship status or other factors."

June 1942 On June 12, the Hawaiian Provisional Infantry Battalion is activated as the all-Nisei 100th Infantry Battalion.

July 1942 On August 12, the first 292 "volunteers" arrive at Heart Mountain Relocation Center.

November 1942 On November 3, army jurisdiction over evicted Japanese Americans ends and authority over them is transferred to the WRA.

January 1943 On January 28, the War Department restores privilege of volunteering for military service to Nisei.

February 1943 On February 1, the 442nd Regimental Combat Team (RCT) is activated. On February 3, the WRA begins administering a loyalty questionnaire to all inmates over seventeen. In early February, the Heart Mountain Congress of American Citizens is formed to challenge the Japanese American Citizen League (JACL) policy of cooperation with the camp administration.

August 1943 On August 21 the 100th Infantry Battalion leaves for active duty in Europe.

January 1944 On January 24, Nisei eligibility for the draft is restored. On January 26, the Heart Mountain Fair Play Committee (FPC) is formally organized.

March 1944 On March 1, 400 Heart Mountain Nisei attend an FPC-sponsored public rally, at which a resolution declaring that men drafted into military service should refuse to report for the physical examination or for induction is unanimously passed.

April 1944 On April 24, Nisei war hero Ben Kuroki is ordered by the War Department on a week-long visit to Heart Mountain during the draft resistance movement to build residents' morale. Thereafter he goes on similar visits to the Minidoka, Idaho, and Topaz, Utah, camps and meets with the same mixed reception as he had at Heart Mountain.

May 1944 On May 10, a federal grand jury indicts sixty-three Heart Mountain draft resisters.

June 1944 On June 26, the 442nd RCT, with the 100th Infantry Battalion as its new first battalion, goes into combat in European theater.

July 1944 On July 18, the earlier indicted sixty-three Heart Mountain Nisei are convicted of draft resistance in the Cheyenne, Wyoming, federal district court and sentenced to three years in federal penitentiary.

August 1944 Seven Heart Mountain FPC leaders and *Rocky Shimpo* editor James Omura are arrested for conspiring to assist draft violation.

November 1944 On November 1-2, Heart Mountain FPC leaders are found guilty and sentenced to federal imprisonment for "unlawful conspiracy to counsel, aid and abet violators of the draft," while journalist James Omura is found innocent of this charge.

December 1944 On December 18, the Supreme Court hands down its decisions in the Korematsu and Endo cases. In Korematsu Executive Order 9066 and the army's eviction of Japanese Americans are upheld, though Justice Frank Murphy dissents from the 6-3 ruling and condemns it as "a legalization of racism." The Endo decision finds that the government cannot detain "concededly loyal" persons against their will. Though this decision precipitates the closing of the camps it does not address the constitutionality of the mass removal and detention of Japanese Americans.

August 1945 On August 11, Japan surrenders to Allies, thus ending World War II.

December 1947 On December 24, Heart Mountain draft resisters (and those from all WRA camps) are pardoned by President Truman.

July 1980 On July 31, President Jimmy Carter establishes the Commission on Wartime Relocation and Evacuation of Civilians (CWRIC) to hold hearings for inquiring into the Japanese American Evacuation and recommending necessary remedies for it.

June 1983 On June 16, CWRIC issues a report, *Personal Justice Denied*, that recommends a formal governmental apology to interned Japanese Americans in World War II and individual payments to camp survivors of $20,000.

October 1987 On October 1, "A More Perfect Union: Japanese Americans and the United States Constitution" opens at the Smithsonian Institution's National Museum of American History. This exhibit examines the constitutional process through the internment experience.

August 1988 On August 10, President Ronald Reagan signs the Civil Rights Act of 1988, thereby enacting into law CWRIC's 1983 recommendations.

February 1995 On February 5, the JACL's Pacific Southwest District, after a heated and emotional debate, approves a resolution to apologize to the Japanese American draft resisters of World War II.

Handout #2: Map

PERMANENT DETENTION CAMPS - called Relocation Centers by the government; housing Internees from March, 1942, and all closed by November, 1945.

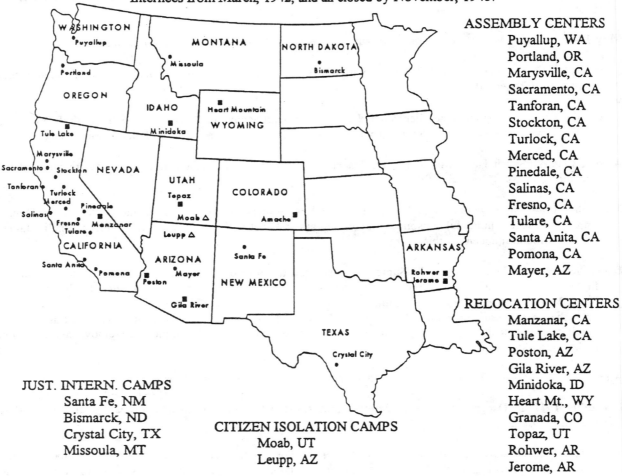

ASSEMBLY CENTERS
Puyallup, WA
Portland, OR
Marysville, CA
Sacramento, CA
Tanforan, CA
Stockton, CA
Turlock, CA
Merced, CA
Pinedale, CA
Salinas, CA
Fresno, CA
Tulare, CA
Santa Anita, CA
Pomona, CA
Mayer, AZ

RELOCATION CENTERS
Manzanar, CA
Tule Lake, CA
Poston, AZ
Gila River, AZ
Minidoka, ID
Heart Mt., WY
Granada, CO
Topaz, UT
Rohwer, AR
Jerome, AR

JUST. INTERN. CAMPS
Santa Fe, NM
Bismarck, ND
Crystal City, TX
Missoula, MT

CITIZEN ISOLATION CAMPS
Moab, UT
Leupp, AZ

ASSEMBLY CENTERS - temporary detention camps in operation from late March, 1942 to about middle of October, 1942, where Internee families were kept until relocated to more permanent detention camps called Relocation Centers.

JUSTICE DEPARTMENT INTERNMENT CAMPS - for non-citizens which included Kibei, Buddhist ministers, newspaper people and other community leaders.

CITIZEN ISOLATION CAMPS - War Relocation Authority Penal Colonies for United States citizens.

SOURCE: Frank and Joanne Iritani, *Ten Visits: Accounts of Visits to All the Japanese American Relocation Centers* (San Mateo, Calif.: Japanese American Curriculum Project, 1995), 3.

Handout 3
Photographs of Frank Emi, Ben Kuroki, and James Omura

"The Loyal Opposition," *San Jose Mercury News/West*, 31 January 1993

Frank Emi and family, taken at Heart Mountain Camp just before the conspiracy trial of the Fair Play Committee in October 1944.

Edward H. Spicer, et al., *Impounded People: Japanese Americans in the Relocation Centers* (U. of Arizona Press, 1969)

Ben Kuroki signing autographs for Nisei admirers at Heart Mountain while on his official visit there in late April 1944 during the camp's draft resistance movement.

Photo courtesy of Hannah Holmes

James Omura standing before a banner paying tribute to him and the Heart Mountain draft resisters held at the Centenary United Methodist Church in Los Angeles, California, on 21 February 1993.

Nikkei Heritage 5 (Fall 1993)

63 Heart Mountain draft resisters as pictured at their indictment in a U.S. district courtroom in Cheyenne, Wyoming, on 10 May 1944.

Handout 4
Comments by and about Frank Emi

"No matter how small a minority, it's not right to violate the Constitution to obtain a certain end. I think the Constitution should be inviolate. That's the only thing we have." Frank Emi, quoted in "Heart Mountain Relocation Camp-A 50 Year Remembrance," *Powell Tribune*, 13 October 1992 (Supplement). Quote appears on pages 3-4 of section of supplement titled "Draft Resisters."

"If Frank Emi and his cohorts of draft-resisters think their position is a popular one, they should talk to some of the Nisei veteran groups. Most of the Nisei vets who served during World War II don't think the draft-resisters should be immortalized or considered martyrs. What will they come up with next? A monument recognizing those who resisted the draft?" George Yoshinaga, "Horse's Mouth," *Rafu Shimpo*, 13 October 1992.

"We could either tuck our tails between our legs like dogs or stand up like free men, and fight for justice. Some of us chose the latter. We were going to resist." Frank Emi, quoted in Takeshi Nakayama, "Heart Mountain Resisters Hold Homecoming," *Rafu Shimpo*, 22 February 1993.

Handout 5
Comments by and about Ben Kuroki

"You have but one country. As a group you [Fair Play Committee draft resisters] are not doing your part as Americans, as Nisei, or for that matter as human beings, in view of the conscientious absolvement of your responsibility." Ben Kuroki, quoted in editorial ("Triumph Over Intolerance"), *Heart Mountain Sentinel*, 29 April 1944.

"I believe that, from what I hear from those who were there, he [Ben Kuroki] was well received in Heart Mountain Camp. Imagine, a parade, people waving the flag, Boy Scouts in uniform in a concentration camp. Could make a good TV drama which could show how a small group (JACL) with the help of the WRA can control a helpless minority. Also, can you imagine a person coming into a camp and be blind to the fact that these innocent people were incarcerated behind barbed-wire fences, watch towers with armed guards. He should have protested the treatment that his fellow Japanese Americans were forced to endure. All he thought was that he was such a great war hero that he became blind to the injustices dealt to a group of unfortunate people. I wonder what he went to fight for." Letter from Mits Koshiyama, former Heart Mountain Fair Play Committee draft resister, to Arthur A. Hansen, 28 October 1994. Housed in the archives of the Japanese American Project of the Oral History Program at California State University, Fullerton.

"My military experience was filled with variety. Shortly after I returned from Europe, Washington ordered me to visit three internment camps in Wyoming, Idaho, and Utah. My job was public relations. . . . I was shocked when I approached the entrance of the Wyoming camp. The armed guards were wearing the same uniform I was wearing. And inside, behind barbed wire, were 'my own people.' They were from three West Coast states, two-thirds of them American citizens and the remainder their alien parents or kin. They were uprooted overnight and denied their rights. Many lost everything in property they took years to accumulate. The Smithsonian Institution, which now has a huge exhibit on the internment, termed it the worst violation of civil rights in the 200 years of the U.S. Constitution." Ben Kuroki, *Nebraska State Historical Society Newsletter* 44 (January 1992), 3.

Handout 6
Comments by and about James Omura

"The removal of Jim Omura as editor of the English edition of the *Rocky Shimpo* was acclaimed, generally, as a very fine thing by Heart Mountain people. Most of them were disgusted with his editorials and apparently were very glad that he was terminated." Memorandum, dated 22 April 1944, from Guy Robertson, Heart Mountain Director, to Dillon Myer, War Relocation Authority National Director.

"By an odd twist, the Japanese American Citizens League, which had gone down the tube with its collaboration policy [during World War II], rose [in the postwar era] out of the shambles to a position of considerable power and influence unmatched in Asian American circles. . . . The League maintains its current prominence by control of the essential process of politics and the media. The major sources of communication are either owned by League officials or beholden to it. Others are easily intimidated by JACL advertisers whose withdrawal of ads means death to the small newspapers of our small minority. In such a deleterious climate, Nikkei news has become managed if not censored." James Omura, "Japanese American Journalism during World War ll," in Gail M. Nomura, et al, eds., *Frontiers of Asian American Studies: Writing, Research, and Commentary* (Pullman, Wash.: Washington State University Press, 1989), 75.

"A lot of you may not know Jimmie's name because he has been written out of history by those who have written our histories for us. I think it's important for us as journalists and writers to go back and discover what is true and what is fake. Know the difference. Go back and recover what has been lost." Frank Abe, as quoted in the *Hokubei Mainichi*, 12 April 1989. Comments derive from the introduction of James Omura by Abe, a reporter for KIRO News radio in Seattle, Washington, on the occasion of Omura being presented a Lifetime Achievement Award by the Asian American Journalists Association on 6 April 1989, in San Francisco, California.

Questions

From Handout 1-Chronology
1. What actions taken by the U.S. government prior to the restoration of the draft in late January 1944 might have led some Nisei to feel that their American citizenship was practically worthless?

2. Defenders of American democracy have argued that, while the system sometimes breaks down in times of crises, the damage is invariably repaired over time in a peaceable manner. Discuss this point in terms of the total chronology.

3. Based on the events covered by the chronology, do you agree with Justice Frank Murphy's dissenting opinion in the Korematsu case that the World War II eviction of Japanese Americans constituted "a legalization of racism"?

From Handout 2-Map
1. Students of history must pay careful attention to maps, for they as well as written narratives "tell a story." What story/ stories does this map tell?

2. Critics of the Japanese American Evacuation have charged that the U.S. government's World War II term "relocation centers" was more euphemistic than accurate and should be supplanted by the term "detention centers." Those opposed to this position have said that the wartime terminology used for these places is a historical fact and that, as such, must be retained to uphold historical accuracy. Analyze, being sure to examine the relationship between language and truth in historical inquiry.

3. The map indicates that some Kibei (U.S. born citizen Nisei who received their formative education in Japan) were among the "non-citizen" population interned in camps administered by the Justice Department. What relationship, if any, does this anomaly have to the Nisei draft issue?

From Handout 3-Photographs
1. It is often said that a photograph is worth a thousand words. What words come to mind when you scrutinize the photograph (within the text) of the sixty-three Heart Mountain draft resisters at their spring 1944 federal indictment?

2. Why do you suppose Frank Emi posed for such a formal family photograph on the occasion of his departure from Heart Mountain for his fall 1944 conspiracy trial with six other Fair Play Committee leaders plus James Omura?

3. The official War Relocation Authority photograph taken during Ben Kuroki's April 1944 tour of Heart Mountain is revealing both for what it shows and for what it omits. Analyze and discuss.

4. The 1993 photo of James Omura at a resisters' tribute was taken by Nisei Hannah Tomiko Holmes, who also made the banner pictured behind Omura. As a young girl she was removed by the government from the Berkeley [California] School for the Deaf and incarcerated at Manzanar in eastern California, even though that camp lacked special facilities for hearing-impaired children. In the 1980s, Holmes became very active in the movement for redress and reparations. Does knowledge of the photographer's background have any bearing on her photo's interpretation?

From Handout 4-Frank Emi

1. It has been observed that customarily in wartime the Constitution gets reduced to "a mere scrap of paper." Why do you suppose that Frank Emi, in light of his World War II experience, does not appear to agree with this cynical proposition?

2. George Yoshinaga's commentary raises many interesting questions. One of them is the relationship between popularity and morality. Another is the diversity of opinion found in all communities, including racial-ethnic ones. Still a third one is the role of monuments in depicting the past. What are some others?

3. Frank Emi's 1993 juxtaposition between "men" and "dogs" can be interpreted as follows: only draft resisters were "men" while all those Nisei at Heart Mountain and the other WRA camps who reported for induction were "dogs"? Does Emi's quoted passage lend itself to other interpretations? How do you suppose George Yoshinaga would react to Emi's statement?

From Handout 5-Ben Kuroki

1. A key aspect of historical education is impressing upon students the importance of context. How does "context" help explain the apparent contrast between the wartime and postwar statements by Ben Kuroki?

2. Increasingly historians have come to accept the notion that, while most historical facts can achieve broad agreement, the interpretation of these same facts depends upon the perspective of the interpreter, whether or not that individual is a professional historian? Put another way, history is seen as having both an objective and a subjective nature. How do Mits Koshiyama's comments about Ben Kuroki's 1944 visit to Heart Mountain apply to this point?

From Handout 6-James Omura

1. To be either a good historian or a good citizen, one must be able to detect bias and to make allowances for it when assessing past or present actions or utterances. Indicate the bias in each of the three statements relating to James Omura and explain what difference you feel it makes to "historical truth."

2. In his unpublished autobiography, James Omura complained that those historians who wrote about the World War II draft resistance at Heart Mountain and his role in it had not taken the time to talk to the people involved. Frank Abe was one person who has interviewed Omura and numerous resisters. What value is oral history to the search for the truth of past reality? How do Abe's comments relate to the role of oral history? And what does he mean, first, when he tells an audience of Asian American journalists that others have written "our histories for us," and then enjoins this group of writers to ferret out "what is true and what is fake" about the Asian American past?

3. Many contemporary historians employ the concept of "hegemony" (that is, that an elite can establish its power only if it exerts a cultural domination over other social classes) in their work. How does this concept apply to Omura's 1989 assessment of the JACL postwar power and influence in the Japanese American community, including the interpretation of its World War II history?

The New Migrants from Asia: Vietnamese in the United States

Statement of Purpose

This is a two-to three-day teaching unit for inclusion in an American history survey course. This brief unit may be included in several places in the course: during discussion of Asian and Pacific immigration history; during discussion of the Viet Nam War and the consequences of that war; and during a discussion of the changing demographics and the potential impacts on race and ethnic relations in the United States.

Introduction

This teaching unit offers an overview history of the Vietnamese American experience. Too often students are left with the impression that Viet Nam was simply the name of a war in which the United States fought, and not the fact that Viet Nam is the name of a real country and that there are more than one million Vietnamese living in the U.S. With additional curricular support, American history teachers can insert this account into their courses without altering the current course format. Teachers can address questions concerning the role of the United States during the Viet Nam War and consider some of the impacts of that war. Students can study American history and its relations with other areas of the world, and the connection between Vietnamese refugees and other Asian Pacific American groups.

Objectives

To examine the perception, common in the United States, that Viet Nam was only the name of a war;

to examine the differences between immigrants and refugees;

to present the arrival of the Vietnamese as new migrants;

to compare the development of the Vietnamese American community with other Asian Pacific American communities; and

to compare the development of the Vietnamese American community with other racial/ethnic minority communities.

Historical Background

The history of Vietnamese Americans began with the end of the Viet Nam War in 1975. On 28 January 1973, after having spent years and millions of dollars financing the Viet Nam War, the United States government reluctantly agreed to withdraw its financial and military assistance after signing the *Agreement on Ending the War and Restoring Peace in Viet Nam*. The peace agreement was signed by representatives of the United States, the Republic of Viet Nam (South Viet Nam), and the Democratic Republic of Viet Nam (North Viet Nam) in Paris. The agreement committed the United States and other signatories to respect the independence, sovereignty, unity, and territorial integrity of Viet Nam, called for prisoners of war to be exchanged, and declared an in-place cease fire.

Soon after the withdrawal of the United States military and economic support, the military situation deteriorated rapidly for the government of South Viet Nam. The flight of the Vietnamese refugees really began within the country, with the North Vietnamese military offensive of mid-March 1975 resulting in the defeats at Pleiku, Kontum, and Ban Me Thuot. As a result of this military offensive about one million refugees poured out of these areas and headed for Saigon and the coast. Most traveled by foot, few were fortunate enough to travel by car, truck, or motor bike. On 30 April 1975, the capital of South Viet Nam, and thus South Viet Nam, came under the control of the Provisional Revolutionary Government. This resulted in the flight of the Vietnamese refugees to the United States.

Before introducing students to the Vietnamese migration to the United States, be sure to include a discussion on the differences between a refugee and an immigrant. *Refugees* are typically people who are reluctant to uproot and resettle because of their social backgrounds and status; but they are forced to do so. Their flight usually results from being persecuted and/or physically harmed for past affiliation with certain political, social, religious, or military groups. *Immigrants*, however, have a choice. They make a "rational" decision based on relatively better economic opportunity, have to prepare for the journey, estimate the cost versus gain, make all the necessary arrangements, and only then, leave their country. Vietnamese refugees were not immigrants who chose to come to the U.S. for better political, social, and economic opportunities. Their migration was for the most part unplanned and out of desperation.

Vietnamese emigration is generally divided into two periods, each with several "waves." The first period began in April 1975 and continued through 1977. This period included the first three waves of Vietnamese refugees in the United States. The first wave of refugees, involving some ten to fifteen thousand people, began at least a week to ten days before the collapse of the government. The second wave, and probably the largest in numbers, involved some eighty thousand, who were evacuated by aircraft during the last days of April. The evacuation of American personnel, their dependents, and Vietnamese affiliated with them was achieved through giant helicopters under "Operation Frequent Wind."

These individuals were relatively well-educated, spoke some English, had some skills that were marketable, came from urban areas, and were westernized. Members of these two waves were primarily Vietnamese who worked for the U. S. government, American firms, or the Vietnamese government. All were thought to be prepared for life in the United States on the basis of their contact with the American government and association with Americans.

The final wave during this period involved forty to sixty thousand people who left on their own in small boats, ships, and commandeered aircraft during the first two weeks of May 1975. They were later transferred to Subic Bay, Philippines and Guam Island after having been picked up, in many cases, by U.S. Navy and cargo ships standing off the coast.

A second period of the Vietnamese refugee migration began in 1978. Since the fall of South Viet Nam in 1975, many Vietnamese have tried to escape the political oppression, the

Gail Paradise Kelly, *From Viet Nam to America* (Boulder, Colo.: Westview Press, 1977)

"Color Me Proud." Fort Indian Town Gap. *Fred Friedman*

A Vietnamese girl at a refugee camp.

major social, and political and economic reforms instituted by the authoritarian government of North Viet Nam. Although the influx continues steadily, the numbers are no longer as massive as they once were. A significant characteristic of this period, especially between the years 1978 to 1980, is the large number of ethnic Chinese migrating out of Viet Nam and Cambodia.

In addition to the ethnic Chinese, there were many Vietnamese who left during this period. These individuals have been called "boat people" because the majority of them escaped in homemade, poorly constructed boats and wooden vessels. Due to flimsy vessels, scant knowledge of navigational skills, limited amount of provisions, and numerous attacks by Thai sea pirates, the death rate of the "boat people" was and is very high. Many of the boat people are awaiting their fate in refugee camps throughout Southeast Asia. In addition, since 1979 many former receiving countries are turning away refugees because of the economic, political, and social strains that they are allegedly precipitating.

The United States Response

At the end of the war, the American public was hostile toward the Vietnamese refugees. A Gallup Poll taken in May 1975 showed that "54% of all Americans opposed . . . admitting Vietnamese refugees to live in the United States and only 36% were in favor with 12% undecided." The common concern of the American public stemmed from economic self-interest—fears of job losses as well as increased public welfare expenditures.

To minimize the social and economic impact of the large

influx of Vietnamese refugees on an American public unfavorable to the Viet Nam War, the United States government adapted the Refugee Dispersal Policy. This policy served four purposes: (a) to relocate the Vietnamese refugees as quickly as possible so that they could achieve financial independence; (b) to ease the impact of a large group of refugees on a given community which might otherwise increase the competition for jobs; (c) to make it easier logistically to find sponsors; and (d) to prevent the development of an ethnic ghetto. If this policy was carried out successfully, the Vietnamese refugees would theoretically assimilate into American society.

As a result, nine voluntary agencies (VOLAGS) were contracted by the government's Interagency Task Force to handle the resettlement of the refugees in the United States. The agencies included the United Hebrew Immigration and Assistance Service, the Lutheran Immigration and Refugee Service, the International Rescue Committee, Church World Service, the American Funds for Czechoslovak Refugees, the United States Catholic Conference, the Travelers Aid International Social Service, and the Council for Nationalities Service. Each refugee family was asked to choose a resettlement agency. If the refugee did not have a preference, an agency was assigned to the family.

The primary task of those agencies was to find sponsors possessing the ability to fulfill both financial and moral responsibilities and to match them with the refugees' families. In short, the sponsors were to introduce the Vietnamese refugees into society, simultaneously helping them to become economically self-supporting. Sponsors included congregations, parishes or affiliates, individual families, corporations, and companies with former Vietnamese employees.

This policy resulted in the relocation of Vietnamese throughout the United States. A few years after this dispersion, however, many Vietnamese began to participate in a secondary migration. That is, since their initial resettlement, many have migrated and relocated to a few states. The 1980 census data on the Vietnamese indicated that the most populated states were California—34.8 percent, Texas—11.3 percent, Louisiana—4.4 percent, Washington—3.7 percent, Virginia—3.9 percent, Pennsylvania—3.3 percent, and Florida—2.9 percent. The 1990 census data also reflect this pattern. The states in which the refugees concentrated their secondary migration are still those states most populated with Vietnamese. With 45.4 percent of the population, California is still the state most preferred by Vietnamese refugees. Texas is still second at 11.3 percent. Washington—4.8 percent and Virginia—3.3 percent have moved ahead of Louisiana—2.9 percent. Florida is still fifth with 2.65 percent while Pennsylvania is now sixth with 2.57 percent. These seven states together have almost 73 percent of the total number of Vietnamese refugees living in the United States. These cultures within these states provide social and psychological support, a warmer climate which is similar to their homeland, and job and economic opportunities.

As a result of the original resettlement, the secondary migra-

tion process, and the length of time since their first arrival in 1975, Vietnamese refugees have been able to establish communities throughout the United States, but are generally located in metropolitan and urban areas.

Since the Vietnamese were forced to leave their country as a result of the war, personal adjustments—such as becoming proficient in English, separating from families, and dealing with war memories—are pressing issues. Because many Vietnamese did not know English, learning a new and different language became an important criterion for adjusting to new living conditions in the United States. In addition, the Dispersal Policy forced many extended families to separate, and some Vietnamese have found themselves in new and unfamiliar communities without family or the community support networks which were of great importance in Viet Nam. Finally, because of the traumatic experiences incurred while leaving their homeland, many experience depression, anxiety, alienation, a sense of helplessness, and recurring war nightmares.

To assimilate into the United States economically as quickly as possible, many Vietnamese were forced to obtain low paying jobs. Even for those who were professionals in their country, their credentials failed to transfer—or simply were not accepted—in the United States. The large number of people who were members of the military had skills which were no longer marketable. And, because many did not have the necessary skills to find high paying jobs, both men and women have had to find employment.

It is easier for women to find employment, especially in the service and low-skill sectors, and women began to occupy positions traditionally held by men. That is, women have succeeded in achieving a degree of economic independence through their employment outside the home. In some cases, women support the entire family while the men receive technical or educational training for occupations with specific skills. Family conflicts between husbands and wives resulted as an unfortunate side effect. Since women were more likely to find jobs than men and in some instances became the only income earner, traditional family roles and authority were changing. Men were no longer the sole provider for the family and their authority was no longer as clear as it was in Viet Nam.

In general, it is easier for immigrant children to adapt to the U.S. After an initial period of confusion, alienation, and uncertainty, most Vietnamese children have resumed their education. In some cases, many have been successful and have continued on to higher education. There are a substantial number of Vietnamese Americans who are attending prestigious colleges and universities throughout America. Upon graduation, these individuals have also become members of the professional group or skilled workers in America.

However, while there has been some success in the field of education, Vietnamese Americans are not a "model minority." After the fall of Viet Nam in 1975, only a small group of children continued their education. Many younger Vietnamese Americans had problems adjusting to American school. Those who seemed to be having the most problems adjusting are those who came either as unaccompanied minors or the recent arrivals. These individuals primarily immigrated after 1975 and most likely came at an age when it was difficult to learn a new language and adjust to a new society; some have turned to gangs, drugs, gambling, and other illegal activities. The formation of youth gangs might have resulted from their inability to catch up with their peers in schools, their unfamiliarity with a strange land, and perhaps their alienation from their families due to cultural gaps.

For the elderly Vietnamese Americans, depression, isolation, loneliness, loss of family and homeland, and a feeling of helplessness are among the most prevalent problems. Because of their inability to speak English, many have experienced difficulties finding jobs commensurate with their skills. In addition, many are frustrated by their lost status and authority, their inability to speak with their children and grandchildren. For them, younger Vietnamese Americans have acculturated too quickly and seem to have discarded many of the values of their parents and homeland, instead substituting new American values. As a result, the traditional authority and status accorded to the elderly has all but disappeared. Finally, elderly Vietnamese Americans are disappointed at not being able to contribute to the welfare and well being of their families in the way they had done in Viet Nam. The traditional Vietnamese family structure has drastically changed for them.

There is evidence that things are stabilizing in many Vietnamese American communities. After a period of social, economic, and familial adjustment, the communities have turned their attention to interaction with the larger society. Those Vietnamese Americans who have spent most of their lives in the United States are coming of age and beginning to exert some of their influence. Because the older generation sacrificed to enable the younger generation to receive a good education and/or obtain the necessary skills for professional employment, many of the youth have returned to build their own communities. While building their ethnic communities, they are simultaneously participating in the larger society through their involvement in political, economic, and social processes.

Despite their recent arrival, Vietnamese Americans have contributed greatly to the American mosaic. Vietnamese communities located throughout the United States do not exist in isolation from the larger society but, rather, are positioned in a relationship with other communities. Furthermore, these communities serve as places for cultural preservation, providing Vietnamese and non-Vietnamese alike the chance to participate in a variety of cultural activities. These activities range from celebrating Tet, or the Lunar New Year, the Mid-Autumn Lantern Festival, new forms of Vietnamese American arts, and religious and cultural ceremonies. ❑

Bibliography

Baldwin, C. Beth. *Patterns of Adjustment: A Second Look at Indochinese Resettlement in Orange County.* Orange County Immigrant and Refugee Planning Center, 1984.

Caplan, Nathan, et al. *The Boat People and Achievement in America: Study of Life, Hard Work and Cultural Values.* Ann Arbor: University of Michigan Press, 1989.

Do, Hien Duc. "The New Outsiders: Vietnamese American in Higher Education." In *Privileging Positions: The Sites of Asian America Studies.* Edited by Gary Y. Okihiro, Scott K. Wong, Marilyn Alquizola, and Dorothy Fujita Rony. Pullman: Washington University Press, 1995.

Freeman, James A. *Hearts of Sorrow: Vietnamese American Lives.* Stanford: Stanford University Press, 1989.

Gliner, Bob and Hien Duc Do. 1994. *"Viet Nam: At the Crossroads."* Video, One Hour. Distributed by San Jose, California PBS/KTEH.

Grant, Bruce. *The Boat People—An "Age" Investigation.* Harmondsworth, England: Penguin Books, 1979.

Haskins, James. *The New Americans: Vietnamese Boat People.* New Jersey: Enslow Publishers, 1980.

Hayslip, Le Ly with Jay Wurts. *When Heaven and Earth Change Places: A Vietnamese Woman's Journey from War to Peace.* New York: Doubleday, 1989.

Hein, Jeremy. *From Vietnam, Laos and Cambodia: A Refugee Experience in the United States.* New York: Twayne Publisher 1995.

Huynh, Jade Ngoc Quang. *South Wind Changing.* Saint Paul: Graywolf Press, 1994.

Kibria, Nazli. *Family Tightrope: The Changing Lives of Vietnamese Americans.* Princeton: Princeton University Press, 1993.

Montero, Darrel. *Vietnamese Americans: Patterns of Resettlement and Socioeconomic Adaptation in the United States.* Boulder, Colorado: Westview Press, 1977.

Nguyen, Qui Duc. *Where the Ashes Are: The Odyssey of a Vietnamese Family.* Reading, Mass.: Addison-Wesley Publishing, 1994.

Rutledge, Paul James. *The Vietnamese Experience in America.* Bloomington: Indiana University Press, 1992.

Schaefer, Richard T. and Sandra L. Schaefer. "Reluctant Welcome: U Responses to South Vietnamese Refugees." *New Community* (1975): 366-70.

Starr, Paul D. "Troubled Waters: Vietnamese Fisherfolk on America Gulf Coast." *International Migration Review* 15 (1981): 226-38.

Strand, Paul J. and Woodrow Jones, Jr. *Indochinese Refugees in America Problems of Adaptation and Assimilation.* Durham: Duke University Press, 1985.

Time, 19 May 1975.

United States Bureau of the Census. Census of Population, 1980.

United States Bureau of the Census. Census of Population, 1990.

Wain, Barry. *The Refused: The Agony of the Indochina Refugees.* New York: Simon and Schuster, 1981.

Hien Duc Do is an assistant professor in the Social Science Department at San Jose State University. His research focuses on race and ethnic relations, and is currently writing a book on the Vietnamese American community in the U.S.

Viet Nam Chronology

1627 French influence begins in Viet Nam when Alexander De Rhodes, a missionary, adapts Vietnamese language to Roman alphabet.

1787 French military intervenes in Vietnamese political affairs.

1861 French military forces capture Viet Nam.

1863 French influence spreads to Cambodia.

1887 France creates Indochina, which includes Viet Nam, Laos, and Cambodia.

1940 Japanese troops occupy Indochina.

1945 World War II ends. France attempts to return to and occupy its former colonies in Indochina.

1954 The French were defeated by the Viet Minh, led by General Vo Nguyen Giap at Dien Bien Phu.

1954 Geneva Conference. Viet Nam was temporarily partitioned under the Geneva Accord. There was to be a national election held in 1956. The national election never took place. The U.S. helped evacuate one million northern Vietnamese Catholic refugees to the South.

1954 Ngo Dinh Diem becomes premier of the Republic of Viet Nam (South Viet Nam). Ho Chi Minh becomes the leader of North Viet Nam.

1963 A coup d'etat and the assassination of Ngo Dinh Diem and Ngo Dinh Nhu.

1964 The Gulf of Tonkin Incident. President Johnson asked Congress to pass the Gulf of Tonkin Resolution. The resolution passed and thus began the "formal" involvement of the U.S. in Viet Nam.

1965 Arrival of American combat troops in South Viet Nam.

1967 After a series of coup d'etat, Generals Nguyen Van Thieu and Nguyen Cao Ky became the president and vice president of South Viet Nam.

1968 The Tet Offensive. Vietnamese communists temporarily occupied South Viet Nam for a few hours, including the U.S. Embassy. Number of American soldiers reaches its peak.

1973 Paris Peace Agreement signed between North and South Viet Nam. This ended the U.S. military involvement in Viet Nam.

1975 Prime Minister Thieu resigned on April 21. North Viet Nam defeated South Viet Nam and captured the country on April 30. More than 100,000 Vietnamese flee their country as refugees.

1980 Passage of the Refugee Act of 1980. This Act defined refugee status and required the federal government to provide assistance to the refugees. Ethnic Chinese were forced to leave Viet Nam.

1987 Amerasian Homecoming Act allowed Vietnamese born of American fathers to emigrate to the U.S.

Vietnamese Population in the U.S. (1990) by State and Percentage

State	Population	Percentage	State	Population	Percentage
Alabama	2,274	0.37	Montana	159	0.03
Alaska	582	0.09	Nebraska	1,806	0.29
Arizona	5,239	0.85	Nevada	1,934	0.31
Arkansas	2,348	0.40	New Hamp.	553	0.09
California	280,223	45.36	New Jersey	7,300	0.12
Colorado	7,210	1.12	New Mexico	1,485	0.24
Connecticut	4,085	0.66	New York	15,555	2.52
Delaware	348	0.06	North Carol.	5,211	0.84
D.C.	747	0.12	North Dakota	281	0.05
Florida	16,346	2.65	Ohio	4,964	0.80
Georgia	7,801	1.26	Oklahoma	7,320	1.19
Hawaii	5,468	0.89	Oregon	9,088	1.47
Idaho	600	0.10	Pennsylvania	15,887	2.57
Illinois	10,309	1.67	Rhode Island	772	0.13
Indiana	2,467	0.40	South Carol.	1,752	0.28
Iowa	2,882	0.47	Tennessee	2,062	0.33
Kansas	6,577	1.07	Texas	69,634	11.27
Louisiana	17,598	2.85	Utah	2,797	.045
Maine	642	0.10	Vermont	236	.04
Maryland	8,862	1.44	Virginia	20,693	3.30
Massachusetts	15,449	2.50	Washington	29,697	4.81
Michigan	6,117	0.99	West Virginia	184	.03
Minnesota	9,387	1.52	Wisconsin	2,494	.40
Mississippi	3,815	0.62	Wyoming	124	.02
Missouri	4,380	0.71	TOTAL	617,747	100

Source: 1990 U.S. Bureau of the Census, *Census Population and Housing: Summary Tapefile 1C.* February 1992. CD90-1C.

Toward Understanding Korean and African American Relations

Introduction

This lesson plan is designed to help students understand the nature of Korean and African American relations in the United States. In the aftermath of the Los Angeles civil unrest (1992) and highly publicized boycotts against Korean American merchants by African American residents in New York (1990) and Los Angeles (1991), the apparent conflict between Korean and African Americans emerged as one of the most visible and explosive issues of urban America. To understand the nature of Korean and African American relations we must examine the economic, cultural, and ideological factors. Equally important, we must understand how Korean and African Americans perceive each other, and situate the role of race and class in Korean and African American relations.

Objectives

To explore the nature of relationships between Korean and African American communities;

to compare and contrast the experiences, concerns, and goals of Korean and African American communities;

to examine and challenge pervasive myths and misinformation about the socio-economic, cultural, and political experiences of Korean and African Americans; and

to examine prospects for coalition-building between Korean and African American communities.

Key Questions

What are the root causes of conflict between Korean and African Americans?

What are the myths and realities of Korean-African American relations?

How did the coverage in the media shape and influence the nature of Korean-African American relations?

How do we look at minority-minority conflict in relation to the declining number of whites, whose power remains dominant but is being transformed?

How can we develop trust and coalitions between Korean and African American communities?

Analysis
Economic, Socio-cultural, and Ideological Factors

Since the early 1980s, Korean-African American conflicts have surfaced in several cities in the United States. With the increase of Korean-owned businesses in African American neighborhoods, complaints, disputes, and boycotts against Korean American merchants have intensified during the 1980s and 1990s. The hostility toward Korean American merchants was fueled by several factors, including the shooting death of Latasha Harlins and subsequent probationary sentence imposed on Soon Ja Du; the over-representation of Korean-owned stores in African American and Latino neighborhoods; and the media perpetuation of images of Korean Americans as rude, greedy, selfish merchants who refuse to learn the English language (1).

The Korean-African American relationship involves immigrant-minority-merchants and native-minority-customers, unique conditions and circumstances that must be examined. In the context of economic despair, many African Americans have perceived Korean American merchants as "aliens" who have "taken over" their communities and are a threat to their economic survival. Some African Americans perceive Korean American merchants as newcomers in a long line of "outsiders" who have exploited African Americans.

Korea underwent rapid industrialization and westernization after World War II and especially during the 1970s. American values and ideals became a part of Korean culture and the national identity. Many Korean immigrants, in this sense, have been exposed to American culture and society even before landing on these shores. In the course of this presocialization, however, some Korean immigrants have been exposed to negative images of African Americans as criminals, welfare recipients, alcoholics, drug addicts, and/or lazy individuals. Additionally, having been exposed to American values, many Korean immigrants believe in the notion of America's meritocracy: one should be able to rise as high as one's talents and abilities permit. This meritocratic ideology is consistent with Confucian values that one's social ranking is determined by one's educational background. Because of the relatively lower educational attainment of African Americans compared with their own high educational background, many Korean immigrants tend to look down on African Americans (2).

Historically, non-African American merchants have dominated the economy of African American communities. The "middleman minority" theory (Blalock, 1967; Bonacich, 1973; Bonacich and Jung 1982; Loewen, 1971) suggests that "because of their economic niche, immigrant groups (i.e., Koreans) are likely to experience friction with at least three important segments of the population: clientele, competitors, and labor unions." Hostility between the middlemen and the customers whom they serve emerges from day-to-day customer/merchant interactions. The middleman minority theory predicts that Korean merchants cannot avoid friction with African American residents because of the built-in conflictual relationship with their African American customers. It is easy to see how the problems can be exacerbated when the sellers are "immigrant" and the buyers are "poor."

The middleman minority thesis provides a very pessimistic future for Korean-African American relations. The theory suggests that Korean immigrants must get out of African American areas, leave the occupation of shopkeeper altogether, or work with the African American community to achieve reconciliation. The economic factor in the merchant-client relationship is, no doubt, one of the main sources of the conflict between Korean and African Americans. However, it does not appear to be the sole, or even the most important, factor.

Cultural misunderstanding between the two groups plays an important role in fueling and sometimes escalating the confrontations. African American customers often complain that Korean merchants treat them disrespectfully, and say the merchants can't communicate with them. "Monocultural people (i.e., Koreans) doing business in a multi-cultural society is potentially problematic. Korean immigrant merchants don't know how to interact with customers," declared Larry Aubry of the Los Angeles County Human Relations Commission. According to Stewart (1993), Koreans and African Americans have different sets of rules concerning proper attitudes and behaviors in the business setting. If the rules are violated, a negative reaction should be expected.

Korean merchants most frequently mentioned loudness, bad language, and shoplifting as inappropriate behaviors by black patrons, stating that African Americans should show respect and courtesy, and should apologize more frequently. African American patrons commonly believed that Korean merchant/employee held negative attitudes toward them, ignoring and watching them constantly, as well as throwing change on the counter instead of placing it in the customer's hand.

Confrontations also derive from the clash of ideology between the two groups. Korean and African Americans seem to have different perceptions about America. For example, becoming an independent entrepreneur represents "success" to many African American residents of the inner city while it is nothing more than an avenue for "making a living" to many Korean immigrants. Because the majority of Korean immigrants came after the Civil Rights movement of the 1960s, they are not cognizant of the long history of racial discrimination and the African American struggle for equality and freedom.

Unaware of the history of oppression and exploitation of minority groups by white America, Korean immigrants believe that America is a "land of opportunities." Korean immigrants often show no respect toward African American customers who are frequently unemployed and dependent upon government programs. African Americans often perceive Korean Americans as a "model minority" who are succeeding and assimilating into American society.

The term "model minority" suggests that minorities (i.e., African Americans and Latinos) should follow the footsteps of Asian Americans who are "making it" on their own without government assistance. High educational attainment levels, over-representation in small businesses, and high family incomes among Korean Americans are compared with other minority groups and are presented as evidence of Korean American success and status as America's model minority.

That notion poses a major challenge to the formation of interethnic coalitions. African Americans may raise the question, "Why should we forge coalitions with Korean Americans, who are more successful than even whites?" In other words, it pits Asian (Korean) Americans against African Americans and Latinos. In summary, confrontations derive from the different historical, economic, and ideological experiences of groups.

Before the 1992 Los Angeles civil unrest, Korean and African Americans tried to improve relations. The murder of four Korean American merchants in April 1986 in South Central Los Angeles facilitated the formation of the Black-Korean Alliance (BKA). Despite the efforts of the BKA and area churches, the situation deteriorated as was evidenced on the 1992 Los Angeles civil unrest. However, it is important to acknowledge that the BKA tried to institutionalize cross-cultural coalition-building.

Implementing the Lesson

Pass out the handouts to students, and have the students respond to the questions. They may work in small groups or individually. For homework, students might look up one or more of the topics or events covered here and report later to the class.

Endotes

1. Edward Taehan Chang and Angela E. Oh, "Korean American Dilemma: Violence, Vengeance, Vision," in *One Nation, Divisible, Multiculturalism and Radical Democracy*, edited by Dean Harris (Greenwood, 1995).
2. Research shows that Koreans have one of the highest educational attainment levels in the United States. For example, 69 percent of Korean household heads in southern California possessed college degrees. See Eui-Young Yu, *Korean Community Profile: Life and Consumer Patterns* (Los Angeles: Korea Times, 1990), 7-9.

Bibliography

Blalock, H. M. *Toward a Theory of Minority Group Relations*. New York: John Wiley 1967.

Bonacich, E. "A Theory of Middleman Minorities." *American Sociological Review* 37 (1973): 547-59.

——— and T. H. Jung. "A Portrait of Small Business in Los Angeles: 1977." In *Koreans in Los Angeles: Prospects and Promises*. Edited by Yu, Phillips Yang. Los Angeles: Koryo Research Institute, California State University Los Angeles, 1982, 75-98.

Chang, E. T. "America's First Multiethnic Riots." In *The State of Asian America. Activism and Resistance in the 1990s*. Edited by Karin Aguilar-San Juan Boston: South End Press, 1994.

——— and Russell Leong, eds. *Los Angeles: Struggles Toward Multiethnic Community*. Seattle: University of Washington Press, 1994.

Inside the L.A. Riots: What Really Happened and Why It Will Happen Again Institute for Alternative Journalism, 1992.

Light, I. and E. Bonacich. *Immigrant Entrepreneurs: Koreans in Los Angeles* Berkeley: University of California Press, 1988.

Loewen, J. *The Mississippi Chinese: Between Black and White*. Cambridge Harvard University Press, 1971.

Yu, E. Y., ed. *Black-Korean Encounter: Toward Understanding and Alliance* Los Angeles: Institute for Asian American and Pacific Asian Studies 1994.

Yu, E. Y. and E. Chang, eds. *Building Multiethnic Coalitions in Los Angeles*. Los Angeles: Institute for Asian American and Pacific Asian Studies, 1995.

Edward T. Chang is Director of the Center for Asian Pacific America and an assistant professor of Ethnic Studies at the University of California, Riverside. He co-edited two volumes on the 1992 Los Angeles civil unrest, and is author of a Korean-language book, Who African Americans Are.

A Chronology of the Black-Korean Encounters in the United States

1872 The first black church established in Los Angeles. The present day First African Methodist Episcopal Church was born out of this church.

1904 The first Korean church (Methodist) in Los Angeles was established on Magnolia Avenue near Pico Boulevard.

1942-50 *Defense Migration.* A large number of African Americans migrated to Los Angeles and settled in the South Central area to work in the defense industries.

1950-53 *The Korean War.* Over 1 million Koreans were killed, and more than 10 million Koreans were separated from their family members.

1981 *Jamaica Boycott, New York.* A dispute between a Korean merchant and an African American customer developed into a boycott of the store. The organized boycott continued for eight weeks.

1983 *Boycott of Korean-owned Stores Urged.* During the months of August and September, a major African American newspaper, the Los Angeles *Sentinel*, ran a five-week series charging that the "African American community has literally been taken over by Asians in the past five years," and urged fellow African Americans to boycott Korean-owned stores.

1984 *Anti-Korean Sentiments Spread.* Black media attacks against Korean Americans intensified in Chicago, New York, and Los Angeles. In Chicago, it was reported that "Koreans are planning to take over Southern Chicago 47th Street District." In New York, it was reported that approximately 40 out of 160 stores on 125th Avenue in Harlem were owned by Korean Americans. In Los Angeles, Korean American merchants were accused of "exploiting the Black community."

1986 *Black-Korean Alliance (BKA).* The deaths of four Korean American merchants in April in South Central Los Angeles triggered the formation of the Black-Korean Alliance. The Alliance continued dialogue until 1992, when it was dissolved.

1988 *Tropic Market Boycott, New York.* A Korean merchant was accused of mistreating an African American woman, and a boycott was organized, lasting for four months. Three separate boycotts targeted Korean stores in Brooklyn, Harlem, and Jamaica.

1989 *Slauson Boycott, Los Angeles.* A Black organization called for a boycott of the Slauson Swapmeet store owned by Korean Americans.

1990 *Red Apple Boycott, New York.* A Haitian woman accused a Korean merchant of assault. It drew national attention as the media sensationalized it as a racial confrontation between Korean and African Americans. The boycott lasted for one year and five months.

1991 *Latasha Harlins Shooting, Los Angeles.* The shooting of Latasha Harlins by a Korean American shopkeeper, Soon Ja Du, in South Central Los Angeles intensified the already volatile relationship between the two communities. Bitterness escalated when Soon Ja Du was released on probation.
  John's Market Boycott, Los Angeles. A shooting death of an African American by a Korean American merchant intensified the racial animosity. Although it was ruled as a justifiable homicide by police, African American organizations called for a boycott of the store. It lasted for four months.

1992 *Los Angeles Civil Unrest.* Civil unrest erupted on April 29 when the news broke that the jury had acquitted the four police officers accused of beating African American motorist Rodney King. The three days of civil unrest resulted in 53 deaths and nearly $1 billion in property damage. South Central Los Angeles and Koreatown suffered major damages. In South Central Los Angeles, more than 560 businesses were destroyed. In Koreatown, more than 300 businesses were burned and looted. Approximately 2,300 Korean American businesses suffered damage as a result of the civil unrest. The total loss to Korean-owned businesses was estimated at $400 million.
  A number of organizations became active in organizing and promoting dialogue and cooperation between racial and ethnic groups in Los Angeles. These included the Coalition of Neighborhood Developers, Multicultural Collaborative, and Colors United. Korean and African American writers and artists initiated various collaborative projects in order to promote racial harmony.

1993 Nineteen Korean Americans were murdered by non-Korean robbers in Los Angeles.

1994 Fifty Los Angeles African American youths were invited to Korea under an annual cultural exchange/scholarship program sponsored by the Korean government. A number of church groups also organized scholarship and Korea tour programs for Black youths and church leaders.

Handout 2
Myths and Realities of Korean-Black Relations

Interethnic misperceptions, conflicts, and tensions between minority groups (i.e., Korean-African American, Latino-African American, Asian American-Latino) in American cities have been an increasing concern. Korean immigrants, like many other new immigrants, have little knowledge of the African American experience, history, and culture. African Americans, due to the media and educational system, have little knowledge of Asian American groups, including Korean Americans.

Reportage on these groups focuses overwhelmingly on negative interactions between minority groups and reinforces negative stereotypes. An example of this is reportage of the Korean-African American conflict in papers such as the Los Angeles *Sentinel*, or of black crime in Asian communities as reported in Asian language papers. In mainstream papers such as the *Los Angeles Times*, *New York Times*, and *Washington Post*, coverage of positive aspects of the African American community is minimal, and coverage of Asian communities often tends to portray them as "model minorities," thereby pitting them against other minority groups such as African Americans and Latinos.

Many observers of Korean-African American relations believe that Korean-owned stores were targeted by rioters during the 1992 Los Angeles civil unrest. Lack of accurate information and adequate education have often created myths and misperceptions. Politicians, the media, and community leaders have exploited the issue by endorsing these myths and stereotypes. To reconcile and begin the reconstruction process, we must separate myths from realities because myths have played an important role in fueling and escalating the confrontation between Korean and African Americans.

Myth 1: Korean immigrants are receiving special loans and assistance from the American government.
Fact: False. Korean immigrants are *not* entitled to receive any special assistance from the government. Southeast Asian *refugees* are entitled to receive special consideration and assistance from the government because of their status as political refugees. However, immigrants are not eligible to receive any special loans or economic assistance from the government.

Myth 2: Korean Americans are rude and disrespectful to African American customers.
Fact: Indeed, some Korean American merchants are rude and disrespectful to their customers. It is equally important to acknowledge that many Korean American merchants have gone extra-miles to accommodate the needs of African American customers. Furthermore, cultural differences are sometimes misinterpreted as being rude and disrespectful. Koreans and African Americans have different sets of rules concerning what is appropriate attitudes and behaviors. For example, Koreans are taught not to make eye-contact with elders and strangers. If you make eye-contact with an elder person, it is considered not only rude and disrespectful, but also a direct challenge to his or her authority. In American culture, however, direct eye-contact is interpreted as respectful during interaction.

Myth 3: Korean American merchants only conduct business in African American communities.
Fact: In Los Angeles, Korean-owned businesses are dispersed all over the city. The clientele of Korean-owned businesses in southern California are as follows: 48 percent white; 22 percent Korean American; 17 percent Latino; and only 10 percent African American. However, the proportion of Korean-owned stores in African American neighborhoods is higher in other areas such as New York, Philadelphia, Chicago, Washington, D.C., and Atlanta.

Myth 4: Korean merchants are foreigners who do not have a right to be in this country.
Fact: Most Korean Americans are here legally and are either permanent residents or American citizens. According to the 1990 census, 67.6 percent of Korean Americans are U.S. citizens by birth or naturalization.

Myth 5: Korean American merchants do not hire African American workers.
Fact: Merchants are in a very difficult position—damned if you do; damned if you don't. During the 1960s, Jewish Americans were accused of operating a "slave market" for underpaying African American workers. Recently, Korean American merchants are being accused of not hiring African American employees. Even if most Korean-owned mom-and-pop stores hired one or two African American employees, it would have very little economic impact on the African American community. Minimum wage-paying jobs are not going to solve inner-city economic problems. Korean American merchants must do more to hire as many African American employees in their stores. However, it is wrong to blame Korean merchants for creating chronic economic problems in the inner city.

Myth 6: Korean American merchants often sell inferior products for a higher price.
Fact: A slightly higher price is normal for all small neighborhood convenience stores and is certainly not limited to Korean-owned stores. In exchange, consumers get the time-saving convenience of shopping close to home. Overall, mom-and-pop stores can neither compete with the large chain stores nor bypass the wholesalers and bargain directly with the manufacturers. A rudimentary understanding of supply and demand should make this situation abundantly clear.

Handout 3
Building Coalitions Between African and Korean Americans

Contrary to popular belief Korean and African Americans share many traits and areas of common concern, including a history of racial oppression, economic exploitation, and political subjugation. Koreans share a history of suffering with African Americans, having endured Japanese colonial rule (1910-45), which undertook genocidal measures against the people and their culture.

To understand Koreans and Korean Americans, one must grasp the concept of *han* which distinguish Koreans from other Asian groups. The deep meaning of *han* can only begin to be understood in feelings of resentment, bitterness, grievance, or regret. Koreans and Korean Americans often express that "they lived life full of *han*," and developed *hwabyong*, a disease of frustration and rage following misfortune. I believe that the Korean ethos of *han* and African American, of soul are very similar concepts.

Korean American churches play a major role in the community, as does the church in the African American community. In the early twentieth century, Korean immigrant churches and church groups played a large role in the nationalistic independence movement of the Korean people from Japanese colonization of their country. African American churches have played a similar historic function in uniting African Americans in independence and civil rights movements. Yet, few Korean immigrants are aware of the role of the African American church, as few African Americans are cognizant of the role of the Korean immigrant church in the United States. These types of knowledge need to be conveyed to the larger Korean and African American communities.

	Korean Americans	African Americans
History	colonized by Japan; contract laborers to Hawaii	forced entry as slaves
Economic	manual labor; the source of cheap labor	no or limited upward mobility
Political	"aliens ineligible to citizenship"	"separate but equal"
Racism	second class citizens	second class citizens
Ethos	*han* and *jung*	soul and blues

Handout 4
Questions

Handout #1
- What contact have you had with Korean or African Americans?
- What are some similarities and differences between the Korean and African American experiences?

Handout #2
- What are some of the media images of African and Asian Americans? How do those images affect inter-ethnic relations, e.g. between Korean and African Americans?
- What are some of the myths and realities of Korean-African American relations?
- How is Korean-African American conflict represented in light of the declining number of whites, whose power remains dominant but is being transformed?

Handout #3
- What are the prospects for Korean-African American coalition-building?
- Did the 1992 Los Angeles civil unrest do anything to bring about an understanding between Korean and African Americans? Or did it exacerbate existing conflicts between the two groups?

Index